RACIALIZED
POLITICS

Studies in Communication, A series edited by Susan Herbst
Media, and Public Opinion and Benjamin I. Page

Racialized Politics

The Debate about Racism in America

EDITED BY David O. Sears
Jim Sidanius
Lawrence Bobo

The University of Chicago Press Chicago and London

DAVID O. SEARS is professor of psychology and political science at the University of California, Los Angeles. JIM SIDANIUS is professor of psychology at the University of California, Los Angeles. LAWRENCE BOBO is professor of sociology and Afro-American studies at Harvard University.

The University of Chicago Press, Chicago 60637
The University of Chicago Press, Ltd., London
© 2000 by The University of Chicago
All rights reserved. Published 2000
09 08 07 06 05 04 03 02 01 00   1 2 3 4 5

ISBN: 0-226-74405-1 (cloth)
ISBN: 0-226-74407-8 (paper)

Library of Congress Cataloging-in-Publication Data

Racialized politics : the debate about racism in America / edited by David O. Sears, Jim Sidanius, and Lawrence Bobo.
    p. cm.—(Studies in communication, media, and public opinion)
    Includes bibliographical references and index.
    ISBN 0-226-74405-1 (cloth : alk. paper).—ISBN 0-226-74407-8 (paper : alk. paper)
    1. Racism—Political aspects—United States Congresses. 2. United States—Race relations—Political aspects Congresses. 3. Racism—United States—Public opinion Congresses. 4. United States—Politics and government—1993– Congresses. 5. United States—Social policy—1993– Congresses. 6. Whites—United States—Attitudes Congresses. 7. Public opinion—United States Congresses. I. Sears, David O. II. Sidanius, Jim. III. Bobo, Lawrence. IV. Series.
E185.615.R2143 1999
305.8'00973—dc21
                                              99-35771
                                             CIP

CONTENTS

This volume is concerned with racial politics in the American mass public as we enter a new century. The unique status of African Americans has been a central political problem for this society since the beginnings of permanent European settlement in North America. The ending of legalized discrimination in the 1960s produced major improvements, but scarcely was successful in wiping the slate clean of the many legacies of more than three centuries of formalized inequality. Since then, our society has been involved in much controversy about what continues to be wrong, and what to do about it. These controversies have, of course, roiled the political world, but they have provoked much academic debate as well. Within the social sciences, they have generated several competing theoretical perspectives, most focusing on whites' resistance to policies intended to increase racial equality. Some emerge from social-psychological theories of prejudice, some derive from sociological theories about structural inequalities in society, and some place conventional partisan politics at the center of the story. These issues are of considerable political and practical consequence and have generated great conflict, both inside and outside of academia.

Our own collaboration on this subject began with a graduate seminar that the three of us co-taught with Professors Marilynn Brewer and Franklin Gilliam, Jr., in the spring of 1991. A crystallizing moment in the seminar occurred at the beginning of the session the day after the videotaped beating of black motorist Rodney King by Los Angeles police officers was released on local television. It stimulated us to increased concern about the unresolved theoretical and empirical controversies in the study of racial politics in America. In 1994, we helped to develop a new Center for the Study of Society and Politics at

UCLA, under the directorship of Professor John R. Petrocik, to facilitate further discussion. The level of conflict and debate in the professional social science literature continued to increase. As a result, in November 1997, we hosted a national conference on the topic of race in mass politics in America. Our intent was to bring all the academic disputants into one room at the same time, presenting their latest original research on the topic. Our hope was that they might begin to talk to each other rather than past each other and that the substantive bases for their always messy, often political, and sometimes racial or personal disagreements might be clarified. To further that end, we also invited a number of outstanding social scientists to serve as outside commentators.

We believe that the conference itself was conducted in a cordial and collegial manner. For this accomplishment, we would like to thank all those who presented papers at the conference as well as Professors Edward Carmines, Jack Citrin, Franklin Gilliam, Jr., Mary Jackman, and Tali Mendelberg, who provided expert commentary. We also owe thanks for financial support to the Institute for American Cultures at UCLA, administered by Professor Shirley Hune, and to Associate Vice Chancellor of Academic Development Raymund Paredes. Logistical support for the conference was provided by the Institute for Social Science Research (ISSR) at UCLA, whose director is David O. Sears and assistant director, Madelyn De Maria.

The volume that has emerged from that process contains the full range of scientific and political views involved in these debates. It is far easier to produce a volume with a narrow range of views from a particular school or faction than it is to capture the full range of a heated debate, one that crosses disciplinary, political, and racial boundaries. Chapters 2 to 9 of this volume are the subsequently refined versions of research papers originally presented at that conference. We are grateful to all these authors for putting up with a difficult and demanding task. We also are grateful to Professors Martin Gilens and Maria Krysan, who presented papers at the conference that were committed elsewhere for publication and so could not be included here.

This volume would not have materialized except for the extraordinary efforts of two individuals. Marilyn Hart of ISSR has kept the project on track with indefatigable conscientiousness, energy, cheerfulness, and occasionally a needed dose of gallows humor. An eerie silence will settle over her position in the national e-mail network and overnight express services when this volume finally appears. John Tryneski, our editor at the University of Chicago Press, has managed to find a seemingly endless succession of rabbits in his hat, always with good humor.

The book itself is organized in five sections. Chapter 1 provides an overview of racial conflicts in the United States, and of the several perspectives that appear in the book. Chapters 2 and 3, by Donald Kinder, David Sears, and their collaborators, present research stemming from the social-psychological approach that focuses particular attention on racial prejudice. Chapters 4 through 7, by Marylee Taylor, Lawrence Bobo, Michael Hughes, Jim Sidanius, and their collaborators, offer several versions of the social-structural approach. Chapter 8, by Paul Sniderman and his collaborators, focuses in particular on the role of conventional politics. Chapter 9, by Thomas Pettigrew, brings an eclectic collection of these factors to bear on the effort to explain ethnic conflict in Europe. Chapters 10 to 12 were commissioned to provide both commentary on the earlier chapters and a broader view of racialized politics in the mass public and were authored by Professors Howard Schuman, Jennifer Hochschild, and Michael Dawson, all renowned experts on American race relations, but with no previous involvement in the debates in question.

There is much contention in the pages that follow. Our belief is that academic debate carried out according to agreed-upon ground rules of methodology and collegiality is good and healthy. Engaging other points of view sharpens and clarifies points of difference, often pointing the way to further research that can illuminate those differences. We feel that the chapters contained herein follow those rules and so will reward even the conflict-averse reader. Not all issues are resolved. And in this process, the editors as well as other participants take some hits. The commentators have the useful perspective of outsiders and perhaps point us to constructive ways of resolving these remaining questions.

We think it is fair to say that everyone involved in this book finds much in the history of American race relations offensive. Beyond that point, there is much disagreement about how far we have come, how far we have to go, and what the prospects are for future progress. Nevertheless, all would share the hope that the American tragedy of race would improve in the next century. Finally, we mark with sadness the passing, during the course of preparation of this volume, of one who did what he could to make that happen, a good friend and colleague, Professor John B. McConahay.

LAWRENCE BOBO is professor of sociology and Afro-American studies at Harvard University and coauthor of *Racial Attitudes in America* (1997).

GRETCHEN C. CROSBY is a doctoral candidate in political science at Stanford University.

MICHAEL C. DAWSON is professor of political science, director of the Center for the Study of Race, Politics and Culture, and chair of the Department of Political Science at the University of Chicago. He is author of *Behind the Mule: Race and Class in African-American Politics* (1994).

CHRIS FEDERICO is a doctoral candidate in psychology at UCLA.

P. J. HENRY is a doctoral candidate in psychology at UCLA.

JOHN J. HETTS is a doctoral candidate in psychology at UCLA.

JENNIFER L. HOCHSCHILD is William Stewart Tod Professor of Politics and Public Affairs at Princeton University and author of *The New American Dilemma: Liberal Democracy and School Desegregation* (1984) and *Facing Up to the American Dream* (1995).

WILLIAM G. HOWELL is a doctoral candidate in political science at Stanford University.

MICHAEL HUGHES is professor of sociology at Virginia Polytechnic Institute and State University.

DONALD R. KINDER is Philip E. Converse Collegiate Professor of Political Science and Psychology at the University of Michigan and coauthor of *Divided by Color* (1996).

RICK KOSTERMAN is a research scientist at the Social Development Research Group, University of Washington.

TALI MENDELBERG is assistant professor of political science at Princeton University.

THOMAS F. PETTIGREW is research professor of psychology at the University of California, Santa Cruz. He is author of *A Profile of the Negro American* (1964) and *How to Think Like a Social Scientist* (1996).

HOWARD SCHUMAN is professor and research scientist emeritus at the Institute of Social Research, University of Michigan, and coauthor of *Questions and Answers in Attitude Surveys* (1981) and *Racial Attitudes in America* (1997).

DAVID O. SEARS is professor of psychology and political science and director of the Institute for Social Science Research at UCLA. He is coauthor of *The Politics of Violence: The New Urban Blacks and the Watts Riot* (1973) and *Tax Revolt: Something for Nothing in California* (1985).

JIM SIDANIUS is professor of psychology at UCLA and coauthor of *Social Dominance: An Intergroup Theory of Social Hierarchy and Oppression* (1999).

PAM SINGH is a doctoral candidate in political science at UCLA.

PAUL M. SNIDERMAN is professor of political science at Stanford University. He is coauthor of *Reasoning and Choice: Explorations in Political Psychology* (1991) and *Reaching beyond Race* (1997).

MARYLEE C. TAYLOR is associate professor of sociology at Pennsylvania State University.

STEVEN A. TUCH is professor of sociology at George Washington University and coeditor of *Racial Attitudes in the 1990s* (1997).

ONE Race in American Politics

Framing the Debates

DAVID O. SEARS

JOHN J. HETTS

JIM SIDANIUS

LAWRENCE BOBO

The place of African Americans in American society has been a controversial question on the political agenda throughout American history. The system of chattel slavery established at the very outset generated intense debates for over two hundred years, even in the framing of the major founding documents of the nation, and ultimately triggered a bloody Civil War. Even after formal emancipation, the Southern "Jim Crow" system of official discrimination and segregation and parallel, though somewhat milder, practices in the North kept blacks in an officially designated lower-caste status.[1]

That began to erode after World War II, perhaps most symbolically in 1954 in the unanimous Supreme Court ruling that racially separate school systems were unconstitutional because they were inherently unequal. Steadily growing institutional strength and political organization in Southern black communities soon led to increasingly numerous civil rights protests. Federal government policy finally shifted dramatically when the 1964 Civil Rights Act provided guarantees of equal opportunity and the 1965 Voting Rights Act secured full black enfranchisement.

Ironically, Northern urban ghettos almost immediately began to erupt in "long hot summers" of violence. Racial problems came to be viewed by the general public as among the nation's "most important problems," and many observers felt that America was in a state of racial crisis.[2] A presidential commission concluded with great pessimism that "our nation is moving toward two societies, one black, one white—

separate and unequal" (Report of the National Advisory Commission on Civil Disorders 1968, 1). And racial issues have been on the political agenda ever since. Beginning in the 1970s, court-ordered busing produced extensive protest and eventually massive levels of "white flight." Racially tinged issues, such as welfare, crime, "permissive judges," and government regulation, have been the subject of strenuous political debate and draconian legislation for three decades. Now referenda aimed at abolishing affirmative action in government are increasingly appearing on state ballots.

It would be surprising if the effects of 350 years of formalized racial inequality could be quickly eliminated. Much progress has been made, of course. But significant racial gaps in most domains of the quality of life continue to exist. And the races are highly polarized about what to do about them. The role of government is perhaps the most centrally contested issue. The authors represented in this volume have major differences of opinion, as will be seen, but they all share the belief that the opinions of the electorate will in the end be decisive.

This book, then, focuses on the nature of public opinion about race in the United States and on its effects on politics. However, public opinion does not exist in a vacuum. It is about something. In our case, that something concerns the reality of blacks' lives in America and what government should be doing about it. This chapter begins, therefore, with a brief appraisal of blacks' situation in America. Though much progress has been made in the last half century, blacks continue to be substantially disadvantaged relative to whites, and that racial gap seems not to have closed much in recent years. We then review how government policy has addressed it over the past four decades. The policies of the 1960s focused on prohibiting explicit racial discrimination against individuals. They were soon supplemented by tougher actions aimed at the tenacious and subtle roots of racial inequality. These in turn have come under increasingly skeptical scrutiny by Congress and the Supreme Court. We then turn to public opinion about racial issues. Although all Americans now overwhelmingly endorse formal racial equality, whites and blacks sharply disagree about most racial policies, and whites themselves are quite divided. Finally, we take up the central thrust of the book, the principal competing theories about the sources of white public opinion about race, variously emphasizing prejudice, social structure, or ordinary politics. The main body of the book consists of the debates among these theories. We hope that collecting in one place this collision of intellectual approaches will represent a valuable contribution.

THE CURRENT STATE OF BLACK AMERICA

In 1965, many were hopeful that the guarantee of formal equal rights would result in the end of most racial inequalities. Since then, there has indeed been much improvement. Nevertheless, blacks today remain at a substantial disadvantage by most standard indicators. This gap between the races has in many respects not narrowed appreciably for the past two decades.[3]

Perhaps the ultimate bottom line is life expectancy. Though blacks' longevity has improved substantially in the past half century, the racial gap in it has scarcely changed at all.[4] To understand such a difference, it is natural to turn first to basic socioeconomic indicators. Blacks have always been substantially more likely to be unemployed than whites. That difference has not varied greatly since the mid-1970s, with the black unemployment rate holding at about double that for whites in good times or bad.[5] To be sure, among the employed, blacks have moved up the occupational ladder substantially. For example, the proportion of black men in white-collar occupations increased from 5 percent in 1940 to 22 percent in 1970 and then again to 32 percent in 1990. But the proportion of whites in such occupations has also substantially increased, so blacks remain severely underrepresented in almost all higher-status occupations.[6]

Blacks' income increased greatly in the years after World War II, both in absolute terms and relative to whites. For example, the black/white ratio in median annual earnings for men increased from 43 in 1940 to 73 in 1980. Since then, blacks' income has continued to increase in absolute terms, but the black/white ratio has not improved further. Moreover, blacks have considerably less economic reserve than do whites. Black households earned about 60 percent as much as the average white household in 1988, but had only 8 percent as much net worth.[7]

Blacks' educational level also showed impressive improvement after World War II. In 1940, 49 percent of the black population had less than five years of schooling, as opposed to only 16 percent of whites. By 1990, blacks were over 90 percent as likely as whites to be high school graduates. But a high school education is no longer as valuable as it once was. Blacks' rate of college enrollment also increased sharply through the 1970s, and the racial gap in initial college enrollment had virtually been eliminated by 1980. But since then, the racial gap in college enrollment has increased substantially, and blacks' rate of college graduation is falling off (see Farley 1996, 231).[8]

Blacks and whites remain surprisingly isolated from one another. Douglas Massey and Nancy Denton (1993, 2) concluded that, as of 1980, "no group in the history of the United States has ever experienced the sustained high level of residential segregation that has been imposed on blacks in large American cities for the past fifty years."[9] At that time, Reynolds Farley and his colleagues (1978) proposed the image of "chocolate city–vanilla suburbs" to describe the phenomenon of black-dominated central cities surrounded by nearly all-white suburban rings. Since then, blacks have increasingly moved into the suburbs. Often that simply reflects the spillover of black residential areas beyond city limits, however, and blacks remain the most residentially segregated minority group.[10] Similarly, blacks are by far the least likely of all minority groups in America to engage in racial or ethnic intermarriage; as of 1990, only about 6 percent of all marriages by young African Americans were interracial (see Farley 1996, 264).[11]

Blacks have become an increasingly important political force in their own right. Black registration and turnout surged following passage of the Voting Rights Act in 1965 and today are comparable to those of whites in the nation as a whole.[12] Black voters are among the most loyal supporters of the Democratic Party at the same time that they generally demonstrate a strong sense of racial solidarity in politics.[13] One result is that the number of black elected officials has increased enormously since the civil rights era, most elected in majority black constituencies.[14] Nevertheless, the racial gap persists in this realm as well. The best rule of thumb is that prominent black candidates tend to split the electorate along racial lines. They usually receive almost all the black vote, while the white vote divides on the basis of racial attitudes, party identification, and ideology.[15] Blacks elected in majority white constituencies are the exception.[16] So while 11 percent of the voting-age population is black, less than 2 percent of America's elected officials are.

The size of the black middle class has increased substantially. The percentage of blacks earning at least twice the poverty-line level of income rose from 1 percent in 1940 to almost 50 percent by the mid-1970s. But in this respect, too, progress has slowed markedly; that proportion has not changed since then (Farley 1996, 255). Also, even this emerging black middle class continues to have much less financial reserves than does the white middle class. As Melvin Oliver and Thomas Shapiro (1993, 93) put it, "An accurate and realistic appraisal of the economic footing of the black middle class reveals its precariousness, marginality, and fragility."[17]

At the other end of the spectrum, the proportion of blacks living in poverty declined sharply until the 1970s, but has remained about constant since then. This is reflected in the concentration of poverty in racially segregated neighborhoods, high levels of male joblessness in central cities, high rates of black involvement in violent crime as both victims and perpetrators, and high rates of female-headed families and out-of-wedlock births (Bobo 1997a; Wilson 1997). For example, at any given time, about one-third of all young black men are enmeshed in the criminal justice system—whether incarcerated, on parole, or on probation. And far more black than white children are born out of wedlock, and far more are living in female-headed households. In these areas, there has been little improvement, either in absolute terms or relative to whites.[18]

At a broad level, then, blacks now have greater opportunity and are much better off than they were before World War II. Still, a substantial racial gap remains in many areas. That much seems to be largely agreed upon. But the trend in those gaps remains a matter of controversy. Some, such as Stephan and Abigail Thernstrom (1997), see a continuing convergence between the races, even if slower in the last two decades, so that the gaps are likely to disappear with time. Others perceive progress as having essentially come to a halt two decades ago. For example, Farley concludes that "black-white discrepancies on the most important indicators of economic status have been persistent for at least two decades" (1996, 263–68).[19] And there are prominent long-term pessimists. Andrew Hacker concludes that the United States confronts "a huge racial chasm . . . and there are few signs that the coming century will see it closed" (1992, 219). Derrick Bell argues that "racism is an integral, permanent, and indestructible component of this society. Indeed, the racism that made slavery feasible is far from dead in the last decade of twentieth century America; and the civil rights gains, so hard won, are being steadily eroded" (1992, ix, 3).

A second matter of dispute concerns the causes of these racial gaps. Some critique black culture. Blacks show a lack of work ethic; they self-segregate rather than taking a chance on living in integrated neighborhoods; they engage in violent crime rather than obeying the law; and they are irresponsible about their families, sexuality, alcohol, and drug use, leading to the continued deterioration of the black nuclear family (e.g., D'Souza 1995; Sowell 1994; Roth 1994; Thernstrom and Thernstrom 1997). Others point to white racism and a wide range of discriminatory practices, such as arbitrary traffic stops by white police, restrictive home mortgage lending policies, differential imposition of the death penalty, and white taxpayers' refusal to provide resources to overcome racial disadvantage.[20] Considerable systematic research has been done on racial discrimination in domains such as employment, housing, education, financial services, health care, the retail market, and the criminal justice system. Recent reviews conclude that it continues to be real and pervasive.[21] Even middle-class blacks prove to be exposed to relentless and ubiquitous personal experiences of discrimination (Feagin and Sikes 1994; also see Hochschild 1993).

FEDERAL RACIAL POLICY

The fate of African Americans, and of race relations in America, will depend on many factors. At this juncture, however, Americans find themselves in a period of great controversy and collective uncertainty about racial problems. Some of the greatest controversies now concern the proper role of government in dealing with those problems.

Between the end of Reconstruction and the end of World War II, the federal government rarely addressed the problem of race, and the two political parties differed little on such questions. In the South, blacks had been effectively disenfranchised, and the Republican Party had virtually disappeared, leaving a nearly uncontested all-white Democratic Party in power. The national Democratic Party shied away from issues of race because its strong Southern base had disproportionate seniority-based influence in Congress. The Republican Party was restrained by its more general ideological caution about governmental action. And blacks themselves were largely politically inactive.

In the early 1960s, however, liberal Democrats began to assert leadership on civil rights, and the parties began to polarize around racial issues.[22] In 1963, the Kennedy administration was somewhat reluctantly pulled into the increasing confrontations between Southern authorities and civil rights activists. Matters escalated quickly, however, and by 1965, landmark civil rights legislation was in place, providing federal guarantees for equal opportunity in a wide variety of domains. Its goal was to remove racial discrimination and so establish a race-blind standard. As Martin Luther King, Jr., said, the hope was that people would be judged by "the content of their character" rather than "the color of their skins." An "intent" standard was set: a violation of equal opportunity could be proven only by demonstrating a specific perpetrator's deliberate intent to achieve a discriminatory outcome.

However, the new laws and affirming court decisions met with much white resistance. It soon became apparent that proving intent in the thousands of daily decisions made by state and local authorities was beyond the capacities of federal agencies or the courts. As a result, beginning in the late 1960s, new techniques to combat continuing racial discrimination began to be employed. They began to replace the "intent" standard with an "effect" standard: a rule could be defined as discriminatory even when it appeared neutral on its face as long as it could be shown to systematically reduce representation of blacks. This naturally increased the intrusiveness of the federal government on behalf of the black population in both the private sector and local government activities. And these policies were potentially especially politically vulnerable because they often were generated by court decision or administrative regulation rather than through legislation (Jaynes and Williams 1989, 224; Thernstrom and Thernstrom 1997).

In fact, in domain after domain, negative reaction has subsequently set in, from the courts, Congress, and conservative presidencies. School desegregation was initially the most visible issue. By the late 1960s, it was apparent that previous decisions had been insufficient to desegregate Southern schools. As a result, the Supreme Court began, in a series of unanimous decisions starting in 1968, to accept proof of mere de facto segregation rather than insisting on proof of intent to segregate. A 1971 decision mandated busing as a desegregation tool, which triggered similar judicial orders throughout the nation. Busing was, however, vastly unpopular among whites. The resulting protest quickly led to a limit on large-scale busing plans, perhaps most visibly in a 1974 decision voiding a metropolitan busing plan in the Detroit area.[23] Confining busing to the city limits allowed "white flight" to largely white suburban schools and perpetuated the de facto segregation of predominantly black schools in central cities.

The 1964 Civil Rights Act set up an Equal Employment Opportunity Commission to carry out the color-blind elimination of racial discrimination in employment. However, it had no powers of enforcement and soon proved to be relatively ineffective. Here, too, government officials concluded that little change would occur as long as intent to discriminate had to be proved and turned to the effect standard. In 1970, racially proportionate hiring targets were mandated for all federal contractors.[24] In 1972, Congress allowed for class-action suits, which soon motivated employers to meet federal guidelines for proportionate hiring voluntarily. However, here, too, an increasingly conservative Supreme Court began to pull back in the late 1980s.[25]

Almost all affirmative action programs in college admissions have been voluntary. They expanded greatly in the 1970s. In the *Bakke v. Regents of the University of California* case in 1978, the Supreme Court outlawed explicit racial quotas, though still allowing race to be used as one factor among many in admissions decisions. But in the *Hopwood v. Texas* case in 1996, it ruled out preferential standards of admission to the University of Texas, and that fall a statewide initiative eliminated affirmative action by state and local governments in California, including by public universities.[26]

Guaranteeing blacks' right to vote had been a central objective of the civil rights movement. The 1965 Voting Rights Act had placed federal officials in specific districts with histories of discrimination in order to facilitate black voter registration. Although this greatly increased black voter turnout, the number of black elected officials still fell far short of proportionality. When that act was renewed in 1982, therefore, Congress and the Justice Department agreed that legislative redistricting plans should be required to maximize the number of "majority-minority" districts, with the goal of increasing minority representation. This, too, was ultimately reversed by the Supreme Court, in *Shaw v. Reno* in 1993 (Thernstrom and Thernstrom 1997, 426).[27]

Finally, the question of "multiculturalism" in educational curricula has pitted cultural minorities' desire for recognition and respect against the goal of assimilating all Americans to the broader society. Controversy has arisen over using languages other than English, teaching ethnic history, broadening the traditional canon to include other cultural traditions, requiring courses in cultural diversity, and even occasionally rewriting the curriculum entirely, as in "Afrocentric" curricula that reinterpret traditional disciplines from an African perspective. These debates also raise more fundamental questions about group-based as opposed to individually based rights, difference-blind treatment, and state neutrality with respect to groups (Glazer 1997; Hollinger 1995; Peterson 1995; Appiah and Gutmann 1996).[28]

Effect standards for the elimination of discrimination, often now described as "race-conscious" remedies, have been intensely debated. Supporters argue that institutional racism and whites' resistance to change have been so deeply and subtly embedded in the entire fabric of American society that little would have changed if more proactive methods had not been used. They argue that demanding findings of intent is beside the point or even a mere distracting excuse; what is needed is proof of equality. Opponents have argued that race-conscious remedies may in fact not have been necessary because substantial progress was already well under way and that such policies actually have slowed racial progress by angering otherwise sympathetic whites (Thernstrom and Thernstrom 1997, 538; Sniderman and Piazza 1993).

PUBLIC OPINION ON RACIAL ISSUES

In a democracy, a natural question about such a long-standing public conflict is what the public wants and why. Addressing those questions is our primary purpose in this volume.

THE JIM CROW BELIEF SYSTEM

A formalized ideology of white racial superiority began to develop in the years prior to the Civil War, in response to abolitionist challenges to slavery. After Emancipation, the Jim Crow system of legalized discrimination and segregation gradually took hold over the later years of the nineteenth century, built on the foundations of that white supremacist ideology. By all accounts, it was broadly accepted in the South and indeed was quite common throughout the nation before World War II.

It had three major components. One was "racialism," the belief that blacks were inherently inferior to whites because of their race. A second was a formal pattern of social distance and segregation, such that blacks were supposed to "stay in their place," separate and subordinate to whites, especially in public. Public facilities were racially segregated, and blacks and whites were not to be personal friends or to date or marry. A third was a legalized pattern of discrimination, such that blacks were not allowed to vote and were provided with separate and inferior schools, while whites were given preference in employment and elsewhere.[29]

This belief system came under attack from intellectuals in the 1930s and 1940s, capped most visibly in 1944 by Gunnar Myrdal's *The American Dilemma*.[30] Fortunately, an early survey by the National Opinion Research Center in 1942 provides benchmark data against which later changes can be measured. Since then, white support for all three elements seems to have precipitously declined. Here we draw principally on the most complete analyses available, those of Schuman et al. (1997). Table 1.1 provides some examples. The belief that blacks are inherently inferior to whites is now at a low ebb. In the 1996 General Social Survey (GSS), only 10 percent of the white respondents to a national survey said the racial differences in jobs, income, and housing arise "because most blacks have less in-born ability to learn" (Schuman et al. 1997, 159).[31]

Support for formal segregation has also sharply diminished. In 1942, most whites supported separate schools for blacks and whites (68 percent) and segregated sections in public transit for blacks and whites (54 percent). In 1958, 96 percent of adult whites disapproved of "marriage between whites and nonwhites," and as late as 1963, 63 percent approved of *laws* forbidding racial intermarriage, as astonishing as that seems today. But support for formal segregation collapsed over the next decade, and today it is practically nonexistent. In the mid-1990s, only 4 percent of white adults believed that black and white children should go to separate schools, and 13 percent supported laws forbidding racial intermarriage.

Before World War II, most whites also thought formal discrimination against blacks was perfectly appropriate, but support for this had also collapsed by the end of the 1960s. In 1942, for example, most (55 percent) thought that whites should have the first chance at any kind of job, but by 1972, only 3 percent thought whites should have such preference.

These changes among whites have largely eliminated racial differences of opinion about the old Jim Crow ideology. For example, in 1995, 99 percent of blacks and 96 percent of whites thought black and white children should go to the same schools rather than to separate schools. In 1996, 97 percent of blacks and 86 percent of whites opposed whites' being able to keep blacks out of white neighborhoods (Schuman et al. 1997, 105, 107, 243). Only on the question of racial intermarriage is there much remaining difference between blacks and whites, as table 1.1 shows (Schuman et al. 1997). Interestingly enough, Myrdal himself had forecast that this might be the most difficult issue for whites to come to grips with.

Several findings in surveys of whites' racial attitudes during the 1960s gave reason for an optimistic view of the future. One was early evidence of generally liberalizing trends in attitudes about the Jim Crow ideology. The others were the substantially greater support for racial equality in the North than in the segregated South and greater support among younger and more-educated whites than among older and less-educated whites.[32] If a vigorous civil rights effort in the South

TABLE 1.1 Increasing Opposition to the Jim Crow Belief System

	White Respondents				Black Respondents
	Early	1960s	1970s	Current	Current
Racial inferiority					
Are blacks' worse jobs, income, and housing because most blacks have less inborn ability to learn? (% No)	—	—	74% (1977)	90% (1996)	89% (1996)
Segregation					
Should white and black students go to the same or to separate schools? (% Same)	32 (1942)	63 (1964)	86 (1972)	96 (1995)	99 (1995)
Do you approve of marriage between blacks and whites? (% Yes)	4 (1958)	—	27 (1972)	67 (1997)	83 (1997)
Favor discrimination					
Should Negroes have as good a chance as whites at any kind of job, or should white people have the first chance at any kind of job? (% As good)	45 (1944)	85 (1963)	97 (1972)	—	—
Existence of discrimination					
Are blacks' worse jobs, income, and housing mainly due to discrimination? (% Yes)	—	—	41 (1977)	34 (1996)	66 (1996)
Do blacks have as good a chance as whites in your community to get any kind of job for which they are qualified? (% No)	—	49 (1963)	18 (1978)	19 (1997)	53 (1997)

Source: Adapted from Schuman et al. 1997, 104–8, 156–60, 240–44, 258–62. All data are from national surveys.
Note: The percentages exclude neutral responses and missing data from the base, including responses such as "haven't thought about it" or insufficient interest to have an opinion. Wording is approximate and minor changes in wording occurred in some items over time.

could reverse three centuries of structural racism in that region and if the white population's educational level continued to rise throughout the nation, ill-educated older whites, steeped in the racism of an earlier day, would gradually be replaced by a new generation of college-educated youths, enlightened by modern social science. Cohort replacement all by itself might gradually erase the Jim Crow ideology.

Current surveys sustain that expectation (Schuman et al. 1997). White public opinion has indeed come to fully repudiate the Jim Crow doctrines so common half a century ago, as we have seen. The way was led by younger, college-educated, and Northern whites (Schuman et al. 1997; also see Glaser and Gilens 1997). This racial caste system had lasted for about 350 years, but it was almost entirely dismantled in the 25 years following World War II. Surrendering it was a truly momentous change in our society, and it came about in a relatively short period of time.

PERCEPTIONS OF DISCRIMINATION

Whites were not blind to the racial double standard that infected our society. As shown in table 1.1, in 1963 about half of the whites (49 percent) believed that blacks in their community did not have as good a chance as whites "to get any kind of job for which they are qualified." But today most whites appear to believe that racial discrimination is no longer a significant factor. For example, 66 percent of the white respondents in the 1996 GSS said that racial differences in jobs, income, and housing were not "mainly due to discrimination." In a 1997 Gallup poll, 81 percent believed that blacks have as good a chance as whites in their own local job market, while 79 percent said that in their community "black children have as good a chance as white children to get a good education," and 86 percent said that they have "the same chance to get any housing they can afford" (Gallup Poll Social Audit 1997).

On this point, blacks and whites part company. Blacks consistently perceive more discrimination and less equal opportunity than do whites. In 1996, blacks were twice as likely as whites (66 percent to 34 percent) to believe that socioeconomic gaps between the races were "mainly due to discrimination" (Schuman et al. 1997, 157, 259).[33] Blacks were far more likely to perceive unequal opportunity in the local job market than were whites (by a 53 percent to 19 percent margin) and more likely to perceive unequal educational and housing opportunities in one's own community as well.[34]

FEDERAL POLICIES

As we have seen, substantial racial gaps remain in most social, economic, and political indicators of well-being. But what, if anything, government should do about them remains a matter of great controversy. Despite whites' increased support for general principles of formal racial equality, they have long been quite divided about the desirability of federal intervention to accomplish such goals. Even government intervention to overcome formal discrimination was highly controversial in the 1960s. In 1964, 63 percent felt that black and white children should go to the same schools, while only 47 percent felt that the federal government should ensure that they did. Similarly, 85 percent felt that blacks should have the same chance at any kind of job, but only 43 percent felt the federal government should intervene to ensure it. These contrasts can be seen by comparing tables 1.1 and 1.2.[35] The white public was then deeply divided about whether the federal government should be involved in guaranteeing equal opportunity.

As indicated earlier, frustration over the ever-changing maneuvers of their opponents led government officials to propose policies that would go beyond guaranteeing equal opportunity and actually ensure greater equality between the races. These have often been described as "outcome-oriented" or "race-conscious" policies because mere evidence of numerical inequalities between the races can trigger remedial action. As can be seen in table 1.2, whites are generally more strongly opposed to these policies than to those that seem to ensure only equal opportunity. Throughout the 1970s and early 1980s, fewer than 20 percent of white adults usually supported busing children to ensure school integration. Opponents typically outnumbered supporters of special help for blacks and other minorities by a two-to-one margin. Special preferences for blacks in jobs and in admissions to higher education have generally been opposed by most whites, and by large margins. Similarly, experimental studies have shown that targeting programs specifically for blacks rather than for poor people in general or using race-conscious as opposed to more universalistic justifications for social programs significantly increases white opposition (Schuman et al. 1997, 123–24, 175; Bobo and Kluegel 1993; Sniderman and Carmines 1997a).[36]

These racial policy proposals not only now draw more opposition than do general principles of racial equality, but also have not shown

TABLE 1.2 Support for Racial Policies

	White Respondents			Black Respondents
	1960s	1970s/1980s	Current	Current
Equal opportunity				
Should the government in Washington see to it that white and black children go to the same schools, or is this not the government's business? (% See to it)	47% (1964)	39% (1972)	38% (1994)	81% (1994)
Should the government in Washington see to it that black people get fair treatment in jobs, or is this not the federal government's business? (% See to it)	43 (1964)	49 (1972)	44 (1996)	91 (1996)
Equal outcomes				
Do you favor or oppose the busing of black and white school children from one school district to another? (% Favor)	—	13 (1972)	33 (1996)	59 (1996)
Should the government in Washington make every possible effort to improve the social and economic position of blacks or not make any special effort because they should help themselves? (% Make every effort)	—	38 (1972)	25 (1996)	66 (1996)
Because of past discrimination should colleges and universities reserve openings for black students or not because such quotas give blacks advantages they haven't earned (% Reserve openings)	—	29 (1986)	26 (1992)	76 (1992)
Because of past discrimination should blacks be given preference in hiring and promotion or not because it gives blacks advantages they haven't earned? (% Give preference)	—	15 (1986)	12 (1996)	59 (1996)

Source: Adapted from Schuman et al. 1997, 123–24, 176–76, 248–50, 266–70. All data are from national surveys.

Note: The percentages exclude neutral responses and missing data from the base, including responses such as "haven't thought about it" or insufficient interest to have an opinion. Wording is approximate and minor changes in wording occurred in some items over time.

the liberalizing trends we saw earlier for those principles. There has been no increase since the 1960s in support for federal action ensuring school integration or equal employment, as shown in table 1.2.[37] Support for outcome-oriented policies has not increased in most other cases either. Similarly, the demographic differences that foreshadowed liberalizing changes about the old Jim Crow doctrines are consistently much reduced concerning racial policy preferences. Younger, college-educated, or Northern whites are in general somewhat more supportive of equal opportunity policies than are older, less-than-college-educated, or Southern whites, but the differences are usually smaller than on the Jim Crow–era issues. These demographic differences are still further attenuated about the more contemporary outcome-oriented policies. To be sure, whites living in the Deep South are still the most conservative on questions such as busing or special government aid to blacks. But such regional differences are less sharp on questions of affirmative action, and sometimes even reversed. Younger cohorts are not uniformly more liberal than older cohorts, and in any case, cohort differences tend to be small. The effects of educational level on attitudes toward these contemporary issues are also somewhat more complex than on the older, Jim Crow–era issues (Schuman et al. 1997).[38]

The result is that blacks and whites are deeply divided over racial policy issues. As can be seen in table 1.2, the vast majority of blacks favor policies to guarantee equal opportunity, while whites are sharply split, or sometimes mostly opposed. Blacks' support is not as monolithic when it comes to outcome-oriented policies, but they still draw majority black support. Both busing and preferential treatment in hiring and promotion were supported by 59 percent of the black respondents in 1996 national surveys, in contrast to the substantial white majorities opposed to them (Schuman et al. 1997).[39]

In short, one goal of the civil rights movement of the 1960s was to outlaw formal segregation and discrimination. That goal is now virtually unanimously accepted. Almost all Americans now accept Justice Harlan's famous dissent in *Plessy v. Ferguson:* "'Our Constitution is color-blind, and neither knows nor tolerates classes among citizens'" (quoted in Thernstrom and Thernstrom 1997, 33). However, the use of governmental action to achieve that goal is at best sharply contested and in some cases strongly opposed by the white majority. There is little evidence of any liberalizing changes over time about such policies, and there are no systematic demographic differences that would suggest that compositional changes in the white population will inevitably lead to greater liberalization. In contrast, blacks strongly support such racially targeted policies, though with more ambivalence about so-called race-conscious policies. This necessarily produces considerable racial conflict about such policies. The contrasts between these two types of issues, and between white and black opinions, represent the starting point for the debates drawn together in this volume. It presents and extends those debates with the hope that we will all better understand our people, our nation, and perhaps even ourselves.

THEORETICAL MODELS OF WHITE OPINION

Explaining opposition to liberal racial policies among whites has been the subject of extensive research and intense debate by American social scientists over the past quarter-century. Here we try to summarize the most prominent alternatives, underlining the areas of strongest controversy. Our intent is to present these alternatives in as impartial a fashion as possible, though surely our own involvement in some of these debates will ensure that we will fall short of that hope.

These models fall into three general categories. The first grows out of the long tradition of sociopsychological analysis of racial prejudice. Such models usually begin with the assumption of early-life socialization of prejudice and social values and also rely on contemporary theories of cognitive processing. The second grows out of the sociological focus on social structure, emphasizing group differences in power, status, and economic resources as the prime movers. Ideology is often treated as a justification for such group interests. The third focuses particularly on the politics of race. It suggests that public opinion on racial policy is now primarily motivated by values and ideologies that are race-neutral. As a result, whites' opinions are strongly influenced by the exact nature of the policy proposals under consideration.

SOCIOPSYCHOLOGICAL MODELS

A variety of sociopsychological perspectives share the assumption that formal racial equality is now a settled issue in this society. But they also suggest that racism has not disappeared; instead, it has taken new forms. They differ about the nature of those new forms and about how racism interfaces with values and attitudes that have no manifest racial content.

SYMBOLIC RACISM, MODERN RACISM, AND RACIAL RESENTMENT One alternative is that such a new form of racism lies behind much of whites' contemporary opposition to racial policies and black political candidates. This originated with David Sears and Donald Kinder's finding that Jim Crow racism had already been repudiated so broadly outside the South by 1969 that it was no longer a useful predictor of whites' political preferences. Instead, they found that other racial attitudes, described as reflecting "symbolic racism," were strongly associated with whites' votes against the black candidate in the close Los Angeles mayoral race in that year (Sears and Kinder 1971).

This evolved into a more general theoretical position. The new form of racism has been variously described as "symbolic racism," "modern racism," or "racial resentment," reflecting slightly different interpretations of the same general reasoning and measurement.[40] This theory embodies several general propositions. First, older forms of racism now predict attitudes toward racial policy or voting behavior only weakly, in part due to the decline in support for them.[41] Second, despite that decline, the socialization of negative affect and stereotypes about blacks continues, leaving a reservoir of racial antipathy decoupled from racialist beliefs. Third, blacks are perceived by many whites to violate such cherished American values as the work ethic, self-reliance, impulse control, and obedience of authority. The new racism is said to derive from a coalescing of negative racial affect with the perceived violation of such traditional values. Finally, the content of the new racism includes the beliefs that discrimination no longer poses a major barrier to the advancement of blacks, that blacks should try harder to make it on their own, that they are demanding too much, and that they are too often given special treatment by government and other elites (see Kinder and Sanders 1996; Sears 1988; Sears et al. 1997; Sears, Henry, and Kosterman this volume).

In a variety of empirical studies, this new racism has been found to make large contributions to explaining whites' attitudes toward racial policy and voting preferences in elections with black candidates, over and above the effects of such alternative predictors as Jim Crow racism, political ideology, party identification, individualism, authoritarianism, or demographic variables (see Kinder and Sanders 1996; Kinder and Sears 1981; McConahay 1986; Sears et al. 1997). Furthermore, whites' opposition to racial policies or black candidacies generally does not reflect a response to real personal racial threats, such as having school-age children in a district with busing or feeling personally vulnerable to being victimized by black crime. These latter findings challenge interest-based accounts of whites' racial attitudes (Sears and Funk 1991).[42]

The symbolic racism approach has stimulated its share of controversies. The major critiques are that the various components of symbolic racism do not represent a coherent belief system, that it is indistinguishable from old-fashioned racism, that it mainly reflects ideological conservatism rather than having much to do with racism, that any association between symbolic racism and racial policy preferences is merely tautological because both measure attitudes toward special treatment of blacks by government, that its origins do not lie in a blend of antiblack affect with perceptions that blacks violate traditional values, that some of the items frequently used to measure symbolic racism can be interpreted as indexing racial threat, that group interest rather than self-interest may be the most powerful form of racial threat, and that the theory is narrowly focused on the case of American race relations rather than being more broadly applicable to cases of intergroup conflict in general (Bobo 1983, 1988b; Sidanius et al. 1992; Sniderman and Tetlock 1986b; Wood 1994).[43]

A number of studies by proponents of the symbolic racism perspective have addressed these issues. First, the various components of symbolic racism do tend to form a coherent belief system, though there is evidence that it consists of two highly correlated subfactors focusing, respectively, on blacks' and on society's responsibilities for blacks' disadvantages (Tarman and Sears 1998). Second, when factor analyzed, symbolic racism and old-fashioned racism form two distinct, though correlated, dimensions. Symbolic racism has the far stronger effect when both are included in multivariate analyses predicting to policy preferences (see Sears et al. 1997; Hughes 1997; McConahay 1986). Third, symbolic racism is indeed correlated with race-neutral conservatism. But when ideology is controlled for, symbolic racism remains the most powerful predictor of racial policy preferences, while ideology tends to have a minor residual effect. Fourth, when measures of symbolic racism are purged of all items referring to government or special treatment policy, the results are essentially unchanged (Sears et al. 1997; Sears, Henry, and Kosterman this volume; Tarman and Sears 1998; also see Alvarez and Brehm 1997).

However, important questions remain. The original theory hypothesized that symbolic racism stemmed from a combination of racial affect and traditional values, especially individualism. The contribution of racial affect seems clear, but most studies to date have not found a strong contribution of individualism, at least not as conventionally measured. The origins of symbolic racism represent the crux of much current research, including that described in several chapters in this volume.[44] Second, it seems clear that neither symbolic racism nor racial policy preferences are much influenced by racial threats to whites personally (i.e., self-interest). But the role of whites' shared group interests in maintaining the racial status quo may have been underestimated.[45] This point, too, is addressed by research in this volume.

SUBTLE, AVERSIVE, AND AMBIVALENT RACISM   Other forms of a "new racism" have been described in related, but somewhat different terms. While the theory of symbolic racism has been criticized as too specific to the United States, Thomas Pettigrew and Roel Meertens have developed an analogous approach that would explain racism in Europe as well as the United States. They suggest that blatant prejudice is being supplanted in both areas by subtle prejudice, which is comprised of the defense of traditional values, the exaggeration of cultural differences, and the absence of positive emotions toward outgroups. Using a large, multinational survey, they provide evidence that subtle prejudice is indeed distinct from (though still related to) blatant prejudice, relatively distinct from political conservatism, and useful in predicting attitudes toward policies relevant to outgroups, such as policies about immigration (Meertens and Pettigrew 1997; Pettigrew this volume; Pettigrew and Meertens 1995).

Aversive racism theorists similarly believe that the decline of old-fashioned racism is genuine and that most whites now are genuinely committed to the principles of racial equality. But, as in the theory of symbolic racism, whites continue to have lingering negative feelings toward blacks. This conflict between egalitarian values and antiblack affect causes anxiety and discomfort, especially in the presence of black people. Such whites therefore are motivated to avoid blacks so that they will not be confronted with their own racist feelings (Gaertner and Dovidio 1986; Kovel 1970).

In this view, whites' avowed dedication to the principles of racial equality is real. In situations that unambiguously call for the application of principles of racial equality, whites will generally respond in nonprejudiced ways. However, in more ambiguous situations, their anxieties about African Americans may lead to the avoidance of interaction. For example, some studies of helping behavior have demonstrated discriminatory behavior against African Americans when the situation offers nonprejudiced explanations for it. When other people are available to help, declining to help a distressed black person can be justified in nonracial terms (Frey and Gaertner 1986; Gaertner and Dovidio 1977). This theory has not been applied to the case of whites' racial policy preferences. But its reasoning would suggest that whites' latent racial anxieties should contribute to greater opposition to racial policies because such opposition can be so readily justified in nonracial terms.

Finally, the concept of racial ambivalence also describes general support for equality coupled with residual negative racial affect. Americans' general support for egalitarian values generates positive feelings toward blacks, but their equally general support for the Protestant ethic generates negative feelings toward them, creating ambivalence. Situations that prime egalitarian values should stimulate positive feelings toward blacks, whereas situations that prime individualism should stimulate negative feelings toward them. This link between negative feelings about blacks and the work ethic bears some resemblance to the theory of symbolic racism. However, the theory of racial ambivalence has stimulated less research to date than have the other approaches (see Katz and Hass 1988; Katz, Wackenhut, and Hass, 1986).

THE AUTHORITARIAN PERSONALITY One of the most influential psychological explanations of racism in the years following World War II was that certain personality pathologies lead to ethnocentrism and outgroup antagonism. Theodor Adorno and his colleagues proposed that individuals raised in a harsh disciplinary environment developed a constellation of personality characteristics including intolerance of ambiguity, cognitive rigidity, submissiveness to authority, conventionality, and intolerance of others who are weaker or different or lower in status. Together, these traits comprised the authoritarian personality syndrome and contributed to generalized ethnocentrism (Adorno et al. 1950).

After much methodological controversy, and a long period of disuse, this construct was resurrected and reorganized by Robert Altemeyer around three core themes: submissiveness to established and legitimate authorities, generalized aggressiveness, and adherence to social convention. In a variety of contexts and countries, Altemeyer's measure of right-wing authoritarianism has proven to be strongly correlated with measures of general ethnocentrism as well as measures of hostility toward a variety of specific outgroups. However, relatively little research has examined the influence of authoritarianism and generalized ethnocentrism on public opinion about racial issues (Altemeyer 1994).[46]

COVERT RACISM A further perspective is that extensive racism still persists, but that new, post-civil-rights-era, normative proscriptions now mute its overt expression. That is, even those with underlying prejudiced beliefs understand that the public expression of racism is no longer acceptable in most circles and usually comply with that norm, at least overtly. A number of sociopsychological methods have yielded evidence of such a dynamic. For example, whites attached to a supposed lie-detector apparatus (e.g., a "bogus pipeline") express more negative attitudes toward African Americans than they do on a standard self-report questionnaire (Sigall and Page 1971). Whites interviewed by black interviewers express less negative racial attitudes than they do to white interviewers (Kinder and Sanders 1996; Schuman et al. 1997). In experimental studies, whites show evidence of covert racism in terms of nonverbal leakage of antipathy toward African Americans, including greater seating distance from them, less time voluntarily spent with them, less eye contact, less verbal fluency, an altered tone of voice, and even variations in electromyographical impulses (Crosby, Bromley, and Saxe 1980; Vanman at al. 1990).

In another line of work, social psychologists have increasingly reported that social behavior and judgments can be mediated by cognition outside of conscious awareness. Implicit, automatic, or nonconscious racial attitudes may therefore be mediated by processes that are relatively unavailable to the individual's own introspection. Such processes are typically measured in terms of the relative accessibility of positive or negative responses to race-related stimuli, such as category labels or pictures presented subliminally. Implicit racial attitudes thus measured are presumably automatically activated in the presence of race-related stimuli (Devine 1989; Dovidio et al. 1997; Fazio et al. 1995).[47]

Though this area clearly represents a promising new avenue of exploration, a number of questions remain. First, studies of the relationship between implicit racial attitudes and "explicit" measures (such as the standard measures of prejudice found in survey studies) have generated somewhat mixed results to date. Second, some interpret the implicit measures of racial attitudes as bona fide "pipelines" to an individual's true racial attitudes, circumventing biases introduced by social desirability and self-presentation (e.g., Fazio et al. 1995). Others suggest that implicit measures instead themselves represent a different type of racism, a set of overlearned, negative, affective associations to blacks (Devine 1989). Third, this research was primarily stimulated by the theory of aversive racism, so it has generally focused on predicting whites' direct interpersonal responses to blacks, such as their nonverbal behaviors. More conscious and deliberative political judgments about racial issues may be better predicted by standard self-report measures of racial attitudes, such as those normally used in survey research (Dovidio et al. 1997).

Because these effects occur automatically and outside of awareness, and even among people low in "explicit" racism, the continued impact of racial attitudes may be even more pervasive than would be clear from considering self-report measures alone. However, there is at least some evidence that implicit racial attitudes may not always be fully activated; that they may in some circumstances be activated, but not applied in judgment; and that processing goals and self-presentational concerns may influence their application (Blair and Banaji 1996; Fazio and Dunton 1997).[48] Even taking into account such modifications, the results so far suggest that the socialization of prejudice may be more insidious and more difficult to undo than often hoped.

SOCIAL STRUCTURAL THEORIES

A second set of theories reflects a sociological emphasis on social structure and group interests. These theories generally share the view that individuals identify with their own racial and ethnic groups, that the competing interests of those groups generate intergroup conflict, and that dominant groups develop ideologies to justify and legitimize their hegemony. Whites' opposition to racially liberal policies thus flows principally from the process of protecting their own interests.

REALISTIC GROUP CONFLICT Donald Campbell organized a number of theories of intergroup relations in anthropology, psychology, and sociology into a general "realistic group conflict theory." He concluded that intergroup attitudes and behaviors tend to reflect the nature of the relationship between the groups' material interests. If the interests of the groups coincide, intergroup attitudes should be relatively positive. However, if the groups are competing over limited resources, intergroup attitudes should be more negative. From this perspective, whites' political responses to racial issues should be driven by zero-sum competition with blacks for jobs, promotions, admission slots to colleges, government contracts, or other goods. Thus, their opposition to racially ameliorative policies—and their antipathy toward the civil rights movement, its leaders, and even blacks themselves—can be explained by the threat blacks pose to whites' privileges (Campbell 1965).[49]

A heavy concentration of blacks may be particularly likely to stimulate a sense of collective threat among whites. V. O. Key, Jr., noted that the most racially conservative Southern political candidates in the Jim Crow South tended to receive their strongest support from whites living in areas most populated by blacks, presumably because white hegemony was most vulnerable in such areas (1949).[50] Such racial-context effects continue to be noted today under the rubric of power theory, especially in the Deep South. For example, in the early 1990s, white voting for the racist candidate for governor and senator in Louisiana, David Duke, was highest in areas of greatest black voter registration (Giles and Buckner 1993, 1995).[51]

Real conflicts of interest may be sufficient to cause negative intergroup attitudes, but they may not be necessary. Relative deprivation theory argues that the perceived discrepancy between one's actual circumstances and others' circumstances may be a stronger determinant of dissatisfaction with one's lot in life than is the absolute level of deprivation. In other words, the mere perception of group deprivation may be sufficient to trigger outgroup antagonism; real conflicts of interest may not be necessary (Vanneman and Pettigrew 1972). Social identity theorists go still further. Tendencies to give favored outcomes to fellow ingroup members and discriminate against outgroup members can occur even in experimentally formed groups without any history of conflict or competition over limited resources, or indeed any prior interaction or relationship with other ingroup members. In fact, such ingroup favoritism exhibits itself even when the randomness of their assignment into such groups is completely transparent to participants (Tajfel and Turner 1986).[52] This perspective has not yet been widely applied to the study of public opinion on matters of race, but it has influenced some theoretical perspectives in the area.[53]

A further distinction between self-interest and group interest has proven important. A considerable body of research has found whites' racial policy preferences to be little affected by their own *self-interest* in such racial issues. Individual whites whose own lives are most affected by issues such as busing or affirmative action generally turn out not to be more opposed to such policies than are whites who are not personally affected at all. However, whites' opposition to liberal racial policies may be more closely related to their sense of how the policy might affect their own group's interests. That is, a sense of group interest may be more important than any sense of individual self-interest.[54] The same is true for relative deprivation. Fraternal deprivation—the sense that one's own group is deprived relative to other groups—is more politically influential than egoistic deprivation—the sense that oneself is deprived relative to other salient individuals (Vanneman and Pettigrew 1972).

THE SENSE OF GROUP POSITION   Much current work is developing a variant of the group conflict perspective, treating prejudice as flowing from "a sense of group position." In this view, "the real object of prejudice ... is beliefs about the proper relation between groups ... [that is,] relative group positions" (Bobo, Kluegel, and Smith 1997, 38).[55] This model contains a number of basic tenets. First, people differentiate themselves from others through the use of group categories, accompanied by a belief in ingroup superiority. Second, ingroup members view members of outgroups as alien and different. Third, members of dominant groups come to believe that such membership confers legitimate proprietary rights to superior status, power, and other resources. Finally, dominant group members readily perceive threats from members of lower-status groups who desire a greater share of those resources. Thus, the sense of group position model views the affective and cognitive underpinnings of prejudice as flowing directly from realistic conflict over group interests and perceptions of threat from inferior groups. Moreover, it goes beyond the concrete economic and political interests that are central to realistic group conflict theory to focus on status as well.

Two general kinds of evidence have been provided for such perspectives. First, whites tend to oppose liberal racial policies more than do blacks, even with controls on a wide variety of demographic, ideological, and racial attitudes. This suggests that the two groups have bedrock conflicts of interest and that those conflicts of interest have important political consequences.[56] However, critics note that it is never possible to control on everything, calling for more direct measurement of the presumed mediators of these racial differences (e.g., Sears and Kinder 1985). Consistent with the group position argument, though, recent research has shown that whites who perceive greater conflict of interest between the races are the strongest opponents of liberal racial policies, again net of the other variables that we have been discussing.[57]

The conceptual boundary between this model and the new racism models is not always sharp, however. On the one hand, proponents of the former view critique some measures of symbolic racism as reflecting group interests or their rationalization. On the other hand, symbolic racism theorists find that the sense of group position model largely abandons the focus on realistic group interests and tangible threats in favor of constructs that can be construed as more symbolic.[58]

Lawrence Bobo's more recent concept of "laissez-faire racism" elaborates further on the sense of group position model. It places the transformation of racial attitudes more fully within its historical context, tracing the ultimate decline of old-fashioned racism back to the demise of labor-intensive agriculture in the South.[59] Such an ideology was no longer required without a continuing need to justify whites' exploitative use of blacks as low-wage agricultural labor. However, that economic change did not undo whites' sense of entitlement to their privileged group position relative to blacks. Thus, a new form of racism developed to defend whites' dominant position within the changed economic context, in which blacks became participants in the broader national economy that is based on free market capitalism. Laissez-faire racism therefore consists of two major components: the continued negative stereotyping of blacks and the placing of responsibility for the socioeconomic racial gap on blacks themselves. In this form, blacks' primary shortcoming is no longer some inherent inferiority, but their cultural resistance to the work ethic.

Like the modern racism perspectives, this theory predicts that laissez-faire racism is distinguishable from old-fashioned racism, is a better predictor of racial policy preferences, and is closely linked to beliefs about the socioeconomic stratification system. An important distinction between the perspectives, however, lies in the purported source of the change in racial attitudes discussed earlier. Laissez-faire racism is not a new brand of racism, but instead reflects the transformation of whites' group interests and their continued defense of those interests. In contrast, the modern racism perspective focuses on the continuing socialization of negative affect toward blacks and perceptions that they violate cherished American values.[60]

SOCIAL DOMINANCE THEORY Social dominance theory also begins with the assumption of a social stratification system that distinguishes dominant and subordinate groups. But unlike the other social structural theories, it regards individual differences in personality within these groups as crucial elements in maintaining that hierarchical system. It first assumes that human societies tend to be structured as

group-based social hierarchies. Dominant groups enjoy a disproportionate amount of power, status, and economic privilege relative to
subordinate groups. Both the categorization into groups and the assignment to dominant and subordinate positions are regarded as arbitrary and socially constructed. The theory suggests that there are three
broad categories of such hierarchies: age-based, in which "adults"
dominate "minors"; gender-based, in which males dominate females;
and a third category that varies across societies, based variously on
such dimensions of stratification as race, caste, ethnicity, nationality,
social class, lineage, or clan. While age and gender systems are said to
be found in all social systems, the third system of social hierarchy is
thought to be restricted to those societies producing sustainable economic surplus (i.e., simple horticultural, advanced agricultural, agrar-
ian, industrial, and postindustrial societies).[61]

The heart of social dominance theory concerns itself with identifying the psychological, ideological, and institutional mechanisms that
produce and sustain these group-based social hierarchies. One of the
most important individual-level forces is *social dominance orientation,*
the desire to establish and maintain such social inequalities. It has
been found to be related to many attitudes about policies that favor
dominant groups and disadvantage subordinate groups. Such findings
have been obtained in quite a number of different cultures and nations.

Social dominance theory argues that group-based social hierarchies
are driven by the interaction and reinforcement of mechanisms at one
level of analysis (e.g., the psychological) with those at other levels of
analysis (e.g., the institutional). For example, people with ethnocentric values are known to self-select into "hierarchy-enhancing" institutions, such as the military and the police. Moreover, such institutions
tend to reward those employees who engage in antiegalitarian behaviors toward members of subordinate social groups.[62] Similarly, those
with egalitarian values will be attracted to careers in "hierarchy-
attenuating" institutions, such as social work or philanthropy. These
institutions will tend disproportionately to allocate positive social
value to members of subordinate groups. They will in turn tend to
reward most strongly those employees who exhibit such egalitarian
behavior toward members of subordinate groups. As a result, institutional treatment of group members is a function of the interaction
between individuals' own preferences and institutional norms.

Within social dominance theory, then, "the American dilemma" is
simply a special case of more general forces that tend to maintain the

relative hegemony of some social groups over others. While the specific operations and transactions that produce group-based social hierarchy will vary from one society and/or historical epoch to another, the underlying and essential hierarchical structure itself should be relatively invariant. Social dominance theorists suggest that better understanding the choreography of these underlying mechanisms will yield both a clearer understanding of the oppressive relationships among groups in general and greater insight into the dynamics of specific group conflicts within specific historical contexts.

Finally, a perspective advanced by Mary Jackman and her colleagues shares aspects of both realistic group conflict theory and social dominance theory. This also centrally features the ideas of an interest-based social hierarchy and the collusion of dominant and subordinate groups to promote stability and avoid conflict (Jackman 1978, 1994, 1996; Jackman and Muha 1984). In contrast with realistic group conflict theory, though, she suggests that dominant groups often attempt to maintain the exploitation of subordinate groups through ideology rather than through open conflict and force. They develop ideologies that justify existing inequalities as fair and just.[63]

Thus, Jackman interprets whites' greater support for general principles of racial equality than for liberal racial policies as primarily reflecting their attempts to maintain their dominant position. A new ideology had to be constructed as the previous ideology began to lose utility. Furthermore, she argues that higher education does not increase racial tolerance. It simply makes whites more aware of their interests and more invested in maintaining their privileges. So more education only provides them with the ability to construct a superficial façade of commitment to equality, masking their underlying resistance to any real change. Thus, educated whites present themselves as unprejudiced without having to do anything that would jeopardize their political, social, and economic dominance over blacks.[64]

POLITICAL THEORIES

A third general theoretical position, associated with Paul Sniderman and his colleagues, emphasizes politics more than it does psychology or social structure. This position arose primarily out of skepticism about the causal role of racism in determining opposition to contemporary racial policies as proposed in the new racism models. It focuses on the fact that citizens get to choose only among the political alternatives organized by political institutions and presented by public leaders. Therefore, it is important to look most closely at the nature of those alternatives. This approach is thus "institution-oriented" rather than "actor-centered." However, these authors have generally not used any particular descriptive label, so we will simply describe it as a "politics-centered" approach.[65]

One proposition in particular stands at center stage: as far as whites are concerned, there is no longer *the* issue of race, no simple, emotional, gut-level response to any racial issue, driven by attitudes toward blacks themselves. Instead, the politics of race has evolved into a variety of distinct "policy agendas," such as equal treatment, social welfare for blacks, and race-conscious policies (e.g., affirmative action). Whites' attitudes vary considerably across these areas in three ways. Their level of policy support varies considerably, with opposition to affirmative action being most intense and pervasive (Sniderman and Carmines 1997a). Their policy attitudes cluster within each area rather than reflecting consistent support or opposition to all racial policies across agendas. And opposition to each set of policies is determined more by its unique politics than by racial animus or group interests. As a result, different predictive models are required to explain opposition to the three different sets of policies (Sniderman and Piazza 1993).

Most important, therefore, is general political ideology because elites tend to frame all domestic issues in ideological terms. Conservatives and liberals differ especially in the value they place on governmental solutions to social problems, so the preferred role of government should perhaps be the most central explanatory factor in whites' attitudes. But general moral values are important as well. For example, fundamental considerations of fairness and equal treatment are especially important in generating opposition to affirmative action because they "thrust in exactly the opposite direction" from it: "in the name of achieving racial equality and tolerance . . . the ideals of equality and tolerance have themselves been upended" (Sniderman and Piazza 1993, 177; Sniderman and Carmines 1997a, 3). College-educated people are especially likely to use their ideology and values in responding to racial issues because they are most practiced with such abstractions. However, this perspective takes issue with the new racism's emphasis on whites' perceptions that blacks violate individualistic values and relegates them to a minor role (Sniderman and Piazza 1993, 56–64; Sniderman and Carmines 1997a, 31–33).

These authors do recognize some continued role of racism in influencing whites' opinions about racial issues. In fact, they frequently allude to the minority of whites who continue to express negative stereotypes of blacks in sample surveys. However, their view of the role of racism is rather circumscribed. Indeed, they present evidence to indicate that opposition to affirmative action is likely to generate racial hostility in addition to being the product of it (Sniderman and Piazza 1993). Prejudice, in their view, is a strong determinant neither of racial policy preferences nor of seemingly nonracial explanatory factors, such as political ideology, egalitarian values, and judgments of the fairness of various policies. Such effects as it has are said to be more prominent among the less educated (Sniderman and Piazza 1993). And in their most recent writings, they emphasize the growing numbers of whites of good will toward blacks and their strengthening desire to see that blacks are better off. They suggest that the racial tolerance exhibited by most whites on matters of principle is genuine by showing that whites generally do not use race-neutral justifications to single out blacks disproportionately for negative treatment, even when given the opportunity to do so (Sniderman and Carmines 1997a, 65–70, 89–92, 135–38).

More recently these theorists have suggested that prejudice may actually be a stronger political force among liberals than among conservatives. Even nonprejudiced conservatives have principled, race-neutral reasons for opposing governmentally based racial policies, whereas prejudiced liberals are torn between their ideological preference for governmental solutions and their prejudice against blacks. They provide evidence both that prejudice has a larger impact on the racial policy attitudes of liberals than on those of conservatives and that liberals show more hesitation in expressing their attitudes toward racial policies, presumably due to their ambivalence. They suggest that liberalism is in crisis because elites' support for race-conscious remedies has generated a great deal of "unacknowledged anger" in the rank and file (Sniderman and Carmines 1997a, chap. 3).[66]

Indeed, so far from race being the quintessentially intractable issue, on which white people are immovably pro or con, these theorists argue that the public can be more easily swayed about racial policies than previously supposed, if convincing moral arguments are made, because attitudes toward racial policy are at heart about politics and not race. They argue for a political reprioritization by liberals because the liberals' race-conscious policy agenda has made things worse, not better. Policies like affirmative action violate traditional American values because such policies are exclusive and race-targeted. They suggest a shift to more universalistic color-blind policies, with justifications that appeal to moral principles reaching beyond race. They provide experimental evidence that particularistic policies have limited appeal irrespective of which particular group they are targeted for. More broadly targeted policies with universalistic justifications are capable of achieving levels of political support that could potentially regalvanize progress toward racial equality (Sniderman and Carmines 1997a, chap. 4).[67]

This approach has earned a substantial audience because of its wide-ranging explication of the role of political values in whites' responses to racial issues and its use of a wide variety of statistical and experimental techniques. Given the heavy volume of research this approach has generated, it is perhaps not surprising that some findings fit the theoretical portrait more closely than others. For example, the most recent work presents the effects of prejudice, and its interaction with ideology, as uniform across all racial policies rather than varying according to "policy agenda" (Sniderman and Carmines 1997a, 59–97; Sniderman, Crosby, and Howell this volume). Second, judgments of fairness and support for equal treatment are thought to mediate the link between race-neutral values and opinions about racial policy, but they are not measured directly and so need to be inferred from differential responses to complexly different political alternatives.[68] Third, a clever, unobtrusive measure of racial attitudes has been developed and seems to indicate that a large number of whites who express racially liberal attitudes on standard survey questions take quite the opposite position when given a covert opportunity to do so. This finding has not been explicitly reconciled with several others interpreted as showing that the good will toward blacks that many whites express on survey questions is quite genuine. Also, conservatives express no more negative attitudes toward affirmative action on this covert measure than do liberals, a puzzling contrast to the view often presented elsewhere that ideology is a central determinant of whites' attitudes toward racial policies (Gilens, Sniderman, and Kuklinski 1998).

Finally, some of the most recent research is troubling with respect to the debate with the new racism theorists. First, at some junctures, the older stereotypes about blacks do seem to have considerable influence, and a "commitment to racial equality" index has strong relationships with attitudes about affirmative action and government assistance to blacks (independent of the justification used for the latter).[69] Second, in some recent experiments, they find that opposition to racial policy is strongest when the proposed recipients are black, described in a stereotype-confirming manner, and among respondents who hold the strongest racial stereotypes: "what is crucial is not race by itself, not welfare in the abstract, not even individual effort considered on its own, but the *conjunction* of all three symbolic elements" (Sniderman et al. 1996, 40, emphasis in original).[70] Moreover, they provide evidence that such a conjunction holds special appeal to political conservatives. Such findings would seem to be quite similar to those central to the new racism theories.

Others have also carried out research that specifically challenges some of the tenets of this political approach.[71] First, despite vastly differently levels of support for different racial policies, factor and regression analyses suggest that they still share an underlying racial component, whether that be racial antipathy, symbolic racism, or group-based antiegalitarianism. In addition, racial attitudes continue to have strong effects on whites' racial policy preferences even when ideology and other political values are controlled (e.g., among many others, Hughes 1997; Pettigrew and Meertens 1995; Sears et al. 1997). Second, this research also has provided evidence that conservative values and racism are in fact substantively related. Some go as far as to suggest that, due in part to the political party realignment around civil rights issues, racism and conservative political values are now inextricably intertwined (for discussion of this realignment, see Carmines and Stimson 1989; Edsall and Edsall 1991a). Third, as education increases, so does the relationship between racism and ideology, as well as the impact of newer forms of racism on attitudes toward racial policy (see, e.g., Sears et al. 1997; Sidanius, Pratto, and Bobo 1996). Fourth, some have begun to contest the notion that a substantial opposition to race-conscious policies stems from a sense that such policies violate color-blind principles of racial egalitarianism. Instead, one usually finds that commitment to egalitarian values strongly predicts *support* for almost any kind of racial policies (see Hughes 1997; Sears, Henry, and Kosterman this volume; Sidanius et al. this volume; Sniderman, Crosby, and Howell this volume).

However these puzzles end up being resolved, this more political approach has played an important role in reviving research on ideological and other political values as sources of opinion on racial policy. More important, it has provided research outlining one possible political framework for placing America back on the path to racial equality.

CROSS-CUTTING THEMES

These theories intersect at several points that it might be useful to underline before previewing the original contributions that follow.

THE ROLES OF RACE AND RACISM

There is substantial disagreement among scholars about the extent to which the term "racism" is appropriately applied to contemporary whites' attitudes.[72] Some see racism as having largely disappeared, along with the formal barriers to equality. Others see it as continuing, but in altered form, as some kind of "new racism." There is even disagreement about whether those "new racisms" are in fact much different from the "old racisms" or indeed about whether they reflect racism at all. In addition, there is some disagreement about the form any such new racism takes.

A central question is whether or not race and racism have major influences over whites' attitudes toward racial policy. Most have answered yes, but for different reasons. Perhaps most extreme are the implicit racism theorists, who suggest that racism matters a great deal and in ways that are outside the awareness and control of even the most egalitarian-minded individuals. The symbolic and aversive racism perspectives suggest that the power of racism can now be found in a conjunction of primitive affective responses to blacks and traditional but nonracial values, while biological racism is largely a thing of the past. The social structural theorists assert that race matters, but primarily as an expression of other forces, such as realistic conflicts of group interest or the desire to maintain the ingroup's position in the social hierarchy. At the other extreme, the politically centered theory says that race matters, but more for questions of principle than policy, and then mainly for the less educated.

There is general consensus about two aspects of the empirical data on this point. One is that blacks are far more supportive of contemporary racial policies than are whites. A second is that the "new racism" measures are quite closely correlated with whites' attitudes toward racial policies (Hughes 1997; Kinder and Sanders 1996; Pettigrew and Meertens 1995; Sears et al. 1997). But at that point, consensus vanishes. Some hold that even old-fashioned (or blatant, or classical) racism still has a substantial effect, while others say it does not.[73] There is controversy over how to interpret measures of the "new racisms." Symbolic racism theorists see them as the consequence of the linkage of racial resentment and ideology stimulated by political elites in the post–civil rights era. Aversive racism theorists see them as the acceptable expression of latent negative affect toward blacks. Group-interest theorists see them primarily as reflecting perceptions of racial threat and manifestations of group interests. Social dominance and ideological hegemony theorists view them as merely measuring one legitimizing ideology among many used to maintain the positions of dominant groups. And the politically centered theorists see them as reflecting nonpolitical ideology and/or redundant tautologies of measures of policy attitudes themselves.

A related area of controversy concerns the level of consistency in white public opinion across racial policy issues. Some believe that a strong current of racial animus underlies whites' preferences about a broad variety of racial issues, whereas others believe that there are now multiple "racial agendas."[74] Support for racial policies varies greatly across issues, as we have seen. Almost all whites support general principles of equal treatment, but are more divided about government action to ensure it, and most oppose race-conscious policies, such as preferential treatment.[75] Race-targeted policies generally draw lower levels of white support than do similar policies targeted more broadly (Bobo and Kluegel 1993; Sidanius et al. this volume; Sniderman et al. 1991; Sniderman and Carmines 1997a). However, there is controversy over whether black-targeted policies are opposed more than policies targeted for other groups, such as women (Sidanius et al. this volume; Sniderman, Crosby, and Howell this volume).

But even if levels of support vary quite widely across issues, a common factor of racial animus or group-based antiegalitarianism could underlie all of them. Statistics such as confirmatory factor analysis yield conflicting findings.[76] A final test of consistency asks if the predictors of these various racial policy attitudes are the same. Here, too, there are conflicting findings. The politics-oriented theorists report that whites arrive at attitudes about equal opportunity, federal treatment, and race-conscious policy on the basis of quite different considerations (Sniderman and Piazza 1993). Others find that symbolic racism is the strongest predictor of attitudes in all areas of racial policy, with relatively little difference across areas (Sears et al. 1997). The debates among these different perspectives have helped to crystallize the alternative possibilities, and further research may advance us to greater consensus.

IDEOLOGY AND TRADITIONAL VALUES

A second theme concerns the role of race-neutral ideologies and values. In the hands of social structuralists, political ideology is to a significant degree a tool used by dominant groups to maintain their hegemony. In contrast, politically oriented theorists argue that it composes principles of self-governance reached through careful consideration and education and plays a central causal role in determining attitudes toward racial policy. In the middle, perhaps, are new racism theorists, who see components of conservative ideology as intertwined with racism, but with both making independent contributions to racial policy preferences.[77]

Beliefs about the causes of inequality similarly play a major role in a number of perspectives. According to social structural theories, they provide dominant groups with justifications for the current state of inequality and the maintenance of a privileged group position. In fact, such theorists have particularly noted the importance of individualistic and the absence of structuralistic explanations of inequality as justifications for opposition to racial policy.[78] This position has culminated in the model of laissez-faire racism, which puts the denial of discrimination and stereotypes about blacks' lack of effort at center stage. Symbolic racism similarly invokes the denial of continuing discrimination and perceptions of blacks' lack of work ethic, though conceptualizing both as measuring a conjunction of antipathy toward blacks and traditional values rather than as being interest-based justifications for structural inequality.

Another major theme concerns traditional American values. Seymour Lipset has argued that "American exceptionalism" is based on a set of core values, of which the most relevant to racial policy issues are individualism and egalitarianism (see Lipset 1996). It has indeed often been observed that this pair of values forms an existential dilemma for many Americans when it comes to matters of race. The primary goal of the civil rights movement was racial equality, the ostensible benefit of which was that each individual, black or white, had the opportunity to succeed on the basis of his or her own merits. In that sense, the two values operated in synchrony. Today they may work in conflicting directions, as the work ethic operates at cross-purposes with racial policies that attempt to correct a free market's tendency to produce unequal outcomes.[79]

Individualism in its own right was one of the building blocks of symbolic racism, along with negative affect toward blacks. It also takes center stage, along with other political values, in the politics-centered theory, where it represents a core tenet of conservatism untainted by racial considerations. In social structural theories, individualism is one among several ideological instruments serving to justify and rationalize group-based inequality and hierarchy. Despite this theoretical importance, however, individualism has empirically usually been only weakly related to attitudes toward racial policy. One difficulty is that many concepts have been gathered under the umbrella of individualism, including self-reliance, the value of work, the work ethic, meritocracy, individualistic attributions for disadvantage, freedom, the primacy of individual rights, and opposition to big government. However, it has generally been measured with a single scale, developed for the National Election Studies in the 1980s, that mainly emphasizes the work ethic (see Feldman 1988). A more systematic attempt at construct development and measurement is perhaps needed.

Egalitarianism was the core value of the civil rights movement, and the removal of racial inequalities remains the central goal of racial policies today. So in some sense treating egalitarian values as predictors of racial policy preferences may lead us into something close to tautology. Nevertheless, it is a central player in several of the theories we have reviewed. The symbolic racism theorists assume that white Americans broadly accept the fundamental principles of equal treatment. Aversive racism theorists see it as a key cocontributor to whites' tension and anxiety about blacks. In the politics-centered view, egalitarianism plays a dual role. Among conservatives, the commitment to color-blindness should be related to opposition to race-conscious policies, such as quotas or set-asides. But among liberals, egalitarianism should be related to support for such racial policies. And, of course, it plays an especially central role in social dominance theory, in the form of social dominance orientation, an individual-difference measure of one's desire to increase or maintain group-based social hierarchy.

Much of the empirical work on egalitarianism has also used a single measure (again, see Feldman 1988). It consistently has strong correlations with attitudes toward racial policy.[80] Another standard measure of social dominance orientation also is closely associated with racial policy preferences.[81] However, the reinterpretation of egalitarianism by Sears and his colleagues in this volume suggests that multiple factors underlie the construct. One potentially reflects "pure" egalitarianism—support for equal treatment—while a second reflects resistance to further advances toward equality, resembling racial resentments and perhaps coming closer to individualism than to what most people think egalitarianism is. Plainly, the field would also benefit from further deconstruction of egalitarianism and careful measurement of its different components.[82]

INTERESTS

The sociopsychological and sociological approaches to intergroup conflict perhaps collide most around the question of interests. The symbolic racism theory, taking a symbolic politics perspective, argued that self-interest (that is, personal racial threats) were not strong motivators of whites' racial attitudes. Realistic group conflict and politics-centered theorists criticized the symbolic racism perspective for emphasizing the role of self-interest and ignoring group interests, which were said to be more central to political life in general (compare Sears and Funk 1991 with Bobo 1983; Sniderman and Tetlock 1986b). Much subsequent theoretical and empirical work has emphasized the importance of the distinction between the two kinds of interests, with even group conflict theorists now concurring in the general weakness of self-interest (see Bobo 1983, 1988b, this volume; Hughes 1997).

Nonetheless, questions remain about the notion of group interests at both the theoretical and the empirical levels. Most obvious, most assume that blacks have a strong interest in the objectives of liberal racial policies: more equality in employment, education, housing, business, and so on.[83] Also, Sears and Kinder offer a distinction between symbolic and realistic group interests (Sears and Kinder 1985). The line has not been sharply defined, however. Even resources as seemingly tangible as money, political power, or territory have their symbolic elements (e.g., Lane 1991). And the sense of group position theory places more emphasis than realistic group conflict theory does on status and other more symbolic, intangible goods.

At a measurement level, there is tension about the use of objective indicators of interests as ignoring real perceived interests and/or insufficient direct measurement of those perceived interests (see Bobo 1983, as opposed to Sears and Kinder 1985). Identification with the white ingroup, for example, has to date not been much explored, and some are skeptical of interpreting the racial differences in policy preferences that remain after controlling on a wide variety of other variables as reflecting differential group interests. There is consensus here at the moment, then, that focusing on group interest is more profitable than an emphasis on self-interest. But there remains considerable theoretical and empirical work to be done.

THIS VOLUME

As with American race relations in general, the contributions in this volume represent a mixture of progress and continued conflict. The

chapters that follow represent the major theoretical positions concerning whites' attitudes toward race and racial policy. They show surprising convergence about the important variables and the most critical unresolved issues. Moreover, they provide a sampling of the
sophisticated theory and methodology that are increasingly the standard for this field. They also reflect the growing trend toward examining the attitudes of groups other than white Americans, a crucial step
to developing broader theory and deeper understanding. Despite this
growing consensus, substantial and heated disagreements remain. We
believe that such debates provide the competitive pressure that has
led, and will continue to lead, to the continued refinement of our understanding of "the American dilemma." Chapters 2 through 9 present research by protagonists in these debates that helps to develop
and crystallize points of similarity and difference from other perspectives. All of them present research original to this volume. Chapters
10 through 12 present comments by experts in American racial politics
who have not themselves been involved in these debates. They provide the valuable perspectives of outside observers. We here briefly
review the chief contributions each chapter makes to the ongoing debates.

Donald Kinder and Tali Mendelberg tackle the critically important
conundrum of the role of individualism in racial politics. Despite its
centrality in most historical accounts of Americans' values, it has consistently had less predictive value in explaining whites' attitudes toward racial policies than the new racism theories would suggest. These
authors suggest that individualism has actually become a *part* of prejudice, in the form of racial resentment. It became incorporated into
the expression of prejudice as whites increasingly abandoned old-
fashioned racism in the aftermath of the 1960s and instead became
preoccupied with black Americans' individualistic shortcomings. They
demonstrate the importance of racial resentment and its specifically
racial nature in three ways. First, they provide a detailed reanalysis of
previous work by Sniderman and Michael Hagen (1985). They show
that racially oriented individualism was a potent component of opposition to racial policy, but not to policies focusing on class or gender. In
contrast, they find that standard measures of race-neutral individualism do not influence attitudes on racial policy issues, although they do
have some effect in domains that are not explicitly racial. Second, using a quite different research approach, they show that people talk
about racial resentment, but not individualism, when they are asked
to think about racial policy. In contrast, other kinds of domestic policy

questions activate thoughts about individualism and the role of government, but not about race. Finally, they provide several rebuttals of the contention that racial resentment merely reflects ideological conservatism and not racial prejudice.

David Sears, P. J. Henry, and Rick Kosterman build on the general consensus that symbolic racism is a most powerful ingredient of opposition to racial policy. But they note the vexing question of its origins. Does it really stem from a mixture of racism and traditional values, particularly individualism, as originally asserted? And what is the role of egalitarian values that have no manifest connection to race? First, they provide additional evidence that symbolic racism is distinctly racial, and distinctive from conservative political ideology, in whites' attitudes. However, it seems to be more closely associated with inegalitarian than with individualistic values. A deconstruction of attitudes about equality yields overwhelming support for the principles of equal treatment and opportunity, but much division about how far to pursue further equality in practice. They find that egalitarianism as ordinarily measured in public opinion data is composed of two separate dimensions. The first again taps whites' broadly consensual commitment to principles of equal opportunity and equal treatment. The second, however, appears to tap resistance to further efforts to increase equality. They then present evidence that the latter is much more closely linked to both symbolic racism and attitudes toward racial policy and, more surprising, to individualistic attributions for poverty and racial disadvantage. This suggests that the apparent link between symbolic racism and inegalitarian values may not be what it seems. Symbolic racism may reflect not opposition to equal opportunity, but resentment of a "free ride" for blacks who are seen as not leading lives consistent with the ethic of individual responsibility. If so, whites' resistance to change would seem to stem more from their perceptions of blacks' lack of commitment to individualism than from inegalitarianism in the usual sense.

Marylee Taylor uses the effects of racial context as a way to assess the role of whites' racial sentiments in influencing their racial policy preferences. Combining survey data and Census information, she measures the size of the black population in the white respondents' environs. As it increases, so does white antipathy toward blacks on such dimensions as traditional prejudice, attitudes toward racial policy, racial resentment, perceived group threat, and individualistic attributions for black disadvantage. In contrast, racial context is not related to attitudes about nonracial social policies. She concludes that such findings strongly suggest that opposition to racial policy is in fact based on racial considerations, and perhaps on racial threats. She anticipates, as do we, further research that outlines the processes that lead to such observed effects of racial context.

Lawrence Bobo highlights and explores three points about public opposition to affirmative action. First, many different types of social policy are grouped under the category heading of "affirmative action," and whites are not equally opposed to all of them. Second, beliefs about its costs and benefits, though a substantial part of the public debate, have not been carefully examined in studies of public opinion. Third, the role of group interests in attitudes toward racial policy has been substantially underestimated because the attitudes of blacks and other minorities have too often been ignored. He finds substantial differences among racial/ethnic groups in their attitudes toward affirmative action: blacks and Latinos are more favorable than whites, while Asians' attitudes tend to resemble whites'. Moreover, these differences survive controls on various attitudinal and demographic variables, suggesting a role for group interests. Bobo finds little evidence that such differences are moderated by education, contrary to Sniderman's politics-oriented theory.

Michael Hughes and Steven Tuch, like Sears and his colleagues, explore individualistic and structural attributions for poverty. Most important, their analysis of stratification ideology is broadened both by examining the views of Asian, Hispanic, and black as well as white respondents and by examining how they apply it to Asian and Hispanic poverty as well as to black poverty. They find that whites are the least likely to make structural attributions. However, whites are also less likely (though not to the same degree) to make individualistic attributions. These differences generally hold irrespective of target group. They also find, as expected, that structural attributions contribute to more liberal racial policy preferences. More surprising, they find that individualistic attributions cancel those effects of structural beliefs, so they, too, suggest renewed pursuit of the role of individualism. In common with other authors, they find substantial effects of racial resentment and, to some degree, political conservatism. Finally, they find substantial group differences that survive controls on a host of attitudinal and demographic variables and, like Bobo, conclude that perceived group interests may play a more substantial role in support for racial policy than previously thought.

Jim Sidanius, Pam Singh, John Hetts, and Chris Federico carry out a critical comparison of social dominance theory with Sniderman's political theory. They find that egalitarianism remains a systematically contested issue rather than being a resolved, consensual, and noncontentious feature of American politics. The greater the general social status of one's ethnic group is, the less committed one is to social equality, even when this equality is defined in terms of equality of opportunity rather than equality of result. In two studies, they find social dominance orientation, based on a fundamentally inegalitarian stance, to be equally or even more strongly associated with racial policy attitudes than are conservatism and individualism. In addition, they find that affirmative action is opposed more if targeted for blacks than for women or the poor. Contrary to the notion that conservatives treat the targets of all such policies similarly on principle, they find that conservatives are more likely to oppose affirmative action for blacks than for other groups, while liberals tend to respond in similar vein to all three groups. Moreover, ideology had stronger effects when the policy was targeted for blacks, suggesting a close link between race and ideology. Also, highly educated conservatives were, if anything, more likely to exhibit a racial double standard than were highly educated liberals. In both studies, comprehensive structural equation models yielded stronger support for social dominance theory than for the politics-oriented view. In addition, the authors present a number of other findings potentially problematic for both the modern racism and the politically oriented positions.

Paul Sniderman, Gretchen Crosby, and William Howell carefully delineate their view that political rather than racial considerations stand at the center of whites' attitudes toward racial policy. One analysis tests the idea that the new racism is a conjunction of individualistic values and antipathy toward blacks. Such a model explains relatively little variance in their data. Second, they challenge the standard account of ideology and opposition to racial policy, presenting evidence of substantial cleavage among liberals over affirmative action. For example, when asked explicitly, conservatives are more likely than liberals to express anger about affirmative action, but liberals have more "unacknowledged anger" about it. Third, racial prejudice exerts stronger influence on racial policy attitudes among liberals than it does among conservatives, presumably because liberal ideology clashes with prejudice, while conservatives tend to be ideologically opposed to governmental solutions irrespective of their racial prejudices. Fourth, they present evidence suggesting that conservatives are not more likely to practice a racial double standard than are liberals. They also highlight the importance of politics in influencing attitudes toward racial policies, finding that support for open housing is much influenced by the specific arguments used to justify such policies. Finally, they provide their own views of areas of agreement and areas of disagreement in this contentious area of research.

Thomas Pettigrew takes on the important task of simplifying the vast number of theoretically and empirically suggested predictors of outgroup prejudice. Furthermore, he conducts these analyses in the context of an impressive multinational survey of prejudice in Europe. Focusing on the responses of the majority groups in each nation, Pettigrew finds that four basic dimensions underlie prejudice: political disengagement, lower social class, traditional conservatism, and lack of cosmopolitanism. He finds that these four dimensions of predictors differ to some extent across types of prejudice, such that lower social class is more critical to producing blatant than subtle prejudice. But similar trends tend to hold across the different national samples and target groups. Most relevant to the controversies central to this volume are two other findings. Traditional conservatism is a strong predictor of all forms of prejudice in all subsamples, and indeed predicted prejudice *more* strongly among the better educated than among the less educated. And prejudice was a strong mediator of the effects of conservatism on opposition to immigration in Western Europe.

Howard Schuman begins with concerns about analyses that infer causal relationships from correlations among racial attitude measures. Sometimes those measures seem so similar in content that the correlations may reflect not a causal relation, but two slightly different measures of the same underlying construct. One safeguard is to correlate indisputably different variables, such as racial context and racial prejudice. However, the distance between such variables opens the door to multiple interpretations. Second, he tends to concur with the central conclusion of the symbolic racism perspective that many whites who opposed racial discrimination in the 1960s later opposed much further racial change. But he notes the important distinction between equal opportunity and equal outcomes, suggesting that attitudes toward them may have different origins. He also wonders if the original assumptions about the role of individualism in symbolic racism are still justified. He notes the invidious nature of the term "racism" and finds it implausible that the many whites who oppose preferential treatment do so simply out of prejudice. He shares the basic social dominance assumption that intergroup hostility is so common as to be a normal condition of human societies. What is unusual in American race relations, then, is the relatively new, but pervasive norm proscribing disparagement of minority groups. He urges greater research attention to whites who promote greater racial equality rather than focusing solely on those who oppose it.

Jennifer Hochschild suggests that some of the debates contained in this volume stem as much from differences in style of intellectual work as from substantive disagreement. Some of the authors are "splitters," who contrast alternate theories in "either-or" fashion, while others are "lumpers," who proceed in "both-and" style. The latter being more to her taste, she is inclined to find merit in all the approaches represented here. She has several suggestions for future research. First, she is critical of the narrowness of the standard conceptualization and measurement of such key concepts as affirmative action, individualism, egalitarianism, and group identity. She believes the field would benefit from a broader range of methods, supplementing the standard survey interview with focus groups, experimentation, intensive interviews, and open-ended questions. She applauds a "multifocal" approach to intergroup conflict, considering not just the American black-white divide, but also other American ethnic groups as well as European ethnic conflicts. Finally, she urges attention to social structure as well as to attitudes—indeed to how social structures may affect the life chances of minority groups without anyone intending it or recognizing it.

Michael Dawson argues that racial attitudes in America must be understood within the context of a continuing racial hierarchy. This hierarchical order has not only structured social and political life in America's past, but also affects many aspects of contemporary American life. He, therefore, generally comes down with the "social structural" rather than the "politics-centered" scholars in these debates. At the same time, he does agree with the latter that politics really do matter: even if many white Americans are unwilling to accept fundamental racial equality, their racial attitudes cannot be exclusively understood in terms of antiblack resentment, antiegalitarianism, or group dominance.

Most pointedly, he goes on to comment on the "racialization" of the research process itself. The research conducted by white and black social scientists tends to be fragmented along racial lines. Not only do minority and white social scientists often occupy separate research communities, primarily investigating opinion within their own racial groups, but also they tend to employ substantially different explanatory models. This racial division of labor may have some malignant consequences. For example, minority researchers often show considerable scholarly "bilingualness" by reading and thinking about the work of both white and minority researchers, while white researchers often tend to ignore the work of minority scholars. Moreover, white social scientists tend to "normalize" their own explanatory models as more "objective" and falling within the range of acceptable scientific discourse, while perceiving the work of minority scholars as politically biased and scientifically suspect. That may not only contribute to the fragmentation of the polity as a whole, but also make it more difficult for us all to understand the intersection between race and politics in American society. Much will be gained if social scientists, like ordinary citizens themselves, make a greater effort to listen to one another across the racial divide. This book is a modest effort in this direction.

FINAL WORDS

In 1903, W. E. B. Du Bois forecast that the defining problem of the twentieth century would be "the color line." By 1944, Gunnar Myrdal had issued a more optimistic prediction: that the color line was not an insurmountable divide because it rested on the fundamentally unstable contradiction of racial prejudice with core American values. Over half a century later, both points of view continue to have their vigorous adherents in American social science.

"Disagreement is a powerful engine of scientific advance. It sharpens conceptual boundaries, directs attention to neglected issues, and, of course, prompts the design of would-be decisive experiments" (Gilovich, Medvec, and Kahneman 1998, 602). We agree with this description of scientific debate. The debate in this field has sometimes been acrimonious, but it has yielded increasingly focused, refined, and testable theoretical perspectives on public opinion toward racial policy. In fact, we find that the debate in this very volume suggests a number of conceptual and theoretical refinements as well as a number of intriguing new directions. Our hope is that this volume will help establish and extend a dialogue that will lead to clarification, among scholars as among peoples of different national backgrounds, of different political preferences, and, yes, of different skin colors.

TWO Individualism
Reconsidered

Principles and Prejudice in
Contemporary American
Opinion

DONALD R. KINDER
TALI MENDELBERG

Individualism occupies a prominent and privileged place in various accounts of the American political tradition, and yet efforts to explain contemporary American opinion on matters of race by invoking individualism have proven remarkably and relentlessly unsuccessful. Reconciling these two colliding observations—both of which we take to be true—is our purpose here.

In the first section of our chapter, we will suggest not only that individualism looms large in descriptions of American politics, but also that it *should:* individualism is written into American institutions and pervasive in American political culture. Despite this, individualism appears to play a negligible role in white Americans' opinions on racial issues, a point we establish in the chapter's second section. Then, in the heart of the chapter, we take up four possible resolutions for this puzzle. In ascending order of importance, they are, first, a methodological solution, that individualism's apparent failure in studies of American racial opinion is apparent only and can be written off to deficiencies in measurement, specification, or estimation; second, the segmentation hypothesis, that *outside* the realm of race individualism *is* important in American public opinion; third, that if individualism is reconceived as an ideological weapon deployed in defense of the racial status quo, then it can be seen to influence white opinion, but in insidious ways that elude conventional analysis; and fourth, the solution we push the hardest, that for reasons of history individualism and prejudice have become entangled: properly conceived, individualism is *in* prejudice. Having restored individualism to its proper place (to our satisfaction, at least), we will conclude with a brief general commentary on the analysis of prejudice and principles in American political life.

INDIVIDUALISM AS A DISTINCTIVE AND DEFINING AMERICAN IDEA

Following his famous visit, Alexis de Tocqueville determined that American political life could be understood only by appreciating the "singular stability of certain principles." Conceding that the American people were in constant motion, Tocqueville claimed that the American political mind remained nevertheless essentially fixed, committed to a few key ideas, among them individualism.

By individualism, Tocqueville meant to emphasize the American habits of separation and self-reliance: "Individualism," he wrote, "is a calm and considered feeling which disposes each citizen to isolate himself from the mass of his fellows and withdraw into the circle of family and friends; with this little society formed to his taste, he gladly leaves the greater society to look after itself." Tocqueville believed that individualism was on the rise in America: "As social equality spreads there are more and more people who, though neither rich nor powerful enough to have much hold over others, have gained or kept enough wealth and enough understanding to look after their own needs. Such folk owe no man anything and hardly expect anything from anybody. They form the habit of thinking of themselves in isolation and imagine that their whole destiny is in their own hands." Tocqueville was no admirer of this development. He thought individualism dangerous for democratic society, and he proposed active engagement in civic affairs as an effective remedy (Tocqueville [1835/1840] 1969, 2:506–8).

Although not always sharing Tocqueville's apprehensions, many other discerning observers have singled out individualism as a defining and distinctive American idea. James Bryce (1900, 270), for example, found individualism to be the American people's "choicest" and most "exclusive" possession. Richard Hofstadter came to essentially the same conclusion; in America, Hofstadter (1948, viii) argued, the "economic virtues of capitalist culture" had been transformed and celebrated as the "necessary qualities" of mankind. More recently still, Robert Bellah and his associates launched their extended complaint against individualism with the sweeping assertion that "[i]ndividualism lies at the very core of American culture." More than any other single idea, individualism, according to Bellah, provides us with a common moral vocabulary; it is, he writes, our "first language" (Bellah et al. 1985, 142, 20).[1]

Just how individualism came to be so prominent in America remains something of a mystery. Resolving it was, of course, a central preoccupation of Max Weber's *The Protestant Ethic and the Spirit of Capitalism* (1958). Weber traced the origins of individualism to Puritan doctrines stressing the need for individuals to arrive at their own accounting with God. In such doctrine, as Weber made it out, work was transformed from a burden into a calling. Work became a vital form of moral activity, just as idleness became a sign of a fall from grace. Under Puritan doctrine, men were required to work in a new way: unceasingly, conscientiously, and diligently. Every moment had to be spent soberly and well.

In Weber's account, Puritans and Quakers carried this view to the New World as articles of faith, where it was reshaped in subtle ways. The idea of calling faded from common speech and with it the idea that in work one labored first for the glory of God. Work came to be seen as serving political and moral purposes rather than directly religious ones. A nervous fear of idleness filled the sermons and essays of American moralists. If sexuality, despair, violence, and radicalism were problems, then work was the solution.

This tendency to define the moral life as a mustering of the will against temptation became increasingly intermixed with the American dream of material success. The nineteenth century witnessed a massive outpouring of popular literature on behalf of the argument that hard work and determination were the keys to wealth. We were a nation of self-made men, or so we were told. "'No boy, howsoever lowly—the barefoot country boy, the humble newsboy, the child of the tenement—need despair. . . . They have but to master the knack of economy, thrift, honesty, and perseverance, and success is theirs'" (quoted in Rodgers 1978, 35). Such was the advice provided the country by John D. Rockefeller, and it was echoed in countless sermons, homilies, and popular tracts.

How the sanctity of work, and especially the moral stain attached to idleness, survived the dramatic transformations brought to American society by industrialization is a remarkable story, well told by Daniel Rodgers (1978). According to Rodgers, as the work ethic became an increasingly abstract ideal, further and further divorced from the reality of work itself, Americans clung to their faith in work as the moral center of life ever more tenaciously. The morally charged language of work and idleness became the "distinctive propaganda of industrial America." Socialists denounced capitalists for their idleness, pointing to "their delicate hands, their yachts and horses, and their ample, brocaded bellies." Conservatives saw in every radical proposal "some device that would enable the idle and incompetent to live at the expense of the frugal and the industrious." European immigrants were regarded as "bummers" and "dead heads," failures who had no place in America. Labor union strikes were portrayed by their opponents as "organized idleness." In short, advocates representing a range of political persuasions helped to fashion work and idleness into "one of the most popular weapons in the arsenal of rhetorical invectives."[2]

The worldly asceticism that Weber identified in Puritan thought is, of course, now rather difficult to detect in the American consumer culture. Still, most Americans continue to subscribe to the intrinsic values of sacrifice and hard work. Herbert McClosky and John Zaller (1984) put this point well: "Long after the strictly theological tenets of Puritanism have lost their status as behavioral imperatives, many Americans continued to view work and wealth through the moral prism of the Calvinist creed" (p. 107). Likewise, individualism remains a prominent feature of American political rhetoric: witness the recent debate over welfare reform or the "individualist fantasy" carried out so successfully by Ronald Reagan (Wills 1987). In short, in America today, idleness is still a moral defect; hard work, in and of itself, a moral virtue; dependence on others, a disreputable condition; economic success, still the American Dream (Feldman and Zaller 1992; Hochschild 1995; Lane 1962; Sennett and Cobb 1972).

THE FAILURE OF INDIVIDUALISM TO EXPLAIN CONTEMPORARY AMERICAN OPINION ON RACE

Despite the many confident pronouncements about individualism's centrality to American political life, we are just now beginning to accumulate systematic evidence on the importance of individualism to flesh and blood citizens (Markus 1993). Moreover, the evidence we do have in hand is not always straightforward to interpret. Like other political principles, individualism is not one idea, but a complicated bundle of ideas (Lukes 1973), and so it is often difficult to know whether all those who claim to be studying individualism are actually investigating the same thing.

Such variety could make a mess of things, but in this case, we think it actually helps. For despite differences in conception and measurement, the relevant literature converges on the same point: that individualism has essentially no role to play in explaining Americans' views on issues of race. This conclusion holds for white and black Americans alike and, as we just suggested, for different kinds of individualism, measured in different ways (see, e.g., Bobo 1991; Feldman 1988; Kinder and Sanders 1996; Kluegel and Smith 1986; Sears 1988; Sniderman and Piazza 1993).

The scholarly consensus on this point is challenged really only by Paul Sniderman and Michael Hagen (1985), who argue in *Race and Inequality* that white opposition to racial equality *is* based primarily in individualism. In their view, whites resist federal efforts to desegregate public schools and oppose government policies that would ensure that blacks are not discriminated against at work out of a principled commitment: Americans—old and young, men and women, rich and poor, white and black—should take care of themselves.

To measure individualism of this variety, Sniderman and Hagen made use of instrumentation originally developed by Charles Glock and his associates. In a sequence of careful studies reported in *The Anatomy of Racial Attitudes* (Apostle et al. 1983), Glock's team questioned Americans about the differences they saw between blacks and whites and especially how they explained those differences. The questions that Sniderman and Hagen pick up and analyze focus on racial differences in economic attainment in particular. The exact questions, which appear in both the 1972 National Election Study (NES) survey and the 1972 Bay Area Study, carried out in San Francisco and Oakland by the Survey Research Center at the University of California at Berkeley, read this way:

> We've asked questions like this of quite a few people by now, both blacks and whites, and they have very different ideas about why, on the average, white people get more of the "good things in life" in America than black people. I will read you some of the reasons people have given, including some things that other people don't agree with at all.

> 1. A small group of powerful and wealthy white people control things and act to keep blacks down.
> 2. The differences are brought about by God; God made the races different as part of His divine plan.
> 3. It's really a matter of some people not trying hard enough; if blacks would only try harder, they could be just as well off as whites.

4. Generations of slavery and discrimination have created conditions that make it difficult for blacks to work their way out of the lower class.

According to *Race and Inequality*, which of these explanations people endorse and which they reject are direct reflections of "basic habits of mind . . . long-standing ideas that make up an important part of a distinctively American outlook on individual achievement, personal responsibility, failure, and inequality" (p. xiv). In particular, by examining patterns of response to these questions, Sniderman and Hagen identified four distinctive types: progressives, fundamentalists, historicists, and, most important for our purposes, individualists. *Individualists* believe that blacks are worse off because they have failed to apply themselves and deny that blacks are worse off because powerful and wealthy whites conspire to keep them in their place.[3]

Individualism, operationalized in this fashion, turns out to be very popular. Of white Americans questioned in the 1972 NES survey, more than one-half—some 57 percent—were classified as individualists, with the remainder distributed rather evenly among the other three types.[4] Individualism emerged as the most favored explanation in the Bay Area Study as well. San Francisco is justly famous for its unconventional politics and unusual traditions, but even there individualism prevailed. Sniderman and Hagen conclude that individualism, more than any other idea, governs how white Americans think about racial inequality.

Individualism's appeal matters greatly, according to *Race and Inequality*, because the explanations that Americans embrace for racial differences affect the policy solutions they are prepared to support. Because individualists explain racial differences by pointing to lack of effort on the part of blacks, they should oppose government efforts to move the country toward racial equality. And they do. Compared to those who single out racial discrimination or the white power structure as the primary cause of racial inequality, individualists are less likely to say that the government in Washington should make certain that blacks receive fair treatment on the job and are less willing to support federal efforts to desegregate public schools.

Based on these results—the popularity of individualism and the association between individualism and opposition to policies designed to promote racial equality—Sniderman and Hagen conclude that white Americans reject equal employment opportunity and school desegregation out of commitment to the "master idea" of individualism. Whites oppose racially egalitarian policies because such policies do for blacks what everyone should do for themselves. It is individualism, the embrace of self-reliance and individual responsibility, that leads white Americans to reject liberal initiatives in the realm of race.

Perhaps, but we don't think so. The heart of our disagreement with Sniderman and Hagen goes to the measurement of individualism. What do people reveal about themselves when they explain economic differences between whites and blacks, especially when they assert that blacks do less well than whites because blacks do not try? *Race and Inequality* says that such a view reveals a settled and durable preference for individualism in general; that in their answers whites reveal nothing about their feelings toward blacks. Asking whites to explain racial differences is merely a convenient and efficient way to get at their values.

This assumption is vital to Sniderman and Hagen's conclusion. Is it right? One critical test is to see whether individualism, measured just as it is in *Race and Inequality*, influences white opinion in the domains of class and gender in addition to race. Do Americans who take an individualistic point of view on racial differences oppose policies that would move the country toward greater equality in general? *Race and Inequality* insists that they must. In Sniderman and Hagen's characterization, individualism is a "folk ideology," a general habit of mind that crosses over the arbitrary boundaries set by race, class, or gender.[5] In contrast, we claim that *Race and Inequality*'s measure of individualism mixes convictions about individual responsibility with resentment directed toward blacks. Consequently, we expect "individualism" to display graduated effects: strongest for opinions on race policy, intermediate for opinions on class (since policies in the realm of class are sometimes racially coded), and weakest for opinions on policy relevant to gender.

To carry this analysis out, we turned to the same 1972 NES survey that supplied the empirical foundation for *Race and Inequality*, measuring individualism, fundamentalism, and the rest exactly as Sniderman and Hagen did. Next we scoured the 1972 survey in order to identify policy questions relevant to race, class, and gender. With respect to race, we went beyond the questions analyzed by Sniderman and Hagen. They examined opinions on integration in principle, neighborhood desegregation, fair employment, and school integration, and so did we. But we also analyzed what appear to be equally relevant questions asked on the same 1972 survey: one regarding public accommodations, another on school busing, and a third on government assistance to blacks. In the domain of class, we found three relevant policy questions: one on whether the federal government should see to it that every person has a job and a good standard of living, another on whether the federal income tax should be made more progressive, and a third on whether there should be a government health plan that would cover all medical and hospital expenses. In the domain of gender, finally, we identified four pertinent policy questions: one on whether women should have an equal role with men in business and in government, another on whether women should stay out of politics, another on whether women with working husbands should be the first to lose their jobs when companies have to lay off workers, and a fourth that registers views on the Equal Rights Amendment (ERA).[6]

With these three sets of policy questions in hand, we can determine whether, as *Race and Inequality* requires, individualism operates as a general value. Our analysis treats individualism, fundamentalism, historicism, and progressivism as a set of binary variables, each defined exactly as in *Race and Inequality,* and we rely on ordinary least squares regression to estimate effects.[7] Does individualism, measured in Sniderman and Hagen's terms, stand in the way of equality in general or in the way of racial equality in particular?

Table 2.1 supplies the answer. For each policy considered separately, table 2.1 presents the estimated effect of individualism on white opinion, given by the unstandardized regression coefficient. The results could hardly be more decisive. On the one hand, individualism has a consistent and sizeable impact on white Americans' views on race policy. Individualists are more likely to oppose government stepping in to prohibit racial discrimination at work, to disapprove of plans to desegregate public schools, to reject the idea that the federal government has any special responsibility to the needs and interests of black Americans, and so on through the complete set. On the other hand, once outside the realm of race, the effect of individualism essentially evaporates. Of the three policies involving class, individualism has a detectable effect on just one: the government's responsibility to provide employment and a decent standard of living. And in the domain of gender, opinion and individualism are utterly unconnected.

These findings undermine Sniderman and Hagen's contention that they have measured individualism in general, and, therefore, also undermine their conclusion that individualism determines white opinion on race.[8] If *Race and Inequality*'s conclusion is set aside, then the empirical record on individualism is virtually unanimous. Individualism,

TABLE 2.1 Impact of Individualistic Explanations for Racial Inequality on White Americans' Policy Opinions in the Domains of Race, Class, and Gender

RACE

Integration in Principle	Residential Integration	Fair Employment	Public Accommodations	School Desegregation	Racial Busing	Government Assistance
.16*	.11*	.26*	.21*	.21*	.09*	.19*
(.04)	(.04)	(.06)	(.05)	(.06)	(.03)	(.03)

CLASS

Guaranteed Jobs	Progressive Tax	Health Insurance
.11*	.00	.02
(.04)	(.04)	(.05)

GENDER

Equal Jobs	Women in Politics	Fire Women First	ERA
.06	.01	.02	.03
(.04)	(.04)	(.06)	(.06)

Source: 1972 NES survey and 1972–76 NES panel study.

Note: Each table entry is the unstandardized regression coefficient with the standard error in parentheses underneath. Each equation includes dummy variables to represent the full set of explanations for racial inequality, one each for individualists, fundamentalists, and progressives, with historicists as the suppressed reference group, and a measure of education. All dependent variables are coded on a 0-to-1 interval, with 1 = the conservative position. For equations based on the 1972 cross-section, the number of cases ranges from 617 to 658; for the two equations based on the 1972–76 panel, the number of cases is 394 for ERA and 423 for Health Insurance.
*p < .05 (one-tailed).

conceived of as a general principle, cannot explain white Americans' opinions on matters of race (Bobo 1991; Feldman 1988; Kinder and Sanders 1996; Kluegel and Smith 1986; Sears 1988; Sniderman and Piazza 1993).[9]

SOLVING THE PUZZLE

It really is a puzzle, then: on the one hand, individualism is assigned a prominent place in accounts of the American political tradition; on the other, individualism appears to be virtually invisible in current studies of American opinion on matters of race. Almost as puzzling, at least to us, is that this jarring juxtaposition has drawn so little attention. Perhaps this is because the two literatures—one consisting of sweeping accounts of political principles across long stretches of American political history, the other made up of detailed statistical investigations of random samples of Americans at particular times—do not often speak to one another.[10] We think they ought to, even when they produce, as here, troubling contradictions. In any case, ours is no ordinary puzzle: a lot rides on how it is resolved. For example, if individualism is as important in American political culture as Tocqueville and others say, then the inability of surveys to find evidence for it provides ammunition to critics who contend that public opinion surveys are incapable of investigating anything important or complex. And if the survey studies are correct, then we are pushed in the opposite, but equally extreme, direction of concluding that Tocqueville and others have nothing to say about the current terrain of American politics. Neither of these positions is attractive; fortunately, as things turn out, neither is where we end up. It will take us a while to get there, but our intention is to persuade the patient reader that Tocqueville *is* still relevant, that the surveys *are* correct, and that individualism, properly reconceived, *is* important in public opinion on race.

METHODOLOGICAL FIXES

One possible resolution takes a methodological line: that individualism's failure in current studies of American racial opinion should be attributed to deficiencies in measurement, specification, or estimation. Measure individualism properly, specify how it influences opinion accurately, estimate its effect sensitively, and the puzzle disappears.

It is hard to argue that methodological standards should not be raised, perhaps all the more so here. The prominence of individualism in historical and comparative studies of American political life points to the real possibility that there is something wrong with current research on public opinion, some technical foul-up that stands in the way of seeing clearly what is actually there.

Among the usual methodological suspects, perhaps the most likely is measurement. Consider this exemplary measure of individualism, developed by Stanley Feldman (1988) and taken verbatim from the 1986 NES survey:

Most people who don't get ahead should not blame the system; they have only themselves to blame.

Hard work offers little guarantee of success.

If people work hard they almost always get what they want.

Most people who do not get ahead in life probably work as hard as people who do.

Any person who is willing to work hard has a good chance at succeeding.

Even if people try hard they often cannot reach their goals.

Now in some respects, these questions seem ideal for measuring individualism as a principle: they are abstract, they make no reference to particular groups or specific policies, and they put individual determination and self-reliance front and center. As such, the questions seem to capture quite well the notion of individualism that Tocqueville, Bryce, Hofstadter, and others had in mind as they described the American political culture.

All survey questions have their limitations, of course, and these are no exception. Their major potential drawback, as we see it, is that they treat individualism as if it were a "cool cognition." That is, the questions are not, with the exception of the first, morally charged. They do not probe reactions to work and idleness treated as ethical categories; they do not inquire as to whether hard work *should* be rewarded. Better would have been more questions in the spirit of the first, which takes up failure and blame in moralistic language.

Various empirical results argue against going very far in this direction, however. First of all, the question that we like turns out to be no more successful a predictor of opinion than the others (Kinder and Sanders 1996). Second, aggregating responses to the six questions into a composite scale produces a reasonably reliable measure. That is,

Americans answer these various questions as if they had one thing prominently in mind.[11] Third, using this scale, the effects of individualism are nevertheless relentlessly unimpressive, and this is so across various plausible specifications and estimation routines (Feldman 1988; Kinder and Sanders 1996).[12] Last and most persuasive, individualism, measured in the standard NES way, *does* influence opinion *outside* the realm of race (we will describe this finding in greater detail in a moment). All these results suggest that the solution to our puzzle lies somewhere other than with methodological improvements, as important as they may be for other reasons. The negligible effects of individualism cannot be written off to technical shortcomings.

SEGMENTATION

Perhaps individualism's troubles are confined to the realm of race. Conceding that individualism is overridden by more compelling considerations on racial matters, it might still be an important ingredient in American public opinion outside the domain of race.

To see if this is so, we turned to the 1986 NES survey and the standard battery of individualism questions introduced in the previous section.[13] We created a composite scale of individualism, based on average responses to the six questions, scaled for convenience's sake onto the 0–1 interval. Table 2.2 presents estimates of the independent effect of individualism, measured this way, on white Americans' views on policy. As table 2.2 implies, these probit estimates take into account the effects due to other plausible causes of opinion, the most notable being racial prejudice and general egalitarianism.[14] The table presents results for six policies, three in the domain of race (whether the government should intervene to ensure that blacks are not discriminated against at work, the role of the federal government in providing assistance to blacks, and affirmative action for blacks in college admissions) and three in the domain of social welfare (the obligation of the government to provide employment and a good standard of living, federal funding for the food stamps program, and the general trade-off between government spending and government services).[15]

Table 2.2 provides strong support for the segmentation hypothesis. Individualism is irrelevant to white opinion on policy initiatives in the realm of race—by now a familiar pattern—but it plays an important role in opinion on various domestic policy matters outside the racial domain. In particular, individualism has a strong effect on whites' views regarding the federal government's obligation to provide work and a decent standard of living and the funding of food stamps and a

TABLE 2.2 Impact of Individualism, Egalitarianism, and Racism on White Americans' Policy Opinions in the Domains of Race and Social Welfare

	RACE			SOCIAL WELFARE		
	Federal Assistance	Fair Employment	College Quotas	Food Stamps	Spending/Services	Jobs/Standard of Living
Individualism	−.19	.13	−.28	−1.34	−.73	−1.45
	(.23)	(.33)	(.26)	(.25)	(.23)	(.23)
Egalitarianism	1.39	1.09	.55	1.44	1.74	1.51
	(.21)	(.29)	(.23)	(.23)	(.21)	(.21)
Racism	−2.01	−1.92	−2.31	−1.07	.48	−.57
	(.20)	(.29)	(.22)	(.22)	(.20)	(.20)
N of cases	808	592	833	826	812	835
Log likelihood	−1328.2	−442.2	−948.7	−807.2	−1458.5	−1422.2
X^2_3	231.3	103.8	169.7	109.8	151.1	85.1
δ_1	−2.00	−.48	−1.27	−1.44	−.90	−1.26
	(.24)	(.32)	(.26)	(.26)	(.24)	(.23)
δ_2	−1.37	−.36	−.62	−.05	−.34	−.68
	(.24)	(.32)	(.25)	(.25)	(.23)	(.23)
δ_3	−.72		.14		.25	−.14
	(.23)		(.25)		(.23)	(.23)
δ_4	.25				1.07	.56
	(.23)				(.23)	(.23)
δ_5	.89				1.67	.98
	(.24)				(.24)	(.23)
δ_6	1.45				2.22	1.32
	(.24)				(.24)	(.24)

Source: 1986 NES survey.
Note: Each table entry is the ordered probit regression coefficient with the standard error in parentheses underneath.

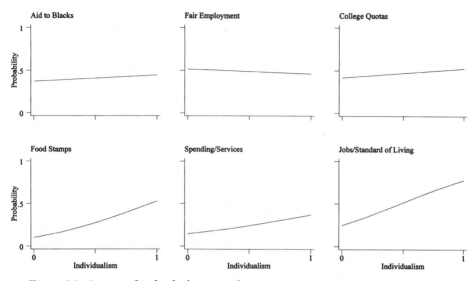

Figure 2.1. Impact of Individualism on White Americans' Opinions in the Domains of Race and Class. *Source:* 1986 National Election Study

more modest, but still noticeable, effect on opinions toward government spending on domestic programs in general.

The magnitude of these effects can be seen more clearly in figure 2.1, which translates the probit coefficients into graphical form. The curves in figure 2.1 are constructed by holding constant the effects due to prejudice and egalitarianism, setting their values to sample averages. The figure presents predicted opinion scores on the various policies (along the vertical axis) as a consequence of variation in individualism (along the horizontal). As the figure makes clear, as individualism increases, white support for various liberal initiatives falls, and falls sharply, as long as the policy initiatives have nothing directly to do with race. But when issues intrude in obvious ways on the fortunes of black Americans, the curves flatten out: individualism becomes irrelevant.

So individualism *is* important. Abstract ideas about individual responsibility and self-reliance do have a place in Americans' views on government policy. That place is social welfare policy, however—not policy bearing on race. This is certainly useful to know, but in a way, these results only add to our mystery. Given that individualism influences how Americans think about social policy generally, why does individualism suddenly disappear when the subject turns to race?

INDIVIDUALISM AS AN IDEOLOGICAL WEAPON

Perhaps it doesn't disappear; perhaps we just need to look for a different kind of individualism. This is the solution that can be drawn out of Mary Jackman's stimulating analysis of the ideological foundations of social inequality (Jackman and Muha 1984; Jackman 1994). Following in some large footsteps, Jackman argues that intergroup attitudes in general and individualism in particular should be conceived of as ideological weapons. In modern capitalist societies, so goes the argument, dominant groups control the means of material and ideological production. Through the latter, dominant groups are able to supervise the creation and distribution of beliefs that justify the current social order; they "routinely manufacture an interpretation of reality and a set of normative prescriptions that serve their interests" (Jackman and Muha 1984, 759). Insofar as such beliefs penetrate the consciousness of subordinate groups, conflict is managed before it begins, and inequality is preserved.

Jackman's major contribution to this general line of argument is to show how the content of such beliefs depends on the nature of the relationship between dominant and subordinate groups. Jackman examines inequalities of race, class, and gender in the contemporary United States. She argues that where inequalities are challenged and contested by the subordinate group, individualism becomes an important element in the dominant group's response and that such a case is provided by current race relations.

More specifically, Jackman argues that in the realm of race, whites come to champion the idea of individualism because it provides them with a principled and apparently neutral justification for opposing policies that are compensatory or preferential toward black Americans. Individualism fits white Americans' political interests perfectly; on Jackman's telling, whites wish to appear both reasonable and responsive, meanwhile making as few real concessions as possible. From this perspective, school integration and affirmative action are wrongheaded because they entail violations of individualism: government privileging the rights of a group over the virtually divine rights of individuals.

Suppose that Jackman is right about individualism. Suppose, as Jackman says, that individualism provides white Americans with an apparently neutral and principled justification for opposing policies designed to upset the racial status quo. Isn't her argument damaged by the finding that served as our empirical point of departure: namely, that white Americans who are especially taken by individualistic doctrines are not especially opposed to government efforts to assist black Americans; that inside the realm of race individualism and policy are unconnected?

Not necessarily. Jackman has something rather different in mind when she refers to individualism. Her notion of individualism is perhaps best thought of, following Steven Lukes (1973), as "political individualism." In Lukes's account, political individualism portrays members of society as "abstract individuals," "independent centers of consciousness." Under political individualism, citizens are the sole generators of their own wants and preferences and the best judges of their own interests. And government, under political individualism, should be limited, its purpose confined to enabling individuals' wants to be satisfied, individuals' interests to be pursued, and individuals' rights to be protected. It is this aspect of individualism that we think Jackman imagines as part of white Americans' defense of racial privilege: not self-reliance, not work and idleness as morally charged categories, but rather the primacy of individual rights.

We take Jackman's solution to the puzzle of individualism's disappearance to be promising, if not yet confirmed by empirical analysis.[16] Her argument is appealing in part because it anchors intergroup attitudes in social structure, in ongoing social inequalities. As Clifford Geertz (1964) points out, this is an advantage enjoyed by "interest theories" of ideology generally, and the gain that such theories thereby provide to an understanding of ideology is both substantial and permanent. All this is worth mentioning because psychologically oriented scholars of prejudice and racism have not always been scrupulous or even serious about situating their analysis within a broader framework of politics and society (as pointed out sharply by Herbert Blumer [1958] and Lawrence Bobo [1988b]). Jackman's analysis is a forceful reminder that prejudice and individualism are forms of intergroup attitudes: they are expressions of both individual conviction and group interest, serving both psychological needs and political purposes.

INDIVIDUALISM *AND* PREJUDICE

That the origins of American race prejudice reach back at least to the middle of the sixteenth century (Jordan 1968) does not mean that prejudice is immutable. It is not. Like other social doctrines, prejudice is subject to occasional and episodic revision. Most of all, it is shaped by alterations in intellectual currents, changes in economic arrangements, and eruptions of political crisis (Fredrickson 1971; Kinder and Sanders 1996).

Our fourth and final possible solution to individualism's disappearance takes this malleability of prejudice for granted. It solves the puzzle by locating individualism *within* prejudice. Today, we say, prejudice's public expression and private language are preoccupied with black Americans' specifically *individualistic* shortcomings: that blacks fail to display the virtues of hard work and self-sacrifice that white Americans claim as central to their own lives and to their society.

Such prejudice appears under various labels: it is "symbolic racism" to David Sears (1988), "modern racism" to John McConahay (1986), "racial resentment" to Donald Kinder and Lynn Sanders (1996), and "laissez-faire racism" to Bobo and Smith (1998). These are closely related concepts; for the most part, the differences here are terminological. As we read them, Sears, McConahay, Kinder and Sanders, and Bobo and Smith agree on a number of important points:

- that biological racism—the doctrine that blacks constitute a separate and permanently inferior race—carries relatively little weight in elite discourse or citizen attitudes today (though it would be a mistake to assume that biological racism has disappeared entirely or permanently);
- that as biological racism has faded to the margins of society, an alternative expression of racism has moved to center stage;
- that like biological racism, symbolic (or laissez-faire) racism legitimates inequalities of wealth, status, and power;
- that symbolic (or laissez-faire) racism is both popular among white Americans and a powerful influence on their political views; and
- that at the center of prejudice today is a deeply felt resentment that blacks choose to live in ways that repudiate individualistic virtues, abiding commitments to hard work, discipline, and self-sacrifice.

The emergence of this form of prejudice can be traced back to transformations set in motion during the racial crisis of the 1960s, as civil disobedience gave way to an epidemic of violence in American cities.[17] On the one hand, the conspicuous and hard-earned successes of the civil rights movement, culminating in landmark legislation that made discrimination illegal and the right to vote real, led many whites to the conclusion that all the obstacles that had stood in the way of black Americans for so long had been successfully removed. The national government had acted forcefully and decisively. The legal foundations for segregation were demolished. Discrimination was illegal. Voting rights were being enforced. In the view of many white Americans, the problem of race had been solved; the nation could now move on to more pressing business.

On the other hand, glaring racial inequalities persisted. Why was it that black Americans continued to fail? Not because of inborn inferiority. Taking their cues from the egalitarian turn in scientific and elite discourse, white Americans were less and less willing to say that racial inequalities in achievement reflected genetic or biological differences between the races. With that line of explanation mostly closed off, whites gravitated instead to individualistic accounts. Whites saw evidence of black failure everywhere—crime, poverty, unemployment, welfare, the explosion of violence and rioting in cities—and they blamed it on defects of temperament and character. Blacks disdained hard work and self-sacrifice and refused to take advantage of the ample opportunities that were now open to them. Racial differences in success were due to lack of black enterprise and initiative. Racial inequality reflected the failure of individualistic virtues to take hold among black Americans.

In short, prejudice today is preoccupied with matters of moral character. At its center are two complementary contentions: that blacks do not try hard enough to overcome the difficulties they face and that, with the connivance of government, they take what they have not earned. Today, we say, prejudice is expressed primarily in the language of individualism; today individualism is part of racism.

With prejudice of this variety in mind, Kinder and Sanders (1996) assembled a set of relevant questions, tested them in a small national survey, and placed the surviving questions into the 1986 NES survey. In keeping with what we take prejudice to mean today, these questions make no reference to genetic inferiority, white supremacy, or racial segregation. Instead, they reflect individualistic resentments: the questions share a sense that blacks have been handed advantages; that government has caved in, showering blacks with special favors; that hard work, self-discipline, and personal sacrifice no longer count for much:

Irish, Italian, Jewish and many other minorities overcame prejudice and worked their way up. Blacks should do the same without any special favors.

Generations of slavery and discrimination have created conditions that make it difficult for blacks to work their way out of the lower class.

It's really a matter of some people not trying hard enough; if blacks would only try harder they could be just as well off as whites.

Over the past few years, blacks have gotten less than they deserve.

Most blacks who receive money from welfare programs could get along without it if they tried.

Government officials usually pay less attention to a request or complaint from a black person than from a white person.[18]

Expressed in these terms, prejudice turns out to be widespread. As table 2.3 reveals, substantial majorities of whites agree that if blacks would only try harder, they could be just as well off as whites; that most blacks who receive money from welfare programs could get along without it if they tried; and that blacks should overcome prejudice on their own without any special favors. Likewise, many reject the assertion that blacks have gotten less than they deserve in recent years, that whites are granted more attention by government officials than blacks, or that generations of slavery and discrimination have created conditions that make it difficult for blacks to work their way into the middle class.[19]

Prejudice is not only popular; it is also powerful. Indeed, to predict white opinion on issues of race, nothing works as well. Typical results are on display back in table 2.2. Earlier we used these probit regressions to establish the point that though individualism is irrelevant to white opinion on racial policy initiatives, it plays an important role in opinion on various domestic policy matters outside the domain of race (e.g., on whites' views regarding the federal government's obligation to provide employment and a good standard of living). Table 2.2 also reveals the power of prejudice. On the role of the federal government in providing assistance to blacks, on whether the government should intervene to ensure that blacks are not discriminated against at work, and on affirmative action for blacks in college admissions, the effects of prejudice are huge. Prejudice's impact is much less noticeable on social welfare issues, coming through strongly on a single issue, support for food stamps. The one exception is interesting, since the food stamps program has figured prominently in public discussions of fraud and abuse in the welfare system and many whites believe that welfare payments go primarily to undeserving blacks (Gilens 1996a, 1996b).

TABLE 2.3 Prejudice among White Americans

1. Most blacks who receive money from welfare programs could get
   along without it if they tried.
Agree strongly	25.4%
Agree somewhat	35.3
Neither agree nor disagree	14.2
Disagree somewhat	18.7
Disagree strongly	6.5

2. Over the past few years, blacks have gotten less than they deserve.
Agree strongly	3.3
Agree somewhat	15.4
Neither agree nor disagree	22.8
Disagree somewhat	38.0
Disagree strongly	20.5

3. Government officials usually pay less attention to a request or
   complaint from a black person than from a white person.
Agree strongly	3.9
Agree somewhat	17.8
Neither agree nor disagree	28.3
Disagree somewhat	30.5
Disagree strongly	19.4

4. Irish, Italian, Jewish and many other minorities overcame prejudice
   and worked their way up. Blacks should do the same without any
   special favors.
Agree strongly	32.9
Agree somewhat	33.7
Neither agree nor disagree	12.4
Disagree somewhat	16.2
Disagree strongly	4.7

[In past studies, we have asked people why they think white people seem to get more of
the good things in life in America—such as better jobs and more money—than black
people do. These are some of the reasons given by both blacks and whites.]

5. It's really a matter of some people not trying hard enough; if blacks
   would only try harder they could be just as well off as whites.
Agree strongly	22.4
Agree somewhat	36.9
Neither agree nor disagree	13.3
Disagree somewhat	19.1
Disagree strongly	8.2

6. Generations of slavery and discrimination have created conditions
   that make it difficult for blacks to work their way out of the lower
   class.
Agree strongly	17.0
Agree somewhat	41.1
Neither agree nor disagree	9.8
Disagree somewhat	19.2
Disagree strongly	12.9

Source: 1986 NES survey.

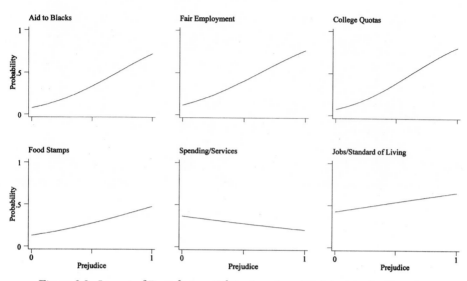

Figure 2.2. Impact of Prejudice on White Americans' Opinions in the Domains of Race and Class. *Source:* 1986 National Election Study

All these effects can be seen more clearly in figure 2.2, which translates the probit estimates into graphical form. Figure 2.2 presents predicted opinion scores on the various policies as a consequence of variation in prejudice, holding constant the effects due to individualism and egalitarianism (by setting their values to sample averages). As figure 2.2 makes clear, for various initiatives in the realm of race—special assistance from the federal government, the prohibition of discrimination at work, affirmative action in college admissions—as prejudice increases, white support declines precipitously.

There is nothing unusual about these findings; they are in fact altogether typical. The same results come booming through, across various specifications, under different political circumstances, and with close attention to alternative and competing explanations. Prejudice is not the only thing that matters for whites' views on racial policy, but it is the most important thing (Kinder and Sanders 1996; Kinder 1998c).

All these findings are a product of familiar and conventional methods: prejudice and opinion are measured independently, and then the relationship between them is estimated statistically. Next we wish to present one additional test of the potency of prejudice, one that draws on fresh evidence and quite different procedures. Here citizens report the thoughts that run through their minds as they contemplate their opinions; these thoughts are recorded and classified; finally, the frequencies of the various categories of thoughts are taken as evidence of the strength of the underlying causes of opinion.

The procedure originates from theoretical work on problem solving by Allen Newell and Herbert Simon (1972). The essential claim is that the verbalizations that people can be induced to provide as they perform various tasks—solving puzzles, learning new concepts, memorizing text, and, here, evaluating policy proposals—illuminate the cognitive processes underlying the tasks. In particular, when properly elicited and analyzed, such verbalizations identify the factors that people take into account as they solve a wide variety of problems (Ericsson and Simon 1993).

Our interest in such procedures is to secure an independent estimate of the influence of prejudice and principles on American opinion. We can actually do this because of innovations introduced by Feldman and Zaller (1992) into the 1987 NES survey. In the spring of 1987, a sample of Americans was questioned on a wide array of political subjects; most important here, people were asked for their opinions on three issues of national policy: one on services and spending, one on employment, and a third on the government's obligation to improve the economic and social position of blacks. Moreover, people were asked about these issues in an unconventional way—two unconventional ways, actually. In the first, immediately after giving their opinions, people were asked:

> Still thinking about the question you just answered, I'd like you to tell me what ideas came to mind as you were answering that question. Exactly what things went through your mind?

> Are there any (other) reasons that you favor [the option you just selected]?

> Do you see any problems with [the option you just selected]?

Under the second procedure, the policy questions were read in the standard way, but without pausing to allow the person to answer, interviewers interjected with the request to "stop and think" before answering:

> Before telling me how you feel about this, could you tell me what kinds of things come to mind when [to take one example] you think about government making sure that every person has a good standard of living? (Any others?)

Now, what comes to mind when you think about letting each person get ahead on their own? (Any others?)

These two procedures for eliciting verbalizations were randomly assigned: half of the respondents in the 1987 survey were asked immediately to recall what was running through their minds as they answered; the other random half were taken through the think-aloud procedure. The advantage of the first is that the probe is entirely general and therefore neutral. The advantage of the second is that it is concurrent rather than retrospective.

Feldman and Zaller designed this portion of the 1987 NES survey, and their analysis of the sample of verbalization materials is full of instructive results.[20] Among other things, Feldman and Zaller (1992) discover that when Americans are asked to come up with opinions on matters of public policy, they are quite likely to have principles in mind: equality, limited government, and, not least, individualism. These results are based on an analysis of just two of the policy questions; Feldman and Zaller set the race question aside. Why? Because the verbalizations reported by people as they came to an opinion on the government's obligation to improve the economic and social position of blacks were different. In particular, many of the comments on government assistance to blacks referred directly to blacks (i.e., discrimination against them or their opportunity to get ahead) or to attributes of blacks. One entirely new category of responses is thus created (negative attitudes toward blacks), and many of the other responses that reflect the same general categories used for the two social welfare questions are intertwined with race (1992, 275, n. 4).

But what is a headache for Feldman and Zaller turns into an opportunity for us. For we wish to compare opinion in the realm of race with opinion in the realm of social welfare, and the Feldman and Zaller questions allow us to do just that.

With this purpose in mind, we analyzed reactions to the two policy questions that, race aside, are closely comparable:

Some people feel the government in Washington should see to it that every person has a job and a good standard of living. Others think the government should let each person get ahead on their own. Which is closer to the way you feel, or haven't you thought much about this?

and

Some people feel that the government in Washington should make every effort to improve the social and economic position of blacks. Others

TABLE 2.4   Prominence of Prejudice and Principles in White Americans' Policy Opinions in the Domains of Race and Social Welfare (Percent)

	GOVERNMENT ASSISTANCE TO BLACKS	JOBS/STANDARD OF LIVING
Prejudice		
Racial resentment	49.8%	0.3%
Biological racism	2.1	0.0
Principles		
Individualism	13.8	67.1
Limited government	5.4	37.2
Equality	25.8	11.2
% No opinion	13.5	14.0
N	333	331

Source: 1987 NES survey.

feel that the government should not make any special effort to help blacks because they should help themselves. Which is closer to the way you feel, or haven't you thought much about this?

Both questions refer to the government in Washington. Both present the policy as a choice between doing more and doing less. Both suggest the same reason for doing less: namely, that Americans should take care of themselves. Both include a reasonably aggressive filter, inviting people who have not thought about the issue to say so rather than making up a casual opinion on the spot. And while the first refers to providing employment and a good standard of living, the second refers to the closely related aspiration of improving social and economic standing. Between the two questions, there is really only a single stark difference, then: the one refers to "every person," while the other refers to "blacks." The many close similarities and the one striking difference mean that the two questions, from our perspective, approximate an ideal experiment.

Table 2.4 presents the results of our analysis.[21] First, consider the question of government assistance to blacks. Table 2.4 shows that on this issue prejudice occupies a prominent place in whites' thinking. Indeed, one variety or another of racial resentment crossed the minds of 49.8 percent of whites questioned in 1987. These included the thought that blacks should help themselves or try harder to make it own their own, that they should stop complaining and do a little bit of work for a change, that they should work like the rest of us, or that they are doing pretty well these days and do not need help. Thus, prejudice that mixes together racial animosity and individualistic values is very prominent. Biological racism, by contrast, is not. As table 2.4 reveals, expressions of biological racism show up at no better than trace amounts. Notice finally that when whites mull over what government should do for blacks, they only occasionally consider individualism in general. References to individualism in the abstract, though not invisible, are scarce.[22]

Turn now to the issue of government providing jobs and a good standard of living. Here the story changes abruptly, but in a way that by now should seem completely familiar. When the question is government extending help to "every person," prejudice simply disappears. At the same time, any number of individualistic themes become commonplace. Now whites say that people should make it on their own, that people must be responsible for themselves, that welfare breeds dependency, that the poor deserve their poverty, that some people are just naturally lazy, that work gives people pride and self-esteem, or that government assistance is unfair to those who do work. Such references seem quite close to what Bryce and Hofstadter meant by American individualism.

In short, relying on radically different methods, we come up with virtually identical results. Individualism looms large when whites think about general social programs and then fades away when they take up issues of race, just as we found in our statistical analysis. Prejudice shows large effects on issues of race, but trifling effects on social programs that distribute benefits and opportunities widely, again just as was the case in our statistical analysis of national surveys. With this striking replication in hand, we say, again, that on matters of race today the most potent force at work in white opinion remains prejudice, prejudice properly conceived, prejudice expressed in the language of individualism.

INDIVIDUALISM AND PREJUDICE?

Not everyone thinks so. One line of criticism is set out by Jim Sidanius and his associates. Sidanius comes to the conclusion that white opposition to liberal initiatives in the realm of race has little to do with racism per se. In Sidanius's framework, racism—old or modern, biological or symbolic—is demoted to the status of myth. Myths provide moral and intellectual justification for policies that reinforce and maintain social inequalities, but they are themselves not the cause of such policies. Racism is a prime example of a legitimizing myth, and so is individualism. Both serve as intermediaries between support for policies that maintain racial inequality, on the one hand, and the real cause of such

views, on the other. The real cause, according to Sidanius, the fundamental driving force behind white conservatism, is "social dominance
orientation." By social dominance, Sidanius means a basic and universal desire to regard one's own group as superior to others. And by
social dominance orientation, he means the extent to which particular
individuals "desire social dominance and superiority for themselves
and their primordial groups" (Sidanius 1993, 209).

At a conceptual level, social dominance bears a striking resemblance to ethnocentrism (Sumner 1906; Adorno et al. 1950; Tajfel
1982; Kinder 1998b). Sidanius situates social dominance within a distinctive theoretical framework, however: one that begins with the
observation of hierarchy in all societies and that locates the universal yearning for group dominance in the imperatives of competition
viewed over evolutionary time. In a series of investigations, Sidanius
finds that social dominance orientation is associated with a wide range
of political ideologies (or as he would have it, legitimizing myths) and,
of more immediate relevance here, that white Americans who score
high on social dominance also are inclined to oppose policies designed
to reduce racial inequalities (Pratto et al. 1994; Sidanius 1993; Sidanius, Devereux, and Pratto 1992; Sidanius, Pratto, and Bobo 1996).

What to make of these results? Sidanius and his associates assess
social dominance orientation through questions that provoke reactions
to equality: "Some people are just more worthy than others" or "In an
ideal world, all nations would be treated equally." It is clear that
people hold reasonably consistent views on the importance and desirability of equality, formulated in this way. With sufficient numbers of
such questions, Sidanius is able to construct a reliable measure—but
of what, exactly? In their abstractness, the questions seem quite dis-
tant from what Sidanius means by social dominance orientation. Except for an occasional reference to "nation," the questions make no
mention of particular groups, primordial or otherwise. To the contrary,
the questions are noteworthy for their abstraction. They put forward
different kinds of equality—equality of opportunity and of result; social, economic, and political equality; and so on—in an entirely general way. Conflict among social groups simply does not come up; nor
does the wish for group dominance. It seems to us that what Sidanius
has reliably measured is general attitudes toward equality.[23]

If social dominance orientation is thought of as antiegalitarianism,
then it is not surprising that Sidanius finds strong empirical connections between social dominance and opinions on policy. Much writing
on the American political tradition, and on American exceptionalism

in particular, takes as a central fact what Tocqueville famously referred
to as the American "passion for equality" ([1835/1845] 1969, 3). We
know from contemporary survey evidence that Americans in fact differ over the importance and desirability of equality and that these differences of principle translate into sharp differences on specific matters
of policy (e.g., Feldman 1988; Kinder and Sanders 1996; McClosky
and Zaller 1984; Rokeach 1973; Schlozman and Verba 1979; Sears,
Huddy, and Schaffer 1986). Sidanius's findings fit neatly within this
tradition. We read his results as reflections of an ongoing and historically contingent dispute in American political life over the meaning
and importance of equality rather than, as Sidanius would have it, the
manifestation of a desire for group domination rooted in evolutionary imperatives.

This difference of interpretation should not obscure an important
empirical convergence. Sidanius finds strong effects of racism on policy views, over and above the effects due to social dominance. That
is, both prejudice *and* egalitarianism (as we would have it) influence
white opinion. This is what Sidanius finds, and it is what we find as
well (Kinder and Mendelberg 1995; Kinder and Sanders 1990, 1996).

A second line of criticism, from quite a different angle, comes from
Sniderman and his colleagues (especially Sniderman et al. 1997 and
Sniderman, Crosby, and Howell this volume; also see Sniderman and
Carmines 1997a; Sniderman and Piazza 1993). Together this work
constitutes an energetic challenge to our conclusion that prejudice
plays a primary role in white opinion on matters of race today. We will
take up this challenge in a moment, but first we want to accentuate
the positive, to identify points where we seem to be in agreement.

First off, like Sniderman and his colleagues, we insist that principles (or values) are indispensable to an adequate comprehension of
American public opinion, both in general and on issues of race in particular (Kinder 1983, 1986, 1998a; Kinder and Sanders 1996). We
agree that policy in the realm of race is complex and that the public
recognizes this complexity: Americans are not simply for or against all
racial policies; their views depend importantly on the details of the
particular policy under examination (Kinder and Mendelberg 1995;
Kinder and Sanders 1990, 1996). We agree that public opinion depends in an important way on how issues are framed and choices formulated—indeed, the final third of *Divided by Color* (Kinder and
Sanders 1996) is dedicated entirely to elaborating and demonstrating
just this point (also see Nelson and Kinder 1996; Kinder and Berinsky

1998; Kinder and Nelson 1998). We agree that the views that citizens take on matters of policy depend on the arguments that the political environment makes readily available—what Sniderman, Gretchen Crosby, and William Howell in chapter 8 call the "rhetorical environment" of issues (Gross and Kinder 1998; Kinder and Sanders 1996).[24] Finally, we agree wholeheartedly on the application of experimental methods to the analysis of public opinion (Kinder and Sanders 1990, 1996; Kinder and Palfrey 1993; Mendelberg 1997).

We do not agree about everything, of course, and we disagree most pointedly about the current political power of racial prejudice. We say that prejudice is the most important force behind white opinion on race; Sniderman and his associates say that prejudice is just one of many, and a not very important force at that (e.g., Sniderman and Piazza 1993, 4–5, 19, 28; Sniderman, Crosby, and Howell this volume).

The results presented in full in *Divided by Color* and more briefly here would seem to make trouble for the claim that prejudice is a "spent force" (Sniderman, Crosby, and Howell, 71), but, of course, this holds only if we have made use of an adequate measure of prejudice. Sniderman argues that we have not, that we have in fact measured something other than prejudice altogether. According to Sniderman, white Americans answer the questions displayed in table 2.3 by calling up general principles, ideological points of view that are themselves racially neutral. If Sniderman is right here, our otherwise troublesome results simply go away. He and his colleagues can then proceed to the conclusion that "[t]he contemporary politics of race is at its core driven by a clash between liberal and conservative values and presumptions, not by racism—old or new" (Sniderman et al. 1997, 28).

This should sound familiar, since it essentially repeats the line of argument Sniderman presented originally in *Race and Inequality* (1985). There, as we showed earlier, Sniderman and Hagen's conclusion hinges decisively on the assumption that asking white Americans to explain racial differences in economic attainment reveals nothing about their attitudes on race. Instead, when white Americans endorse the claim that blacks could be just as well off as whites if they would only try harder, they are simply revealing a general and principled position on individual responsibility and self-reliance. Earlier in our chapter, we have shown this assumption to be unsustainable; indeed, Sniderman can now be counted among those who have given up on individualism conceptualized and measured in this way.[25]

But with individualism abandoned, the general line of argument nevertheless presses ahead, with individualism replaced by egalitarianism. Sniderman and his colleagues are now saying that the questions shown in table 2.3 actually reveal long-standing ideas on equality. Thus, when whites say that the Irish, the Italians, the Jews, and many other minorities overcame prejudice and worked their way up and that blacks should do the same without any special favors, they are displaying their enduring and general views on equality. Once again, such answers have nothing to do with race. Once again, politics is an entirely honorable business, an exchange of competing ideas.

There is room in politics for principles and ideas, of course, but we cannot agree with Sniderman and his colleagues that intending to measure racial prejudice, we measured general egalitarianism instead. Consider these results, each prominently featured in chapter 5 of *Divided by Color:*

- Prejudice (as we will continue to call it) is diminished in the presence of black Americans. That is, when whites are questioned by black interviewers, they express less of it than when they are questioned by whites.
- Prejudice, as measured in table 2.3, is a powerful predictor of racial stereotyping. White Americans who endorse the sentiments expressed in table 2.3 also believe that, compared to whites, blacks are lazy, dangerous, and stupid.
- The huge impact of prejudice on whites' views on racial policies, as shown in figure 2.2, is over and above the effects due to other plausible explanations, *including egalitarianism.* White Americans disagree over the importance of various kinds of equality to society and politics; these differences of principle have strong effects on policy opinions, in the domain of race as in others. But taking these effects of egalitarianism into account, the impact of prejudice remains enormous.
- The impact of prejudice is most pronounced on policies that deal explicitly and unambiguously with race (school desegregation, fair employment, affirmative action, and the like); is modest, though still sizeable, on what might be called "covert" racial issues (policies such as welfare reform and capital punishment that do not explicitly refer to race, but may be widely understood to have racial implications); and vanishes altogether on broad social programs (Medicare, federal support for public education, Social Security).

All these results make perfect sense if we actually succeeded in measuring racial prejudice, and little or no sense if we instead and inadvertently measured general egalitarianism.

Thus, the conclusion that racial politics today is only (or even primarily) about principles or ideology cannot be right. White Americans oppose policies like fair employment and affirmative action to an important extent (not exclusively) for reasons of race. Prejudice is still with us.

CONCLUSIONS AND IMPLICATIONS

How is it that individualism can be accorded such a privileged place in so many insightful characterizations of the American political tradition and, at the same time, play such a negligible role in explanations for contemporary American opinion on racial matters? The best answer for this mystery, we have argued here, is to recognize that a potent form of American racism has recently come to prominence, one that incorporates individualistic values. Properly understood, individualism is part of racism.

Prejudice today is distinctive partly in its differentiation from the doctrine of biological racism that it has largely replaced (at least for the time being). Biological racism began as a rationale for slavery and then for various post-Emancipation forms of racial oppression (Fredrickson 1971). At its center was the contention that blacks were an inherently and permanently inferior race. Prejudice today does not presume this form of white supremacy, nor does it set out a defense of segregation and discrimination. Prejudice today is preoccupied instead with matters of character and temperament, alleging first and foremost that blacks do not try hard enough to overcome the modest difficulties they face and that they take what they have not earned.

What is *not* new in contemporary expressions of racism is the mixing together of animosity and principle. Prejudice is *always* expressed in language that white Americans find familiar and compelling (Bobo 1988b). Limited government and states' rights are principles—but when they are used to defend slavery or to protect segregation as a way of life, they become part of the prejudice of the times. For reasons of history pointed to earlier in our chapter—because of the intricate conjunction of compelling events that comprised the racial crisis of the 1960s—today prejudice is expressed primarily in the language of individualism.

Nor do we mean to imply, by emphasizing recent events, that the form taken by prejudice today has no precedents. Familiar-sounding formulations can be found at previous moments in American history: occasionally in arguments over slavery, for example, or at the high point of Social Darwinism near the end of the nineteenth century, for another. Depending partly on the opportunities provided by events, so long as Americans continue to be drawn to the idea of individualism, some leaders will find it to their advantage, and some citizens will find it satisfying, to explain racial inequalities in individualistic terms.

If, as we maintain, racism is not some fixed and eternal doctrine, but subject to and participant in the vicissitudes of political life, the same should be said for principles. Too often, it seems to us, principles are treated as if they transcend the context of their times—if not quite eternal, then as essentially unchanging and unchangeable. Thus, Gunnar Myrdal's (1944) reference to the American Creed, an ideological inheritance he traces back in a straight line to Enlightenment ideals. Or Seymour Lipset's (1963) argument that the entire length of American political history can be read as a perpetual and ongoing struggle between two essentially fixed ideas, equality and achievement. Or Tocqueville's observation, where our chapter began, that "[t]wo things are surprising in the United States: the mutability of the greater part of human actions, and the singular stability of certain principles. Men are in constant motion; the mind of man appears almost unmoved" ([1835/1845] 1969, 2:506–8).

We do not think so. Principles like individualism are not fixed, but rather are always in (slow) motion, always evolving. Furthermore, this evolution is a story of politics: a story, as Rodgers puts it, of "contention, argument, and power." Following Rodgers, we argue that principles should be understood in how they are "put to use, and in this way fashioned and re-fashioned: not what the American political tradition *means,* but how various aspects of the Creed have been *used:* how they were employed and for what ends, how they rose in power, withered, and collapsed, how they were invented, stolen for other ends, remade, abandoned" (Rodgers 1987, 3).

Understood in this way, principles are nevertheless real: real to citizens struggling to figure out "who is *good* and what is *right*" (Stoker 1992, 370) and real as well to analysts struggling to decipher the forces driving public opinion. It would be surprising if a full and rounded account of public opinion on matters of race turned out to reserve no room for principles. Still more surprising, by the evidence laid out here, would be an account that omitted prejudice.

THREE Egalitarian Values
and Contemporary
Racial Politics

DAVID O. SEARS
P. J. HENRY
RICK KOSTERMAN

The "dark passage" began to people the shores of North America with African slaves almost immediately upon the beginnings of European settlement. Though slavery was abolished more than two centuries later, formal legal and political equality was not extended to the descendants of those Africans until the aftermath of World War II, nearly three and one-half centuries after the first slaves arrived. In the years since, formal equality has been institutionalized in countless ways. Official inequality, such as de jure segregation or laws against interracial marriage, is almost entirely in the past. There has been much successful integration of the workplace, higher education, and political life. Blacks have narrowed their historic disadvantages relative to whites in such domains as income, education, housing, health, and longevity (Farley 1996; Thernstrom and Thernstrom 1997). And relatively few Americans now believe in whites' racial superiority or support de jure segregation or discrimination against blacks (Schuman et al. 1997).

The process of advancing racial equality has not been painless. Nor is it by any means complete. Indeed, not long after the decisive civil rights breakthroughs of the early 1960s, the National Advisory Commission on Civil Disorders (the Kerner Commission) concluded that "our nation is moving toward two societies, one black, one white—separate and unequal" (Report of the National Advisory Commission on Civil Disorders 1968, 1). Pockets of the virulent older forms of racism still remain, as indicated by the substantial vote for ex–Ku Klux Klan leader David Duke in gubernatorial and senatorial campaigns in

Louisiana (Kuzenski, Bullock, and Gaddie 1995), the persistence of small white supremacist and racist "skinhead" groups, and the continuing incidence of racially based hate crimes. Even in mass surveys, some traditional racial prejudice and negative racial stereotyping can still be detected, though it appears to be much diminished (Bobo and Kluegel 1997; Schuman et al. 1997).

More politically important has been intense white opposition to policies explicitly intended to increase racial equality, such as busing, affirmative action, and vigorous enforcement of fair employment and fair housing regulations (Citrin 1996; Schuman et al. 1997; Sears, Hensler, and Speer 1979; Steeh and Krysan 1996). Whites have also preferred tough-minded welfare and crime policies in recent years. Race is periodically a salient factor in political campaigns, as suggested by the Bush campaign's use of the Willie Horton case in 1988 and Jesse Helms's 1990 campaign ad depicting a white person losing his job because of "racial quotas."

Moreover, blacks and whites remain severely polarized over racial issues. Most whites believe that discrimination has been greatly reduced and that equal opportunity does in fact exist, while most blacks believe that discrimination remains at high levels and that opportunities are not equal (see Hochschild 1995). In most elections pitting black against white candidates, the votes are split quite sharply by race, and racial prejudices tend to be strongly predictive of which whites will oppose the black candidate (e.g., Kinder and Sanders 1996; Kleppner 1985; Sears, Citrin, and Kosterman 1987). The hopes stimulated by the society's general acceptance of formal racial equality must therefore be tempered by numerous indications of continuing political conflict over race and of white resistance to change. Indeed, in 1997, President Clinton concluded that the tensions created by racial inequality continue to be such potent forces in American public life that he called for an intensive renewal of national discussion of the subject.

CONTEMPORARY WHITE RACISM

If almost all whites now accept the general idea of formal equality, why do they so strenuously resist social changes intended to promote it? One possibility is that divisions over equality continue to drive political controversies over race, as whites protect their privileged position in the stratification system (Bobo, chap. 5; Sidanius et al., chap. 7). Another possibility is that other values drive this resistance, such as a preference for limited government, while "prejudice is very far from a dominating factor in the contemporary politics of race" (Sniderman and Carmines 1997a, 73).

Our own view is that the acceptance of formal equality is genuine, but that racial animus has not gone away; it has just changed its principal manifestations. Before the civil rights era, there was much white support for Jim Crow racism, particularly beliefs in the innate inferiority of blacks and support for state-enforced racial segregation and formal discrimination, a package of beliefs described variously as "generalized inegalitarianism" (Sears and Kinder 1971), "old-fashioned racism" (McConahay 1986), and "blatant prejudice" (Pettigrew and Meertens 1995). Those beliefs have largely disappeared, we argue.

Instead, the politically most potent racial attitudes take a different form today, which we have described as "symbolic racism."[1] Its main themes are that (1) blacks no longer are especially handicapped by racial discrimination, but that (2) they still do not conform to traditional American values, particularly the work ethic, as well as obedience to authority (as in schools, the workplace, or law enforcement) and impulse control (concerning such issues as alcohol, drugs, sexuality, and prudent use of money). Nevertheless, (3) they continue to make illegitimate demands for special treatment, and (4) they continue to receive undeserved special treatment from government and other elites.[2]

Symbolic racism is represented as a new form of racism. In terms of its content, that seems to be the case. Few whites now support the core notions of old-fashioned racism (Schuman et al. 1997). The main themes of symbolic racism are mostly recent developments, at least in their current incarnations. To be sure, the belief that blacks do not work as hard as they should, or as hard as whites, has been a central racial stereotype since the early days of slavery (Allport 1954; Jordan 1968). But the existence of racial discrimination was not seriously questioned during the era of Jim Crow. Whites have long resented blacks' demands for better treatment, but these demands are now perceived as demands for *special* rather than equal treatment. Similarly, resentment of supposedly undeserved special treatment from elites has some resonance with complaints as far back as Reconstruction, but it plainly has a new flavor in the post–civil rights era context.

A considerable number of studies have demonstrated the close association of symbolic racism with opposition to racially targeted policies and black political candidates. Symbolic racism is, among racial attitudes, consistently the strongest predictor of such political preferences, and usually considerably stronger than such nonracial values and attitudes as political ideology (see, most recently, Bobo, chap. 5; Kinder and Mendelberg, chap. 2; Hughes 1997; Kinder and Sanders 1996; Sears et al. 1997). That no longer seems to be a particularly controversial point.

Our central focus in this chapter is on the origins of symbolic racism. In one widely quoted conceptualization, it was described as a "resistance to change in the racial status quo based on moral feelings that blacks [in particular] violate such traditional American values as individualism and self-reliance, the work ethic, obedience, and discipline" (Kinder and Sears 1981, 416). That is, it was thought to conjoin two long-standing products of earlier socialization: antiblack affect and traditional nonracial values, merged in the perception that blacks in particular violated those values.

The first point, then, was that symbolic racism represented a modern version of the antiblack racism that had long infected American society, but in a form more suited to the realities of the post–civil rights era. The term "racism" was defined as a category-based affective response to attitude objects that have to do with race. If an individual responds systematically more negatively to attitude objects associated with blacks than to other comparable objects, we infer a "racist" response because it is a racially based negative response that overrides any other differences between attitude objects associated with blacks. This is analogous to the use of "anti-Semitism" to describe any form of systematic prejudicial or discriminatory response to Jews on the basis of group membership.[3]

It seemed to us quite unlikely that several centuries of broadly based antiblack prejudice had somehow abruptly disappeared within the relatively few years since the successes of the civil rights movement. However, others argue that whites' racial policy preferences (and symbolic racism itself, as customarily measured) can be explained without assuming an important effect of racial prejudices per se. For example, opposition to racial policies or black candidates could, like opposition to any other policies or candidates, simply stem from perceived deficiencies in those political options themselves. As Byron Roth (1990, 34) says, "[P]eople might honestly consider quotas and busing unwise and counterproductive" (also see Kuklinski et al. 1997). Or in the "politics-centered" view of Paul Sniderman and his colleagues (chap. 8; Sniderman and Piazza 1993), such opposition could be rooted primarily in racially neutral values and attitudes. Ideological conservatives might oppose any liberal policies and candidates, racial or not, simply because they embody excessive government power or violate basic values of personal responsibility and self-reliance. "The contemporary debate over racial policy is driven primarily by conflict over what government should try to do, and only secondarily over what it should try to do *for blacks*" (Sniderman and Carmines 1997a, 4).

Two general research strategies have been employed to test for the contribution of racism to racial policy preferences and symbolic racism. One has been to test directly for the impact of whites' racial attitudes on their policy and candidate preferences. Numerous studies have demonstrated the pervasive effects of various kinds of racial attitudes on preferences about racial policy issues, black candidates, racist white candidates, and ostensibly nonracial issues, such as crime, welfare, and tax cuts, and even issues mainly involving other minority groups.[4] However, when measures of symbolic racism have indexed racial attitudes in such studies, some have described them as being "confounded" with attitudes such as political ideology.[5] When this has been tested by controlling for the relevant nonracial values and attitudes, the effects of symbolic racism usually remain nearly at full strength, while the nonracial controls themselves have little effect.[6]

A second strategy has been to demonstrate the direct impact of antiblack affect on symbolic racism. Antiblack affect is difficult to measure without resorting either to older, somewhat dated measures, such as traditional stereotypes, or to blatant measures that seem likely to raise problems of social desirability biases, such as thermometer measures of group liking. Nevertheless, within that limitation, antiblack affect does have a significant impact on symbolic racism (Hughes 1997; Sears et al. 1997). The evidence derived from both strategies, then, would seem to us clearly to point to an important role for racial animus in whites' racial policy preferences and in the origins of symbolic racism.

The second point is that symbolic racism is not merely racial, but also an intimate blend of this antiblack affect with race-neutral traditional American values. Those traditional values were originally specified in quite general terms. For example, Donald Kinder and David Sears (1981) and John McConahay and Joseph Hough (1976) alluded to a wide variety of conservative values, such as individualism, the work ethic, obedience to authority, moral traditionalism, sexual repression, delay of gratification, patriotism, and reverence for the past. Subsequent writing has most often cited individualism. But variations in commitment to individualistic values seem generally not to have had the expected empirical effects, either on racial policy preferences or on symbolic racism itself.[7] This finding might not be disconfirming in itself. Symbolic racism theory suggested that perceptions that blacks violate traditional values were more important than absolute levels of commitment to the value itself. That is, one might or might not be Calvinist enough to believe that work was the path to salvation. The problem would arise if blacks fell short of one's own standards, whatever they were.[8]

As a result, a more important problem for the theory was that a number of studies have instead reported that inegalitarian values are highly associated with both symbolic racism and opposition to racial policies.[9] The theory specifically identified inegalitarian values as *not* central to any new racism. Indeed, it portrayed symbolic racism as a replacement for an outdated and widely rejected "generalized inegalitarianism," not as a product or expression of it (Sears and Kinder 1971). Our central purpose here is to provide a deeper analysis of whether or not inegalitarian values remain pivotal points in the politics of race.[10]

AMERICANS' BELIEF IN EQUALITY

From the beginnings of the nation, in 1776, some principle of equality has by almost all historical accounts been a central element in Americans' value systems. Gordon Wood (1992), in writing about the ideological foundations of the American Revolution, says that "equality was the most radical and most powerful ideological force let loose in the Revolution" (p. 232). The phrase incorporated into the Declaration of Independence, "all men are created equal," was not anomalous; it grew out of a broad sentiment of the time. Alexis de Tocqueville, too, writing a half century later, was struck by the widespread egalitarianism of American society. Looking back from a contemporary vantage point, Seymour Lipset (1996) places equality in a short list of five basic values that have been central to American democracy ever since. Indeed, Jack Citrin and his colleagues (1990) find a belief in equality is perceived by the general public as the *most* central attribute of "a true American."

Why equality became so important to those early Americans, and precisely what they meant by it, is more debatable. This was a new nation, with no inherited aristocracy or social order. Land was readily available, with only a relatively small urban proletariat. The "social contract" of eighteenth-century American civil society was widely thought to have rested on the consent of the governed, in that sense equalizing their stake in the whole. The nation was founded in a philosophical climate hospitable to equality, amidst Enlightenment ideas of natural law and natural rights. And as a Christian society, many accepted the notion that all are equal in God's eyes, and equally responsible to God. At a more mundane level, many colonists felt considerable political resentment in the 1770s because certain onerous laws were applied to them and not to their English cousins (Pole 1993).

Slavery was the most visible exception to this egalitarian spirit.[11] The African slaves were usually not thought to have been "created equal," and they plainly were not treated equally. The anomalous status of the black slaves was not a mere oversight. The distinctive constraints on their rights were firmly codified surprisingly early in the English colonization of North America, during the 1660s and the decades immediately thereafter (Jordan 1968; Wood 1997). The Continental Congress deliberately excised Jefferson's language abolishing slavery from the Declaration of Independence, and their successors consciously acquiesced in its legitimacy when writing the Constitution.

As opposition to slavery crystallized in the nineteenth century, however, the principle of racial inequality became ever more clearly contested. For example, in the 1820s, abolitionists began using the phrase "all men are created equal" to bolster their own rhetorical side of the debate over slavery. Abraham Lincoln ultimately invoked that phrase at Gettysburg to legitimize his emancipation of the slaves (see Maier 1997). The Fourteenth Amendment was intended to extend some measure of equality to blacks soon after the Civil War, but it was soon interpreted so narrowly by the Supreme Court that it had little effect (Pole 1993). The system of racial inequality received new ideological justification in the late nineteenth century, when social Darwinists and other racialists provided supposedly scientific evidence that some races were inherently superior to others (Fredrickson 1971). By the beginning of the twentieth century, the Jim Crow system was firmly in place in the American South, founded on the widespread belief that it was legitimate to give blacks inferior treatment (both officially and in private life). Half a century later Gunnar Myrdal (1944) argued that although egalitarian values were fundamental to the American Creed, their relevance to the question of race continued to be contested.

We argue that the political question of extending formal equality to African Americans was irreversibly resolved in the 1960s. That pivotal decision was made in a relatively short time, contributed to by people at all levels of the society, ordinary people sitting in and marching in the streets, congressmen voting civil rights legislation, presidential executive orders, faceless bureaucrats making and implementing regulations, and courts making decisions decreeing political and legal equality for all races. Nevertheless, whites continued to be divided about many concrete racial policies. Debates over equality itself were central to those division, with racial liberals invoking egalitarian principles to justify the civil rights agenda, while racial conservatives defended the inegalitarian racial status quo.

However, the full application of the principle of equal rights to African Americans is now no longer seriously contested among elites. Even conservatives rarely defend inequality itself. Indeed, the completeness of this victory is illustrated by the fact that both liberals and conservatives now justify their positions on disputed racial issues in terms of explicitly egalitarian values. For example, a conservative Supreme Court expresses its skepticism about affirmative action as a violation of "color-blindness." We will show below that this consensus is now fully reflected in public opinion as well.[12] We would even argue that this consensus now extends well beyond race, to a widespread belief that it is illegitimate to use any ascriptive group membership by itself to disadvantage individuals.

EGALITARIAN VALUES AND CONTEMPORARY RACIAL POLICIES

But if so, why does variation among whites regarding egalitarian values emerge as a powerful predictor of their attitudes about contemporary racial policies? Addressing this question is the primary purpose of this chapter. We can think of three possible explanations. One is that we are wrong about that presumed consensus. Perhaps many white Americans have not renounced the general principle of racial inequality after all and today continue to resist changes that would threaten their privileged positions in the existing social hierarchy. Their apparently increasing support for general principles of racial equality may merely reflect dissembling, as Mary Jackman (1994; Jackman and Muha 1984) argues. Or they may support equality in the abstract, but resist any real and costly practical implementation (Bobo, chap. 5; Sidanius et al., chap. 7). Either way, political debates over race would still revolve, in the end, around issues of racial equality, with left and right playing their traditional roles.

A second possibility is that general principles of racial equality have indeed been accepted broadly and consensually in American society.

But the civil rights agenda of the political left may have shifted from providing blacks with equal opportunity to providing them with preferential treatment. If so, political cleavages over equality might now depend on which issue is at stake. Government regulations to ensure equal opportunity may be opposed by conservatives out of dislike for big government. But some policies, such as preferential admissions to college may be construed as racial discrimination against whites and be opposed as violations of egalitarian principles (e.g., Thernstrom and Thernstrom 1997). *Opposition* to policies such as affirmative action rather than support for them might, therefore, be motivated by a commitment to egalitarian values.[13]

The theory of symbolic racism suggests a third possibility, one that takes a somewhat more complex view of egalitarian values. To start with, there are markedly different kinds of equality (Pole 1993; Rae 1981). Some relatively pure egalitarian values are often described as "equality of opportunity" or "equal treatment." The clearest include legal and political rights, such as equal treatment by the courts regardless of wealth or religion and equal rights to vote and run for office. They also include some economic rights, such as the right to attend a movie or take out a home loan regardless of one's group membership. Support for the egalitarian principle underlying these beliefs is now a matter of general consensus, we will argue. The gender and racial asterisks once qualifying the phrase "all men are created equal" are now almost completely erased. As a result, this set of purely egalitarian values is not likely to be at the heart of today's divisions of opinion about racial issues.

But this consensus regarding egalitarianism begins to erode when considering other kinds of beliefs about equality. Even if people generally agree with equal *treatment* for all as a goal to which we should aspire, there is much disagreement about the extent to which the society should interfere with market mechanisms for determining *outcomes*. At one extreme, few would support ensuring equal outcomes for all. And few oppose any effort to help the disadvantaged. But in between, much political controversy centers on policies intended to increase equality of outcomes.

Opposition to them, we argue, arise from individualistic values about working hard and putting forth effort to succeed. Racial policies that seem to promote more equal outcomes are often perceived as illegitimate interferences with the fundamental individualistic principle of meritocracy. Consider the metaphor of comparing life to a footrace, and birth to a starting line. Almost all now agree that at that starting line all contestants should be equal, none formally handicapped by their group membership. But how they fare in the footrace should depend on other factors, such as their own abilities and efforts. Jennifer Hochschild (1995) puts it well in her description of "the American Dream"; its first tenet is that everyone must be allowed to participate equally in the search for success, but close behind is the belief that achieving success depends on one's own efforts. Promoting more equal outcomes, therefore, can be perceived as political interference with market mechanisms and as coming at the expense of rewarding individual effort and ability. In this sense, individualistic values should drive beliefs about trying to increase equality of outcomes. Beliefs about equality of outcomes, then, are likely to be more contested and politicized than beliefs about equality of opportunity because of this sense that equality of outcomes violates individualistic values.[14]

We would argue further that this second version of beliefs about equality, much influenced by individualistic values, is particularly central to racial issues. As Lyndon Johnson recognized in applying the footrace metaphor to the racial context, the peculiar history of African Americans has complicated the question of equality at the starting line (see Bobo, chap. 5). Racial differences in outcomes could be attributable to blacks' continuing handicaps at the starting line, or they might be due to lack of ability or effort. The question inherently creates great disagreement, since conclusive facts are not easy to assemble. As a result, the effort to increase racial equality often is construed as violating the cardinal individualistic principles that one's gains should be linked to one's own efforts and that there should be no free lunch. It also has perhaps been inevitable that racial animus would continue to dog such efforts.

In short, the man-in-the-street definition of equality deals with equal treatment and equal opportunity; people should not be treated unequally just because of their group membership. But this form of egalitarianism may no longer be strongly contested or centrally involved in differences of opinion among whites about racial issues. However, efforts to increase equality of outcomes draw concerns about violations of individualism, especially in the racial context. This form of inegalitarianism, based in individualistic values and racial animus, returns us to the original concept of "symbolic racism."[15]

These alternative explanations for the apparent role of egalitarian values are addressed below in an empirical analysis of white public opinion. We begin by replicating the finding that symbolic racism is currently the most powerful determinant of whites' preferences on racial policy issues. Then we focus on the origins of symbolic racism and why it plays this central role. We pursue five specific hypotheses:

1. *Symbolic racism has a central racial component:* The influence of symbolic racism is partly due to race per se; antiblack attitudes should make an important contribution to both symbolic racism and racial policy preferences, even with nonracial attitudes controlled.

2. *Violation of traditional values:* Perceptions that blacks violate individualistic values significantly influence both symbolic racism and racial policy preferences.

3. *Varieties of egalitarianism:* Beliefs about equality are more multidimensional than has been recognized. Whites today consensually support equal treatment and equal opportunity for all. Issues that involve equality and other values are more contested.

4. *Formal equality:* Individual differences in support for the principle of equal treatment may not be central to symbolic racism.

5. *Contested mixture of egalitarianism and individualism:* Some beliefs about equality reflect its mixture with individualism, and they are more strongly contested. They also tend to be racialized and particularly closely associated with symbolic racism.

METHOD

SAMPLES

Our analyses used the National Election Studies (NES) 1986, 1990, and 1992 election surveys, based on large representative cross-sectional samples of American adults, and the 1983 and 1985 NES pilot studies, based on smaller subsamples of respondents initially interviewed in the 1982 and 1984 postelection surveys, respectively.[16] Black respondents were excluded in all analyses, leading to the following sample sizes: 1983, $N = 284$; 1985, $N = 397$, weighted $N = 614$; 1986, $N = 922$; 1990, $N = 1,151$; 1992, $N = 2,110$. We also use data from the 1997 Los Angeles County Social Survey (LACSS), a random-digit-dial survey of adult residents of Los Angeles County. Hispanic, Asian, and African-American respondents were excluded in these analyses, leaving $N = 277$. Finally, we also report analyses on white respondents in the 1996 LACSS. The relevant methodological details are described in Sidanius et al. (chap. 7).[17]

RACIAL POLICY ATTITUDES

Questions on racial policy preferences in the 1985 and 1986 surveys were grouped into three general areas (see Kinder and Sanders 1996 and Sniderman and Piazza 1993 for parallel groupings), yielding separate scales for each area. A *federal assistance* scale (the role of the federal government in delivering services and assistance to blacks) was developed for both surveys, based on items on (1) "aid to minorities," asking whether the government should help blacks (and other minority groups) or whether these groups should help themselves and (2) federal spending, asking whether government spending to assist or improve the conditions of blacks was "too little" or "too much" or whether it should be increased or decreased. Reliabilities for these scales are .64 in 1985 and .59 in 1986.

Scales on the obligation of the federal government to guarantee *equal opportunity*, especially in employment, housing, and education, were based on (1) the government's role in seeing to it that black and white children go to the same schools, (2) the government's guarantee of fair treatment in jobs and job opportunities, (3) guaranteed "equal opportunity to succeed," and (4) the government's role in fair housing (1985 only). Reliabilities for the *equal opportunity* scales are .75 in 1985 and .63 in 1986.

Affirmative action scales (extending special preferences to blacks in employment and education) included (1) the preferential hiring and promotion of blacks and (2) university quotas to admit black students.[18] Reliabilities for the *affirmative action* scales are .73 (form A) and .74 (form B) in 1985 and .74 in 1986.

A four-item *racial policy* scale in the 1997 LACSS was created by combining all available items from the general areas mentioned above. This general *racial policy* scale included two federal assistance items, an equal opportunity item, and an affirmative action item (see the Appendix) and had a reliability of .73.

INDEPENDENT VARIABLES

Almost all contemporary analyses of the link between nonracial values and racial policy preferences have measured both egalitarian and individualistic values with six-item scales evenly divided between items keyed for "agree" and those keyed for "disagree" (see Feldman 1988). In the 1985 and 1986 NES surveys, reliabilities for the *individualism* scale are .59 and .60, respectively, and for the *egalitarianism* scale, .56 and .65 (as well as .62 and .70 in the 1990 and 1992 NES surveys), respectively.[19] The distinction between individualism and egalitarianism holds up well empirically. Factor analyses of the twelve items in the 1985 and 1986 surveys yielded the expected two-factor solutions, with minimal interfactor correlations ($\phi = -.16$ and $-.17$, respectively). The Pearson correlations between the two scales are negative, but modest in size: $-.21$ and $-.15$, respectively. An eight-item *traditional morality* scale in 1985 and 1986 focused on tolerance of different lifestyles, the breakdown of moral standards, and so on; reliabilities are .76 and .81. Sixteen items measured *social dominance orientation* in the 1996 LACSS (see Sidanius et al., chap. 7), and six items did so in the 1997 LACSS ($\alpha = .68$).

The *symbolic racism* items used in the 1985, 1986, 1996, and 1997 surveys are shown in the Appendix. They yielded scales with reliabilities of .66, .71, .59, and .85, respectively. *Antiblack affect* was measured with the standard "feeling thermometer" item.

A variety of attribution items were included in three of the studies. In 1985, a scale of *individualistic attributions for poverty* was based on three items measuring how much the respondent agreed that lack of effort, lack of thrift, and loose morals, respectively, were the cause of poverty. Reliability was .65. Also in 1985, a *structural attributions for poverty* scale was based on four items measuring how much the respondent agreed that low wages, poor schools, insufficient jobs, and being taken advantage of by rich people, respectively, were the cause of poverty. Reliability was .64 in 1985.[20]

In 1997, an *individualistic attributions for crime* scale was created out of four items measuring blame of individual criminals for crime, in terms of lack of morals and breakdown of the family as causes of crime, and the death penalty and "three strikes" legislation as good solutions for crime. Reliability for this scale was .56. Also in 1997, a *structural attributions for crime* scale was created out of four items measuring how much the respondent agreed that lack of jobs and lack of good schools were causes of crime, and that reducing poverty and providing education and job training were good solutions for crime. Reliability for this scale was .56.[21]

Finally, the 1985, 1986, and 1997 surveys included several items on *attributions for black disadvantage,* measuring whether lack of hard work, slavery and discrimination, lack of ability, "God's will" (1985 and 1986 only), and lack of jobs and a good education (1997 only) were responsible for blacks' lower status in society. These items were analyzed individually rather than being scaled in the analyses that follow.[22]

Several control variables were employed in all studies. In the NES surveys, *party identification* represented the mean of standardized versions of the standard NES seven-point summary variable (running from "strong Democrat" to "strong Republican") and the difference score between the thermometer ratings of the two parties. Similarly, *political ideology* used a seven-point liberal-conservative scale (running from "strong" or "extremely" liberal to "strong" or "extremely" conservative) combined with the difference between the liberal and conservative thermometers.[23] In the LACSS, the thermometer items were not available. Most regression equations also included standard demographic controls—age, education, income, social class, and sex—plus dummy variables for region, marital status, and Fundamentalist, Catholic, and Jewish religious preferences.

TESTING THE THEORY OF SYMBOLIC RACISM

According to our theory, symbolic racism should be a more powerful determinant of whites' racial policy preferences than other racial attitudes (such as old-fashioned racism) or the major nonracial values and political attitudes.[24] As mentioned above, this has already been demonstrated in several earlier studies. This chapter rests most heavily on the 1985 and 1986 NES surveys and the 1997 LACSS because they contained the most extensive measures of beliefs about equality, symbolic racism, and policy preferences.

That central role of symbolic racism also holds in these three surveys. To test for this, racial policy preferences were regressed on both racial attitudes (symbolic racism; antiblack affect) and nonracial attitudes (egalitarian, individualistic, and moral values; party identification and ideology) as well as basic demographic variables. In each case, symbolic racism was the strongest predictor of racial policy preferences.[25] Since these findings simply replicate those reported elsewhere, we will not go into further detail about them. Instead, we move to the question of the origins of symbolic racism.[26]

THE ROLE OF RACIAL ANIMUS

Our first hypothesis is that racial animus is an important determinant both of whites' opinions toward racial policy preferences and of symbolic racism. Neither can be explained adequately on the basis of race-neutral attitudes alone. We here present three different tests of this hypothesis, all of which point to a meaningful racial contribution.

TABLE 3.1 Antiblack Affect and Traditional Values as Predictors of Opposition to Racial Policy: Regression Analyses

	FEDERAL ASSISTANCE		EQUAL OPPORTUNITY		AFFIRMATIVE ACTION	
	1985	1986	1985	1986	1985	1986
Antiblack affect	.21°°	.25°°	.25°°	.11°	.13°	.17°°
Traditional values						
Egalitarianism	.39°°	.29°°	.30°°	.30°°	.16°	.15°°
Individualism	−.06	.07°	.06	.11°	−.04	.07°
Morality	.07	.00	.10°	−.02	.00	.09°
Political predispositions						
Party identification	.27°°	.07	.11	.02	−.12	.11°
Ideology	−.05	.16°°	−.04	.11°	.17°	.06
Adjusted R^2	31.7%	34.8%	23.7%	22.2%	10.6%	14.7%

Sources: 1985 NES pilot study and 1986 NES survey.
Note: The 1985 results are based on the weighted *n*. Each entry contains the standardized regression coefficient from an equation that includes all indicated variables as well as demographic controls described in the text. All items are keyed so that a conservative response is high.
°$p < .05.$ °°$p < .001.$

First, antiblack affect, as measured by a feeling thermometer, significantly influences these racial policy preferences even with controls on nonracial values and predispositions. Its regression coefficients are significant in all three policy domains in both the 1985 and the 1986 NES surveys, as shown in table 3.1, indicating considerable robustness of the effect. Second, these effects of antiblack affect on policy preferences are quite similar across all three domains of racial issues. This further supports the notion that whites' attention is mostly captured by the racial content of these issues. Finally, there is a demonstrable component of racial animus in symbolic racism itself. Table 3.2 presents bivariate correlations of symbolic racism with various racial and nonracial predictors from the two NES surveys. It shows that antiblack affect is consistently strongly related to symbolic racism (although affect toward whites is not). Table 3.2 also presents regression equations that also show a strong effect of antiblack affect on symbolic racism. The effect is at about the same level in both surveys, indicating substantial robustness of the finding as well.

In short, racial animus has been shown in three ways to contribute to both racial policy preferences and symbolic racism. Antiblack affect significantly influences racial policy preferences, even with the major nonracial values and attitudes controlled. It has approximately the same effect across three very different domains of racial policies, suggesting that whites are responding to the common racial theme under-

TABLE 3.2 Origins of Symbolic Racism

	1985		1986	
	r	β	r	β
Racial group affect				
Antiblack affect	.27°°	.27°°	.28°°	.18°°
White affect	.00	−.09	N.A.	N.A.
Traditional values				
Egalitarianism	.41°°	.28°°	.39°°	.24°°
Individualism	.30°°	.20°°	.24°°	.19°°
Morality	.20°°	.12°	.28°°	.09°
Political predispositions				
Party identification	.26°°	.12°	.11°	.01
Ideology	.26°°	−.02	.29°°	.12°
Adjusted R^2		28.8%		35.2%

Sources: 1985 NES pilot study and 1986 NES survey.
Note: The 1985 results are based on the weighted n. Each entry under β includes the standardized regression coefficient from an equation that includes all indicated variables as well as demographic controls described in the text. All items are keyed so that a conservative response is high.
°$p < .05$.   °°$p < .001$.

lying them as much as to their political idiosyncrasies. And, finally, it makes a consistently significant contribution to symbolic racism itself. All these findings are replicated in two different surveys. The specifically racial component in both symbolic racism and preferences in these diverse policy domains would seem to be contrary to the notion that racial issues have become deracialized and are now primarily evaluated in terms of broader political and ideological principles or of each issue's political idiosyncrasies, as in the politics-centered theory favored by Sniderman and his colleagues (see Sniderman and Carmines 1997a; Sniderman, Crosby, and Howell, chap. 8). For whites, race as well as politics is centrally involved in these policy questions.

TRADITIONAL VALUES

Our second hypothesis is that blacks' violations of individualistic values are an important source of symbolic racism, while whites' commitment to formal equality should now be sufficiently consensual to render egalitarian values peripheral to disputes about racial issues. However, egalitarian values had surprisingly strong effects, consistent with previous findings cited earlier. The equations in table 3.1 show that when symbolic racism is not considered, beliefs about equality make a strong and significant contribution to explaining policy preferences in every case, yielding an average regression coefficient of .27.

Individualism has much weaker effects, with an average coefficient of only .04, failing even to be statistically significant half the time.

Egalitarianism also had stronger effects on symbolic racism than did individualism, though the differences were not as dramatic. Both its bivariate correlation with symbolic racism and the regression coefficients are consistently larger for egalitarianism, as shown in table 3.2. However, individualism does have a significant effect in both equations, so the evidence does not completely contradict the hypothesis.

This surprisingly greater centrality of egalitarian values has potentially important implications for the theories we are concerned with. First of all, these data are clearly inconsistent with the theory expounded by conservative elites that whites reject policies like affirmative action because racial preferences violate fundamental egalitarian values. It is the *in*egalitarians, not the egalitarians, who oppose such policies. Second, they seem to suggest that white Americans still retain politically consequential differences of opinion about racial equality. That is consistent with social-structural theories emphasizing the powerful forces maintaining traditional racial hierarchies. But, third, they are contrary to the symbolic racism perspective, which views individualism-based criticism of blacks as central to today's racial politics and formal racial equality as a largely settled issue, and so no longer very relevant.

WHITE AMERICANS' ATTITUDES TOWARD EQUALITY

Are fundamental principles of equality still as contested as these findings suggest? To address this question, we draw on several surveys with extensive measurement of beliefs about equality. We begin by distinguishing several different types of equality and assessing how white Americans feel about each.

CONSENSUS: EQUAL OPPORTUNITY AND EQUAL TREATMENT

Our third hypothesis is that almost all white Americans unite behind the egalitarian ideas at the core of the American Creed: that all individual Americans should have equal opportunity to succeed and that no American should be denied equal treatment just because of his or her ascriptive group membership (see Hochschild 1995; Pole 1993). Indeed, as shown in the top panel of table 3.3, on average 89 percent concur that "our society should do whatever is necessary to make sure

TABLE 3.3 Whites' Support for Equality

	PERCENTAGE SUPPORTING EQUALITY	YEAR OF SURVEY
Consensual beliefs		
(1) All individuals should have equal opportunity.		
Our society should do whatever is necessary to make sure	89	(1983)
that everyone has an equal opoprtunity to succeed.[1]	89	(1985)
(Agree)	86	(1986)
Increased social equality.[3] (Agree)	91	(1997)
Mean	89	
(2) All groups should be given equal treatment.		
It would be good if groups could be equal.[3] (Agree)	91	(1997)
We should do what we can to equalize conditions for different groups.[3] (Agree)	85	(1997)
Our society should do whatever is necessary to make sure that blacks' opportunities to succeed are equal to those of whites. (Agree)	85	(1983)
Our society should do whatever is necessary to make sure that women's opportunities to succeed are equal to those of men. (Agree)	86	(1983)
Mean	87	
(3) Differences between groups do not justify unequal treatment.		
Inferior groups should stay in their place.[4] (Disagree)	93	(1997)
Sometimes other groups must be kept in their place.[4] (Disagree)	84	(1997)
If certain groups of people stayed in their place, we would have fewer problems.[4] (Disagree)	78	(1997)
Some whites are just better cut out than blacks for important positions in society. (Disagree)	92	(1983)
We should give up on the goal of equality since blacks and whites are so different to begin with. (Disagree)	88	(1983)
Some whites are better at running things than blacks are and should be allowed to do so. (Disagree)	86	(1983)
We should give up on the goal of equality since men and women are so different to begin with. (Disagree)	83	(1983)
We should give up on the goal of equality since people are so different to begin with. (Disagree)	79	(1983)
Some men are just better cut out than women for important positions in society. (Disagree)	74	(1983)
Some men are better at running things than women are and should be allowed to do so. (Disagree)	75	(1983)
Mean	83	

TABLE 3.3 *continued*

	PERCENTAGE SUPPORTING EQUALITY	YEAR OF SURVEY
Contested beliefs		
(4) Inequality in our society is still a problem.	80	(1983)
If people were treated more equally in this country we would have many fewer problems.[1] (Agree)	73	(1985)
	57	(1986)
If blacks and whites were treated more equally in this country we would have many fewer problems. (Agree)	70	(1983)
If men and women were treated more equally in this country we would have many fewer problems. (Agree)	65	(1983)
It is really not that big of a problem if some people have more of a chance in life than others.[2] (Disagree)	45	(1985)
	47	(1986)
One of the big problems in this country is that we don't give everyone an equal chance.[1] (Agree)	54	(1983)
	43	(1985)
One of the big problems in this country is that we don't give blacks an equal chance. (Agree)	48	(1986)
	49	(1983)
One of the big problems in this country is that we don't give women an equal chance. (Agree)	45	(1983)
Mean	53	
(5) We worry too much about inequality in this country.		
This country would be better off if we worried less about how equal people are.[2] (Disagree)	33	(1985)
	37	(1986)
We have gone too far in pushing equal rights in this country.[2] (Disagree)	41	(1985)
	33	(1986)
Mean	36	
Consensually rejected beliefs		
(6) All individuals have the same abilities.		
Some people are just better cut out than others for important positions in society. (Disagree)	15	(1983)
Some people are better at running things and should be allowed to do so. (Disagree)	7	(1983)
Mean	11	

Sources: 1983 and 1985 NES pilot studies, 1986 NES survey, and 1997 LACSS.
Note: Exact wording is given.
[1]Included in index of "less equal treatment" (NES).
[2]Included in index of "we've gone too far" (NES).
[3]Included in index of "less equal treatment" (LACSS).
[4]Included in index of "dominance" (LACSS).

that everyone has an equal opportunity to succeed" and/or support the value of "increased social equality." Panel 2 shows an almost equal level of commitment (87 percent) to the belief that all *groups* should be treated equally, in that "it would be good if groups could be equal" and "we should do what we can to equalize conditions for different groups." There is a consensus among whites that people should not be discriminated against because of their group memberships.

There is also a strong post–civil rights era consensus that any existing group differences do not justify treating groups unequally. People in a disadvantaged group should not be deliberately kept in a subordinate status simply because of that group membership. As shown in panel 3 of table 3.3, on average 83 percent believe that even acknowledging differences among people or groups does not justify giving up on the goal of formal equality. For example, whites now overwhelmingly reject the old-fashioned racism belief that "inferior groups should stay in their place." Few whites feel that even the many obvious ways in which women differ from men do not justify giving up the goal of giving them equal treatment.

CONTESTED: DO WE STILL HAVE A PROBLEM?

Other versions of egalitarianism remain highly contested. The white public is sharply divided about whether or not inequality is still a serious social problem. On average, only about half agree that "if people were treated more equally in this country we would have fewer problems," that "one of the big problems in this country is that we don't give everyone an equal chance," or that "it is really not that big of a problem if some people have more of a chance in life than others" (see panel 4 of table 3.3). These questions combine the general principle of equality (for which, we argue, there is consensual support) with the additional assertion that our society continues to have insufficient equality and repairing that flaw would improve the society (which, we argue, is highly contested). Whites are deeply split about whether or not the problem of inequality is behind us.

And most whites believe that we do not have a serious problem with discrimination any longer and that people worry about equality too much, complain about it too much, and spend too much time pushing for it. For example, about two-thirds on average agree with such inegalitarian statements as "this country would be better off if we worried less about how equal people are" or "we have gone too far in pushing equal rights in this country" (see panel 5 of table 3.3). Although these items do not mention blacks, these beliefs have obvious relevance to race: others have noted the widespread belief in the white mass public that blacks are no longer denied equal opportunity (e.g., Hochschild 1995), and elite analysts argue that such beliefs contain much factual truth (e.g., Thernstrom and Thernstrom 1997).

REJECTED: ALL INDIVIDUALS HAVE THE SAME ABILITIES; ALL SHOULD HAVE THE SAME RESOURCES

A central feature of traditional American thinking has been to accept that individuals vary both in their abilities and in their motivation to utilize them and that their returns should (and do) depend mainly on those two factors. Indeed, this belief has long been held responsible for American hostility to socialism. So not surprisingly almost all whites agree that "some people are just better cut out than others for important positions in society" (15 percent) and that "some people are better at running things and should be allowed to do so" (7 percent; see panel 6 of table 3.3). Here there is consensual support for *inequality*.

But this highlights a critically important contrast: whites consensually reject the notion that *group* differences per se justify differential access to important roles in society (as shown earlier in table 3.3, panel 3). Yet they consensually accept the idea that *individual* differences in capacity on exactly the same dimensions justify differential access to valued resources (panel 6).[27]

Finally, these surveys have no items on radically egalitarian distribution of outcomes, such as the proposition that the government should guarantee that all individuals have equal income. On the basis of much other past research, however, we can confidently say that the idea of real economic leveling usually gets little support in America (Hochschild 1995; Lipset 1996; McClosky and Zaller 1984). Equalizing outcomes by formula is rejected in part because Americans feel it would rob people of their (individualistic) motivation to succeed. Sometimes, they think, gains in equality would come at the expense of individualistic values (Lane 1962).

THREE KINDS OF EGALITARIAN BELIEFS

We showed earlier that egalitarianism, as measured with the NES scale, has surprisingly strong effects on whites' racial policy preferences and symbolic racism (tables 3.1 and 3.2). But egalitarianism is, as we have seen, not a unitary matter. Conceptually, it encompasses numerous ideas and domains. Empirically, these diverse ideas attract very different levels of support among whites. As we will see, some versions of egalitarian beliefs prove to be considerably more closely associated with symbolic racism than others and, for that reason, play quite different roles in the politics of race.

How can different kinds of egalitarianism best be distinguished? For the purpose of characterizing overall levels of support for equality, we have loosely divided them in table 3.3 into six categories on the basis of both shared content and approximate levels of support. But to determine their real psychological clustering requires the use of more formal statistical criteria. Factor analyses of these measures yield three distinctive clusters. One resembles the value of equality as understood in common discourse, focusing on equal treatment and equal opportunity. Such principles of equality are now broadly accepted. A second set reflects the interdependence of egalitarian and individualistic values, and they are considerably more contested. A third set involves the notion of keeping subordinate groups "in their place," which is rejected by the vast majority of whites.

The first two clusters emerge quite reliably from factor analyses of the six NES egalitarianism items. These analyses, using the 1985 and 1986 NES surveys, are shown in table 3.4, along with analyses using the 1990 and 1992 NES surveys to provide greater contemporaneity. Each analysis yields the same two factors. Their distinctiveness is underlined by the modesty of their intercorrelations. Three-item subscales generated to reflect each factor yielded Pearson correlations of .25, .27, .25, and .31 in the four surveys, respectively. This factor solution seems quite stable, since the results are strikingly parallel across the four surveys: the same items load most heavily on the same two factors in each case, the loadings are quite similar in magnitude, and the interfactor correlations are very similar.[28]

What is the substantive difference between these two clusters of beliefs? The factor labeled "more equal treatment" seems to embody true egalitarian values as understood in ordinary language, focusing on equal opportunity ("our society should do whatever is necessary to make sure that everyone has an equal opportunity to succeed" and "one of the big problems in this country is that we don't give everyone an equal chance") and equal treatment ("if people were treated more equally in this country we would have many fewer problems"). On balance, these items yield considerable, though not uniform, support for equality, with an average of 66 percent supporting equality on these items in the 1985 and 1986 NES surveys (see table 3.3).

TABLE 3.4 Factorial Structure of Egalitarian Values

Factor	YEAR OF THE SURVEY							
	1985		1986		1990		1992	
	1	2	1	2	1	2	1	2
More equal treatment								
Our society should do whatever is necessary to make sure that everyone has an equal opportunity to succeed. (reverse coded)	.24	.40	.28	.47	.39	.16	.21	.39
One of the big problems in this country is that we don't give everyone an equal chance. (reverse coded)	.16	.49	.23	.59	.63	−.11	.31	.73
If people were treated more equally in this country we would have many fewer problems. (reverse coded)	.32	.53	.27	.71	.69	.05	.28	.77
We've gone too far								
We have gone too far in pushing equal rights in this country.	.56	.27	.51	.24	−.02	.50	.67	.27
This country would be better off if we worried less about how equal people are.	.66	.28	.77	.28	−.05	.70	.81	.29
It is not really that big of a problem if some people have more of a chance in life than others.	.36	.20	.55	.26	.09	.44	.57	.33
Interfactor correlation (phi)		.43		.47		.36		.43

Sources: 1985, 1986, 1990, and 1992 NES surveys.

Note: The entries are loadings drawn from the structure matrix using principal axis factor analysis with an oblique rotation. The larger factor loadings for each item are boxed.

The other factor involves the perception that "we've gone too far" and seems to capture a resentful response to efforts to increase equality: "we have gone too far in pushing equal rights in this country," "this country would be better off if we worried less about how equal people are," and "it is really not that big of a problem if some people have more of a chance in life than others." Many fewer whites are egalitarians in these terms, with an average of only 39 percent supporting equality on these items in the 1985 and 1986 NES surveys (see table 3.3). These beliefs are more contested, we argue, because they capture the potential clash of egalitarianism with individualism rather than pure egalitarianism itself. Underlying them is a belief that, however desirable equality might be, it cannot be externally imposed, but can be achieved only through individual effort.

Another measurement approach capitalizes on the assessment of beliefs about equality in measures of "social dominance orientation" (see Sidanius et al., chap. 7). This personality predisposition distinguishes individuals who support group hierarchies from those who oppose such hierarchies. It is operationally defined in terms of two separate components. One indexes attitudes toward social equality in terms similar to the NES "more equal treatment" factor, calling for agreement with "increased social equality" and the statements that "it would be good if groups could be equal" and "we should do what we can to equalize conditions for different groups." The second is a "dominance" component that focuses on restricting inferior groups to their subordinate positions in the social hierarchy, using force if necessary: "inferior groups should stay in their place," "sometimes other groups must be kept in their place," and "if certain groups stayed in their places we would have fewer problems." This dominance component has no obvious counterpart in the NES items.

A factor analysis of these six social dominance orientation items in the 1997 LACSS study yielded the expected two-factor solution, distinguishing the three general egalitarianism items from the three dominance items. Neither set loads much on the other factor, and the correlation between the two factors is small (with an oblique rotation, $\phi = .20$).[29] We interpret the first factor as another relatively pure measure of support for egalitarian values. However, it is considerably more skewed than its counterpart in the NES studies, since about half the sample falls at the most extreme egalitarian point of the ten-point scale and only 8 percent are on the inegalitarian side of the midpoint. This may be due in part to the fact that these items mostly refer explicitly to equality among groups, whereas the NES items refer to equality for individuals. If so, it would reinforce two of our earlier claims, that almost all white Americans now support formal political and legal equality for all groups and that the principle of equal treatment for groups seems to be even more broadly based than that of equal treatment for individuals.

The beliefs captured by the "dominance" factor, on the other hand, reflect the idea that traditional group hierarchies must be maintained. Few whites today agree very much with this viewpoint: only 12 percent fell on the dominant side of neutral in the 1997 LACSS. This idea has had its clearest application in recent American history in the old-fashioned racism belief system, which insisted that blacks must stay within the confines of their lower-caste position. As a result, we might speculate that "dominance" might now mainly be linked to what little remains of old-fashioned racism, even though these items do not explicitly refer to race.

The NES egalitarianism and the LACSS social dominance orientation measures, then, yield three subtypes of beliefs about equality: "more equal treatment," beliefs in the general principles of equal opportunity and equal treatment; "we've gone too far," the belief that too much attention has been paid in recent years to equality; and "dominance," a belief in enforcing existing group hierarchies. Our goal in the remainder of this chapter is to see if this distinction helps to explain the link between symbolic racism and the overall NES egalitarianism scale reported earlier. To do so, we have created three-item scales to measure each subtype. Since we are specifically interested in understanding the origins of symbolic racism and whites' opposition to racial policies, in the remainder of the chapter we reverse the scoring of "more equal treatment" such that high scores reflect greater *in*egalitarianism, and we relabel it as expressing the desire for "less equal treatment." The other two subtypes, "we've gone too far" and "dominance," are naturally keyed with high scores reflecting inegalitarian beliefs, so they have not been reversed.

THE LINK TO SYMBOLIC RACISM

Taken at face value, the findings of close links between inegalitarianism and both racial policy preferences and symbolic racism shown above in tables 3.1 and 3.2 would seem to suggest that fundamental disputes about equality continue to be central to racial politics, and more central than individualistic values. If true, this would be contrary to the symbolic racism and other "new racism" perspectives, since they view opposition to formal equality as so diminished in strength as to be peripheral to contemporary racial issues. But this assertion should not apply equally to all three subtypes of inegalitarian beliefs. The successful resolution of the civil rights struggles of the 1960s should indeed have rendered beliefs in "less equal treatment" and in "dominance" obsolete, but it is not so clear that the same could be said for "we've gone too far." Are all three equally implicated in the association of inegalitarianism with symbolic racism?

To test this, we repeated the analyses of the origins of symbolic racism shown in table 3.2, with three key modifications. First and most important, we substituted the three subscales just described for the overall egalitarianism scale. Second, we substituted indicators of old-fashioned racism for white affect, which had not had any significant effects in the earlier analyses. Third, the individualism and morality value scales had originally had significant, but secondary effects. The former was a disappointment because symbolic racism had been thought to stem in part from perceived violations by blacks of traditional values, especially individualism. However, the NES individualism scale used in those analyses is not fully appropriate for testing the symbolic racism hypothesis because it measures support for the work ethic itself rather than a perception that blacks violate it. A more racialized way of measuring individualistic thinking is available in these surveys in attributions about the root causes of racially tinged social ills, such as poverty and crime, so they were substituted for those value scales.

In these new analyses, indicators of antiblack affect and conservative ideology again have significant effects in most cases. More important, though, differentiating the three subtypes of inegalitarianism proves to be quite revealing. The regression coefficients for pure inegalitarianism, as indexed by the NES "less equal treatment" subscale, are quite small in the two NES surveys (.07 and .05, respectively) and not statistically significant. The results are quite parallel across the two studies, as shown in table 3.5, increasing our confidence in this null finding.[30] Still, both these estimates rely on the same three-item subscale, and any conclusions that rely so heavily on a specific measuring instrument place a heavy burden on the instrument itself. The findings prove to be about the same for the "less equal treatment" subscale drawn from measures of social dominance orientation in the 1996 and 1997 LACSS studies. Again, "less equal treatment" is not a strong predictor of symbolic racism, yielding regression coefficients of .12 and .13 in the two studies, respectively, and only the latter is statistically

TABLE 3.5   Origins of Symbolic Racism

	1985 NES	1986 NES	1996 LACSS	1997 LACSS
	β	β	β	β
Inegalitarian values				
Less equal treatment	.07	.05	.13°	.07
Dominance	—	—	.06	.11
We've gone too far	.33°°	.31°°	—	—
Racial attitudes				
Antiblack affect	.19°	.18°°	.22°	.01
Blacks less able	−.11°	.01	.04	.13°
God's will	.09	.17°°	—	—
Nonracial attributions				
Individualism	.12°	—	—	.30°°
Structuralism	.07	—	—	.22°°
Political predispositions				
Party identification	.10	−.01	.13	.17°
Ideology	.05	.17°°	.26°	.15°
Adjusted R^2	28.6%	29.4%	26.2%	39.6%

Sources: 1985 NES pilot study, 1986 NES survey, and 1996 and 1997 LACSS studies.
Note: The entries are the standardized regression coefficients with the full symbolic racism scales. Nonracial attributions for poverty were measured in 1985; attributions for crime were measured in 1997. A high score means, respectively, more negative racial attitudes, more belief that it is God's will that blacks are less well off, less egalitarianism, stronger Republican, more conservative, more blaming poverty/crime on the individual, and more blaming poverty/crime on societal problems.
°$p < .05$.   °°$p < .001$.

significant, as shown in table 3.5. Finally, "dominance" would seem to share some of the features of "less equal treatment," since it, too, represents a fundamental repudiation of formal equality and lives on in only a small minority of whites. And it, too, proves to have only small and nonsignificant associations with symbolic racism once other variables are controlled, as shown in table 3.5 (β = .06 in the 1996 LACSS study and .11 in 1997).[31]

In four surveys, then, regressing symbolic racism on the most straightforward measure of inegalitarian values, "less equal treatment," yields an average coefficient of only .09, and just one of the four is significant. "Dominance," support for traditional group hierarchies, fails to predict symbolic racism significantly in either of two surveys, with an average regression coefficient of .08. We would conclude that neither pure inegalitarianism nor a preference for traditional social hierarchies has much to do with the symbolic racism belief system. The explanation for the oft-reported association between symbolic racism and inegalitarianism as measured in NES surveys must lie elsewhere.

The third subtype of inegalitarianism, "we've gone too far," would seem to be a more promising candidate. Its content sounds more like the resentments of continuing complaints and demands by minorities that are captured in the symbolic racism belief system. Consistent with that view, its bivariate correlations with symbolic racism are about twice as high as those of either of the other subtypes of inegalitarian beliefs.[32] And in the regression equations, "we've gone too far" has a robust and highly significant relationship with symbolic racism, with an average coefficient of .32, far higher than those for "less equal treatment" or "dominance."

The association between the overall inegalitarianism scale and symbolic racism apparently does not mean what it originally seemed to, therefore. Opposition to general principles of equal opportunity and equal treatment is not closely linked to the symbolic racism belief system, contrary to the interpretation usually placed on findings such as those in table 3.2. Rather, symbolic racism is closer to the resentments that are captured by "we've gone too far."

RACIALIZED INDIVIDUALISM

Those earlier findings also did not provide strong evidence that the symbolic racism belief system has roots in perceptions that blacks violate such traditional values as individualism. The new analyses shown in table 3.5 use attributions about the causes of racially tinged social problems for this purpose. Individualistic attributions about poverty had a statistically significant effect on symbolic racism in the 1985 NES survey, while structural attributions did not. Individualistic attributions about crime had a stronger effect on symbolic racism in the 1997 LACSS study than did structural attributions (though in this case structuralism did have a significant effect).[33] Whites' symbolic racism is closely related to such individualistic attributions about blacks, then. Racialized individualism, not individualism per se, may be at the heart of the symbolic racism belief system.

So far we have shown that symbolic racism is considerably more closely linked to "we've gone too far" and individualistic attributions for racially tinged social problems than to the other two subtypes of inegalitarianism. At this point, we need to reconsider the causal model implicit in our analysis. Like others who have tested this model (e.g., Hughes 1997; Sears 1988; Sniderman, Crosby, and Howell, chap. 8), we have assumed a causal ordering that places "basic" prejudices and values as antecedents to symbolic racism, which in turn is treated as prior to racial policy preferences. That sequence assumes that prejudice and values are fundamental psychological predispositions, perhaps acquired early in life. But we are not confident that "we've gone too far," the active ingredient in the standard measure of inegalitarian values, belongs in the category of early-acquired basic values. Rather, it may reflect resentments about contemporary American society like those captured by the symbolic racism belief system. It seems prudent to proceed on this more cautious assumption about its causal role than to presume its priority. But doing so requires changing our analytic strategy from sequencing these beliefs in an overall causal flow to trying to unpack the belief system that we describe as "symbolic racism." For the remainder of the chapter, then, we switch from using regression analysis, implying causality, to using simple bivariate correlations to assess the clustering of related beliefs.

Does "we've gone too far," like symbolic racism, embody racialized individualism? Many whites may believe that "we've gone too far" because they believe that blacks no longer face great handicaps at that metaphorical starting line. That is, they may see any remaining racial inequalities as primarily attributable to blacks themselves, to their lack of work ethic or impulse control, their irresponsibility, and other internally controllable factors. To test this, we need to look for associations between "we've gone too far" and indicators of racialized individualism and for null relationships with beliefs thought to fall outside the symbolic racism syndrome.

If "we've gone too far" is closely tied to racialized individualism, it should correlate more with individualistic attributions for racial problems than with either structuralist ones or those that do not explicitly concern race. The available attributions in the NES surveys focused on poverty and attributions for blacks' disadvantages. The data are supportive in two ways. First, "we've gone too far" is indeed more closely associated with individualistic (average $r = .35$) than with structural attributions (average $r = .18$), as shown in table 3.6. Second, it is racialized. It correlates more strongly with attributions about racial disadvantage (average $r = .32$) than with comparable attributions about poverty (average $r = .14$).[34] In sum, there is a close link between the beliefs reflected in "we've gone too far" and individualism, especially when race is explicitly involved. Racialized individualism is the clearest common ground between "we've gone too far" and symbolic racism.[35]

TABLE 3.6   Correlates of Different Versions of Inegalitarianism

	We've Gone Too Far		Less Equal Treatment			Dominance
	1985	1986	1985	1986	1997	1997
Attributions for poverty/crime						
Individualistic	.25°	—	.06	—	.11	.17
Structural	.04	—	.43°	—	.31°	.03
Attributions for racial disadvantage						
Individualistic	.41°	.39°	.13	.09	.22°	.35°
Structural	.29°	.20°	.18°	.16°	.22°	−.01

Sources: 1985 NES pilot study, 1986 NES survey, and 1997 LACSS studies.
Note: Attributions for poverty were measured only in 1985; attributions for crime were measured only in 1997. A high score means more inegalitarianism. For poverty and crime attributions, a high score means blaming poverty/crime on the individual and on societal problems, respectively. For racial disadvantage attributions, a high score means blaming racial disadvantage on lack of hard work on the part of blacks, and on slavery and discrimination, respectively.
°$p < .001$.

"LESS EQUAL TREATMENT": NONRACIALIZED CONSERVATISM

The logic of pure egalitarian values would lead us to expect that they would not be much connected to individualism. Providing equal rights to all does not depend on anything done by those granted the rights because all have the rights by birth rather than having to earn them by good behavior. Indeed, "less equal treatment" is essentially uncorrelated with individualistic attributions for social problems; only one of the five correlations is statistically significant, and they average just $r = .12$, as shown in table 3.6. In contrast, all five of the correlations of "less equal treatment" with structural attributions are significant, and they average .26.

Is this form of pure inegalitarianism peripheral to all racial issues or just to symbolic racism? The two NES surveys each had two measures of "old-fashioned racism": beliefs that blacks' disadvantages are due to an inherent lack of ability or due to God's will. The former was also measured in the two LACSS studies. But "less equal treatment" has very little relationship with old-fashioned racism either. Only one of its six correlations with these beliefs is statistically significant, and the average correlation is only .02. This is summarized in table 3.7.[36] A second indication that "less equal treatment" is not particularly racialized is that its correlations with attributions for social problems are actually substantially *lower* when the problems are explicitly racial; the

TABLE 3.7   Average Correlations of Inegalitarianism with Old-Fashioned Racism and Political Predispositions

	WE'VE GONE TOO FAR	LESS EQUAL TREATMENT	DOMINANCE
Old-Fashioned Racism			
Low ability	.25	.12	.38
God's will	.24	−.08	—
Political predispositions			
Party identification	.20	.29	.05
Ideology	.26	.29	−.02

Sources: The first column is based on the 1985 and 1968 NES surveys, the third column is based on the 1996 and 1997 LACSS studies, and the middle column is based on all four surveys (except that "God's will" was asked only in the two NES studies).

Note: A high score means less egalitarianism/more dominance, blaming racial disadvantage on blacks' lesser ability or on God's will, and more Republican or more conservative.

average correlation is .12 regarding blacks' disadvantages and .26 for poverty or crime.[37] Unlike "we've gone too far," then, pure inegalitarianism is not closely associated with either individualism or race. Such null findings strengthen the case for a special connection between symbolic racism and racialized individualism.

"DOMINANCE": A VESTIGE OF OLD-FASHIONED RACISM

We earlier speculated that the "dominance" form of inegalitarianism is largely a vestige of the old-fashioned racism of two generations ago. Indeed, in both LACSS studies it proves to be strongly correlated with blaming blacks' disadvantages on low intelligence, as shown in table 3.7. It is considerably more closely associated with old-fashioned racism ($r = .38$) than it is with symbolic racism (average $r = .22$).[38] But if "dominance" is mainly a residue of old-fashioned racism, it should be largely irrelevant to contemporary political divisions. And it does have almost no association at all with conventional partisan predispositions: all four correlations with party identification and ideology are close to zero, averaging .02. By way of contrast, the other subtypes of inegalitarianism are woven quite thoroughly into contemporary politics; the average correlation of "we've gone too far" with partisan predispositions is .23, and for "less equal treatment," .29, as shown in table 3.7 (also see Miller and Shanks 1996).

The three subtypes therefore have somewhat different connections to racial policy preferences. "Dominance" is largely peripheral to such issues; its correlation with the racial policy preference scale in the 1997 LACSS was .16, while "less equal treatment" correlated strongly

(r = .45) with that scale. "We've gone too far" also yielded an average correlation of r = .31 with policy preferences in the two NES surveys; the comparable correlation for "less equal treatment" was .27. Genuine egalitarian values remain relevant both to politics in general and to racial politics in particular. But unlike "we've gone too far," the reason is not any link to newer forms of racism. Rather, it stems from the continuing association of egalitarianism with conventional partisan predispositions.

In sum, these three versions of inegalitarian beliefs have quite different linkages to racial politics. The purest version of inegalitarian values, "less equal treatment," has no consistent association with racial attitudes, whether new or old. "We've gone too far" seemingly reflects resentment of the efforts made in American society over the past few decades to increase equality. It is the most closely linked to symbolic racism and seems to have roots in racialized individualism. "Dominance" is also racialized, but is linked more closely to the vestiges of the older, pre–civil rights era caste system than to contemporary racial politics. Distinguishing these three kinds of inegalitarianism gives us some further purchase on the origins of symbolic racism, then. Previous findings relating it to inegalitarianism apparently do not mean what they seem. Symbolic racism reflects misgivings about the pace of racially egalitarian reforms in American society due to their clash with individualistic values rather than because of a lack of support for the principle of equal treatment itself.[39]

DISCUSSION

The theory of symbolic racism proposes that few whites now adhere to the old-fashioned racism belief system, so it now has little effect on their political responses to racial issues. Instead, their racial policy preferences are most heavily influenced by symbolic racism, expressed in beliefs that racial discrimination is no longer a serious constraint, that blacks have insufficient work ethic, and that they are, therefore, making excessive demands and receiving undeserved special advantages.

SUMMARY

Empirically, we began by replicating the finding that symbolic racism is a strong predictor of whites' preferences about racial policies. Our main goal, however, was to understand the origins of symbolic racism. The original theory suggested that it results from a blend of two residues of earlier socialization, antiblack affect and traditional values. We report several kinds of evidence that it does in fact have a strong racial component: antiblack affect does influence racial policy preferences even with major nonracial political attitudes controlled; its effects are very similar across quite different domains of racial policies, suggesting that their common racial component captures much of whites' attention, above and beyond the individual political contents of these policies; and it has significant effects on symbolic racism itself.[40] These findings support Kinder and Mendelberg's (chap. 2) view that prejudice is still with us and continues to play an important role in forming racial policy preferences. It is contrary to the view of Sniderman and his associates (e.g., Sniderman, Crosby, and Howell, chap. 8; Sniderman and Carmines 1997a) that race now plays a relatively minor role in these issues.

Our second hypothesis was that individualism is the traditional value most implicated in symbolic racism and racial policy preferences. However, using the measures that have been used in a number of other recent studies, we found that individualism has weaker effects than do egalitarian values. This is an important potential departure from the symbolic racism theory because the hypothesized repudiation of old-fashioned racism should have eliminated politically consequential divisions of opinion about formal racial equality.

To better understand this apparent disconfirmation, we turned to an examination of egalitarian values themselves. White Americans feel very differently about different kinds of equality. We find that whites now broadly and consensually support the traditional ideal of formal equality that involves ensuring equal treatment and equal opportunity for all groups. However, they are sharply divided about the extent to which inequality remains a serious problem in our society.

Because different versions of beliefs about equality appear to get such different responses, we pursued this distinction more systematically. We began by factor analyzing the items in the most commonly used egalitarianism scale, that developed by the National Election Studies. It yielded the same two factors in each of four national surveys. We then subjected a standard measure of social dominance orientation (see Sidanius et al., chap. 7) to the same factor analytic treatment. It yielded two factors as well. This multidimensionality of two scales that previously have been treated as homogeneous turns out to be quite consequential for their predictive values in the area of racial attitudes.

We then keyed all these factors such that high scores reflected opposition to equality and relabeled them accordingly. One factor that emerges from both sets of factor analyses seems to reflect pure inegalitarian values. We described it as "less equal treatment." It is a significant dimension of division in partisan politics, but it proves to have little association with symbolic racism and is not discernibly racialized in any other way. As we had initially expected, then, the pivot point of the debate about race has indeed moved away from any serious questioning of formal equality.

A second factor, specific to the measures of social dominance orientation, was labeled "dominance" and reflects the belief that subordinate groups should be kept in their places. Because that was such a strong theme in white supremacist thinking for so long, it is perhaps not surprising that "dominance" is more closely linked to old-fashioned racism than to the conventional political debates of the 1990s and does not relate closely to conventional partisan attitudes, symbolic racism, or racial policy preferences.

The third factor focuses on questions about which whites are substantially less egalitarian: is inequality still a big problem in America, and have we gone too far in trying to eliminate it? We described this as the "we've gone too far" perspective. In essence, "we've gone too far" seems to tap a resentful response to efforts to produce more group equality. These beliefs are more highly contested and more racialized than are the pure inegalitarian beliefs reflected in the first factor. They are especially closely linked to symbolic racism and also to racialized and individualistic attributions for racially tinged problems. Most important, they seem to reflect a belief that further action by the broader society will not help blacks' situation; the rest of the distance is up to blacks to travel themselves. This view returns us to the original theory that symbolic racism reflects a mixture of antiblack feeling and individualistic interpretations of social problems.

The theory is modified by the present findings, however, to incorporate a clearer understanding of the interdependence of inegalitarian and individualistic beliefs than originally envisaged. The standard measures of egalitarianism do indeed contain some items that tap support for equal treatment and equal opportunity, as originally intended. But the NES measure also contains items that involve a mixture of inegalitarian beliefs (opposition to further collective efforts to force more equality) and individualistic beliefs (further equality can come

about only through the efforts of the disadvantaged individuals themselves). Our main point is that it is a mistake to interpret such measures as reflecting pure inegalitarian values.[41]

METHODOLOGICAL CONCERNS

We should briefly address three possible methodological issues. First,
the three subtypes of inegalitarian beliefs have different levels of support among whites. Variations in skewness could potentially threaten
any comparisons of their relationships with other variables. However,
tables 3.6 and 3.7 show that each subtype has relatively stronger correlations with some variables and relatively weaker correlations with still
others. It is the specific pattern of those associations that differentiates
these three versions of beliefs about equality, not differences among
the three in the overall magnitude of their associations with other variables.

Second, we empirically documented a specifically racial component
to both symbolic racism and racial policy attitudes using the standard
methods of regression analysis with controls on relevant nonracial attitudes. But in doing so, we run the risk of "circularity," as Schuman
(chap. 10) has put it. That is, correlations among those dimensions
might merely reflect moderately consistent responses to different
ways of asking about the same underlying construct—in this case,
general racial attitudes. One safeguard he proposes is to correlate only
variables that are indisputably different, such as Taylor's (chap. 4) correlation of objective racial context with racial attitudes.[42] However,
this does not seem to us to be a viable solution for hypotheses that
are intrinsically concerned with subjective states, such as that long-
standing racial attitudes influence racial policy preferences. Nor do
we think it wise to abandon the test of hypotheses that are theoretically, socially, and/or politically important when they happen to pose
difficult methodological challenges.

Nevertheless, such methodological problems should not be ignored. In social science, there is usually no perfect solution to any
problem. So we have offered several partial answers. One is to compare whites' responses to diverse racial policy issues. It is clear that
the nature of the issue matters; whites are more supportive of some
racial policies than others, as several of the authors in this volume
forcefully remind us (Kinder and Mendelberg, chap. 2; Bobo, chap.
5; Sniderman, Crosby, and Howell, chap. 8; also see Sniderman et al.
1997; Steeh and Krysan 1996; Stoker 1998). But racial attitudes have
quite consistent effects across policy issues. There is some variation

across issues, but the distinctions are not sharp, and it is hard to see clear systematic trends (also see Kinder and Sanders 1996; Sears et al. 1997). This suggests that whites see each policy issue through the lens of prior racial attitudes as well as in its own right.

A second approach is to use "side information" from longitudinal studies, which suggests that general racial attitudes (including symbolic racism) are relatively stable over time (Converse 1975; Converse and Markus 1979; Kinder and Sanders 1996; Sears 1981; Sears and Funk 1999). From that, we could infer that they are causally prior to attitudes toward more transient policy options.

A third approach is to vary experimentally the presence of race in materials presented to respondents, as in the race targeting of policies, the race of welfare recipients or criminal perpetrators, or the group identified in measures of symbolic racism. In most such cases, racializing reduces policy support and/or interacts with underlying racial attitudes, as we would expect.[43] In the end, though, any model will be convincing only with converging evidence of different kinds, replicated over multiple studies.

The symbolic racism model proposes a particular causal ordering of key variables, but tests it with cross-sectional survey data. This opens the door to alternative models that place the same variables in different causal orders. Most obvious, the sense of group position model (Bobo, chap. 5) and social dominance theory (Sidanius et al., chap. 7) both treat the beliefs captured by measures of symbolic racism primarily as components of a dominant ideology that invokes meritocracy and free market ideology to legitimize an inegalitarian social structure. That is, they treat such beliefs more as consequences of social stratification than as root causes of policy preferences. The differences among these perspectives probably cannot be resolved by simply rearranging the causal orders of the same set of variables when all are measured in a single cross-sectional survey.[44]

More convincing would be pinpointing variables or processes central to one model and not another. For one thing, symbolic racism theory asserts the long-term stability and motivating power of attitudes about African Americans; evidence on that point is presented elsewhere (Sears 1981; Sears and Funk 1999; Sears and van Laar 1999). According to social dominance theory, social dominance orientation should also have long-term stability and strong independent causal force. In contrast, current interests are central constructs in the group position theory (Bobo, chap. 5). From an objective point of view, the benefits to blacks of programs like affirmative action may be considerable, but the costs to whites may not be very great (Bowen and Bok 1998). From a subjective point of view, whites may or may not perceive very high levels of zero-sum competition with blacks (see Bobo and Hutchings 1996). Second, there is an important distinction between self-interest and group interest. Considerable evidence indicates that self-interest has relatively little direct impact on attitudes about racial issues (Sears and Funk 1991; also see Bobo 1988b). Perceptions relevant to group interests often seem to have stronger effects (Bobo and Hutchings 1996; Kinder and Sanders 1996; Sears and Jessor 1996). However, the conceptual distinction between the symbolic racism and group position formulations about the nature and role of group interests remains somewhat murky (compare Sears and Kinder 1985 with Bobo and Hutchings 1996; also see Hughes 1997). This would suggest that further conceptual and empirical work on group interest is needed.

CONCLUSIONS

In conclusion, we would argue that the often-reported associations between measures of egalitarian values and those of racial policy preferences or symbolic racism do not mean what they seemed to at first glance. Though replicable, they have perhaps been interpreted too literally. They may reflect the impact of racialized and individualistic beliefs about societal problems more than they do a central role for pure egalitarian values in racial issues. African Americans seem to be especially common targets of this racialized individualism (also see Kluegel and Bobo 1993; Pettigrew 1979). And white Americans who perceive racial problems as primarily the responsibility of individual blacks rather than of the society at large are not likely to believe that governmental racial policies will be successful or that they are desirable.

To be sure, our analysis of "less equal treatment" suggests one path by which egalitarianism may affect racial policy preferences free of racial prejudice. In the 1985 and 1986 NES surveys, its average correlation with racial policy preferences is .27. Even after symbolic racism is partialled out, a significant correlation remains (average partial $r =$ .22). At first blush, this finding would seem to support the speculation offered by Sniderman and his colleagues that whites resist contemporary racial policies in part because "the ideals of equality and tolerance have been upended" in such policies (Sniderman and Carmines 1997a, 3).

But that view is inconsistent with the empirical evidence in two ways. First, it attributes whites' resistance to their belief that contemporary racial policies violate fundamental egalitarian principles. That has it backwards: it is *in*egalitarianism, not egalitarianism, that is associated with opposition to racial policies, as shown in table 3.1. That association is pervasive, replicated across surveys and over several types of issues and over different kinds of measures (e.g., Hughes 1997; Kinder and Sanders 1996; Sidanius et al., chap. 7).

Stephan Thernstrom and Abigail Thernstrom (1997), like Sniderman and his colleagues (Sniderman and Piazza 1993; Sniderman and Carmines, 1997a), argue that affirmative action is a particular case in point, that commitment to egalitarian principles is responsible for widespread white opposition to such "preference-based" or "race-conscious" policies. Elite critics of affirmative action sometimes do indeed justify their positions with egalitarian rhetoric, as in the quotes from Martin Luther King, Jr., calling for a color-blind society that were used to bolster the 1996 California initiative campaign to repeal governmental affirmative action programs. But in mass opinion, it is the inegalitarians who most oppose affirmative action. For example, in the 1997 LACSS, conducted shortly after that initiative campaign, our measure of pure inegalitarian values, "less equal treatment," was strongly correlated with opposition to racial policies ($r = .45$). At the national level, the correlation between "less equal treatment" and opposition to affirmative action was $r = .26$ in the 1986 NES survey. Similar findings have been reported by others (e.g., Hughes 1997; Sidanius et al., chap. 7).

More generally, the "politics-centered" theory misses the most powerful dynamic in whites' preferences about racial policy issues. Recent research, some reported in this volume and some elsewhere, has begun to find that individualism does indeed have an important role in the racial resentments captured in the symbolic racism belief system—*when individualism is racialized.* The analyses reported in tables 3.1 and 3.2 above, as well as those reported by Kinder and Mendelberg (chap. 2) and Sniderman and his colleagues (chap. 8), do indeed find that nonracial individualism has relatively little impact on racial policy preferences or symbolic racism. But racialized individualism—whether measured in the form of symbolic racism or racial resentments (Sears et al. 1997; Kinder and Mendelberg, chap. 2), individualistic attributions for racial disadvantage (Kinder and Mendelberg, chap. 2; Kluegel and Bobo 1993), or negative stereotypes of blacks as lazy (Gilens 1998)—has markedly stronger effects on racial policy preferences than does nonracial individualism. Kinder and Mendelberg (chap. 2) also report both that racialized individualism has substantially stronger effects on racial policy preferences than on attitudes about other forms of social policy and that whites' spontaneous thoughts about racial policies are laden with racial resentment, whereas those about nonracial policies tend not to be.

Converging evidence about the role of racialized individualism also comes from recent experimental studies. Stereotypes about blacks' poor work ethic significantly predict negative attitudes toward welfare mothers and welfare policy, but only when the welfare recipients are black and only when they behave consistently with that negative stereotype. Those stereotypes have no significant effect on attitudes about white welfare recipients or black recipients who violate the stereotype (Peffley and Hurwitz 1998; Peffley, Hurwitz, and Sniderman 1997). Negative impressions of black welfare mothers are also more predictive of negative attitudes about welfare policy than are negative impressions of white welfare mothers (Gilens 1998). The conjunction of being black and violating fundamental individualistic values seems to be the lightning rod that attracts opposition to liberal racial policies.

Finally, what can our findings tell us about how racial divisions and inequalities can be reduced? Both Bobo (chap. 5) and Sniderman and his colleagues (chap. 8; Sniderman and Carmines 1997a) suggest that greater public support might result from shifting attention from questions of racial prejudice to the actual merits of policies themselves, whether in terms of their costs and benefits or their congruence with white Americans' values and basic sense of fairness. Consistent with that view, much research shows that white opinion is not at all uniform across racial policy issues; the nature of the policy itself seems to have a great deal to say about how it is evaluated (Kinder and Sanders 1996; Sniderman and Carmines 1997a; Sniderman and Piazza 1993; Stoker 1998; Steeh and Krysan 1996; also see Kinder and Mendelberg, chap. 2; Bobo, chap. 5; Sniderman, Crosby, and Howell, chap. 8). But as common as this observation is, and as much speculation as has been devoted to explaining such differences, little hard research has been devoted to the question of *why* those differences in support across issues occur, so such explanations remain largely speculative.[45]

One thing that can be said with some confidence is that all racial issues tend in some measure to draw whatever racial prejudices individual whites possess (see, inter alia, Sears et al. 1997; Kinder and Mendelberg, chap. 2). We believe that this unpleasant fact of life poses a problem for a dialogue about real conflicts of interest and the actual costs and benefits of different policy proposals (Bobo, chap. 5). We would agree with Bobo that the political system is better suited to negotiating solutions to conflicts of interest than to resolving moral disagreements.[46] And he does find that whites' evaluations of affirmative action are strongly correlated with their perceptions of its effects. But he also finds that symbolic racism is the strongest predictor of whites' assessments of those effects. It is difficult to conclude that very many whites are, at this time, capable of dispassionately appraising the effects of such policies free of whatever racial attitudes they bring to the table.

A non-race-targeted "new liberal agenda" might, therefore, seem to be more promising, since it avoids having to confront directly the continuing racial animus in many white Americans (Bobo and Kluegel 1993; Sniderman and Carmines 1997a; Wilson 1987). Of course, there is the obstacle of Americans' broad preference for market criteria of "earned deserts" rather than political remedies for inequalities (Carmines and Merriman 1993; Lane 1986; also see Bobo, Kluegel, and Smith 1997 on "laissez-faire racism"). That aside, ostensibly non–racially targeted safety net and redistributional policies have also tended themselves to become racialized over time, seeming inevitably to get sucked into the cauldron of racial politics. Gilens (1998, 1999) has presented persuasive evidence of the racialization of universalistic social welfare programs, and we would agree with his conclusion that "this negative 'racialization' of welfare calls into question the 'hidden agenda' strategy for fighting racial inequality" (1998, 194).

Almost all white Americans have ultimately come to the view that formal, legalized discrimination is wrong, and most of those now support policies to make it illegal (Schuman et al. 1997). But other persisting racial inequalities several decades after the end of the Jim Crow system present a more difficult dilemma. As we have seen, white Americans divide on the question of who is responsible for continuing inequality. The many who place responsibility on blacks themselves tend not to support public policies that are intended to help. Those who place responsibility on the society are more supportive of government action. The theme that binds the past to the present is the continuing influence of racial prejudices in creating both these persisting divisions of opinion and the resulting political coalitions. If in the end individualism is woven inextricably into American culture, whites' special antagonism toward African Americans need not be. We continue to believe that is what needs to be addressed.

APPENDIX

The symbolic racism items used in the 1996 LACSS are as follows:

(1) If blacks work hard they almost always get what they want. Do you strongly agree, agree, disagree, or strongly disagree?

(2) Hard work offers little guarantee of success for blacks. Do you strongly agree, agree, disagree, or strongly disagree?

(3) Irish, Italian, Jewish and many other minorities overcame prejudice and worked their way up. Blacks should do the same without any special favors. Do you strongly agree, agree, disagree, or strongly disagree?

(4) Blacks are getting too demanding in their push for equal rights. Do you strongly agree with this, somewhat agree, somewhat disagree, or strongly disagree?

The symbolic racism items used in the 1997 LACSS include (3) and (4) above as well as the following:

(5) How much discrimination against blacks do you feel there is in the United States today, limiting their chances to get ahead? A lot, some, just a little, or none at all?

(6) Government officials usually pay less attention to a request or complaint from a black person than from a white person. Do you strongly agree, agree, neither agree nor disagree, disagree, or strongly disagree?

(7) Some say that the civil rights people have been trying to push too fast. Others feel that they haven't pushed fast enough. How about you: Do you think that civil rights leaders are trying to push too fast, are going too slowly, or are they moving at about the right speed?

(8) Most blacks who receive money from welfare programs could get along without it if they tried. Do you strongly agree with this, somewhat agree, somewhat disagree, or strongly disagree?

(9) Over the past few years, blacks have gotten less than they deserve. Do you strongly agree, agree, neither agree nor disagree, disagree, or strongly disagree?

(10) Has there been a lot of real change in the position of black people in the past few years, only some, not much at all?

(11) Do blacks get much more attention from the government than they deserve, more attention, about the right amount, less attention, or much less attention from the government than they deserve?

(12) It's really a matter of some people not trying hard enough; if blacks would only try harder they could be just as well off as whites. Do you strongly agree with this, somewhat agree, somewhat disagree, or strongly disagree?

(13) Generations of slavery and discrimination have created conditions that make it difficult for blacks to work their way out of the lower class. Do you strongly agree with this, somewhat agree, somewhat disagree, or strongly disagree?

The general racial policy scale used in the 1997 LACSS included the following items:

(1) Equal opportunity for blacks and whites to succeed is important but it's not really the government's job to guarantee it. Do you strongly agree, agree, disagree, or strongly disagree?

(2) Should spending for programs that assist blacks be increased, decreased, or kept about the same?

(3) Some people feel that the government in Washington should make every effort to improve the social and economic position of blacks and other minorities. Others feel that the government should not make any special effort to help minorities because they should help themselves. Do you feel the government should help improve the position of blacks and other minorities, or that blacks and other minorities should help themselves? [Measured on a five-point scale anchored at "Government should help minorities, to a great extent" and "Minorities should help themselves, to a great extent."]

(4) Proposition 209 on last November's statewide election ballot had to do with state and local laws relating to affirmative action. A yes vote was a vote to end race and gender-based affirmative action programs in public employment, education, and contracting. Regardless of how you felt at the time, is that something you favor now, or would you prefer to continue race-based and gender-based affirmative action programs?

The NES variables are as follows:

- Federal assistance: V7231 and V7311 in 1985; V334 and V522 in 1986.
- Equal opportunity: V7106, V7412, V7414, and V7416 in 1985; V485, V506, and V522 in 1986.
- Affirmative action: V7421 and V7425 (form A) or V7423 and V7427 (form B) in 1985; V476 and V478 in 1986.

- Symbolic racism: V8214, V8215, V8218, and V8222 through V8226 in 1985 (including LACSS items 3, 5, 6, 8, 9, 12, and 13 above); V559, V565 through V568, V579, and V580 in 1986 (the same as LACSS items 3, 6–9, 12, and 13 above).
- Equality: V2169, V2172, V2175, V2178, V2250, and V2256 in 1983; V8201, V8203, V8205, V8401, V8403, and V8405 in 1985; V364 through V369 in 1986; V426 through V431 in 1990; V6024 through V6029 in 1992.
- Racial equality: V3200, V3202, V3204, V3206, V3224, and V3226 in 1983 (form B).
- Gender equality: V3192, V3194, V3196, V3198, V3216, and V3220 in 1983 (form A).
- Individualism: V8202, V8204, V8206, V8402, V8404, and V8406 in 1985; V508 through V513 in 1986.
- Morality: V7101 through V7103 and V8101 through V8105 in 1985; V525 through V532 in 1986.
- Attributions for poverty: V8235, V8236, V8238, V8240, V8241, V8243, and V8244 in 1985.
- Attributions for black disadvantage: V8213 through V8215 and V8217 in 1985; V578 through V580 and V582 in 1986.

FOUR The Significance of Racial Context

MARYLEE C. TAYLOR

Do white Americans' racial policy opinions revolve primarily around race, or are they a function of broader ideological preferences? Paul Sniderman and his associates have concluded that prejudice is less important and broad policy preferences more important than commonly assumed (see, for example, Sniderman et al. 1993; Sniderman and Piazza 1993). "A quarter century ago, what counted was who a policy would benefit, blacks or whites," say Sniderman and Thomas Piazza (1993, 4–5); now, however, "ideological differences over racial public policies represent genuine differences of political outlook rather than covert racism" (1993, 13).

David Sears and his colleagues disagree. Most recently Sears et al. (1997) used data from four major surveys to compare the strength of "symbolic" and "traditional" racial attitude scales with ostensibly non-racial measures as predictors of racial policy opinion. Compared to ideology, party identification, social welfare attitudes, individualism, morality/sexuality, and authoritarianism, these researchers found racial attitudes, particularly "symbolic racism," to be the most powerful predictor of whites' opinions about provision of equal opportunity, federal assistance to blacks, and affirmative action.

Though framed differently, aspects of Lawrence Bobo and James Kluegel's (1993) article turn the argument of Sniderman and his colleagues on its head. Seeking to explain the lower white support for race-targeted than for income-targeted policies, these researchers compared the predictive potency of racial prejudice, stratification beliefs, perceived discrimination, and group self-interest in determining white support for race-targeted and income-targeted "equal outcomes" and "opportunity enhancement" programs. Their overall conclusion stressed the importance of white group self-interest. But they noted findings that raise interesting questions about the role of racial attitudes in shaping policy opinion and policy-related beliefs.

In particular, Bobo and Kluegel found racial prejudice to be a significant predictor of opinions on income-targeted opportunity enhancement policies, suggesting that many whites superimpose racial status on poverty and disadvantage, hearing "black" when they read "poor." These authors also suggested that assessments of discrimination, a strong predictor of support for race targeting, may be "theory driven" (an outgrowth of white resistance to racial change) rather than "experience driven" (a logical product of whites' perceptions of their world).

In other words, where Sniderman and his associates claim racial prejudice has *less* sweeping impact on policy opinion than commonly supposed, Bobo and Kluegel suggest the impact of racial prejudice may be *more* sweeping.

My own research has asked how aspects of the local racial context affect racial views. "How White Attitudes Vary with the Racial Composition of Local Populations: Numbers Count" (Taylor 1998) assesses the impact of local minority concentration on traditional prejudice, opposition to race targeting, and policy-related beliefs. For all three dimensions of racial views, the answer is clear: white negativity swells as the local black population grows, especially outside the South.

The proposition that sizeable minorities often increase white hostility has a long history in social science (see, e.g., Allport 1954; Williams 1947). As Lincoln Quillian (1996) points out, negative white reaction to black population concentrations is virtually always described as a threat response. However, the multiple strategies employed in my earlier work (Taylor 1998) did not provide evidence that either economic or political threat is responsible for the link between black numbers and negative white attitudes.

As pointed out in my 1998 article, the role of threat in mediating the impact of black numbers on white racial attitudes may be difficult to document because threat is not simply a precursor of prejudice: the two may be inextricably intertwined. Writing about racial proportions effects four decades ago, Gordon Allport said:

> [T]he principles of relative size and gradient of density cannot stand alone. . . . Some ethnic groups seem more menacing than others—either because they have more points of difference or higher visibility.

Growing density, therefore, is not in itself a sufficient principle to explain prejudice. What it seems to accomplish is the aggravation of whatever prejudice exists. (1954, 22)

In a similar vein, Donald Kinder and Lynn Sanders find whites' sense of personal threat and "group threat" from blacks so closely linked to "racial resentment" that the researchers conclude:

[T]he perception of threat has a systematic foundation, but the foundation is provided not by actual conditions of conflict and competition but by feelings of racial resentment. Threat is not so much a clear-eyed perception as it is an emotion-laden attitude. Whites feel racially threatened because they are predisposed to look at the world that way; they see danger and risk when others, more sympathetic in their racial sentiments, do not. (1996, 90)

These insights suggest a strategy other than interattitude correlational analysis for assessing the role of racial sentiment in shaping white Americans' views. Beliefs and preferences that are independent of racial prejudice should also be insensitive to the impact of local population composition. Views that are bound up with racial sentiment should reveal themselves in their responsiveness to the race composition of the local population.

The purpose of this chapter is to outline the dimensions of white residents' sensitivity to local racial context. Using the impact of black numbers on traditional prejudice as a benchmark, the goal is to assess the impact of black population share on

1. racial policy opinion,
2. racial policy–related beliefs, and
3. ostensibly nonracial views often taken as alternative explanations of racial policy opinion.

Results will be used to reflect back on the debate about the role of racial and purportedly nonracial influences on white Americans' racial policy opinions. If Sniderman and his associates are correct when they claim that racial sentiment has minimal impact in the policy realm, there should be few cases where local racial proportions affect whites' views. If, instead, racial sentiment has extensive impact on white Americans' policy opinions (Sears et al. 1997; Bobo and Kluegel 1993), we should see evidence in widespread effects of local black population share on whites' opinions and beliefs.

Where informative, the impact of another dimension of the local racial context will be examined as well—the relative economic status of local blacks and whites.

DATA AND ANALYSIS

Data for this project come from two micro/macro data files that link responses to the 1990 and 1994 General Social Surveys, respectively, with 1990 Census information about respondents' localities.

The General Social Survey (GSS) has long been a central source of information about views and opinions related to race (Firebaugh and Davis 1988; Smith and Sheatsley 1984). The 1990 GSS was chosen to serve as the micro side of one data file because it contains a special module on Racial/Ethnic Tolerance, an extensive battery of items tapping race-related attitudes and beliefs (see Davis and Smith 1990 for details). The Multiculturalism module of the 1994 GSS makes that survey a rich source of micro data for our second data file (Davis and Smith 1994).

The multistage stratified sampling procedure used for the 1990 GSS drew respondents from 84 localities—61 metropolitan areas and 23 nonmetropolitan counties, pairs of counties, or (in one case) a collection of communities. The 1994 GSS respondents were drawn from 100 localities, just over two-thirds of which were metropolitan areas. Response rates were high in both years—74 percent and 78 percent, respectively—yielding 1,150 white respondents to the 1990 GSS and 1,216 white respondents to the Multiculturalism module of the 1994 GSS. Locality identifiers provided by the National Opinion Research Center were used to link the two survey data files with macro Census-based descriptors of the metropolitan and nonmetropolitan areas in which respondents lived.

Many analysts (e.g., Fossett and Kiecolt 1989; Wilcox and Roof 1978) have persuasively argued that the metropolitan area, the locality unit for most GSS respondents, is probably the psychologically important unit in which the impact of racial and ethnic mix in the population is felt.

A BENCHMARK—TRADITIONAL PREJUDICE

The 1990 GSS provides a rich set of traditional prejudice measures. Some eighteen questions were used to construct subscales representing stereotyping, aversion to contact, and antiegalitarianism, which were then combined into a Traditional Prejudice summary scale. Confirmatory factor analysis guided scale construction (as detailed in Taylor 1998).

Traditional prejudice measures in the 1994 GSS are more limited. For the 1994 GSS data, stereotyping is represented by the single difference in respondents' placement of "whites in general" and "blacks" on a seven-point scale representing industriousness. Aversion to contact is simply respondents' reactions to sending a child to school with varying proportions of black enrollment. The 1994 GSS does allow construction of the same antiegalitarianism scale as used in the 1990 GSS. For both years, high scores on the Traditional Prejudice summary scale represent prejudiced responses.

FOCAL DEPENDENT MEASURES

RACIAL POLICY OPINION Following Sniderman and Piazza (1993), this chapter distinguishes among "equal treatment," "race-conscious," and "social welfare" policies, with only the first and second meriting treatment as explicitly racial. For Sniderman and Piazza, fair housing is a quintessential *equal treatment* issue: "not whether blacks should be able to obtain a benefit . . . others cannot," but "only whether blacks should be able to do what most other Americans can do, and believe they have a clear right to do" (1993, 111). The *race-conscious* category used here takes the label at face value: it is broader than Sniderman and Piazza's, referring not just to preferential treatment and quotas (the earlier authors' focus), but also to the range of race-targeted programs discussed by Bobo and Kluegel (1993), along with busing. (Some such policy questions were treated by Sniderman and Piazza [1993] as social welfare issues. Following their definitions rather than their practice, I reserve the *social welfare* label for policies that benefit the poor and disadvantaged without explicit racial criteria, as detailed later.)

Both 1990 and 1994 GSS respondents were asked whether the government should enforce Fair Housing, Sniderman and Piazza's prime representative of *equal treatment.*

The bank of *race-conscious* items is richer. For the 1990 GSS, a broad Race Targeting summary scale was built from two subscales and an additional item. An equal outcomes subscale (Bobo and Kluegel 1993) indexes opinions about whether the history of discrimination has created a special obligation for the government to help blacks and assessments of current spending levels for "assistance to blacks"/"improving the conditions of blacks." (These split-ballot questions were combined into a single measure.) A second subscale represents three items constituting one condition of a split-ballot experiment registering reactions to what Bobo and Kluegel (1993) labeled opportunity enhancement for blacks—efforts to address poverty and unemployment among black Americans by giving tax breaks to business and industry for locating in affected areas, spending more money on early education, and providing special college scholarships. A measure of opposition to busing is the last inclusion. Busing is similar to other scale constituents in its explicit use of race as a criterion for treatment, though it differs in having desegregation rather than the redistribution of tangible resources as its immediate purpose. Confirmatory factor analysis guided this scaling (as detailed in Taylor 1998).

The 1994 GSS included the constituent items for the equal outcomes subscale as well as the measure of busing support; these constitute the Race Targeting summary scale for 1994.

The 1994 data also included two measures not available in 1990, tapping opposition to affirmative action that involves preferential hiring. These were used to construct a Preferential Treatment scale.

All measures of racial policy opinion are scored with opposition high. (As a dichotomous measure, the fair housing question would have been subjected to logistic analysis were it not for the advantage of providing comparable results across this set of policy measures.)

RACIAL POLICY-RELATED BELIEFS Attributions of black disadvantage to effort, as well as assessments of the discrimination faced by blacks, figure prominently in Sniderman and Piazza's analysis (1993; see especially chaps. 4 and 5). The role of beliefs about discrimination in shaping white policy opinion is important as well in Bobo and Kluegel's work (1993). Here attributions about black disadvantage and assessments of discrimination are represented with scales supported for the 1990 data by confirmatory factor analysis (and used in Taylor 1998).

Victim Blame indicates endorsement of inborn ability and motivation/will power explanations of black disadvantage in jobs, income, and housing; System Blame indexes the rejection of discrimination and educational opportunity explanations; Denial of Discrimination registers assessments of the discrimination faced by blacks in getting good-paying jobs and in buying or renting housing wherever they want. The denial of discrimination items were not used in 1994; victim blame and system blame were operationalized in the 1994 data as they had been in the 1990 data. High scorers on these measures explain racial inequality in terms of individual failings, deny that blacks face structural barriers, and minimize discrimination and continuing inequality.

Another form of policy-related belief will be examined as well: the 1990 and 1994 files each contain an Advantage scale. Constituent items say or imply that blacks are receiving more than their share of valued social outcomes. Some of the items have been described as racial group threat measures by earlier researchers (Kinder and Sanders 1996; Fossett and Kiecolt 1989) and indeed by myself (Taylor 1998). Most could also be construed as measures of relative deprivation (Runciman 1966; Vanneman and Pettigrew 1972; Taylor 1979). Some of these questions serve to measure Kinder and Sanders's (1996) racial resentment. Because each of these GSS questions was phrased to ask respondents' perceptions to as matters of fact, I include them in the policy-related beliefs category, although most can be read as expressions of evaluation as well as perception.

The 1990 GSS contained just two Advantage measures. One concerns *job advantage,* tapping respondents' belief that white candidates often lose out on jobs or promotions to (equally or) less qualified blacks. The second, respondents' sense of black *socio/political advantage,* is the difference between respondents' assessments of the influence held by whites and that held by blacks over American life and politics.

The 1994 data contain a richer set of Advantage measures. The *job advantage* measure described above was included, with this refinement: in 1994, the question was asked as a split ballot, with half the respondents given the 1990 wording and the other half asked about losing out simply to "less qualified" blacks. For use here, the alternate versions of the 1994 split-ballot question were combined into a single measure. A parallel *college advantage* question asked respondents to estimate the frequency with which whites lose out on college admission to "less"/"less or equally" qualified blacks. Again, data from the two versions of the split ballot were combined into a single measure. *Government advantage* assesses the attention blacks receive from government in comparison to the attention given whites. And *personal job disadvantage* estimates the likelihood that, because of affirmative action, the respondents themselves or their family members will lose out to blacks on jobs or promotions. For the Advantage scales, high scores represent the view that blacks are given an advantage.

OSTENSIBLY NONRACIAL VIEWS The 1990 GSS data contained numerous measures of ostensibly nonracial policy opinions and their potential predictors.

Political Philosophy, a central construct in Sniderman and Piazza (1993) and a predictor of policy opinion in Sears et al. (1997), is registered through respondents' reports of their political party identification and their self-placement on a scale of conservatism. High scores are assigned the Republican and conservative poles of these continua.

Authoritarianism is claimed by Sniderman and Piazza (1993) to be a more important predictor of political attitudes than individualistic values. In response, Sears et al. (1997) included authoritarianism in their analyses of race policy opinions. In the 1990 data, authoritarianism registers respondents' belief that children should not be allowed to talk back to their parents and their conviction that people can be divided into two classes—the weak and the strong. (These latter two items constituted the Authoritarianism scale used in Schuman, Bobo, and Krysan 1992.) High scores represent the authoritarian position.

Among stratification beliefs, individualism has received substantial attention in discussions of contemporary racial attitudes (e.g., see Sears 1988; Kluegel and Smith 1986)—too much attention according to Sniderman and Piazza (1993). Bobo and Kluegel (1993) make the useful distinction between normative individualism, the belief that social hierarchy is a good thing, and existential individualism, the belief that a merit-based reward system actually exists in this country. In the 1990 data, Normative Individualism is indexed by three items measuring agreement that large income differences are necessary to promote individual effort in general and advanced study for professional work in particular and that rewards should be based on work, not needs. Existential Individualism is represented by two items attributing poverty to drunkenness/loose morals and lack of effort. The three-item Anti-structuralism scale represents denial that poverty is explained by inadequate schools or insufficient jobs and affirmation that all Americans receive an equal chance. As the scale labels suggest, high scores represent the individualistic response on the first two scales and the avoidance of structuralist response on the third.

The final ostensibly nonracial outcome measures assess opposition to social welfare programs—defined here as programs that address poverty and unemployment without regard to race. These programs include, but are not limited to, the income-targeted policies considered in Bobo and Kluegel (1993). There is some overlap with the Social Welfare scale used by Sears et al. (1997) to predict race policy attitudes.

Opposition to social welfare programs is well represented in the 1990 GSS. The Welfare scale summarizes measures of opposition to explicitly labeled "welfare" (support for "workfare" and for the reduction of welfare benefits to make work more attractive), supplemented for half the sample by evaluations of current government spending on "welfare." The Poor Aid scale summarizes responses to an extensive battery of items that asked about assistance to the poor or disadvantaged with no explicit reference to race or to "welfare": one item assessing denial of a U.S. government responsibility to improve the standard of living for all poor Americans; two items assessing opposition to government job creation; four items asking about government responsibility to create a safety net by other means than job provision (viz. by providing a decent standard of living for the unemployed, reducing income differences between the rich and the poor, giving financial assistance for college to those from low-income families, and providing decent housing for those who cannot afford it); six items tapping opposition to government spending on various forms of "safety net" programs aimed at children from poor families (prenatal care for poor mothers, health care for uninsured children, preschool programs like Head Start, child care for poor families, housing for poor families with children, and nutrition programs for children from poor families); and the other half of the split-ballot items represented in the race-targeting measure, registering opposition to programs that address poverty and unemployment among poor Americans by giving tax breaks to business and industry for locating in affected areas, spending more money on early education, and providing special college scholarships. For half the sample, these components were supplemented by evaluations of current government spending on "assistance to the poor." High scores represent opposition.

In the 1994 data file, Political Philosophy is measured as it had been for the 1990 file. In the 1994 Authoritarianism scale, the choice of obedience as a top-priority value for children is accompanied by a measure of agreement that obedience and respect for authority are the most important virtues for children and the conviction that obedience is more important in preparing children for life than thinking for themselves. Stratification belief measures are not available in the 1994 data. The 1994 Welfare measure, available for only half the sample, consists solely of an evaluation of current government spending on "welfare." Poor Aid assesses denial of a U.S. government responsibility to improve the standard of living for all poor Americans, supplemented for half the sample by evaluations of current government spending on "assistance to the poor." In all cases, direction of scoring parallels that for the 1990 GSS data.

INDIVIDUAL-LEVEL PREDICTORS

Conventionally used individual-level background characteristics serving as controls in this analysis include education (years of schooling), occupational prestige (the Hodge, Siegel, and Rossi index; see Siegel 1971), full-time work status (full-time work versus all other), sex, and age/cohort.

LOCALITY-LEVEL "CONTEXTUAL" PREDICTORS

Total and race-specific population counts for the 83 eligible localities in the 1990 data file and the 100 localities in the 1994 data file are ingredients for the key contextual measure in this research—the proportion of African Americans in the local population (PROPORTION BLACK). (Locality population breakdowns based on racial identity and Hispanic ethnicity were manipulated so that PROPORTION BLACK represents an estimate of the *non-Hispanic* black population share.)

An important supplement to PROPORTION BLACK is a measure of the relative economic status of blacks and whites in the locality, BLACK/WHITE ECONOMIC STATUS. This scale summarizes black-to-white ratios of male employment rates and proportions of families with income greater than $25,000.

In addition to these focal contextual measures, several locality-level variables serve as controls. The natural logarithm of Total Population Size is an important inclusion in all analyses because this variable has the potential to suppress any effects of black population share: total population size and black population share are positively correlated across cities; however, large localities are generally home to progressive attitudes (Wilson 1985, 1991; Tuch 1987), whereas black population concentrations are hypothesized to engender negative racial views among whites. Also included is a measure of WHITE ECONOMIC STATUS; this control makes more interpretable any effects of the BLACK/WHITE ECONOMIC STATUS ratio. Finally, a key contextual predictor derived from the GSS data is region, SOUTH versus non-South.

ANALYSES

This micro/macro data set invites multilevel modeling. Exploratory analysis with ordinary least squares regression was confirmed using the HLM/2L hierarchical linear modeling program (Bryk, Raudenbush, and Congdon 1994). Tables 4.1 through 4.3 present the HLM results.

RESULTS

Tables 4.1 through 4.3 present the most relevant estimates—the unstandardized regression coefficients for central contextual variables after controlling for individual characteristics and total population of the locality. (Full results for the regression of each outcome on the seven individual-level predictors and the entire set of contextual predictors are available from the author.)

For all social psychological outcome measures, the impact of black population share (PROPORTION BLACK) is reported before and after controlling for region (SOUTH). SOUTH and PROPORTION BLACK are, of course, substantially correlated. In the 1990 data, the bivariate correlation is .48: for the average Southern white 1990 GSS respondent, the local population was 18 percent black; for white GSS respondents living outside the South, the local population averaged only 7 percent black. Any impact of SOUTH and PROPORTION BLACK on racial views will thus be confounded. Many readers will give primary attention to the conservative estimate, the net PROPORTION BLACK effect after region is controlled; however, the more liberal estimate without the region control is presented as well, in acknowledgment of the ambiguity created by the confounding of SOUTH and PROPORTION BLACK.

For racial policy–related beliefs, estimates are reported for a third model, which includes a measure of the relative economic position of local blacks and whites (BLACK/WHITE ECONOMIC STATUS), accompanied by an appropriate control (WHITE ECONOMIC STATUS).

Results for analyses of 1990 traditional prejudice and some 1990 measures of racial policy opinion and racial policy–related beliefs have been discussed earlier (Taylor 1998).

A BENCHMARK—TRADITIONAL PREJUDICE

As backdrop for the remaining discussion, the first panel of Table 4.1 reports effects of local black population share on 1990 and 1994 scales representing traditional prejudice, shown in previous research to be sensitive to local racial proportions (Fossett and Kiecolt 1989; Taylor 1998). The 1994 scale of Traditional Prejudice is predictably less reliable because fewer component measures were available, but it joins

TABLE 4.1   Effects of Black Population Share and Region on Traditional Prejudice and Racial Policy Opinion

	1990 GSS		1994 GSS	
	Model 1	Model 2	Model 1	Model 2
Traditional Prejudice				
PROP. BLACK	3.62°°°	2.72°°	1.16°°°	.87°°
SOUTH		.32		.10
Racial Policy Opinion				
Equal Treatment				
Fair Housing				
PROP. BLACK	.56°°	.36	.31ᵗ	.28
SOUTH		.07		.01
Race-Conscious				
Race Targeting				
PROP. BLACK	3.85°°°	2.99°°	1.58°°°	1.29°°
SOUTH		.30		.11
Preferential Treatment				
PROP. BLACK			.38	.19
SOUTH				.07

$^t p < .10.$ $°p < .05.$ $°°p < .01.$ $°°°p < .001.$

the 1990 scale in showing a highly significant ($p < .01$) effect of PROPORTION BLACK, even after region is controlled. To convey a sense of the magnitude of the 1990 effect after all controls are in the model, my 1998 article reported that a ten-point rise in the local percentage of blacks is predicted to bring an increase in traditional prejudice by about the same amount as 1.9 additional years of education would decrease it.

RACIAL POLICY OPINION

The impact of local black population share on racial policy opinion is reported in the second panel of table 4.1. These results bear directly on the claim of Sniderman and his associates that opinion on many racial policies has little to do with racial sentiments.

As an "equal treatment" issue, Fair Housing opinion would be expected to reflect racial sentiments to some degree, and thus to be sensitive to the local black population share. Table 4.1 shows there is a tendency in the predicted direction, but the impact of PROPORTION BLACK on Fair Housing opinion is not strong enough to remain significant after region is controlled.

The story is quite different for Race Targeting, the primary representative of opinion on race-conscious policy. In both years, the im-

pact of PROPORTION BLACK on Race Targeting is highly significant ($p < .01$). As reported in my 1998 article, after controls, a ten-
point rise in the local percentage of blacks is predicted to bring an
increase in opposition to race targeting by about the same amount as
3.3 additional years of education would decrease it.

Table 4.1 also reveals the absence of a significant effect of PRO-
PORTION BLACK on a 1994 measure of Preferential Treatment,
similar to that discussed by Sniderman and Piazza (1993).

In sum, these data are congruent with Sniderman and Piazza's
(1993) contention that opposition to race-conscious programs has
little to do with racial sentiment *only* if race-conscious policy is construed as narrowly as the earlier researchers' operationalization and
confined to racial preferences and quotas. Opposition to other forms
of race-conscious policy—from spending to "improve conditions for
blacks" to offering race-targeted college scholarships—is quite sensitive to the local racial context. This makes it highly implausible that
racial sentiments play no role.

RACIAL POLICY–RELATED BELIEFS

As discussed in my 1998 article, white 1990 GSS respondents' attributions for black-white inequality are responsive to local racial proportions, even when region is controlled. This is reflected in the effects
of PROPORTION BLACK on Victim Blame and System Blame in
table 4.2. Whites in localities with large black population shares are
more likely to blame blacks themselves and less likely to blame structural factors than are whites living in localities with few blacks. Such
attributions are often interpreted as causes of racial policy attitudes.
However, their sensitivity to racial proportions makes them look more
like expressions of racial sentiment.

Parallel attribution measures in 1994 show the same general pattern of sensitivity to racial proportions, but the effect drops and becomes nonsignificant once region is controlled. As noted earlier, region and PROPORTION BLACK are substantially correlated. Given
the inextricable linkage of black population concentration with Southern history, some readers may find the PROPORTION BLACK effect
assessed without the control for region to be the more credible estimate.

Denial of Discrimination, measured only in the 1990 GSS, does not
show an effect of PROPORTION BLACK after region is controlled.
My earlier article (Taylor 1998) offered a hypothesis to explain the null
partial relationship: black numbers may have countervailing effects on

TABLE 4.2 Effects of Black Population Share, Region, and Economic Status Indicators on Racial Policy–Related Beliefs

	1990 GSS			1994 GSS		
	Model 1	Model 2	Model 3	Model 1	Model 2	Model 3
Victim Blame						
PROP. BLACK	.61°°°	.44°	.43¹	.33°	.09	.15
SOUTH		.04	.06		.09°	.08°
W ECON. STATUS			-.02			-.03
B/W ECON. STATUS			-.02			.01
Rejection of System Blame						
PROP. BLACK	.62°°°	.59°°	.60°°	.51°°	.02	.07
SOUTH		.01	.01		.18°°°	.17°°°
W ECON. STATUS			-.02			-.03
B/W ECON. STATUS			-.01			-.01
Denial of Discrimination						
PROP. BLACK	1.03°°	.39	.27			
SOUTH		.24°°	.27°°			
W ECON. STATUS			.04			
B/W ECON. STATUS			-.01			
Advantage						
PROP. BLACK	1.35°°°	1.35°°°	1.50°°°	1.31°°°	.89°	.93°
SOUTH		.00	-.03		.16¹	.16¹
W ECON. STATUS			-.06			-.02
B/W ECON. STATUS			.01			.00

¹$p < .10$.   °$p < .05$.   °°$p < .01$.   °°°$p < .001$.

the cognitive and motivational antecedents of discrimination estimates, prompting a rise in whites' impulse to justify opposition to race
targeting, but also bringing elevated residential segregation and other
signs of racial division that make discrimination hard to deny.

The final set of racial policy–related beliefs, represented in the Advantage scale, is particularly important because of its pertinence to
opinions about affirmative action. Table 4.2 shows Advantage to be
highly sensitive to local racial population proportions in both 1990 and
1994. If whites in localities with substantial black populations more
often feel at a racial disadvantage, readers may reasonably ask if this
might be a realistic perception. Supplemental analysis using the 1990
GSS data showed whites from substantially black localities to be no
more or less likely to report affirmative action at their workplace. Also,
whites from heavily black localities are not disproportionately likely to
say that their financial circumstance relative to other families is bad
or that they have experienced financial decline. These patterns argue
against the realistic perception interpretation.

A more systematic investigation of the realistic perception interpretation was undertaken as well. For all the racial policy–related beliefs examined here, cognitively based responses of white residents to
local racial context should be sensitive to the *character* of the local
black population as well as its size. In fact, cognitively based responses
should be more responsive to character than size. For example, where
black male employment rates and black family incomes are relatively
low, whites who do not recognize the structural impediments faced
by blacks may often conclude that personal failings of blacks explain
the existing racial inequality. The opposite contextual circumstance—
relatively high male employment and family income among local
blacks—might plausibly encourage whites' sense of disadvantage, raising scores on the Advantage scale.

To investigate these possibilities, the focal BLACK/WHITE ECO-
NOMIC STATUS measure was added to the model, along with the
control variable WHITE ECONOMIC STATUS. In table 4.2, the
third column of 1990 and 1994 results reports the estimates for these
economic status measures. The upshot is clear. Economic status
showed no hint of a relationship reaching or approaching significance
with any outcome in either year. The most reasonable interpretation
of these findings is this: the view that blacks have an edge on whites is
not just a cognitive phenomenon, a clear-headed perception of local
realities. Instead, it looks more like a racially motivated sentiment.

TABLE 4.3 Effects of Black Population Share and Region on Ostensibly Nonracial views

	1990 GSS		1994 GSS	
	Model 1	Model 2	Model 1	Model 2
Political Philosophy				
PROP. BLACK	.24	.43	.52°	.54
SOUTH		−.06		−.01
Authoritarianism				
PROP. BLACK	.72°	.28	.09	−.34
SOUTH		.15°		.15°
Normative Individualism				
PROP. BLACK	−.02	−.02		
SOUTH		.00		
Existential Individualism				
PROP. BLACK	1.27°°°	1.19°°		
SOUTH		.03		
Antistructuralism				
PROP. BLACK	.18	.05		
SOUTH		.05		
Welfare				
PROP. BLACK	1.11°°°	.87°	.02	.17
SOUTH		.08		−.05
Poor Aid				
PROP. BLACK	.24	.01	.52¹	.33
SOUTH		.08		.06

¹$p < .10$.   °$p < .05$.   °°$p < .01$.   °°°$p < .001$.

OSTENSIBLY NONRACIAL VIEWS

The dependent measures represented in table 4.3 are virtually always considered alternatives to racial beliefs and attitudes. The purpose of the analyses reported here is to ascertain whether these predictors are indeed nonracial or whether they themselves are sensitive to racial context.

The pattern of results revealed in table 4.3 is easy to summarize. Neither Political Philosophy nor Authoritarianism relates reliably to local PROPORTION BLACK after region is controlled in 1990 or in 1994. As for stratification belief scales, available only in the 1990 data, a highly significant effect of PROPORTION BLACK was shown on only one—the Existential Individualism measure of the belief that individual failings are responsible for poverty. The Poor Aid scale, which indexes opposition to social welfare programs in general, was not sensitive to local racial proportions in either 1990 or 1994. In contrast, opposition to Welfare in particular did increase as the local PROPOR-TION BLACK increased in one survey year—1990.

The absence of PROPORTION BLACK effects on most ostensibly nonracial views may be considered a validity check, reassuring us that the sensitivity of central dimensions of racial policy opinion and racial policy–related beliefs to local PROPORTION BLACK is not the product of some methodological artifact.

The sensitivity of opposition to Welfare in 1990, but not in 1994, is interesting, and perhaps not all that puzzling. The 1990 data were collected only two years after a victorious 1988 Republican presidential campaign infamous for its reliance on the "race card," largely through use of code words for race, such as "crime" (Kinder and Sanders 1996). "Welfare" was another such widely used code word. By 1994, the Democrats were in the White House and talking about welfare in very different terms, arguably dissipating the racial connotation of welfare in the minds of the white American public. In fact, the indication that racial sentiment underlay victim blaming for poverty in 1990 may not have been replicated if parallel 1994 data were available, for the same reason that the PROPORTION BLACK effect on 1990 welfare opinion was not replicated in 1994—the political climate had changed.

CONCLUSIONS

The role of racial sentiment in shaping white Americans' racial policy opinions and racial policy–related beliefs has been a matter of controversy. The strategy of this chapter has been to use sensitivity to local racial proportions as an indication that racial sentiment is implicated in the respective dimensions of whites' views.

Effects of local racial proportions on the traditional prejudice of white respondents to the 1994 GSS replicate patterns reported earlier for the 1990 GSS: traditional prejudice rises as the local black population share swells. The magnitude of this effect rivals those of the more powerful individual-level predictors of prejudice. The pronounced sensitivity of traditional prejudice to the local black population share supports the use of local racial proportion effects to detect the influence of racial sentiment on policy opinions and related beliefs.

Finding that opposition to race-targeted programs rises directly with the local proportion of blacks is centrally important. Based on narrow evidence about opposition to preferential treatment and quotas, Sniderman and Piazza (1993) conclude that white opinion on race targeting has little to do with racial sentiment. As noted in my 1994 article, affirmative action often entails measures such as open advertising and targeted recruiting, stopping far short of quotas or even softer forms of preferential selection. Charlotte Steeh and Maria Krysan (1996) clearly demonstrate that our understanding of public opinion about affirmative action is badly warped by the near exclusive concentration of surveys on preferential treatment. Furthermore, even broadly defined, affirmative action is only one form of race-conscious policy. Results presented above are starkly incongruent with the conclusion that white opinions about race-conscious policies *in general* have little to do with race. Among the race-conscious policies referenced here, only white opposition to preferential labor market treatment is insensitive to the local racial context. For equal outcomes and opportunity enhancement policies, white opposition clearly swells as local black numbers increase, an effect that persists even with a comprehensive battery of controls. Of course, these data do not discredit claims that racial policy opinions are influenced by broader political considerations—only claims that such opinions are unaffected by racial dynamics.

Among policy-related racial beliefs, the 1990 assessment of discrimination does not relate reliably to black population share, perhaps because perceptual and motivational tendencies countervail—black numbers bring antipathy, but also greater segregation and discrimination that cannot easily be denied. In contrast, victim-blaming and system-blaming attributions for racial inequality are markedly sensitive to local black numbers in the 1990 data, though less so in 1994. Beliefs that blacks have advantages over whites in the labor market, education, and politics show pronounced sensitivity to local racial proportions in both the 1990 and the 1994 data.

Cognitively driven, "rational" views about the extent of discrimination, the causes of inequality, and the extent of black advantage over whites should reasonably respond to the local *economic* realities. White respondents might be more likely to see black inability and irresponsibility as causes of inequality in localities where large numbers of black men are not working and where many black families are poor. Conversely, such localities should be less likely to foster the sense that blacks have an edge over whites. The absence of any such economic context effects bolsters our conclusion that many of these racial policy–related "beliefs" have more to do with sentiment than cold, clear perception.

Among the ostensibly nonracial views examined here, political stance, authoritarianism, normative individualism, antistructuralism, and support for most programs serving the poor showed no marked or consistent relationship to local black numbers. On the other hand, in 1990, opposition to "welfare" and attribution of poverty to failings of the poor were more common in localities where the black population share was large. This pattern may very well reflect the Republican use of code words to attract votes of racially prejudiced whites in the 1988 campaign.

Altogether, examining the sensitivity of white public opinion to the local racial context seems a promising means of detecting the role of racial sentiment in shaping public opinion, a useful supplement to information provided by intercorrelations among social-psychological measures. Contrary to the claims of Sniderman and his associates, these data suggest that racial sentiment underlies whites' opposition to most race-targeting programs as well as many racial policy–related beliefs and opinions on ostensibly nonracial issues that have been used in political campaigns to evoke prejudiced responses.

An important next step is to learn more about the local social processes that mediate the contextual effects reported here. Fuller understanding will require attention to the voices of local media, politicians, and other opinion leaders.

FIVE Race and Beliefs
about Affirmative
Action
*Assessing the Effects of
Interests, Group Threat,
Ideology, and Racism*

LAWRENCE BOBO

INTRODUCTION

Race remains among the central fault lines of American political
life, with race-conscious social policy increasingly under attack.
Indeed, the legal and political assault on affirmative action gathered
force throughout the 1990s. The decade opened with the elevation of
Clarence Thomas, arguably a beneficiary of affirmative action, but also
a committed opponent, to a place as the 106th justice of the U.S. Supreme Court. Federal court rulings ended affirmative action programs
in higher education in the case of the University of Texas Law School
and in the public schools in the case of the prestigious Boston Latin
School. Voters in the states of California and Washington passed, by
solid margins in both instances, ballot initiatives calling for an end to
affirmative action programs.

Although these events suggest that the times may have decisively
turned against affirmative action, it is particularly disappointing to realize that a full and constructive political dialogue about affirmative
action has not yet taken place (Skrentny 1996; Sturm and Guinier
1996; Guinier 1998). Instead, the debate over affirmative action often
seems to involve two warring camps, each of which stakes a mutually
exclusive claim to moral virtue (Edley 1996). Defenders of affirmative
action cast themselves as the champions of racial justice and the keep-
ers of Dr. King's dream. Opponents of affirmative action cast themselves as the champions of the true "color-blind" intent of cherished

American values. In the eyes of affirmative action defenders, the latter are, at best, apologists for racism. Opponents see their antagonists as advancing a morally bankrupt claim to victim status and the spoils of racial privilege for African Americans and other racial minorities. Advocates within both camps increasingly turn to research on public opinion to validate their assertions. Yet the morally judgmental character of both advocacy and the extant body of research on public opinion is problematical. Both misread the meaning of race in the American experience and the role of group interests intrinsically raised by affirmative action politics.

Two sharply opposed views of public opinion on affirmative action dominate research. In one account, the controversy and often the intense opposition to affirmative action among white Americans is centrally rooted in antiblack racism (Kinder and Sanders 1996; Sears et al. 1997). In the opposing account, whites' deep discomfort with affirmative action is said to reflect high-minded value commitments and little if any antiblack animus (Lipset and Schneider 1978b; Sniderman and Piazza 1993). In either view, ironically, affirmative action policies are seen as unlikely to fare well at the bar of white public opinion.

Although there is a debate here of serious scholarly moment, I wish to bring into critical focus three features or presumptions shared by both the racism school of thought and the values and ideology (read: principled objections) school of thought about public opinion. First, both approaches contribute to the distorted view that opposition to affirmative action among whites is monolithic. It is not (Steeh and Krysan 1996).[1] Affirmative action policies span a range of policy goals and strategies (Chermerinsky 1997), some formulations of which (e.g., race-targeted scholarships or special job outreach and training efforts) can be quite popular (Bobo and Kluegel 1993; Bobo and Smith 1994).

Second, the racism and the principled objections arguments focus on one element of public opinion: policy preferences themselves. Perceptions and beliefs about the possible benefits and costs of affirmative action are almost never explored. From the vantage point of making a constructive contribution to the policy process, this is disappointing. It is much easier to envision changing such beliefs than ending racism or fundamentally reshaping values and ideological identities. While what one believes about the effects of affirmative action does not singularly determine policy views in this arena, such beliefs surely are an important element in the larger politics of affirmative action.

Third, scholarship advancing both types of accounts shares an emphasis that has thoroughly marginalized the opinions of African

Americans and other racial minorities.[2] This has had unfortunate consequences for theory development and for the capacity of public opinion analysts to make useful contributions to the larger public discourse. Ignoring the voices of people of color results chiefly in a severe underestimation of the role of group interests in the politics of affirmative action and facilitates the stalemate of opposing claims of moral virtue on the left (i.e., the valorous nonracists) and the right (i.e., the valorous color-blind). Ironically, a focus on interests might better facilitate constructive dialogue and compromise. Interests should be understood in both the short-term and the long-term senses. Whereas the short-term interests of racial groups in affirmative action may seem zero-sum in character, the long-term interests most assuredly are not. What is more, our legal and political system routinely grapples with how to reconcile conflicting interests and arrive at sustainable compromises. Such compromises are, after all, the art of politics. Our institutions have a much harder time adjudicating opposing claims of rights and of moral virtue as compared to those based on interests. Left at this level of discourse, a sort of self-righteous tyranny of the majority is ultimately likely to prevail.

Thus, in this chapter, I examine beliefs about the costs and benefits of affirmative action. I pursue a multiracial analysis, assessing the views of black, white, Latino, and Asian respondents to a set of questions contained in the 1992 Los Angeles County Social Survey (LACSS). I expressly examine the effects of perceived group competition and threat on beliefs about the effects of affirmative action. All of this is done while taking seriously the ideas advanced in the racism and principled objection schools of thought about public opinion on affirmative action.

BACKGROUND

General assessments of public opinion on affirmative action point to three noteworthy patterns. First, there has been considerable stability in basic policy views. Contrary to the tenor of media framing, which both claims and in its own portrayal embodies a more sharply negative trend in recent years (Entman 1997), the general trend has been for stability in public opinion (Steeh and Krysan 1996). Second, the exact wording of questions heavily influences the observed level of support for affirmative action. This pattern is unlikely to involve a simple methodological artifact. It appears to reflect substantively important differences in the character of the policy goals and strategies used.

Elsewhere I have discussed this as a difference between opportunity-enhancing forms of affirmative action and outcome-directed forms of affirmative action (Bobo and Kluegel 1993; Bobo and Smith 1994; see also Lipset and Schneider 1978b). Programs with the goal of improving the human capital attributes of minorities tend to be far more popular than those aimed at equalizing outcomes. And programs that call for the application of quotas and clear-cut racial preferences are highly unpopular, even among blacks (Schuman et al. 1997). Third, opinions on affirmative action usually differ by race, with blacks a good deal more supportive than whites (Kluegel and Smith 1986; Kinder and Sanders 1996). Indeed, depending on the exact question and policy, the situation is often one of majority black support for a specified form of affirmative action and majority white opposition, though neither group is univocal in outlook (Jaynes and Williams 1989).

There are few scholars who would dissent from this summary. The debate is joined, however, over the question of the social wellsprings of white opposition to affirmative action. Here the research literature divides between those arguing for the importance of racism and those arguing for the importance of cherished values and ideological commitments.

THE RACISM HYPOTHESIS

The large body of work on symbolic racism (Sears 1988; Sears et al. 1997) and isomorphic arguments about abstract racial resentments (Kinder and Sanders 1996) posits that a new form of antiblack racism has risen. This racism is more subtle than the coarse racism of the Jim Crow era, which bluntly advocated racial segregation, discrimination, and the inherent inferiority of blacks to whites. It involves a blend of early learned antiblack feelings and beliefs with traditional American values of hard work and self-reliance. It is expressed in resentment and hostility toward blacks' demands for special treatment and toward government recognition of blacks' demands and in unreasoned denial of the modern potency of racial discrimination or bias. It has no meaningful dependence on material contingencies in the private lives of individual whites: it is a learned attitude rather than a reflection of socially rooted instrumentalities.

This new attitude is elicited when political leaders or discourse invokes issues or labels that call to mind blacks. Whites respond in terms of this underlying psychological animus against African Americans. One effect of this symbolic racism is the rejection of policies such as affirmative action. Research has shown that measures of such attitudes are the central factor—more important than ideology, values, personal risk of loss, and perceived group threat—in determining whether whites support or oppose affirmative action–type policies (Kinder and Sanders 1996; Sears et al. 1997).

It is quite important in this research that specific types of attitudes and their effects on policy views be understood as "racism." These outlooks are held to rest heavily on fundamentally irrational antiblack feelings and fears rather than objective, realistic conflicts of interest (Sears 1988). The symbolic racism researchers are quite explicit in the judgment that such attitudes and their political effects are morally wrong and deserving of approbation, no matter the exact terminology. As David Sears argued, "There is no doubt that *racism* is pejorative, but so is *prejudice;* none of us like to think we are either racist or prejudiced" (1988, 79, emphasis in original). This point is pressed further by Donald Kinder and Lynn Sanders, who claim that most other prominent analysts of white racial attitudes have "white-washed racial prejudice" (1996, 269–72).

By implication then, the symbolic racism approach would expect to find that beliefs about the effects of affirmative action are heavily tainted by racism. Viewed from this vantage point, such beliefs constitute little more than a polite vocabulary for ventilating the underlying racial resentments. As a result, the theory suggests, we are likely to find a strong, if not central, association between symbolic racism and beliefs about the effects of affirmative action for blacks.

THE PRINCIPLED OBJECTIONS HYPOTHESIS

The symbolic racism research has been criticized on a remarkably wide variety of grounds. The most widely discussed and accepted alternative theoretical account of views of affirmative action posits that important values and ideological outlooks, thoroughly devoid of antiblack animus, prompt many whites to reject affirmative action. As Paul Sniderman and Thomas Piazza argued: "At the deepest level though, racial politics owes its shape not to beliefs or stereotypes distinctly about blacks but to the broader set of convictions about fairness and fair play that make up the American Creed" (1993, 176).

This hypothesis about principled bases of objections to affirmative action has a special twist. To wit, not only is racism a small part of the modern politics of race, but also it is only among the politically unsophisticated that racism carries force. Among politically sophisticated individuals who understand what it means to hold a conservative identity and values, it is these high-minded and race-neutral considerations that motivate opposition to affirmative action (Sniderman and Piazza 1993).

Accordingly, the influence of racism has been vastly exaggerated by the symbolic racism researchers (indeed in a manner and to a degree that has led to a harmful politicization of social science scholarship; see Sniderman and Tetlock 1986; Tetlock 1994). Furthermore, Sniderman and Piazza suggest that as the larger civil rights movement shifted its focus from fundamental civic equality and a rhetoric of color-blindness to a focus on equal social rewards and a rhetoric of race-based entitlements, it lost the moral high ground. Blacks and their allies placed themselves in fact at odds with the values embodied in the American Creed (Sniderman and Piazza 1993).

The broadest implication of this approach is that beliefs about the impact of affirmative action for blacks should be most negative among those who identify themselves as politically conservative and among those who most strongly adhere to the values of the work ethic. Apprehension about the consequences of race-based social policy should flow naturally from their conservative inclinations and underlying value commitments. If the full perspective is correct, we should find that the association between political ideology and values and beliefs about affirmative action is strongest among highly educated whites. Viewed from this perspective, believing that affirmative action has unwanted consequences is a legitimate, uncontrived, and indeed logical expectation, given some individuals' ideological and value orientations.

THE GROUP POSITION AND PERCEIVED THREAT HYPOTHESIS

This approach springs from sociologist Herbert Blumer's (1958) theory of race prejudice as a sense of group position. He argued that critical elements of prejudice were feelings of entitlement to social resources, status, and privileges and perceived threats to those entitlements posed by members of other groups. In this view, any social system with long-standing racial identities and institutionalized racial inequality in life chances sets the stage for "realistic" or meaningful struggle over group interests defined along racial lines (Bobo 1997c).

The core argument here is that racial politics unavoidably involves a nettlesome fusion of racial identities and attitudes with racial group interests. It suggests that many whites will oppose affirmative action not so much because they see a race-based policy as contravening their loftiest values or because they have learned a new, politically relevant set of resentments of blacks, but rather because they perceive blacks as competitive threats for valued social resources, status, and privileges.

In short, the group position approach contends that there are real interests at stake in the debate over affirmative action. A policy aimed at the reduction of educational and employment disadvantages faced by racial minorities (and by women), to the extent it is effective, of necessity means a diminution of the privilege previously enjoyed by white males. From the vantage point of those in the fields of law and disciplines other than political psychology (e.g., economics and sociology), the inherent clash of interests raised by affirmative action policies seems obvious. As economist Lester Thurow put it: "Yet any government program to aid economic minorities must hurt economic majorities. This is the most direct of all of our zero-sum conflicts. If women and minorities have more of the best jobs, white males must have fewer. Here the gains and losses are precisely one for one" (Thurow 1994, 240). Or as sociologist Stephen Steinberg explained: "[O]ne thing is clear: without government, both as employer and as enforcer of affirmative-action mandates, we would not today be celebrating the achievements of the black middle class. Indeed, it is precisely because the stakes are so high that affirmative action is so fiercely contested" (Steinberg 1995, 167–68).

It is essential to counter some misperceptions about an interest-based argument. One can recognize a basis in interests for the politics of affirmative action without accepting the disingenuous claim that discrimination against minorities and women is replaced by equally illegitimate discrimination against white males, without endorsing the ahistorical view that affirmative action policies were motivated solely by a desire to serve the interests of a particularistic group, and without accepting the claim that coalition formation and consensus building become impossible. Affirmative action is mainly pursued in order to stop discriminatory practices that unduly privilege white males. It is aimed at eliminating the routine "mobilization of bias" that would otherwise reproduce unfair white male advantage (Carnoy 1994). Doing so does, therefore, come at some cost to many white males, but it does not render them the victims of discrimination in reverse. Contrary to the now conventional media labeling, affirmative action, at its core, is not about "special preferences." As the eminent stratification sociologist Barbara Reskin recently explained:

> Affirmative action does not replace one form of favoritism with another, it replaces cronyism with objective personnel practices. Its suc-

cesses have not been achieved through discrimination against white men. Federally mandated affirmative action programs neither require nor allow employers to give preference to workers because of their sex or race. Giving preference to an unqualified candidate because of her or his race or sex constitutes illegal discrimination, regardless of whether the beneficiary is male or female, white or minority. In the early 1970s, some employers reserved a specific number of jobs for women and minorities, but this practice virtually disappeared after the courts ruled that it violated the 1964 anti-discrimination law. While the affirmative action efforts of some contemporary employers are undoubtedly unfair to individual whites or men, reverse discrimination is rare. (1998, 90)

On two counts, the claims that a discourse of interests vitiates support for affirmative action and that the policy springs from a narrowly particularistic logic are incorrect. First, it is precisely in order to obtain fair access to education and employment opportunities that affirmative action programs are pursued. Thus, contrary to the position taken by Sniderman and his colleagues, the rationale for the policy has always made an appeal to broad American ideals of opportunity, justice, and fair play. This was true when John F. Kennedy campaigned for the presidency and made civil rights an important component of his agenda. It was clearer still when early in his administration he issued Executive Order 10925, which first used the phrase "affirmative action." According to historian Carl Brauer, Kennedy's executive order established:

> [t]he President's Committee on Equal Employment Opportunity (PCEEO) by combining two existing but largely ineffectual committees. He directed the new panel to "ensure that Americans of all colors and beliefs will have equal access to employment within the government." In addition, he ordered the committee to conduct a racial survey of the government's employment practices in order to provide a "yardstick by which to ensure future progress." (1977, 79)

Of course, the turning point in launching affirmative action policy and in articulating the principled basis for affirmative action came with Lyndon Johnson's Executive Order 11246 in 1965 and his associated speech at Howard University. The speech makes explicit the goal of appealing beyond merely racial considerations in order to achieve fairness. As Johnson remarked in the oft-quoted speech:

"But freedom is not enough. You do not take a person who, for years, has been hobbled by chains and liberate him, bring him up to the starting line of a race and then say, 'you are free to compete with all the others,' *and still justly believe that you have been completely fair.* Thus it is not enough just to open the gates of opportunity. All our citizens must have the ability to walk through those gates. This is the next and more profound stage of the battle for civil rights. We seek not just freedom but opportunity—not just legal equity but human ability—not just equality as a right and a theory but equality as a fact and as a result." (Quoted in Steinberg 1995, 113–14, emphasis added)

Given the historic and long-standing effort to justify affirmative action on the grounds of American values of fairness, justice, and opportunity, it is ironic that some public opinion analysts proceed as if the only basis for the policy has been an abstract desire for race targeting (see Sniderman and Carmines 1997a).

Second, taking a long-term view makes it clear that the societal benefits are substantial. According to a recent comprehensive study of the impact of affirmative action for minorities at elite colleges and universities, there are several broad benefits that flow from taking race into account in admission practices. William Bowen and Derek Bok (1998) found that affirmative action in higher education contributed substantially to the expansion and solidification of a black middle class, served to more fully integrate blacks into American society, and exposed both blacks and whites to positive integrated environments. Furthermore, they found that the black graduates of these elite institutions were somewhat more likely than their white peers to obtain professional degrees in the fields of law, business, and medicine. The black graduates were substantially more likely to be highly civic-minded and socially involved individuals as well.

The group position framework also maintains, then, that much of the white opposition to affirmative action springs from a desire to maintain a privileged position in the American racial hierarchy. The theory holds that this desire is manifest politically in perceptions of group threat and competition from minority groups members. Hence, the greater the sense of competitive threat felt from blacks in general is, the more negative the beliefs about the likely effects of affirmative action should be. Although it would be appropriate to interpret such an explicitly racialized motive for opposition to policies aimed at racial equality as an aspect of racism, doing so is not essential to the group position and perceived threat argument.[3] Indeed, since racial identities and racial group interests are seen as historically emergent and contingent, the crucial implication is that it is the understandings of group interests and what affects those understandings that is analytically and politically most important. With respect to the rhetoric of racial politics then, the group position and perceived threat argument stands in sharp contradistinction to both the symbolic racism and the principled objections arguments. Judgments of the moral worth of the bases of views of affirmative action can certainly be made, but at some level, interests and perceived threats are simply that: interests and perceived threats.

DATA AND MEASURES

The data come from the 1992 Los Angeles County Social Survey, a countywide, random-digit-dialed, computer-assisted telephone survey of adults living in households. The survey oversampled telephone numbers in zip code areas with high concentrations of blacks (65 percent or more) or Asians (30 percent or more) to generate larger numbers of black and Asian respondents. To capture Los Angeles's large Latino population, a Spanish version of the questionnaire was developed. A total of 1,869 respondents were interviewed: 625 whites, 483 blacks, 477 Latinos, and 284 Asians. Owing to a split-ballot design, this analysis is based on a randomly selected third of respondents who were administered the questions on affirmative action for blacks.[4]

Symbolic racism was measured with a scale based on three Likert-response-format items: "Most blacks who receive money from welfare programs could get along without it if they tried"; "Government officials usually pay less attention to a request or complaint from a black person than from a white person"; "Irish, Italian, Jewish and many other minorities overcame prejudice and worked their way up. Blacks should do the same without any special favors." Scale scores range from 0 to 1, with higher scores reflecting higher levels of symbolic racism.

The principled objections hypothesis was tapped with three different measures concerning political ideology, inegalitarian outlooks, and commitment to the work ethic or individualism. *Political ideology* was measured by self-identification on a one- to seven-point scale ranging from extremely liberal to extremely conservative. *Inegalitarianism* was measured by using responses to two Likert-type items: "Some people are just better cut out than others for important positions in society";

"Some people are better at running things and should be allowed to do so." *Individualism* was measured using responses to two Likert-type items: "If people work hard they almost always get what they want"; "Most people who don't get ahead should not blame the system: they really have only themselves to blame." Both sets of measures are drawn from the measures of core American values developed for the National Election Study (NES) surveys by Stanley Feldman (1988).

Perceived threat was measured with responses to four Likert-type items: "More good jobs for blacks means fewer good jobs for members of other groups"; "The more influence blacks have in local politics the less influence members of other groups will have in local politics"; "As more good housing and neighborhoods go to blacks, the fewer good houses and neighborhoods there will be for members of other groups"; "Many blacks have been trying to get ahead economically at the expense of other groups." These items and their properties are discussed in fuller detail elsewhere (Bobo and Hutchings 1996). It is worth noting here that these items constitute a conservative approach to tapping perceived threat. The items always expressly invoke at least two groups, speak to relatively concrete resources, specify a zero-sum relationship, and use neutral language. All of these steps are taken in order to avoid the type of conceptual ambiguity and confusion that still surrounds the notion of symbolic racism.

We also introduce controls for two other aspects of racial attitudes that tap important dimensions of antiblack attitudes. Intergroup *affect* is measured with a feeling thermometer score ranging from 0 to 100, with high scores indicating more positive affect. Racial *stereotypes* are measured with an index composed of three items that used seven-point bipolar trait ratings. Respondents rated blacks on the trait dimensions of intelligent/unintelligent, prefer to be self-supporting/prefer to live off of welfare, and easy to get along with/hard to get along with.

ANALYSIS AND RESULTS

RACE AND BELIEFS ABOUT AFFIRMATIVE ACTION

Are beliefs about the effects of affirmative action sharply divided by race, with racial minorities perceiving overwhelmingly positive outcomes and whites perceiving overwhelmingly negative outcomes? Responses to the four questions on the impact of affirmative action, shown in table 5.1, present a somewhat more complicated pattern. To

TABLE 5.1   Race/Ethnicity and Beliefs about the Impact of Affirmative Action for Blacks

	STRONGLY AGREE	AGREE	NEITHER	DISAGREE	STRONGLY DISAGREE	TOTAL	N
Affirmative action for blacks is unfair to whites.							
White	11%	34%	24%	23%	8%	100%	216
Black	5%	13%	17%	45%	20%	100%	173
Latino	5%	25%	32%	35%	2%	99%	160
Asian	4%	30%	35%	25%	6%	100%	88
Affirmative action in education gives an opportunity to qualified blacks who might not have had a chance without it.							
White	9%	50%	22%	16%	3%	100%	217
Black	29%	55%	5%	10%	1%	100%	172
Latino	8%	58%	22%	11%	2%	101%	161
Asian	8%	46%	29%	16%	1%	100%	87
Affirmative action for blacks may force employers to hire unqualified people.							
White	13%	47%	13%	21%	6%	100%	217
Black	5%	22%	10%	44%	19%	100%	173
Latino	3%	36%	20%	38%	3%	100%	161
Asian	7%	32%	20%	37%	5%	101%	87
Affirmative action in the workplace for blacks helps make sure that the American workforce and economy remain competitive.							
White	2%	27%	24%	39%	8%	100%	216
Black	17%	43%	17%	18%	4%	99%	173
Latino	2%	53%	24%	18%	4%	101%	160
Asian	5%	32%	28%	31%	5%	101%	87

be sure, there is a large and significant racial group difference in response to each item, with blacks (especially) and Latinos usually more likely to adopt favorable views of affirmative action than are whites. However, Asians' views are typically closer to those of whites than to those of blacks or Latinos. And in no instance does even the black-white difference reflect diametrically opposite views. Indeed, to a degree that should discomfit both the racism school and the principled objection school, white opinion is neither monolithic nor uniformly negative. Nearly one-third of whites (29 percent) perceived affirmative action for blacks as helpful to American economic competitiveness, one-third rejected the idea that affirmative action is unfair to whites, and nearly 60 percent agreed that affirmative action provides educational opportunities for qualified blacks who might not otherwise get a chance. The point where affirmative action encounters the most negative perceptions among whites is acceptance of the idea that it leads to hiring unqualified blacks (60 percent gave agreeing responses).

This picture of quite real, but muted racial differences in perceptions of the effects of affirmative action is more readily appreciated by examining results for a simple summary scale based on the four items (α reliability = .66), as shown in figure 5.1. Scores of 0 on the scale indicate maximally favorable perceptions of affirmative action, and scores of 5 indicate maximally negative views of affirmative action. First, there are highly reliable race differences in the likelihood of perceiving affirmative action as having negative effects [$F(3, 625) = 18.09$, $p < .00001$]. Second, even among whites, the mean score on the Perceived Negative Effects of Affirmative Action scale rises just above the midpoint of 3.0. Third, the figure highlights what some would interpret as an American racial hierarchy in views of affirmative action. At the bottom of the racial hierarchy, and thus least likely to hold negative perceptions of affirmative action, are African Americans, followed by Latinos and then Asians; whites, at the top of the hierarchy, are most inclined to hold negative perceptions.

To this point, the results provide at least some initial suggestive evidence for a more interest-group-based understanding of views of affirmative action. Views are differentiated by race in predictable ways. Blacks, the group whose historical experiences in the United States have most consistently embodied a lower-castelike status, are the least willing to embrace negative views of affirmative action.

It is entirely possible, however, that what appear to be race-based differences in opinion are really differences in socioeconomic background or other demographic composition characteristics (e.g., native-born status) that we should be cautious to interpret as reflecting racial group interests. In order to address this issue, table 5.2 estimates a series of regression equations where perceived negative effects of affirmative action are the dependent measure. Model 1, which includes only a set of dummy variables identifying black, Latino, and Asian respondents (with white respondents as the omitted or contrast group) reiterates the results of figure 5.1. There are significant differences between blacks and whites and between Latinos and whites. However, there is no statistically discernible difference in the likelihood that Asians and whites view affirmative action as having negative effects. Overall, a simple control for race explains about 12 percent of the variation in beliefs about the effects of affirmative action.

Does the impact of race on views of affirmative action diminish

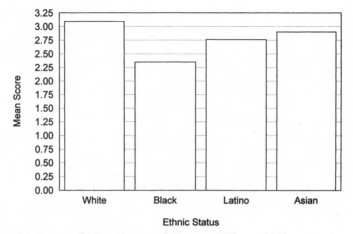

Figure 5.1. Race and Mean Perceived Negative Effects of Affirmative Action (1992 LACSS)

upon introducing controls for social class characteristics, such as education and income, and other demographic factors, such as age, sex, and native-born status? No. Indeed, if anything, the black-white and the Latino-white differences grow larger after introducing social class and demographic characteristic controls (compare model 2 to model 1). The black-white gap widens by about 10 percent, and the Latino-white gap widens by about 8 percent.

Those arguing from the principled opposition point of view might reasonably conjecture, however, that much of what appears as a "race" difference is rather a difference in ideology and values that, primarily for historical and political reasons, overlaps with race. If this is true, we should find that controlling for ideological conservatism, inegalitarian values, and individualism should considerably diminish racial group differences. As model 3 shows, controlling for ideology and values slightly reduces the black-white difference (9 percent) and the Latino-white difference (2 percent), but still leaves highly reliable racial group differences in each case. It should be noted that in this race-pooled model there are no significant effects of inegalitarianism or individualism on perceived negative effects of affirmative action. Only ideological identification itself appears to matter.

For the sake of completeness, we take the further step of introducing a battery of explicit racial attitude measures (model 4). Even this, however, fails to eliminate significant race effects. Most dramatically, once we remove the impact of several types of arguably "antiblack"

TABLE 5.2 OLS Regression Models of Perceived Negative Effects of Affirmative Action for Blacks ($N = 497$)

	MODEL 1	MODEL 2	MODEL 3	MODEL 4
Race/ethnicity				
White (omitted)				
Black	−0.127°°°	−0.134°°°	−0.123°°°	−0.092°°°
	0.015	0.016	0.015	0.015
Latino	−0.048°°	−0.052°°	−0.051°°	−0.056°°
	0.016	0.019	0.018	0.017
Asian	−0.024	−0.008	−0.001	−0.015
	0.020	0.022	0.022	0.020
Social background				
Education		−0.006	−0.006	−0.000
		0.004	0.004	0.004
Age		0.000	−0.000	−0.000
		0.000	0.000	0.000
Male		0.019	0.016	0.013
		0.012	0.012	0.011
U.S. native		0.029†	0.030†	0.042°°
		0.017	0.016	0.015
Family income ($10,000s)		−0.007°	−0.007°	−0.003
		0.003	0.003	0.003
Ideology and values				
Conservatism			0.020°°°	0.015°°°
			0.004	0.003
Inegalitarianism			0.040	0.004
			0.033	0.031
Individualism			0.047	−0.028
			0.032	0.031
Racial attitudes				
Affect				0.000
				0.000
Stereotypes				−0.006
				0.035
Perceived threat				0.235°°°
				0.041
Symbolic racism				0.252°°°
				0.041
Constant	0.602°°°	0.677°°°	0.541°°°	0.255°°°
	0.011	0.060	0.065	0.071
Adjusted R^2	0.121	0.132	0.190	0.316

Note: Figures listed are unstandardized regression coefficients and standard errors.
†$p < 0.10$.   °$p < 0.05$.   °°$p < 0.01$.   °°°$p < 0.001$.

attitudes, the Latino-white difference actually grows larger. To be sure, the black-white difference narrows nontrivially (about 25 percent), but it remains sizeable.

To borrow Cornell West's (1993) pithy observation: race matters! Beliefs about the consequences of affirmative action are importantly shaped by racial group membership and therefore, we would infer, by the differential short-term stake or interest that racial groups have in affirmative action policies (see Jackman 1994 for a similar argument).

WHITES' BELIEFS ABOUT THE NEGATIVE EFFECTS OF AFFIRMATIVE ACTION

It could be argued that by pooling the responses of blacks, whites, Latinos, and Asians we are masking potentially important distinctive patterns in the views of white respondents. In particular, both the principled objection school and the racism school arguments were formulated initially as accounts of the attitudes of white Americans. To this end, table 5.3 reports regression models of the determinants of the perceived negative effects of affirmative action measure among white respondents only. This part of the analysis also considers the claim of the principled objections theorists that the views of the highly educated exhibit less dependence on racial attitudes and a greater influence of ideological and value-based reasoning. We do so by specifying interactions among level of education and each of the values and ideology measures and the two theoretically central racial attitude measures: perceived threat and symbolic racism. For this part of the analysis, level of education is treated as a dummy variable distinguishing college graduates from those without college degrees. Among whites, virtually no LACSS respondent had fewer than eleven years of schooling, and a very high fraction (fully 40 percent) had completed college. Thus, this is an admittedly truncated examination of the education interaction hypothesis, but a truncation that reflects the real distribution of education levels among white adults in Los Angeles County.

Consistent with the results from the pooled race models (table 5.2), the only element of the values and ideology argument to exhibit a significant relation (at conventional levels of statistical discernability, $p <$ .05) to perceived negative effects of affirmative action is conservative self-identification. If a more generous criterion for statistical discernability is applied ($p < .10$), which may be justifiable in this instance, given the overall small number of cases and the arbitrariness of the conventional standard, then both *inegalitarianism* and *individualism*

TABLE 5.3 OLS Regression Models of Perceived Negative Effects of Affirmative Action for Blacks (White Respondents Only, $N = 163$)

	MODEL 1	MODEL 2
Constant	.178 (.080)°	.127 (.091)
Social background		
College degree	−.002 (.021)	.128 (.123)
Age	.001 (.001)	.001 (.001)
Male	.028 (.021)	.030 (.021)
Family income ($10,000s)	.008 (.005)	.008 (.005)
Ideology and values		
Conservatism	.020 (.006)°°	.022 (.009)°
Inegalitarianism	.119 (.012)†	.116 (.028)†
Individualism	−.122 (.062)†	−.151 (.080)†
Racial attitudes		
Affect	−.000 (.001)	−.000 (.001)
Stereotypes	−.109 (.080)	−.115 (.082)
Perceived threat	.218 (.089)°	.184 (.111)
Symbolic racism	.380 (.081)°°°	.498 (.107)°°°
Interactions		
College ° conservatism	—	−.003 (.013)
College ° inegalitarianism	—	.013 (.121)
College ° individualism	—	.052 (.127)
College ° perceived threat	—	−.007 (.179)
College ° symbolic racism	—	−.264 (.156)†
Adjusted R^2	.332	.327

Note: Cell entries are unstandardized regression coefficients. Figures in parentheses are standard errors.

†$p < 0.10.$ °$p < .05.$ °°$p < .01.$ °°°$p < .001.$

influence beliefs about affirmative action. The effect of *individualism,* however, is in the opposite direction of that expected under the principled objections hypothesis: the more whites are committed to notions of reward for hard work, the less likely they are to hold negative beliefs about the effects of affirmative action for blacks.

The effects for perceived threat and symbolic racism are more straightforward. Both significantly enhance whites' perception of negative impacts of affirmative action, particularly for symbolic racism. And these two variables contribute the lion's share to the overall 33.2 percent of the variance explained in perceptions of the negative effects of affirmative action under model 1.

Model 2 allows for possible interactions between level of education and the values and ideology measures as well as the perceived threat and symbolic racism measures. None of the interaction terms meets conventional criteria of significance. Given the small Ns, however, it is worth noting that the effect of symbolic racism does appear to be smaller among the college educated ($p < .10$). However, there is no evidence of a heightened effect of ideology for either value measure among the better educated. There is no sign that the effect of perceived threat is contingent on level of education. The model including the interaction terms, furthermore, does not yield a meaningful improvement in variance explained over the model specifying no interactions. On the whole then, the education-interaction hypothesis is not borne out. The relatively limited capacity of education to reduce the level or impact of some forms of intergroup negativism has, of course, been anticipated by Mary Jackman's ideological refinement thesis (Jackman and Muha 1984).

RELATION TO POLICY PREFERENCES

This analysis is primarily concerned with beliefs about the consequences of affirmative action. Such beliefs have been unstudied and may help identify a way for more constructive dialogue between public opinion analysts and those trying to fashion a progressive coalition for affirmative action (Sturm and Guinier 1996; Bowen and Bok 1998; Guinier 1998). Still, the question arises of how these beliefs relate to policy preferences on affirmative action. While it is beyond the scope of this analysis to develop a model of the determinants of affirmative action policy views, preliminary results suggest a very close association between beliefs about the effects of affirmative action and actual policy preferences. Among white respondents, the perceived negative effects scale has a Pearson's correlation of .68 ($p < .001$) with a three-item scale of affirmative action policy views.[5] Among the social psychological variables examined to this point, this is the single strongest bivariate correlation with affirmative action policy views. In addition, the perceived negative effects of affirmative action have a strong net impact, even if added to a regression equation predicting opposition to affirmative action policy, only after controlling for education, age, sex, family income, conservatism, inegalitarianism, work ethic, symbolic racism, and perceived threat (partial $b = 3.17$, $p < .001$, where the dependent opposition to affirmative action variable runs from a low score of 0 to a high score of 5.0). Hence, there is a sound empirical basis to expect beliefs about the effects of affirmative action to play a part in the actual policy views individuals are likely to hold.

SEVERAL INTERPRETATIVE ISSUES

THE PROBLEM OF RATIONALIZATION

From one vantage point, the seeming importance of the perceived costs and benefits of affirmative action is misleading at best. Beliefs about the impact of a policy, while putatively quite pragmatic and defensible on their face, may simply mask less honorable motives for opposing the policy. In this case, opposition to affirmative action, while actually rooted in some form of animus toward blacks, may be cloaked in the language of sensible concern with unwanted effects of the policy. Certainly, the impact of symbolic racism can be interpreted in this fashion. But three patterns argue against a strong version of this interpretation. First, there is a degree of internal complexity to the perceived costs and benefits of affirmative action, as there is to the policy views themselves. Why should fully 59 percent of the white respondents concede that "affirmative action in education gives an opportunity to qualified blacks who might not have had a chance without it" if all they are interested in doing is masking opposition to affirmative action? It would be cognitively simpler to deny any positive or beneficial effects.

Second, racial background itself, ideological conservatism, perceived threat, and symbolic racism are significantly related to the beliefs about the impact of affirmative action for blacks. What one believes about affirmative action's effects is thus not neatly reducible to an underlying antiblack animus. In the light of these multiple sources and the intractable ambiguity of what measures of "symbolic racism" actually mean, it is inappropriate to treat such beliefs as mere rationalization.

Third, even when pitted against other concepts, the perceived negative effects measure has highly significant effects on affirmative action policy views. Most important, even if the perceived costs and benefits variable is the last measure introduced into the equation, it continues to have significant direct effects on opposition to affirmative action. That is, even if we stack the deck against it by including first the other putatively more important measures (i.e., symbolic racism), we still find effects for perceived negative effects of affirmative action. If these views were merely a stalking horse for symbolic racism or for perceived group threat, or for both, then in the presence of these other factors it should add nothing more to our capacity to account for the level of opposition to affirmative action. Instead, it has considerable net effects.

To be sure, the potential problem of rationalization is not fully resolved by these considerations. Further research will be necessary to accomplish such a goal. For example, it would be useful to conduct survey-based experiments that include either accurate information or persuasion efforts directed at influencing the perceived consequences of the policy. If either the perceived consequences or the actual affirmative action policy attitudes, or both, go unchanged in the presence of a credible and persuasive message, then indeed the roots of the perceptions and attitudes reside elsewhere.

ON SCOPE AND THE DIFFICULTY OF DISCUSSING GROUP INTERESTS

It would be a mistake to interpret the argument or the evidence presented here as positing the singular and overarching importance of group interests to the dynamics of race politics. This research is not advanced as an effort to identify a new master motive or another "simple and sovereign" approach. First, it is a beginning effort to correct a serious omission in our thinking about affirmative action and about the politics of race more broadly. To wit, prior scholarship on public opinion about affirmative action has been preoccupied with a stark dichotomous choice: it is a matter of values and ideology, *or* it is a matter of antiblack attitudes of some kind. Such formulations are needlessly simplistic and overlook altogether both what people perceive about the likely impact of a policy and the role for group interests in shaping the perceptions of policy consequences and the policy attitudes themselves. Second, it is an effort to place public opinion research on firmer, more credible ground for speaking constructively to the modern politics of race. Ignoring or minimizing a substantial factor in what makes affirmative action a controversial matter is a counterproductive form of intellectual "denial."

Given the logical implication of affirmative action policy (Thurow 1994; Steinberg 1995), the empirical evidence on race-based differences in opinion, and the importance of perceived threat among whites, why are scholars so reluctant to consider group interests as one element in the politics of affirmative action? One aspect of the problem is the strong bias toward "either/or" formulations. For instance, Sniderman and Edward Carmines, in a flight of hyperbole, argue that it is both "wrong and wrong-headed" (1997a, 115) to see a conflict of interest involved in the politics of affirmative action. They contend that "if the issue of race really were to reduce to group interests, given that blacks constitute only a small fraction of the citizenry, there never would have been a successful biracial effort in behalf of racial justice" (p. 115). This declaration reflects astonishingly simplified either/or thinking rather than a careful consideration of the available evidence.

A hypothetical example drawn from academe can quickly illustrate the extremity and shortsightedness of the claim made by Sniderman and Carmines. In the current period of resource scarcity in higher education, more and more academic departments find that when faculty retire, they are not automatically granted a replacement slot. Instead of simply allocating slots to departments, there are often college- or divisionwide competitions for a finite number of slots. The department that persuades the dean gets the slot. Imagine then, if you will, a scenario wherein a History department and a Political Science department have each had a recent retirement. The dean responds by offering only one replacement slot, to be granted to the department that makes the best case for a new hire. This is a zero-sum conflict of interest between the History department and the Political Science department. Imagine further that most members of both departments ardently defend their own department's "right" to make the next hire, though neither accomplishes complete internal unanimity on this point. That both departments have an unambiguous "interest" in securing the slot foreordains neither deep and irreconcilable conflict between the departments nor complete unanimity within departments on how to respond. Real conflicts of interest, based on some corporate or group characteristic, frequently arise without necessitating (1) that the corporate or group interest at stake be the only operative factor, (2) that mutual within-group unanimity of viewpoints emerge, or (3) that a pitched "warre of all against all" be the only avenue of response. It would indeed be foolish to conclude that the only evidence of a significant role for group interests requires that such interests be the singular, monolithic, and irreconcilable source of a dispute. Yet this is effectively the standard that Sniderman and Carmines suggest be applied.

In a scenario like the "one slot" situation, I suspect that the perceived benefits (or costs) of obtaining the slot, how generally vulnerable or threatened (or secure) members of a department feel about their status within the university, and some general ideas and values about the elements of a proper liberal education would all come to bear to differing degrees. But I also suspect that the odds would run strongly against departmental affiliation having *no* bearing on how most individuals responded precisely because real, short-term interests are at stake. It is in this sense that I argue interests are a necessary element of our thinking about the politics of affirmative action and, further, that the reluctance to recognize the role of interests simultaneously does damage to social scientific theory and weakens the capacity to forge a progressive political strategy.

Yet a second possible basis for the reluctance to see interests as part of the politics of affirmative action has to do with the nature of racial groups. To speak of "interests" in the context of race seems to accord "race" a deeper ontological reality than the concept should rightly possess. This reluctance has a sensible foundation inasmuch as the concepts of race and racial groupings are social constructions rather than naturally occurring categories. As such, racial categories and identities derive their force and power from the human capacity to create socially significant symbols or meaning. It is in direct recognition of this consideration that I draw a fundamental distinction here between short-term and long-term interests. Racial categories and identities are ultimately malleable rather than fixed. As a result, there can be no fundamental, long-term conflicts of interest between racial groups. However, in the presence of socially significant racial identities and communities that also embody sharp race-linked divisions in the command of economic resources, access to and command of political resources, and enjoyment of broad social esteem, there are quite profound material and socioemotional "stakes" in the politics of race. Social policies designed to greatly reduce or eliminate those race-linked inequalities of necessity entail a reduction in the extent of group privilege for some and a corresponding improvement in condition for others.

There is yet a third possible basis for the reluctance to recognize the role of interests, which involves the taken-for-granted nature of white privilege and the traditional rhetoric and strategy of the civil rights movement. It is, I suspect, simpler for many liberals to treat the race problem as an abstract moral question than it is to confront the reality of racial privilege. Ironically, it is what we now regard as the moral power and rhetoric of traditional civil rights leaders that reinforces this tendency. In conventional analyses, whether advanced by the racism school or the principled politics school, there are "good guys and bad guys," and it is easy to view one's self as standing in the camp of the morally virtuous. The rub, however, is that white skin privilege is a categorical benefit, not merely something enjoyed by those openly hostile to blacks or other minorities. Such a recognition means forfeiting some degree of claim to innocence, and that is a cognitively difficult task, even for the well-intentioned. As a result, analysis and discourse that confront group-based interests and privileges can make uncomfortable even those of genuine goodwill. And it does, therefore, run the risk of making coalitions more difficult to forge. But coalitions forged on the basis of partial understanding or plainly erroneous beliefs are just as fragile, if not more fragile, because the underlying social reality will inexorably assert itself.

One of the important, but paradoxical accomplishments of the civil rights movement has been to cast open bigotry into deep disrepute. It is an important accomplishment inasmuch as the sacrifice, courageous struggle, and lofty rhetoric of civil rights crusaders gave witness to a nation that it had to change if it wanted to live up to its highest ideals. For most white Americans, this accomplishment is seen in the sweeping positive transformation in racial attitudes that has occurred over the past five decades (Schuman et al. 1997), a transformation that much social scientific evidence suggests runs deep enough that most white Americans want to preserve a self-image as racially egalitarian individuals (Gaertner and Dovidio 1986). The accomplishment is paradoxical in that large and systematic racial inequalities persist and are actively justified in the absence of coarse bigotry. That is, there is still extensive white privilege in life chances and the systematic reproduction of such privilege without Jim Crow racism and the historic political actors who once advocated for it. The dilemma of the new "laissez-faire racism," as I have developed more fully elsewhere (Bobo, Kluegel, and Smith 1997; Bobo and Smith 1998), is that you don't need coarse, biological racism to facilitate the maintenance of white skin privilege and black disadvantage. Yet in the popular mind, racism is now narrowly equated with cross burnings, hooded Klansmen, and the Jim Crow rantings of the likes of George Wallace and Lester Maddox. The failure to recognize interests and privilege, as well as the justification of such conditions, as part of the problem of racialized politics is a serious constraint on the capacity to understand the social phenomenon under investigation and impedes constructive response to the current racial divide.

CONCLUSIONS

The empirical results support several conclusions. *First, whites and racial minority group members do not hold diametrically opposed views of the costs and benefits of affirmative action for blacks.* Although much of the media discourse about affirmative action highlights intense group conflict, especially between blacks and whites, there is far more overlap in outlooks than such packaging recognizes (Entman 1997). While the results point in manifold ways to the central importance of race to affirmative action politics, the arena for potential common ground is larger than the general discourse or the tenor of recent scholarship on public opinion about affirmative action has properly acknowledged. To be sure, beliefs about the effects of affirmative action do not foreordain specific policy positions. Yet much of the "politics" of affirmative action is a discourse about the effects of such a policy. These results point to some useful wellsprings of favorable and potentially more consensual views of affirmative action.

Second, much of why "race matters" would appear to reflect group-based interests. This is, we submit, the only reasonable interpretation of the powerfully robust racial difference in opinion that separates the views of blacks and of Latinos from those of whites. Certainly, this is not a context where one would argue for a heritable proclivity to favor affirmative action. Yet group differences are just one possible indication of an interest basis to public opinion. But even in terms of understanding the effects of perceived group threat and, to a degree, of symbolic racism on whites' beliefs, it is something about how individuals understand their "place" in the American *racial order* that appears to be at stake. That is, it would be a mistake to interpret these results as simply confirming the advocacy of those on the left who wish to don the armor of moral superiority and classify opponents of affirmative action as transparent racists. These are racial attitudes situated in a powerfully racialized economic and political context where there is a meaningful and indisputable short-term difference in group interests.

William Julius Wilson (1987) convincingly argued that liberals lost their hegemonic position in the discourse on social welfare and poverty policy because they failed to acknowledge important, if often unsettling, realities about the nature of life in poor ghetto communities. Liberal analysts of public opinion on affirmative action have effectively committed the same error by ignoring or disparaging the all too transparent social reality of the differing stakes that blacks and Latinos, on the one hand, and whites and to a degree Asians, on the other hand, have in the preservation and implementation of affirmative action. By not addressing the role of interest groups and perceived group interests and by stressing instead moralistic judgments of who is and who is not a racist, the door was opened wide to a conservative response that cast opponents of affirmative action as the truly moral figures in the debate. Thus, the transparent fact that political advocacy for affirmative action has come principally (though far from exclusively) from the traditional civil rights community, especially from black organizations explicitly seeking to advance the interests of the black community, is not addressed at all by liberal analysts of racial attitudes. The extent of this failure remains so great that even the most recent efforts to revive symbolic racism theory (e.g., Sears et al. 1997) commit again the grave error of classifying attitudes toward civil rights leaders and black political activism as an "abstract racial resentment," namely, symbolic racism (see Bobo 1988a; Bobo 1988b; Tuch and Hughes 1996b; and Hughes 1997 for a critique). By having legitimated and made central a discourse of values and morality, liberal analysts have made it easy for conservative analysts to cast the demands made by blacks and other minorities as morally corrupt self-aggrandizement.

Third, and perhaps above all else, the talk of values and ideology— of a putatively principled basis of objection to affirmative action— receives very limited support in this analysis. To be sure, ideological identification has a real net effect on beliefs about the impact of affirmative action among whites. However, part of the gross effect of ideology stems from its correlation with explicitly racial attitudes, and, what is more, the effects of perceived threat and of symbolic racism are a good deal more consequential.

Of course, it has been easy to overplay the argument from principles. Those on the right who wish to don the armor of moral innocence in their war against affirmative action are ready to accept this view. Certainly, seminal elite treatises (Glazer 1975) and media discourse (Entman 1997) have placed such exaggerated and inappropriate emphasis on the term "preferences" and have so routinely packaged affirmative action as a profound break with an American tradition of resisting government recognition of "groups" that the real historical record is easily misunderstood. Explicitly race-based policies, usually actively antiminority in design, have characterized major social policies in the United States almost from the very founding of the nation (Takaki 1994)—so much so that the logic of affirmative action policies, rather than contradicting the American historical pattern, is actually entirely consistent with it. As eminent historian John Higham explained:

There was nothing novel or constitutionally irregular about governments or private bureaucracies favoring a class of citizens who need special help. Consider, for example, the Freedman's Bureau, which Congress created in 1866 to assist newly freed former slaves in the conquered South, or the long history of federal water policy, tax laws, and veterans legislation—all of which singled out a particular group for government benefits. (1997, 20)

Indeed, given the historic intertwining of race and the understanding of values in the United States, it is somewhat paradoxical, if not Orwellian, that a "values and ideology" argument is ever credibly positioned as completely race-neutral. Eminent historical sociologist Orlando Patterson argues persuasively that conservative scholars have pursued a disingenuous argument against group-based claims in the racial context when in fact they vigorously support group, or "corporate," claims in many other contexts. He writes:

The fundamental flaw in conservative thinking is the refusal to acknowledge the peculiar demands of representational behavior and collective life. Insisting that the representative should treat individuals exactly the same as in face-to-face interactions is perverse, hypocritical, and downright obtuse, in light of the treatment of corporate constituencies.

American conservative representative leaders are in hopeless intellectual disarray on this matter. Not only is the socioeconomic system that they cherish founded on the principle of corporate responsibility and action, but conservatives, more than any other group, are prone to appeal to collective ideals and agency when it suits them. Which group of people urges their fellow Americans to be patriotic and gets most upset when protesters exercise their First Amendment right to burn the flag? And what is patriotism if not the most extreme commitment to a belief in a supraindividual entity called the nation? Which group of Americans wants us all to pursue a common national culture with a single common set of virtues and ideals grounded on a common set of religious beliefs? (Patterson 1997, 116)

Patterson goes on to deride the conservative claim that government should never recognize racial groups in the form of affirmative action as a matter of principle. He argues, "That the conservatives object to such a policy on the grounds that collective agency and liability do not exist is sheer hypocrisy and self-contradiction. Collective reparation is a well-established principle in the law of nations" (Patterson 1997, 122).

Race, at least in terms of the traditional black-white divide, has long been the axis along which full and genuine membership in the polity was established and which set the boundaries for determining what constituted appropriate or inappropriate treatment of individuals (Bobo 1988b; Prager 1987; Steinberg 1995). Race has been so profoundly implicated in American politics that it played the central role in reshaping national partisan political identities and party alignments in the post–World War II period (Carmines and Stimson 1989; Edsall and Edsall 1991a).

In sum, neither U.S. history nor the wellsprings of public opinion provides much support for the values and ideology position. Given the resounding rejection of this "theory" in a range of studies using different samples and measures, the time may have arrived to lay it to rest with finality (see Bobo 1991; Kinder and Sanders 1996; Meertens and Pettigrew 1997; Sears et al. 1997; Sidanius, Pratto, and Bobo 1996). Absent some powerful new evidence, the principled objection hypothesis stands as at best a logical possibility, albeit historically implausible and repeatedly disconfirmed by a number of empirical analyses.

Students of public opinion on affirmative action will better understand the social phenomenon they study and make more useful contributions to the national dialogue on race if (1) research reaches beyond policy preferences to include beliefs about the effects of affirmative action, (2) race and racial group interests are repositioned to a more central analytical place, and (3) multiracial analyses and comparisons become more commonplace. Without denying that racism remains a problem or that ideological conservatism matters for whites' attitudes, affirmative action is also very much about the place racial groups should occupy in American society.[6]

Blacks and Latinos face real and tangible disadvantages and systematic modern-day racial discrimination. They are more likely to live below the poverty line, indeed far below it as compared to whites (Harrison and Bennett 1995); they are far less likely to complete college degrees (Hauser 1993), a form of certification that increasingly draws the line between a middle-class standard of living and a life of constant economic hardship (Danziger and Gottschalk 1996); and they will almost certainly face discrimination in searching for a place to live (Massey and Denton 1993) or for employment (Holzer 1996; Kirschenman and Neckerman 1991; Turner, Fix, and Struyk 1991). The removal of affirmative action in higher education has immediate and potentially disastrous effects on the positions of blacks and Latinos (Weiss 1997). It is increasingly clear that lessening the pressure brought by government for affirmative action and for activist civil rights enforcement produces real and often drastic declines in the economic and educational fortunes of blacks and Latinos (Carnoy 1994). Despite all the high, abstract, and moralizing rhetoric, affirmative action is simultaneously about concrete matters of who gets what.

A rhetoric centered around a mutual recognition and accommodation of legitimate interests is a far more promising basis for racial progress than are the brickbats of moral superiority now wielded so vigorously by those on the left and those on the right. Furthermore, advocates of affirmative action would do well, first, to shed the perception that white public opinion is monolithic on this question and, second, to set about the eminently political task of promoting ideas and values consistent with affirmative action, as did leaders from the civil rights era, such as Kennedy, Johnson, and King. Such framing of issues by elites is a critical factor shaping public opinion. The far from overwhelming vote in California in favor of Proposition 209 and more recently the defeat of an anti–affirmative action measure in Houston suggest that there is more promise of an effective pro–affirmative action strategy than the current air of liberal defeat recognizes. As I have argued elsewhere:

> The assumption that public opinion is known or fixed in a certain direction is probably more constraining than is public opinion itself. Reformers of the left or the right who take the contours of public opinion for granted or who assume that there is little need to promote actively particular issue frames and reinforce the values, assumptions, symbols, and catch phrases that lend meaning to questions of public policy are likely to falter before the bar of public opinion. (Bobo and Smith 1994, 395)

Lani Guinier is quite right. In order to move beyond race, we will most assuredly have to work through race in all its implications (Guinier 1998, 240). This will require a sensible and honest focus on the things that are really at stake. But if we do so, there are good reasons to believe that a progressive coalition for policies such as affirmative action and an even broader sense of "sustainable community" can be achieved.

six How Beliefs about
Poverty Influence
Racial Policy
Attitudes

A *Study of Whites, African
Americans, Hispanics, and
Asians in the United States*

MICHAEL HUGHES
STEVEN A. TUCH

INTRODUCTION

Few issues are as controversial, or generate as much debate, as race-targeted social policies, especially affirmative action. Hailed by proponents as an appropriate remedy for past racial injustices and rejected by opponents as unfair reverse discrimination, race targeting continues to be one of the most divisive issues in late-twentieth-century American social and political life. While antiblack and anti-integrationist sentiment among whites has declined markedly over the past several decades (Bobo, Kluegel, and Smith, 1997; Jaynes and Williams 1989; Schuman et al. 1997), resistance to race targeting persists (Tuch and Sigelman 1997; Steeh and Schuman 1992; Sigelman and Welch 1994).

One of the factors thought to explain the contradiction between whites' support for general principles of racial equality, on the one hand, and their rejection of policies aimed at redressing racial inequities, on the other, is stratification ideology, especially beliefs about the causes of poverty (Tuch and Hughes 1996a, 1996b; Kluegel and Smith 1986). Unfortunately, nearly all past research on racial and ethnic differences in poverty beliefs has focused exclusively on whites and blacks, usually examining whites' attributions about blacks' poverty and the effect of these attributions on racial policy attitudes (see Hunt

1996 for an exception). As a result, we know little about whites' views of the causes of poverty among other minority groups, the beliefs of minority group members themselves about their own and other groups' poverty, whether stratification ideology affects policy attitudes among minority groups in the same way that it does among whites, and whether stratification beliefs and racial ideology explain differences between whites and minority group members in support for egalitarian racial policy.

In this study, we take a step toward filling these gaps. Employing a unique, nationally representative data set that includes oversamples of African Americans, Hispanics, and Asians, we address four main questions: (1) Are there differences between ethnic groups in causal attributions of minority poverty? (2) Do causal attributions of minority poverty differ depending on the target group (i.e., the group the attributions are made about)? (3) How do causal attributions of minority poverty influence racial policy attitudes? (4) Do stratification beliefs and racial ideology explain group differences in support for egalitarian racial policy?

BACKGROUND

CAUSAL ATTRIBUTIONS ABOUT MINORITY POVERTY

Two kinds of poverty beliefs concern us here (Feagin 1975): individualistic attributions that focus on supposed characteristics of the poor themselves, such as lack of effort or ability or weak attachment to a work ethic, and structuralist attributions that emphasize the role of such factors as poor education, lack of jobs, and discrimination in structuring socioeconomic outcomes.[1] Past research has established that high socioeconomic status (SES) is associated with individualistic beliefs about the causes of poverty and low SES with more structuralist beliefs, but these associations are not strong (Kluegel and Smith 1986; Hunt 1996). Evidence also suggests that both African Americans and Hispanics, who are more likely than whites to be of low SES, are also more structuralist than whites (Hunt 1996), though we know far less about Hispanics' than African Americans' thinking in this area. No previous study has examined the stratification beliefs of Asians.

In a study of whites, blacks, and Hispanics, Matthew Hunt (1996) demonstrated that ethnic differences in beliefs about poverty are not merely reflections of SES; rather, these differences remain after education and income are controlled. In explaining these findings, Hunt argued against an economic self-interest hypothesis and in favor of a group identification effect; that is, that minority group members identify more with the poor than whites do. Hunt also found that African Americans and Hispanics are more individualist in orientation than whites. This finding is consistent with other research that has shown that the two attributions, individualistic and structuralist, are not contradictory, but can, and often do, coexist (Kluegel 1990; Kluegel and Smith 1986). In other words, to a considerable extent, even those who have not fared well in the stratification system nonetheless endorse individualistic accounts of the causes of achievement and failure, an indication of the pervasiveness with which a dominant individualistic ideology permeates all segments of society. Basing his reasoning on the work of Lawrence Bobo (1991) and Michael Mann (1970), Hunt argued that structuralist ideology exhibits more across-group volatility than does individualistic ideology. Structuralist thinking is more common in periods of economic crisis than in other times, but never gains prominence, since its most ardent supporters never accumulate enough power to turn it into social policy. Individualistic ideology, being more stable, retains the appearance of ideological hegemony in American society and is internalized by both minority and dominant group members. As a result, Hunt argued, members of minority groups are more likely than whites to experience a "dual consciousness," simultaneously subscribing to both structuralist beliefs (by virtue of group identification) and individualistic beliefs (as a result of acculturation to dominant American values that are relatively stable).

What role do causal attributions about minority poverty play in shaping attitudes toward race- and ethnic-targeted policies? Past research indicates that whites who believe that racial inequality is caused by structural factors tend to be supportive of race targeting aimed at improving African Americans' life chances (Tuch and Hughes 1996a; Kluegel 1990; Kluegel and Smith 1986). Presumably, the belief that social structure is an important determinant of economic outcomes makes whites more receptive to taking effective action to change that structure in order to reduce inequality.

Another prominent account of the role of causal attributions in influencing policy attitudes treats the belief that poverty is caused by the behavior of poor people as a form of victim blaming that legitimates doing nothing to change the structure of social and economic inequality in U.S. society (Ryan 1971). However, the evidence that such individualistic thinking influences white attitudes about policies designed to reduce African-American inequality is poor and inconsistent (Tuch and Hughes 1996a; Bobo and Kluegel 1993).

Whether, and if so, how, whites' policy attitudes are similarly driven by stratification ideology concerning Hispanics and Asians is not known; nor is it known how stratification ideology influences the race-targeted policy attitudes of minority group members themselves.

Most published accounts of structuralist and individualist ideology assume that these are polar opposites rather than separate dimensions. As noted above, Hunt (1996) presented evidence that this is not the case, but rather that the two dimensions are independent of each other and are correlated. Thinking of these apparently separate dimensions as polar opposites has deterred researchers from exploring how individualistic ideology may combine with structuralist ideology to affect racial policy attitudes. For instance, although previous research has shown that individualism may not have a main effect on racial policy attitudes, it may interact with structuralism, reducing support for racial policies among those who reject structural explanations of poverty, but not among others.

RACIAL POLICIES

What do we mean by "race-targeted policies"? Unlike generic or "color-blind" social programs, which apply to the economically disadvantaged regardless of race, race-targeted policies are explicitly designed to redress social, economic, or political inequalities between whites and racial and ethnic minorities. Racial policies differ widely in form and objective, however. Some, such as compensatory job training and special education programs, are nearly universally supported by whites and blacks alike; others, such as preferential treatment in hiring, promotion, or college and university admissions, are nearly unanimously rejected by whites, who view such programs as violating principles of fairness. Preferential treatment is not universally accepted among blacks either. Some conservative African Americans reject race targeting on the grounds that such programs, on balance, do more harm than good by perpetuating the racist stereotype that blacks are unable to succeed without government assistance (see Boston 1988 for a review). Little is known about the attitudes of Hispanics and Asians toward affirmative action programs designed for them. In this analysis, we focus on two dimensions of racial policy attitudes: (1) an index measuring opposition to affirmative action and (2) the belief that whites have no responsibility to compensate blacks, Hispanics, and Asians for past discrimination.

RIVAL EXPLANATIONS

Stratification ideology is just one of several factors identified in the race attitudes literature as an explanation for whites' tendency to reject policies that would reduce or eliminate racial inequality. If ideology is a potent explanation, its effects on race targeting must persist net of rival explanations. A good deal of disagreement exists in the literature over how best to account for racial policy attitudes, however (see, e.g., the exchange between Steven Tuch and Michael Hughes [1996b] and Darren Davis [1996], David Sears and Tom Jessor [1996], Mary Jackman [1996], and Laura Stoker [1996]). Below we present an overview of the major alternative theoretical accounts.

MINORITY OPPORTUNITY Several studies have reported a marked tendency on the part of whites to view blacks' opportunity as plentiful (Sigelman and Welch 1994; Kluegel and Smith 1986). Since support for race targeting requires, at a minimum, the recognition of at least some constraints on blacks' opportunity, this account of racial policy views interprets opposition to race targeting as a reflection of whites' tendency to deny the existence of obstacles to blacks' opportunity. Whether beliefs about Hispanics' and Asians' opportunity similarly shape attitudes toward affirmative action for these groups is not known.

RACIAL RESENTMENT The work of Donald Kinder and Lynn Sanders (1996) on racial resentment and Sears (1988) and Sears and his colleagues (Sears and Kinder 1971; Kinder and Sears 1981) on symbolic racism suggests that traditional racial prejudice has been replaced by a "modern" version of racism that is grounded in early racial socialization experiences and in whites' beliefs that blacks violate such traditional American values as self-reliance and hard work. The result, according to this account of racial policy attitudes, is a new form of racial prejudice that is the principal contemporary ideological dimension influencing whites' racial policy attitudes (Hughes 1997). However, we do not know whether this kind of resentment influences the racial policy attitudes of Hispanics, Asians, and/or African Americans.

MINORITY INDIVIDUALISM The abstract ideology of individualism has been important for the theoretical grounding of racial resentment (i.e., "symbolic" or "modern" racism) (Kinder and Sears 1981; Sears 1988; Kinder and Sanders 1996). However, research has not con-

firmed that individualism is an important predictor of racial policy attitudes (Hughes 1997; Tuch and Hughes 1996a; Sears 1988), and while
it has a relationship with racial resentment, individualism cannot be
implicated in how racial resentment (or "symbolic racism") influences
racial policy attitudes (Hughes 1997).

There is some evidence that *racial* individualism is associated with
racial policy attitudes, however (Tuch and Hughes 1996a). We argue
that racial individualism is a form of racial prejudice in which the ideology of individualism is used as a moral yardstick to judge racial minorities, but not others. In our view, this dimension is at the core of
the concept of symbolic racism, and we believe it is the mechanism
by which individualism could be involved in the impact of symbolic
racism on racial policy attitudes.

Since, in the present study, our measure of minority resentment is
narrow and such resentment is measured in a nonstandard way (see
below), we also include a measure of minority individualism (focusing
on "minorities" rather than a particular racial group) to tap this important dimension of symbolic racism.

DENIAL OF DISCRIMINATION To the extent that acknowledgment of
the existence of discrimination toward blacks and other minority
group members is a necessary prerequisite for support of policies
aimed at dismantling discrimination's effects, those who deny that racism and discrimination are problems are likely to oppose race- or ethnic-targeted policies (see, e.g., Kluegel and Smith 1986).

MINORITY THREAT Also referred to as group threat (Quillian 1995,
1996; Fossett and Kiecolt 1989), group interest, or group conflict
(Bobo and Kluegel 1993; Pettigrew 1985) theories, the minority threat
account of opposition to race targeting focuses on the role played by
defense of white privilege in structuring policy views. According to
this perspective, to the extent that whites views blacks' social and political advancement as a threat to their own advantaged position, any
social programs that promote egalitarianism will be rejected.

CONSERVATIVE OPPOSITION Some analysts (e,g, Roth [1994] and
Sniderman and Piazza [1993]) have stressed the possibility that whites'
opposition to racial policies reflects a "principled" view of government
responsibility that sees any intrusion of government into private affairs
as unacceptable. According to this account, opposition to race target-

ing has no racial overtones, but rather reflects deeply held conservative views about the proper role of government.

As noted above, much of the research on racial policy attitudes has focused on finding an explanation for whites' lack of support for racially targeted social policies. Arguments in the literature cited above strongly suggest that stratification ideology and the racial and political attitudes just reviewed are the important factors. If these are the factors that make whites distinctive in their lack of support for race-targeted policies for reducing inequality, a multivariate analysis should indicate that they explain the differences between whites and minorities in support for race-targeted policies. If not, other, unmeasured factors must also be important determinants of race-targeted policy attitudes.

THE PROBLEM

Past research has found that explanations of minority poverty influence support for racial policy. However, nearly all of this research has examined whites' attributions of the causes of blacks' poverty, ignoring the role of stratification beliefs in shaping whites' attitudes toward policies earmarked for Hispanics and Asians. We know even less about the views of these minority group members themselves toward race targeting. This chapter attempts to fill this void by analyzing structuralist and individualist beliefs about the causes of black, Hispanic, and Asian poverty among members of each of these minority groups as well as among whites.

We are especially interested in (1) whether causal attributions of minority poverty depend on the ethnicity of the target group and whether attributions vary by the ethnic affiliation of the respondent and (2) how race-specific attributions of poverty and other racial and political attitudes influence racial policy views. No previous work has simultaneously examined the attitudes of whites, African Americans, Hispanics, and Asians toward race and ethnic targeting.

Stratification ideology is not the only explanation of racial policy preferences, however. In examining the influence of poverty beliefs, we take account of the possibly confounding effects of alternative explanations of policy views as well as the effects of such sociodemographic variables as ethnic group membership, education, gender, and age. Our goal is to determine whether causal attributions of minority poverty have any explanatory power net of the influences of these other factors. Thus, a third major goal of this study is to determine whether structural and individualistic attributions and racial ideology explain racial/ethnic differences in support for egalitarian racial policies.

To accomplish these goals we use a unique, nationally representative data set that includes measures of whites', blacks', Hispanics', and Asians' attitudes toward a range of affirmative action policies. Below we describe this data set and our analytic strategy in more detail.

DATA AND METHODS

DATA

The data for this study come from a 1995 *Washington Post* telephone survey of race relations attitudes. The data were collected by Chilton Research Services during July, August, and September of 1995. The sample of 1,970 persons eighteen years of age and older was designed to be representative of the U.S. population and included oversamples of African Americans, Hispanics, and Asians. The final sample had 802 whites, 451 African Americans, 251 Hispanics, and 352 Asians. (The 110 persons who indicated another race and the 4 persons whose race could not be ascertained were excluded from analysis.) Completed interviews were obtained from 43 percent of eligible respondents selected for interview at the household level. Because this response rate is not optimal, readers should view our results with appropriate caution.

SUBSAMPLES

Most of the questions in the survey were asked of all respondents. These include questions about ideology and attitudes about racial policy. However, questions about attributions of poverty within different ethnic groups were asked of different subsets of respondents. The entire sample was randomly divided into three subsamples, with each subsample asked about the causes of poverty among only one ethnic group. Thus, one-third of the entire sample was asked about the causes of African-American poverty, one-third was asked about the causes of Hispanic poverty, and one-third was asked about the causes of Asian poverty.

The analyses we report were performed within each of these three independent subsamples. We will be able to examine race differences in attributions about each group and the impact of attributions about each group on racial policy attitudes. However, given the design of the survey, it is impossible to determine how beliefs about the causes of, say, African-American poverty are related to beliefs about the causes of Asian poverty.

MEASUREMENT

ATTRIBUTIONS ABOUT POVERTY Each of the three subsamples described above was asked the following question, with "African American(s)," "Hispanic American(s)," and "Asian American(s)" inserted in the blanks for each respective subsample:

> Here is a list of things some people have mentioned as reasons for the economic and social problems _____ face today. For each one, please tell me if you think it is a major reason for the problems _____ face, a minor reason, or not a reason at all?

> Past and present discrimination.
> Lack of educational opportunities.
> Lack of motivation and their unwillingness to work hard.
> Lack of intelligence.
> Whites don't want _____ to get ahead.
> Language problems.
> Lack of jobs.
> The breakup of the _____ family.

"Major reason" was coded 3, "minor reason" was coded 2, and "not a reason at all" was coded 1.[2]

Principal components factor analyses were performed in each subsample on the eight reasons for "economic and social problems." In the subsamples asking about African Americans and Hispanic Americans, two clear factors emerged: structural attributions (past and present discrimination, lack of educational opportunities, whites don't want _____ to get ahead, and lack of jobs) and individualistic attributions (lack of motivation and their unwillingness to work hard, and lack of intelligence). Reliability analysis yielded an alpha of .72 for the African-American structural items and .69 for the Hispanic structural items. Alpha for African-American individualistic items is .54 and for Hispanic individualistic items is .57.

The two additional items (language problems and the breakup of the _____ family) did not consistently load on the different factors for each group. Subsequent analyses showed that neither item is an important predictor of policy attitudes in any of the three subsamples, so these items were dropped from the analysis.

The results of the factor analyses of the items about Asian Americans in the third subsample were not as clear as for the other two subsamples. When the four structural and two individual items concerning Asian poverty were included in a single factor analysis, the education item loaded on the first factor with the motivation and intelligence items, while the discrimination item and the item about whites' wishes to hold minorities back loaded on the second factor. The lack of jobs item was split between these two factors. However, when only the four structural items were entered into a single factor analysis, they loaded strongly on one factor, and reliability analysis yielded an alpha of .66 for these four items. The two individual items identified above (motivation and intelligence) have a correlation of .60, yielding an alpha of .75.

In the interests of parsimony and simplicity of analysis and interpretation, we constructed the same two variables for attributions about Asian poverty as for African-American and Hispanic poverty. However, it is clear from our factor analyses that attitudes about Asian poverty are not structured in the same way as those about African-American and Hispanic poverty. In particular, individual and structural attributions are not so clearly differentiated as those for African Americans and Hispanics are. In our analysis, this is reflected in the stronger correlation between structural and individual attributions about Asian-American poverty.

In sum, in each subsample we have two attributions indices: a structural attributions index and an individualistic attributions index. In subsample A, these two indices refer to beliefs about African-American poverty; in subsample B, to Hispanic poverty; and in subsample C, to Asian poverty.

MINORITY OPPORTUNITY Respondents were asked about the opportunities of African Americans, Hispanic Americans, and Asian Americans relative to those of whites. For one random half of the sample, the specific question was:

> Do you feel that _____ have more opportunity, less opportunity, or about the same opportunity *to live a middle class life as whites?* (Emphasis added)

For the other random half of the sample, the specific question asked was:

Do you feel that _____ have more opportunity, less opportunity, or about the same opportunity as whites *to be really successful and wealthy?* (Emphasis added)

Each question was asked with reference to each of the three ethnic groups. "More opportunity" was coded 3, "about the same opportunity" was coded 2, and "less opportunity" was coded 1. Because the variation in wording for these questions did not yield a substantial difference in the distribution of the variables or in how they correlated with other variables, the difference in wording was ignored, and three variables were constructed to reflect opportunity attitudes, one for each ethnic group.

RACISM IS A PROBLEM Respondents were asked: "How big a problem is racism in our society today? Is it a big problem, somewhat of a problem, a small problem, or not a problem at all?" Coding was from 1 ("not a problem") to 4 ("big problem").

RESENTMENT OF MINORITIES Respondents were asked: "In general, would you rather have: (A) The federal government provide more services, even if it costs more in taxes, or (B) The federal government cost less in taxes but provide fewer services?" If respondents answered "B," wanting less taxes, they were also asked to respond to the following:

I'm going to read you a list of reasons some people have given for why they would rather have the federal government cost less and provide fewer services. For each one, please tell me if it is a major reason, a minor reason, or not a reason at all why you feel that way.

One of the six reasons provided in the list was "The federal government is spending too much on low-income minorities." Respondents were also asked: "Of these, which is the most important reason?"

The minority resentment variable was constructed from the above questions. If government spending on low-income minorities was the most important reason, respondents were coded 4; if this was given as a major reason, they were coded 3; minor reason was coded 2; and respondents saying it was not a reason and respondents who were willing to pay more taxes were coded 1. An unavoidable problem with this variable is that some of those who are willing to pay more taxes may nevertheless be resentful, but are being coded the same as those who say spending on low-income minorities is not a reason they want lower taxes. However, this means that estimates of the effect of resentment will be conservative, understating its actual influence.

MINORITY INDIVIDUALISM This variable is represented by a single item. Respondents were asked to respond to the following:

> Some people have made the following statements about the future of America and the role of low-income minorities in it. Please tell me if you agree or disagree with each statement.

One of the statements was "Low-income minorities need to take more individual responsibility and become less dependent on government." Responses were agree (1) and disagree (0).

MINORITY THREAT Respondents were asked: "Compared to 10 years ago, do you think people like you are closer or farther away from attaining the American Dream?" Those who said "farther away" were then asked: "Is each of the following a major reason, a minor reason, or not a reason at all why people like you are farther away from attaining the American Dream?" Eight reasons were offered, including the following:

> Preferences given to other racial and ethnic groups threaten my job opportunities.
> The growing number of other racial and ethnic groups is eroding my way of life.

Each of these items was coded as follows: "major reason" = 2, "minor reason" = 1, "not a reason at all" = 0, and a response of "closer to the American Dream" on the filter question = 0. These two items were then summed into a single variable. As with the resentment variable, this measure will provide conservative estimates of the effect of minority threat on the dependent variables.

CONSERVATISM Respondents were asked: "Would you say your views in most political matters are very liberal, liberal, moderate, conservative, or very conservative?" Responses were coded from 1 ("very liberal") to 5 ("very conservative").

RACIAL POLICY ATTITUDES Our data set includes four measures of respondents' racial policy attitudes. The first three of these are general policy questions that do not reflect attitudes specific to a particular racial or ethnic group. We combined these items into a factor-weighted composite index of opposition to affirmative action (standardized item α = .56). The fourth measure is specific to the racial/ethnic groups asked about in subsamples A, B, and C. The three items composing the opposition to affirmative action index are as follows:

• *Affirmative Action Is a Good Thing.* Respondents were asked: "Generally speaking, do you think affirmative action is a good thing or a bad thing for the country, or doesn't it affect the country that much?" Responses were coded as follows: 3 = "bad thing," 2 = "doesn't affect the country much," and 1 = "good thing."

• *Hiring Should Be Strictly by Merit.* Respondents were asked the following question:

> Which of these statements comes closer to the way you feel?
>
> A. Diversity benefits our country economically and socially, so race or ethnicity should be a factor when deciding who is hired, promoted, or admitted to college.
> B. Hiring, promotion, and college admissions should be based strictly on merit and qualifications other than race or ethnicity.

If respondents answered "A," they were asked the following:

> Would you still feel that way if it meant that more qualified whites sometimes lost out to less qualified minorities for jobs, promotions, or college admissions?

If respondents answered "B," they were asked the following:

> Would you still feel that way if it meant that minorities were underrepresented in some types of jobs, or that few or no minorities were hired by some companies or admitted to certain colleges?

Responses to these questions were combined into a single variable that was coded as follows: a code of 1 means that race/ethnicity should be a factor even if whites sometimes lose out; a code of 2 means that race/ethnicity should be a factor, but not if whites sometimes lose out; a code of 3 means that hiring, promotions, and admissions should be based on merit, but not if that means that minorities would be underrepresented; and a code of 4 means that hiring, promotions, and admissions should be based on merit even if minorities are underrepresented.

• *Congress Should Limit Affirmative Action.* Respondents were asked to respond to the following:

> I'm going to read you a list of issues being considered in Congress. For each one, please tell me if you think it is something Congress should do or not do.

After receiving an answer for each issue, the interviewer asked if that was something the respondent felt strongly that Congress should or should not do. One of the issues in the list was "Limit affirmative action." This variable was coded as follows: 4 = "strongly feel Congress should do"; 3 = "feel Congress should do, but not strongly"; 2 = "feel Congress should not do"; and 1 = "strongly feel Congress should not do."

The second measure of affirmative action attitudes is as follows:

• *Whites' Responsibility to Make Up for Past Discrimination.* Respondents in each of the three subsamples described above were asked a question about whites' responsibility to make up for past discrimination against African Americans, Hispanics, or Asians, depending on the subsample. Analysis of these group-specific dependent variables in each subsample allows us to determine if attributions about the causes of a particular group's poverty impact racial policy attitudes relevant to that group.

Respondents were asked to respond to the following:

> When people talk about what white Americans should be willing to do to help _____ in this country, which of the following two statements comes closer to your view?
>
>> White Americans have benefited from past and present discrimination against _____, so they should be willing to make up for these wrongs.
>>
>> Most white Americans have not benefited from past and present discrimination against _____, so they have no responsibility to make up for these wrongs.

This variable is a dichotomy; respondents who agree that whites have no responsibility to make up for past discrimination are coded 1, and those who agree that whites should be willing to make up for past discrimination are coded 0.

AGE, EDUCATION, AND GENDER Age, measured in years, ranges from eighteen to eighty-eight, with a median of forty-two. Education has six categories: 1 = eighth grade or less, 2 = some high school, 3 = graduated from high school, 4 = some college, 5 = graduated from college, and 6 = postgraduate. Gender is a dummy variable coded 1 = female and 0 = male. Because past research has shown these sociodemographic variables to be related to policy attitudes (Kluegel 1990), we control on each in our models. In the analysis that follows, we fit ordinary least squares or logistic regression models to the data as appropriate, depending on the measurement level of the dependent variable.

FINDINGS

Prior research has noted that structural and individual attributions about poverty are not opposite ends of a single continuum, that people may (and oftentimes do) simultaneously attribute poverty to both causes, and that such "dual consciousness" is more likely among minorities than among whites. We calculated correlation coefficients between the individual attributions index and the structural attributions index within each subsample and within each race/ethnicity group. In subsample A, which was asked about causes of African-American poverty, individual and structural attributions have an overall correlation of .13 ($p \leq .001$). Among whites, it is .10 (n.s.); among African Americans, .16 ($p \leq .05$); among Hispanics, .19 ($p \leq .10$); and among Asians, .12 (n.s.). In subsample B, which was asked about causes of Hispanic poverty, the overall correlation is .20 ($p \leq .001$). Among whites, it is .22 ($p \leq .01$); among African Americans, .15 ($p \leq .05$); among Hispanics, .08 (n.s.); and among Asians, .13 (n.s.). In subsample C, which was asked about causes of Asian-American poverty, the correlation is substantially higher, as suggested by the factor analyses described above: .50 ($p = .001$) overall, .41 ($p \leq .001$) among whites, .62 ($p \leq .001$) among African Americans, .55 ($p \leq .001$) among Hispanics, and .51 ($p \leq .001$) among Asians.

These findings support the idea that individual and structural attributions are correlated,[3] but do not strongly support the argument that the correlation is generally higher among minority groups than among whites. When the indices refer to causes of poverty among Hispanics, the correlation is highest among whites. When the indices refer to African Americans or Asians, whites do have the lowest correlation, but it is not substantially different from that among the other racial/ethnic groups.

RACIAL/ETHNIC DIFFERENCES IN POVERTY ATTRIBUTIONS

Figure 6.1 displays means for the structural (top panel) and individual-istic (bottom panel) poverty attributions indices by ethnicity within each subsample. The means are adjusted for education, age, and gender and are calculated on attribution variables that have been trans-formed into standard scores (with a mean of 100 and a standard devi-ation of 10) in order to make direct comparisons across the two distributions possible. The top panel in figure 6.1 shows that white respondents are least likely, and minority respondents most likely, to attribute poverty to structural causes regardless of the target group. Analysis of variance on these means with subsample and ethnicity as independent variables (with $p = .05$) indicates that ethnicity is a sig-nificant predictor, that the subsample is nonsignificant, and that the interaction between subsample and ethnicity is nonsignificant. Post hoc tests ($p \leq .05$) on overall differences between ethnic group means indicate that Asians and Hispanics do not differ significantly from each other, but that whites are significantly less structural and African Americans are significantly more structural than all other groups. Overall, these findings indicate that structural attributions depend on the ethnic group of the respondent, but not on the ethnicity of the target group.

The bottom panel of figure 6.1 indicates that whites are not more likely than other groups to make individualistic attributions of poverty. With one major exception, whites are least likely and Asians are most likely to make individualistic attributions. The major exception is that Asians are not particularly likely to make individualistic attributions about their own group. Overall, these findings are more complex than those for structural attributions are. In an analysis of variance (with $p \leq .05$), we found again that ethnicity is a significant predictor and the subsample is nonsignificant. However, in this case, the ethnicity by subsample interaction is significant. Post hoc significance tests ($p \leq .05$) found a different pattern of significant differences within each subsample. In subsample A, where attributions are of African-Ameri-can poverty, Asians are significantly more individualistic than all others. In addition, whites are significantly less individualistic about black poverty than are Hispanics. In subsample B, where attributions are of Hispanic poverty, whites are significantly less individualistic than African Americans and Asians. In subsample C, where attributions are of Asian poverty, African Americans were significantly more individu-alistic than whites or Asians (there were too few Hispanic cases to

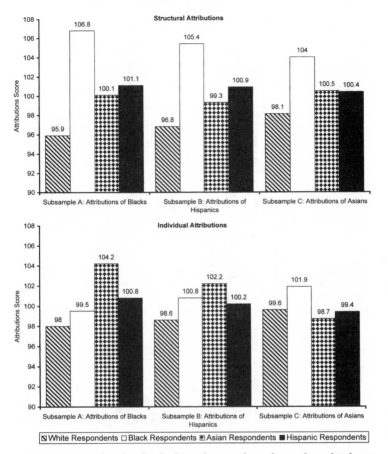

Figure 6.1. Structural and Individual Attributions by Subsample and Ethnicity
Note: See text for significance of differences across subsamples and ethnic groups.

produce significant differences). Overall, these findings indicate that individualistic attributions depend on both the ethnicity of the target group and the ethnicity of the respondent.

THE IMPACT OF RACE/ETHNICITY AND POVERTY ATTRIBUTIONS ON RACIAL POLICY ATTITUDES

Table 6.1 presents the results of regressing both racial-policy-attitude-dependent measures on race/ethnicity, structural and individual attributions, ideology, and sociodemographic variables, by subsample. Coefficients in the columns labeled "beta 1" are standardized estimates

TABLE 6.1 Regressions of Opposition to Affirmative Action on Race/Ethnicity, Poverty Attributions, and Other Variables; Standardized Coefficients and Odds Ratios

	SUBSAMPLE A: ATTRIBUTIONS OF AFRICAN AMERICANS			SUBSAMPLE B: ATTRIBUTIONS OF HISPANICS			SUBSAMPLE C: ATTRIBUTIONS OF ASIANS		
	Zero Order	β 1	β 2	Zero Order	β 1	β 2	Zero Order	β 1	β 2
	Opposition to Affirmative Action Index (OLS Regressions)								
Race/ethnicity**									
Black	-.34°	-.20°	-.15°	-.42°	-.30°	-.22°	-.39°	-.33°	-.29°
Asian	-.09†	-.07	-.01	-.23°	-.20°	-.16°	-.16°	-.12°	-.10°
Hispanic	-.19°	-.15°	-.13°	-.14°	-.13°	-.09°	-.17°	-.15°	-.13°
Structural attributions***	-.38°	-.32°	-.18°	-.40°	-.32°	-.23°	-.26°	-.27°	-.20°
Individual attributions***	.12°	.17°	.02	-.02	.09°	.00	.02	.17°	.08
Minority individualism	.17°	—	.06	.14°	—	.09°	.12°	—	.03
Minority opportunity***	.29°	—	.09°	.28°	—	.08†	.04	—	-.02
Racism is a problem	-.26°	—	-.08†	-.22°	—	.03	-.19°	—	-.06
Resentment of minorities	.40°	—	.19°	.39°	—	.22°	.36°	—	.23°
Minority threat	.18°	—	.15°	.00	—	.04	.08°	—	.08†
Political conservatism	.33°	—	.19°	.34°	—	.18°	.22°	—	.13°
Age	.02	—	.02	.07†	—	.03	.04	—	-.05
Education	-.04	—	-.08†	-.07†	—	-.04	-.04	—	-.04
Gender	.05	—	.05	.07†	—	.06	.01	—	.00
R^2		.21°	.35°		.25°	.36°		.19°	.29°

WHITES HAVE NO RESPONSIBILITY TO MAKE UP FOR PAST DISCRIMINATION AGAINST TARGET GROUP°°° (LOGISTIC REGRESSIONS)

	Zero Order	OR 1	OR 2	Zero Order	OR 1	OR 2	Zero Order	OR 1	OR 2
Race/ethnicity°°									
Black	.21°	.36°	.46°	.19°	.29°	.30°	.35°	.44°	.47°
Asian	.49°	.57°	.66	.49°	.55°	.55°	.42°	.47°	.39°
Hispanic	.56°	.67	.87	.26°	.26°	.31°	.52°	.57†	.58
Structural attributions°°°	.73°	.75°	.79°	.66°	.69°	.70°	.80°	.81°	.85°
Individual attributions°°°	1.01	1.13	1.05	.93	1.10	1.12	.94	1.11	1.05
Minority individualism	1.61	—	1.07	1.89†	—	1.85	2.39°	—	2.03°
Minority opportunity°°°	1.97°	—	1.16	1.85°	—	1.21	1.01	—	.84
Racism is a problem	.53°	—	.80	.69°	—	1.09	.65°	—	.81
Resentment of minorities	1.39°	—	1.14	1.51°	—	1.20†	1.21°	—	1.05
Minority threat	1.03	—	1.01	.95	—	1.09	1.12†	—	1.17†
Political conservatism	1.28°	—	1.09	1.14	—	.93	1.20°	—	1.31°
Age	1.01	—	1.01	1.00	—	.99	1.00	—	.99
Education	.90	—	.92	1.04	—	1.14	.97	—	1.02
Gender	.77	—	.73	1.30	—	1.49†	1.23	—	1.27
Model χ²		78.00°	82.00°		119.83°	122.43		40.81°	53.14°

†$p < = .10$ (two-tailed).
°$p \leq = .05$ (two-tailed).
°°Zero-order coefficients for race/ethnicity come from a regression of dependent variables on race/ethnicity dummies together.
°°°Variables are specific to target group.

from models that fit the ethnicity and attributions predictors only; co-efficients in the columns labeled "beta 2" are estimates from our fully specified models—that is, models that increment the beta 1 models by adding the ideology and sociodemographic factors.

RACE/ETHNICITY The comparison category for the race/ethnicity dummy variables is whites. The consistent finding across subsamples and dependent variables is that members of minority groups are more favorable than whites to policies that would reduce racial inequality and are more likely to deny that whites have no responsibility to make up for past discrimination. In general, attribution variables, racial ideology, and sociodemographic characteristics do not explain the differences between minority groups and whites.

In every case, across all six comparisons, African-American respondents are more favorable than whites toward racial policies, both before and after controls. Asians and Hispanics also differ significantly from whites on four of six comparisons before and after controls. On the second dependent variable, African Americans are consistently more likely than whites to believe that whites have a responsibility to make up for past discrimination regardless of the target group. With the notable exception of the African-American target group, Asians are also more likely than whites to believe that whites have an obligation to redress past discrimination. On the other hand, Hispanics are significantly different from whites, after controls, only when asked if whites have a responsibility to do anything about discrimination against Hispanics. In short, stratification ideology and racial ideology variables do not explain ethnic group differences in racial policy attitudes, clearly indicating that some of the differences between whites and others in opposition to race-targeted policies are due to other factors.

THE IMPACT OF STRATIFICATION IDEOLOGY VARIABLES, WITH AND WITHOUT CONTROLS FOR SOCIODEMOGRAPHIC VARIABLES The structural attributions index has a substantial zero-order correlation with racial policy attitudes for both dependent variables within each sub-sample, indicating that the more respondents believe that an ethnic group's poverty is caused by structural factors, the more they support policies that would reduce racial inequality, and the more likely they are to deny that whites have no responsibility to make up for past discrimination. In every case, this association is weakened, but not rendered nonsignificant, by controlling for race/ethnicity. In sum, belief in structural causes of poverty is an important determinant of racial policy attitudes whose impact is not explained by race/ethnicity and sociodemographic variables.

Controlling for race/ethnicity, belief in individual causes of poverty is significantly associated with the opposition to affirmative action index in all three subsamples, indicating that the impact of individualistic attributions does not depend on which racial/ethnic group one is making attributions about. However, this impact is not as strong as that for structural ideology, and it is not found for the other dependent variable.

THE IMPACT OF RACIAL IDEOLOGY AND SOCIODEMOGRAPHIC VARI- ABLES Though in the present study we are not focusing on the effects of racial ideology variables beyond controlling for dimensions known to affect policy attitudes, the findings for these variables are interesting and revealing. For the opposition to affirmative action index, the most important of the ideology variables are resentment of minorities and political conservatism, both of which have substantial zero order correlations with the dependent variable in each subsample. The resentment and conservatism variables remain the most important, or among the most important, predictors when all other variables are in the equations.[4] Otherwise, the racial ideology variables have generally weak and inconsistently significant effects on racial policy attitudes. The beliefs that racism is a problem and that members of minority groups have plenty of opportunity are not consistent predictors. Notably, neither minority threat nor the belief that minorities should be more individualistic has a proximate impact on racial policy attitudes. Since some of these variables have strong zero order associations with policy attitudes, their weakness as predictors is due to their associations with race/ethnicity, poverty attributions, resentment of minorities, conservatism, and sociodemographic factors. The findings for resentment are particularly impressive, given that the measure is poor, as noted above, and that the estimate of its effects is likely to be conservative.

Though previous studies have found age to be an important predictor of social policy attitudes, the present study does not. Nor do education and gender significantly impact attitudes toward these policies. The effects of the ideology and sociodemographic variables on respondents' views about whether or not whites have a responsibility to redress past discrimination are less consistent. Although several significant zero order correlations exist, few of these persist when controls for race/ethnicity and causal attributions are introduced. The responsibility dependent variable clearly taps a dimension of racial attitudes that is not strongly influenced by these ideology and sociodemographic factors.

THE IMPACT OF STRATIFICATION IDEOLOGY VARIABLES WITH CONTROLS FOR SOCIODEMOGRAPHIC AND RACIAL IDEOLOGY VARIABLES   As shown in the third column of each model in table 6.1, the impact of structural attributions on race-targeted policy attitudes remains statistically significant when controls are added for racial ideology, indicating that structuralism has an independent effect on race-targeted policy attitudes. In contrast, individualistic attributions have no significant impact with controls for racial ideology. Overall, these findings indicate that the impact of structuralist attributions is not due to its correlation with other attitudes, and they are consistent with previous studies that have shown that individualism does not seem to be an important determinant of racial policy attitudes.

ETHNIC GROUP–SPECIFIC EFFECTS OF INDEPENDENT VARIABLES   In an effort to uncover ethnic group differences in the effects of stratification and racial ideology variables on racial policy attitudes, we performed regression analyses (not shown) within each ethnic group (whites, African Americans, Hispanics, and Asians) that were analogous to those presented in table 6.1. Because the sample design in this study results in sample sizes for ethnic groups within subsamples that range from 64 to 269, we do not have the statistical power to do a definitive analysis of the interaction of stratification ideology and racial ideology variables with ethnicity in predicting racial policy attitudes. As a result, this part of our results can be only suggestive and should be viewed with some caution.

For both the structural and the individualistic attributions indices, we found that, in general, the pattern observed in table 6.1 is reproduced in analyses of each ethnic group. The only significant exceptions are that, among African Americans, individualistic attributions of Asian poverty increase opposition to affirmative action and individualistic attributions of Hispanic poverty increase the belief that whites should be willing to make up for past discrimination against Hispanics.

For the racial ideology variables, the general pattern of table 6.1 is also reproduced, but with two exceptions. First, political conservatism is a consistent predictor of opposition to affirmative action only among whites. Second, resentment, though a significant predictor of opposition to affirmative action for whites, Asians, and Hispanics, is not significant and is very nearly zero in magnitude among African Americans.

THE INTERACTION OF INDIVIDUALIST ATTRIBUTIONS WITH STRUC- TURAL ATTRIBUTIONS As noted above, though theory suggests that individualism and individualistic attributions should influence racial policy attitudes, research, including that in the present study, has not shown that such factors are important. This may be because research- ers have thought of individualism and structuralism as polar ends of a continuum and not as separate dimensions whose combined influence may be important. Though not important in its own right, individual- ism might increase opposition to egalitarian racial policies among those whose belief in structuralism is weak. If this is true, the effect of the interaction should be negative, indicating that as structuralism becomes stronger, the effect of individualism diminishes.

We investigated this hypothesis by adding a structuralism × indi- vidualism interaction term to each of the regression analyses pre- sented in table 6.1 (analyses not shown). This interaction term is sig- nificant ($p \leq .05$) in four of the six analyses. For the opposition to affirmative action index, the interaction term is significant in subsam- ples A and C, and for the white responsibility item, it is significant in subsamples A and B. However, in all four cases, the interaction be- tween these two variables is positive, meaning that as each variable increases, the effect of the other becomes more positive.

This is not what we expected. We did not find that individualism has a strong effect on opposition to race-targeted policies that weakens as structuralism increases. After doing additional analyses (also not shown) to investigate the exact nature of the significant interactions, we found that as individualism increases, the effect of structuralism in reducing opposition to egalitarian policies is reduced. In all four instances, structuralism is not a significant predictor of racial policy attitudes among those whose belief in individualistic attributions is strong.

CONCLUSIONS

We derive several conclusions from the analyses presented in this chapter. First, structural and individual attributions about poverty are positively correlated. These correlations are somewhat stronger among minorities than among whites, but this difference is not so great that we would argue that minorities have a dual consciousness about the causes of poverty and whites do not. In fact, both ideologies seem to coexist among whites as well as among others.

What accounts for the apparent anomaly of Americans simultaneously endorsing both structural and individual explanations of poverty? All Americans are exposed to common sources of cultural indoctrination, especially by the media, the educational system, and traditional religion. Because both sorts of messages are components of socialization, it is not surprising that people believe both. It is also possible that in general people recognize that human behavior is complex and that life conditions are produced by a multiplicity of causes. As others have noted (Hunt 1996; Kluegel and Smith 1986), structural beliefs about the causes of poverty seem to be "layered onto" (Hunt 1996) an existing individual base.

Second, whites are somewhat more likely to reject both structural and individual attributions of poverty than are members of minority groups. Put another way, consistent with Hunt's (1996) study, minorities are at once more structuralist and more individualistic than whites. We extend this finding to Asians. For the most part, the differences between whites and minorities on the structural attributions index are not explained by sociodemographic variables, supporting Hunt's group identification hypothesis in regard to group differences in attributions. The making of structural attributions about poverty is consistent regardless of target group. However, variation in individual attributions is responsive to both the ethnicity of the respondent and that of the target group, suggesting that individual attributions are somewhat more volatile than suggested by Hunt (1996).

Third, our findings indicate that structural attributions increase support for race-targeted policies across ethnic groups regardless of which group is the focus of attributions. This suggests that making structural attributions about poverty is a general belief that has the same influence on policy attitudes regardless of which group is the focus of attributions. In addition, such attributions seem to have the same influence on policy attitudes in the dominant group as they do among minority group members.

Fourth, although making individualistic attributions about poverty does not directly influence racial policy attitudes, its importance may be that it cancels the effect of structural beliefs. This conclusion stands in contrast to the position we have taken in previous work and to that taken in recent studies in the symbolic racism/racial resentment literature (Sears 1988; Kinder and Sanders 1996; Hughes 1997; Tuch and Hughes 1996a) that individualism is probably not an important determinant of racial policy attitudes. In the present study, we found that as individualism increases, the effect of structuralism decreases to nonsignificance. This is quite important, given that structural attributions are consistently the strongest influence, or among the strongest influences, on racial policy attitudes. We strongly suggest that before researchers studying racial policy attitudes abandon individualism as an important factor in racial attitudes, they fully probe the role of individualism as a moderator of the influence of other ideological dimensions.

Fifth, in spite of our poor measure of minority resentment, it emerges here, as it has in other studies (Kinder and Sanders 1996; Hughes 1997), as an important determinant of racial policy attitudes. It is also notable that our measure of minority threat is a poor predictor. Recent studies by Marylee Taylor (1998), Lincoln Quillian (1995, 1996), and Mark Fossett and Jill Kiecolt (1989) strongly suggest that feelings of threat produced by the size of minority and ethnic group populations is an important determinant of racial/ethnic attitudes. One possible reason for the differences in findings may be that we have only perceptions and these other studies have data on the relative sizes of population groups. It may be that the impact of minority population size on policy attitudes does not involve an intermediate perception of threat. Also plausible is the idea that the measure itself is a very conservative estimate of the impact of minority threat and that what is notable is that we found anything at all.

Sixth, and finally, minority groups are substantially more likely than whites to support egalitarian racial policies, even after we have controlled for structural and individualistic attributions about poverty, a variety of racial ideology dimensions, and sociodemographic variables. The differences are most consistent for African Americans, but are clearly in evidence for Hispanic and Asian Americans as well.

Because variables tapping respondents' beliefs and world views about racial matters and inequality do not explain the differences between minority groups and whites in support for egalitarian racial policy, our findings strongly suggest these differences are produced by a combination of perceived group interest and group identification. Minority group members share a group position in U.S. society that is distinct from the majority. While minority groups differ substantially from each other culturally and economically, their social and political positions have historically been very similar. We hypothesize that be-cause of their dominant position, whites do not identify with minorit-ies and do not sense that they can in any way gain from supporting egalitarian racial policies. Further research to probe the precise mech-anisms sustaining racial/ethnic differences in support for egalitarian racial policies is clearly warranted.

SEVEN It's Not Affirmative
Action, It's the Blacks

*The Continuing Relevance of
Race in American Politics*

JIM SIDANIUS
PAM SINGH
JOHN J. HETTS
CHRIS FEDERICO

A great deal of effort has been devoted to understanding the origins of popular attitudes toward race-targeted redistributive policies, such as affirmative action. Much of this work has explained these attitudes in terms of two main factors: (1) psychological antipathy or prejudice against blacks and other minority groups (e.g., Kinder and Sanders 1996; McConahay 1983; McConahay and Hough 1976; Sears 1988; Wright 1977) and (2) political ideology and values such as self-reliance, individual responsibility, fairness, and equity (Glazer 1975; Sniderman and Hagen 1985; Sniderman et al. 1991; Sniderman and Piazza 1993; Sniderman and Carmines 1997a, 1997b; Sowell 1984). Recently a number of scholars have argued that the latter has supplanted the former as the principal source of the public's opposition to race-specific policies, at least among the well-educated. Moreover, this view has been echoed by a number of public intellectuals, commentators, and politicians. Together they argue that "race-neutral" values of justice, equality, and equity are the primary determinants of public opposition to race-targeted policies—a position that has been bolstered by scholarly findings indicating only a weak association between antiblack affect and opposition to such policies.

Given the prominence of such claims in contemporary American discourse, we feel it is incumbent on us to examine the various propositions associated with this explanation of attitudes toward racial policy, an explanation that we will refer to as the *principled politics (PP) approach.* In particular, we shall focus on (1) the model's conception of "racism"; (2) its prediction that ideology and the values of individualism, fairness, self-reliance, and equality are the principal sources of opposition to various race-targeted policies; (3) its claim that racism and conservatism are essentially orthogonal to each other, especially among the educated; and (4) its presumption that education *reduces* the effect of racial concerns on the rejection of policies such as affirmative action. To be sure, others have examined the links among affect, ideology, and racial politics. However, most of these investigations have been conducted in a piecemeal fashion and do not constitute a comprehensive or systematic inquiry into the claims of the principled politics model.

Our purpose in this chapter is twofold. First, we will examine the extent to which rejection of racial policies is grounded in the political, ideological, and moral concerns of respondents. Second, we will compare the PP model to an alternative approach, *social dominance (SD) theory* (Sidanius 1993; Sidanius and Pratto 1993a; Sidanius and Pratto 1999), a model that advances a substantially different understanding of the motives underlying opposition to race-targeted policies and challenges the prevailing claim that such opposition is best understood through the prism of sovereign "political" and moral values. Instead, it argues that the desire for group dominance is among the most important motives underlying opposition to race-specific policies.

PRINCIPLED POLITICS MODEL

The PP model emerged as a critical response to symbolic racism theory, which suggested that negative affect had fused with traditional values, such as individualism and broader conservative ideological principles, to produce a new form of racism (see Sears 1988). Rejecting this claim, the PP theorists have argued that racial animus is no longer a central factor in the organization of racial policy beliefs and, more broadly, that the politics of race is about politics, not about race. For example, in *The Scar of Race,* Paul Sniderman and Thomas Piazza write:

> Prejudice has not disappeared, and in particular circumstances and segments of the society it still has a major impact. But race prejudice no longer organizes and dominates the reactions of whites; it no longer leads large numbers of them to oppose public policies to assist blacks across-the-board. It is, as we shall show, simply wrong to suppose that

the primary factor driving the contemporary arguments over the politics of race is white racism. (1993, 5)

In a more recent statement of their views, Sniderman and Edward Carmines claim that attempts to demonstrate that opposition to affirmative action is shaped by racism are "empirically false and politically self-defeating" (1997b, 471). This claim has been made somewhat plausible by the consistent finding that "racism"—defined as antiblack affect—is only weakly related to attitudes about racial policies, such as affirmative action, busing, fair housing, and so on.

How, then, are to we understand the politics of race? The answer, the PP theorists aver, lies in a set of political, ideological, and moral concerns, particularly core American beliefs about fairness, equality of opportunity, and equity. In their most recent work, *Reaching beyond Race* (1997a), Sniderman and Carmines argue that the idea of preferential treatment is considered fundamentally *unfair* by most people. Race-targeted policies unduly advantage certain groups and are perceived as violating the egalitarian rules of the game. From this angle, race-neutral considerations, such as the proper role of government and the importance of personal merit, rather than white prejudice underlie public rejection of policies like affirmative action. The debate over race-targeted policies is, therefore, no different from debates over other government policies involving issues of fairness, individual responsibility, and government activism.

The PP theorists also reject the claim that opposition to race-targeted policies is restricted to conservatives or to those less tolerant or less committed to racial equality. They note that liberals are as likely as conservatives to be "angry and upset" about policies involving preferential treatment (Sniderman and Carmines 1997b, 468). Moreover, they contend that those who are firmly committed to achieving equality for blacks are just as likely to oppose affirmative action policies. The underlying assumptions, then, are that most Americans are firmly committed to the notion of equality and, therefore, that equality is no longer a contested issue, and that opposition to preferential policies should not be seen as a manifestation of racism. In fact, say the PP theorists, it was precisely this *commitment to equality* that prompted Americans to dismantle de jure discrimination and racism in the 1960s:

Just because so many Americans are committed—imperfectly to be sure, but genuinely all the same—to the values of liberty and equality, they had no *principled* basis to object to the original civil rights move-

ment; on the contrary, so far as the Creed was relevant, it pushed them
to support equal treatment. (Sniderman and Piazza 1993, 177)

The proposition that Americans believe strongly in racial equality
and that opposition to race-specific policy is not grounded in antipathy
toward blacks has been endorsed by other "end-of-racism" commentators and scholars, most recently by Stephan and Abigail Thernstrom
in *America in Black and White* (1997).

This is not to suggest that the PP theorists completely discount the
role of racial animus in the public's reaction to race-targeted policies.
However, they note that the effects of "racism" are restricted to policies that involve the principle of "equal treatment" (e.g., fair housing
laws) or that call for sustained contact with blacks. For instance, the
authors find that there is little relationship between ideology and attitudes toward fair housing (Sniderman and Piazza 1993, 122). In contrast, social welfare (e.g., Aid to Families with Dependent Children)
and other race-conscious agendas (i.e., affirmative action) center primarily around issues of effort, fairness, and equity and not around the
color of one's skin. The relative importance of racism is thus contingent on the nature of the policy issue.

It is also contingent, according to the PP theorists, on a person's
level of intellectual sophistication. They argue that it is the less educated whose attitudes are most likely to be influenced by racial animus
and prejudice regardless of the racial policy issue. In contrast, the policy reasoning of the "cognoscenti" is governed more by political and
ideological concerns. The PP theorists develop this argument in a series of articles in which they argue that cognitive/"political" models
account for the policy choices of those best equipped to understand
abstract ideas and principles, whereas affective/"prejudice" models account for the thinking of the less sophisticated (Sniderman et al. 1986;
Sniderman, Brody, and Kuklinski 1984). Because their reasoning processes are governed by abstract ideas and principles, the educated are
more likely than the less educated to be consistent in their views
across different racial policies. To illustrate, by varying experimentally
the recipients of government assistance in their Group Opportunity
Experiment, Sniderman and his colleagues (Sniderman et al. 1991)
found that *college-educated* liberals and conservatives do not differentiate between government support for women or blacks. In contrast,
the responses of the less educated suggest a double standard, in which
government support for blacks was likely to find disfavor. But as the
authors note, poorly educated conservatives and poorly educated lib-

erals are both prone to this double standard. Thus, they conclude that it is *education* and not *ideology* that explains the racial double standard in public evaluations of redistributive policies. They claim that it is simply incorrect to say (as symbolic racism theorists have done) that conservatives are more likely to practice a double standard because of a presumed link between traditional values and racism. They state:

> It simply cannot be correct to argue that racism nowadays is driven by the values of the right if the readiness to practice a racial double standard is weakest among those who best understand those values and is strongest among those who least understand them. (Sniderman et al. 1991, 437)

They echo the claim of others that education encourages consistency across policy beliefs and has a salutary effect on racial tolerance more generally. Sniderman and Piazza write:

> Contrary to the common suggestion that formal schooling teaches people primarily the socially desirable thing to say, education is the institution in contemporary American society that contributes most powerfully to establishing genuine racial tolerance, and its contribution not only shapes how whites feel toward blacks but their willingness to treat them the same as whites. (1993, 13)

In sum, the PP model makes the following claims: (1) that Americans are strongly committed to the value of equality; (2) that opposition to policies such as affirmative action and quotas is grounded not in prejudice or racial animus, but in political and ideological values, such as individualism and fairness; (3) that conservatives are no more likely than liberals to practice a racial double standard in evaluating government-sponsored policies for different target groups; (4) that racism and political conservatism are essentially independent of one another, at least among the educated; and (5) that it is respondents' education, not their ideological orientation, that explains the differential support for policies targeted toward different groups.

SOCIAL DOMINANCE THEORY

An alternative approach to understanding public opposition to race-specific policies is the group dominance approach. While there are a number of different models of racial and ethnic conflict that can be regarded as variants of this general perspective,[1] all share three core ideas. First, societies are typically organized as group-based hierarchies, with a dominant group enjoying a disproportionate share of positive value (e.g., power, wealth, education) and at least one subordinate group suffering a disproportionate share of negative value (e.g., low-status jobs, poor health). Second, politics can be thought of as an exercise in *intergroup* competition over scarce material and symbolic resources. Third, one of the primary functions of values and ideologies (e.g., liberalism/conservatism, racism, the Protestant work ethic) is to legitimize the disproportionate allocation of desired social outcomes to the dominant group and to maintain the structural integrity of the system of group-based social hierarchy. In this chapter, the particular version of the general group dominance approach we will concern ourselves with is SD theory (see Sidanius 1993; Sidanius and Pratto 1999).

From this perspective, both the unequal distribution of value to different groups in the social system and the desire of the dominant group to maintain its privileged position make it unlikely that people from different positions in the social status hierarchy will reach complete consensus on issues of justice and equity. The SD approach asserts that one's commitment to equality is likely to be related to the social status of one's group, with members of dominant groups being more resistant to the redistribution of resources and less likely to endorse principles of equality. Moreover, SD theorists reject the PP claim that Americans—or for that matter, people from any society— are uniformly committed to equality, irrespective of their social status. Most important, SD theorists reject the claim that it is commitment to equality itself that is a source of opposition to race-targeted policies. On the contrary, SD theorists emphatically claim that it is precisely the commitment to *antiegalitarianism* that is the primary engine behind resistance to redistributive policies, such as affirmative action, especially among dominants.

The SD perspective also questions the PP claim that ideology and social values are the only or primary motives behind white opposition to race-targeted policies. Rather, it suggests that the policy attitudes and institutional preferences of dominants will tend to favor the powerful over the powerless. While ideological and moral concerns may indeed mediate dominants' attitudes toward various policies, the SD approach adds that these "race-neutral" beliefs also are shaped by a desire to maintain a position of dominance within the hierarchical social structure.

While SD and PP theorists are thus at loggerheads on many fronts, there is one important point on which they almost completely agree.

Namely, both groups of theorists argue that antiblack affect explains relatively little of the variance in public opposition to race-targeted policies. However, in contrast to the PP theorists, the SD theorists also argue that racial animus toward blacks probably *never was* the primary motive behind racial oppression in America. Rather than being motivated by negative affect, SD theorists argue that these discriminatory social policies were primarily motivated by the desire to exercise dominion, superiority, and power over the "essentialized other." More precisely, SD theorists claim that the most consistent feature of dominant group attitudes is a belief in the moral and intellectual superiority of the ingroup—a belief that may or may not be accompanied by negative affect toward subordinate groups. Consider, for instance, Pierre van den Berghe's (1967) observation that the attitudes of whites were characterized by relatively positive or neutral affect toward blacks in the slave systems of both the antebellum American South and the British Caribbean. Despite this absence of strong and widespread negative affect toward blacks, no serious scholar would argue that notions of racial superiority—or race itself—were irrelevant in that period. The SD approach thus proposes that "racism" be defined in terms of inferiority-superiority and not in terms of affective evaluations. On this basis, one can reject the PP claim that a failure to observe high correlations between antiblack affect and/or negative stereotypes and racial policy beliefs implies that racial considerations have become irrelevant. The data imply nothing of the sort. Rather, by looking at the dimension of "affect," one is simply looking in the wrong direction.

Among other things, SD theory posits the existence of a personality dimension specifically related to beliefs about group equality. This dimension, known as *social dominance orientation (SDO),* reflects the degree to which people desire unequal, dominance-oriented relationships among groups within the social system. According to SD theory, individuals who exhibit high levels of SDO are more likely to view group relations in terms of zero-sum conflict and to oppose ideologies and policies calling for a more equitable division of resources among social groups. Moreover, extensive research has shown the SDO measures to have high construct validity and reliability (Altemeyer 1998; Gray et al. 1997; Kemmelmeier, Cameron, and Chaiken 1998; McFarland and Adelson 1996; Pratto et al. 1994; Sidanius and Pratto 1999). The construct validity of SDO has been confirmed not only in the United States, but in several other nations and cultures as well, including Canada, Sweden, the former Soviet Union, Israel, the Palestinian

Territories (e.g., the West Bank and Gaza), New Zealand, Taiwan, and the People's Republic of China (see Sidanius and Pratto 1999). Research has also provided evidence for the discriminant validity of the SDO construct, clearly distinguishing it from a number of related constructs, such as conservatism, authoritarianism, racism, and interpersonal dominance (see Altemeyer 1998; McFarland and Adelson 1996; Pratto et al. 1994; Sidanius and Pratto 1999).

While much of the research undertaken by SD theorists is relevant to the claims advanced by the PP model, perhaps the most relevant of these studies concerns the relationship among racism, political conservatism, and SDO (e.g., Sidanius, Pratto, and Bobo 1996). Three findings are of particular importance here. First, when racism is defined in terms of ideologies of racial superiority—rather than simply in terms of negative affect—racism and conservatism are found to be positively associated rather than independent of one another, contrary to the claims of the PP theorists. The greater the political conservatism of respondents is, the more likely they are to endorse notions of white superiority and black inferiority. It should be noted that this positive relationship between political conservatism and racism has been found not only in the United States, but in a variety of other nations as well, including England, Holland, New Zealand, Australia, and Sweden (see Sidanius, Ekehammar, and Ross 1979; Sidanius and Pratto 1993b; Wilson and Bagley 1973). Moreover, Jim Sidanius, Felicia Pratto, and Lawrence Bobo (1996) find that the relationship between racism and conservatism disappears once SDO is partialed out. Consistent with the assumptions of SD theory, this, of course, suggests that political conservatism and racism are united by a common streak of group-based antiegalitarianism. Evidence for this contention has been found in other countries as well (e.g., Sweden; see Sidanius and Pratto 1993b).

Second, in contrast to the claims of the PP model, the relationship between racism (defined as racial superiority) and political conservatism is stronger among more well-educated respondents. The finding is also consistent with the SD model, which suggests that it is the educated who will have the most complete understanding of how various sociopolitical beliefs relate to issues of status and hierarchy within society. Therefore, it is among the educated that political ideologies can best be understood in terms of desires for group dominance.

Third, contrary to the predictions of the PP model that opposition to race-targeted policies among the educated is driven primarily by political and ideological motives, it has been found that higher levels of education are associated with an increase in the relationship between racism and SDO, on the one hand, and with affirmative action opposition, on the other, even after controlling for political conservatism. From the SD perspective, this, too, makes sense: since educated members of dominant groups should best understand how redistributive policies impinge on the material and symbolic interests of their group, their opposition is *more likely* to be grounded in the desire to maintain and enforce group-based hierarchies (see also Jackman 1978; Jackman and Muha 1984).

Perhaps the cleanest example of these SD principles one is likely to come across in concrete American politics is a pair of decisions concerning affirmative action taken by the Board of Regents of the University of California in the late 1990s. On July 20, 1995, the University of California Board of Regents decided to abolish affirmative action in student admissions on the basis of race and gender. The practice of using race as one of several criteria in admissions seemed to violate, as Governor Pete Wilson noted, "fundamental fairness, trampling individual rights to create and give preference to group rights" (*Los Angeles Times*, 21 July 1995). Echoing the arguments of the PP theorists, Wilson noted that the elimination of preferential treatment would ensure "equal opportunity" for all applicants.

However, it is noteworthy that this vigilant protection of fairness and equality seems not to have included other "targets" of preferential treatment, such as athletes, children of politicians, "legacy" admissions, and the children of large contributors to the university (i.e., "VIP set-asides"). For example, on July 18, 1998, while eschewing special admissions, the University of California Board of Regents still decided against forbidding the admission of the children of well-connected and wealthy contributors to the university, even when these children were clearly not competitive on the basis of their own academic merit. In other words, while affirmative action for blacks is now institutionally unacceptable, affirmative action for the very wealthy is institutionally acceptable. From a group dominance perspective, this decision makes perfect sense and illustrates that objections to race-based policies are not primarily grounded in ideology, political values, or abstract principles of "fairness." Rather, these institutional decisions will tend to favor the powerful over the powerless and be motivated by the desire of dominant group members to maintain their dominant positions within the hierarchical social structure.

In light of these findings, there is reason to suspect that, contrary to the claims of the PP theorists, dominance motives are likely to structure public opposition to racial policies and to have different effects depending on the targets of the policy. More specifically, the SD model would predict that the desire to maintain a group-based non-egalitarian structure is related to white opposition to affirmative action policies for blacks in particular. The reason for this prediction lies in our assumption that, although conflict over material and symbolic resources (in this society) has been organized around race, class, and gender, it is the enforcement of racial hierarchy that has involved the greatest degree of force and aggression. We would, therefore, predict SDO to be most strongly related to policy issues involving *race-targeted policies designed to benefit blacks*. Moreover, since they are best equipped to understand that race-targeted policies affect the existing character of power and status relationships, we would expect that, among the educated, SDO would be most strongly related to opposition to policies targeted for blacks, but not necessarily to policies targeted for women or the poor. Finally, while SD theorists have no doubt that whites will object to affirmative action because of its assumed "unfairness," they would also suggest that this perceived unfairness is not an exogenous variable. Rather, among whites, the perceived fairness or unfairness of affirmative action will itself be a function of group-based antiegalitarianism. In other words, affirmative action will be perceived to be "unfair" because it threatens the social dominance of whites.

Thus, the PP and SD perspectives lead to very different predictions concerning the relationship among affect, political ideology, group dominance, and racial politics. Using data from two different samples, and a combination of survey and experimental techniques, we shall attempt to answer the following questions:

1. What is the relationship between ethnic group status and commitment to values of equality? The PP model suggests that Americans are uniformly committed to the value of equality. Social dominance theory, on the other hand, would suggest that group-based antiegalitarianism is related to one's position within the ethnic hierarchy, with higher-status groups being less positively disposed toward equality.

2. What are the roles of affect and ideology in public opposition to race-targeted policies? The PP model suggests that whites'

resistance to redistributive social policies can be explained largely in terms of political ideology and norms of fairness and equity rather than antiblack affect. While SD theory also predicts that negative black affect should be of little importance, it would predict the desire for group dominance to be the primary determinant of whites' racial policy attitudes, a motive that PP theorists continue to ignore altogether.

3. What is the relationship among group dominance, political ideology, and racial policy attitudes? Since PP theorists do not see opposition to race-targeted policies as being rooted in desires for group dominance, they would predict both political ideology and policy beliefs to be independent of such motives. In contrast, the SD position suggests that political ideology and racial policy attitudes are driven by the same underlying factor, namely, SDO.

4. What is the relationship between political ideology and support for policies targeted toward different groups? Is there a double standard in public support for policies targeted toward women, blacks, and the poor? The PP model predicts that conservatives are *no more likely* than liberals to practice a racial double standard (i.e., to more strongly oppose government policies targeted for blacks than those targeted for other groups). However, based on the previously demonstrated relationship between SDO and political conservatism, the SD model would predict that conservatives are in fact more likely to practice a double standard, with the greatest opposition reserved specifically for policies targeted toward blacks.

5. What are the effects of education on public support for policies targeted toward different groups? Does intellectual sophistication eliminate the practice of a double standard? The PP model predicts that it does. The model suggests that among the educated—both liberals and conservatives—varying the recipient of the policy should have no impact on the level of support for the policy. Social dominance theory, on the other hand, would expect education to increase the practice of a racial double standard, particularly among conservatives.

6. What is the relationship between SDO and support for affirmative action policies, controlling for the effects of political conservatism? While the PP theorists ignore the SDO con-

struct altogether, the SD model predicts that the relationship between SDO and opposition to affirmative action should become stronger—not weaker—with increasing levels of education.

7. Finally, rather than being sovereign and unrelated to desires for group-based dominance, SD theory would expect perceptions of "fairness" to be strongly related to these dominance motives (i.e., SDO). Moreover, perceptions of "fairness" and "unfairness" should mediate a substantial portion of the relationship between SDO and general opposition to affirmative action.

To test these hypotheses, we relied on two data sets. The first three hypotheses were tested using a student data set collected at the University of California, Los Angeles, in 1993. A large oversample of Hispanic and African-American students in that study allowed us to examine group differences in commitment to the value of equality with a good deal of precision and statistical power. We also used this data set to assess the relationship among racism (defined as antiblack affect), ideology, and group dominance orientation as well as the relative influence of these variables on race-targeted policies. The data set had items measuring three distinct dimensions of racial policy attitudes: (1) support for government policy ensuring equal access to public accommodations, (2) generalized redistributive government policy, and (3) affirmative action policy. Thus, we could also test the claim of PP theorists that policy attitudes within each dimension are motivated by different considerations. Unfortunately, when it came to testing our remaining four hypotheses, this data set presented us with several problems. First, given that a university sample imposes a potential restriction of range on intellectual sophistication, we were unable to test one of the core claims of the PP model—namely, that increased education attenuates the impact of racism and boosts the influence of ideology on racial policy attitudes. Second, because this data set did not vary the potential recipients of government assistance or assess perceptions of "unfairness," we were unable to test for the effects of education or ideology on the practice of a racial double standard in public support for government-sponsored policy. Consequently, we assessed hypotheses 3–7 using data from a random sample of adults drawn from a much broader spectrum of the educational continuum. In addition, the study used a split-ballot methodology that allowed us to experimentally vary the potential beneficiaries of government assistance.

STUDY I: METHOD

PARTICIPANTS AND PROCEDURE

The data in study I were collected through a mail survey of 631 UCLA undergraduates (43.1 percent male, 56.9 percent female) in the fall of 1993. Hispanic and African-American students were oversampled, resulting in a final sample consisting of Asians (25.7 percent), whites (28.6 percent), Hispanics (18.2 percent), blacks (16.3 percent), and Others (11.2 percent). The median age was 21.16 years. The survey assessed student attitudes concerning multiculturalism and intergroup relations.

INDEPENDENT VARIABLES

DEMOGRAPHICS This consisted of the standard set of variables, including (1) socioeconomic status (SES), which was assessed by the use of two indices—estimated family income and self-classification of one's family into one of five social class categories ("poor," "working class," "middle-class," "upper-middle class," and "upper-class"); (2) gender (males = 1, females = 2); (3) age; and (4) American citizenship (0 = noncitizen, 1 = American citizen).

POLITICAL CONSERVATISM Conservatism was measured in the standard fashion by asking respondents to classify themselves into one of seven categories, ranging from 1 = "very liberal" to 7 = "very conservative."

PROTESTANT WORK ETHIC Endorsement of the Protestant work ethic was measured using four items (Cronbach's α = 0.75): (1) "If people work hard they almost always get what they want"; (2) "Most people who don't get ahead should not blame the system, they really have only themselves to blame"; (3) "In America, getting ahead doesn't always depend on hard work"; and (4) "Even if people work hard, they don't always get ahead."

RELATIVE AFFECT TOWARD BLACKS To assess this, respondents were first asked to indicate their feelings toward their own ethnic group and toward blacks on seven-point scales, ranging from 1 = "very negative" to 7 = "very positive." The relative-affect measure was then generated by subtracting respondents' rating of blacks from their rating of their own ethnic group.

SOCIAL DOMINANCE ORIENTATION Social dominance orientation, or group-based antiegalitarianism, was measured using the complete sixteen-item Social Dominance Orientation Scale ($\alpha = 0.89$). Respondents answered on a seven-point scale, ranging from 1 = "strongly disagree/disapprove" to 7 = "strongly agree/favor." This scale, as noted above, assesses the degree to which respondents endorse hierarchical and dominance-based relationships among salient social groups. Extensive item analysis has shown the scale to have high convergent validity, discriminant validity, and reliability (Pratto et al. 1994; see Appendix).[2]

DEPENDENT VARIABLES

Respondents were also asked to indicate their attitudes toward a range of racially relevant government policies. All items were answered on a seven-point scale, ranging from 1 = "strongly agree/favor" to 7 = "strongly disagree/disapprove." We analyzed three distinct racial policy dimensions: redistributive government policy, public accommodations policy, and affirmative action policy.

REDISTRIBUTIVE GOVERNMENT POLICY This was assessed with the following five items ($\alpha = 0.81$): (1) "Government should see to it that minorities get fair treatment in jobs"; (2) "Government should not pass laws concerning the hiring of ethnic minorities"; (3) "Government should ensure that Whites and minorities go to the same school"; (4) "Government should do what it can to improve the economic condition of poor ethnic minorities"; and (5) "Government has no business trying to improve the economic condition of poor ethnic minorities."

PUBLIC ACCOMMODATIONS POLICY This was assessed using two items ($\alpha = 0.76$): (1) "Government should ensure that minorities can go to any hotel or restaurant they can afford," and (2) "Government has no business trying to ensure minority access to hotels and restaurants."

AFFIRMATIVE ACTION POLICY This variable consisted of respondent reactions to a single item: "Affirmative Action."

STUDY I: RESULTS AND DISCUSSION

GROUP-BASED ANTIEGALITARIANISM AND ETHNIC STATUS

Principled politics theorists—like Alexis de Tocqueville, Louis Hartz, and other analysts of American liberalism before them—assume that

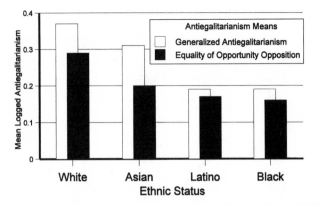

Figure 7.1. Mean Antiegalitarianism as a Function of Ethnic Status (UCLA Student Sample)

equality is among the nation's core values. In fact, they argue that the gradual demise of racial hierarchy in the United States can be attributed to Americans' universal commitment to the principle of equality. The logic of the SD model, however, suggests that we should find differential commitment to the principle of equality, with dominant groups being more in favor of hierarchical social relationships among social groups. To assess whether group-based antiegalitarianism is uniformly distributed across status lines, we conducted analyses of variance using a refined measure of group-based antiegalitarianism as the dependent variable and group status as the independent variable. A comprehensive antiegalitarianism scale was computed by using the seven items from the SDO_6 Scale (i.e., items 9–15; see Appendix; see also figure 7.1).

A look at figure 7.1 reveals the kinds of differences in group-based antiegalitarianism that SD theorists would expect. Rather than finding uniform commitment to equality, we can see that whites show relatively high levels of group-based antiegalitarianism, while Hispanics and blacks show relatively low levels of antiegalitarianism, with Asians in between ($F(3, 615) = 35.67$, $p < 10^{-12}$; $\eta = .38$; remember that these are logged values). Thus, these findings confirm that commitment to *group-based* antiegalitarianism is not uniformly distributed throughout the social system. Rather, it is strongly related to one's position within the ethnic hierarchy. To make this point even clearer and to distinguish between the issues of "equality of opportunity" (claimed to be at the core of the American Creed) and "equality of result," we used two items from the SDO Scale that deal specifically with equality of opportunity rather than equality of result (i.e., "All groups should be given an equal chance in life," and "We would have fewer problems if we treated different groups more equally"). Here endorsement of equality of opportunity was even more clearly and systematically related to the social status of the groups involved. Once again, whites were most opposed to equality of opportunity, while blacks were least opposed to equality of opportunity ($F(3, 620) = 24.73, p < 10^{-11}$; $\eta =$ .33; see figure 7.1).

CAUSAL MODELS OF THE RELATIONSHIP AMONG GROUP DOMINANCE, POLITICAL IDEOLOGY, AND RACIAL POLICY ATTITUDES

Principled politics theorists make two major arguments concerning the determinants of racial policy attitudes: (1) antiblack affect should have little or no effect on public opposition to policies such as affirmative action and racial quotas, and (2) ideological and political values should be the most important predictors of public opposition to such policies. In contrast, SD theorists argue that (1) antiblack affect should be only weakly related to public attitudes about affirmative action, (2) group-based antiegalitarianism (i.e., SDO) should be strongly associated with attitudes toward redistributive public policies (e.g., affirmative action), and (3) part of the relationship between SDO and affirmative action opposition should be mediated via seemingly "principled" ideologies, such as political conservatism and the work ethic. Moreover, this relationship should be particularly strong among the most cognitively sophisticated respondents.

In order to gauge the relative validity of these competing claims and to examine the overall degree to which each of these models actually fits the empirical data, we conducted a series of path analyses using LISREL (Jöreskog and Sörbom 1993). We restricted these analyses to the Euro-American respondents ($n = 148$), using maximum-likelihood estimates and correlation matrices as input. In each model, seven variables were considered: gender, SES, SDO, antiblack affect, political conservatism, endorsement of the Protestant work ethic, and overall opposition to a given racial public policy (e.g., public accommodations, affirmative action).

THE PRINCIPLED POLITICS MODEL For example, the PP model of white attitudes toward affirmative action is depicted in figure 7.2.[3] Following the claims of the PP theorists, this model assumes that the primary, proximal antecedents of affirmative action opposition are po-

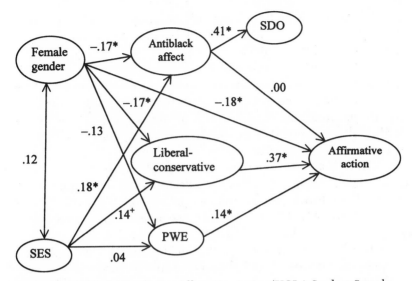

Figure 7.2. PP Model Predicting Affirmative Action (UCLA Student Sample, Whites Only). $\chi^2 = 43.93$, df = 8, $p < .0001$, AGFI = .76; $^\circ p < .05$.

litical conservatism and commitment to the Protestant work ethic rather than antiblack affect. These two ideological variables in turn are assumed to be driven by gender and SES. In the spirit of the PP model, SDO is assumed to have no effect whatsoever on whites' attitudes about affirmative action, although it is allowed to have a relationship with antiblack affect.

Consistent with the PP perspective, both political conservatism and the Protestant work ethic were significant predictors of affirmative action opposition ($\beta = 0.37$, $p < .01$; and $\beta = 0.14$, $p < .01$, respectively). Also not surprisingly, females were significantly less opposed to affirmative action than males ($\gamma = -.18$, $p < .05$). Female gender and SES in turn were significant predictors of political conservatism ($\gamma = -.17$, $p < .05$; and $\gamma = 0.14$, $p < .05$, respectively). Females had significantly lower levels of antiblack affect than males ($\gamma = -.17$, $p < .05$), while SES was positively correlated with antiblack affect ($\beta = 0.18$, $p < .05$). Moreover, consistent with expectations, SDO was found to be significantly and strongly related to antiblack affect ($\beta = 0.41$, $p < .05$). However, neither gender nor SES was found to have significant relationships with endorsement of the work ethic ($\gamma = -.13$ and $\gamma = 0.04$, respectively).

Despite the fact that these relationships are generally consistent with the predictions of the PP model, an examination of the goodness of fit statistics reveals that the model did not provide an acceptable or satisfactory fit to the empirical data (i.e., $\chi^2 = 43.93$, df $= 8$, $p < .0001$; AGFI $= 0.76$; see also table 7.1).

Two additional variations of the PP model were estimated as well: one substituting attitudes toward redistributive government policy for the affirmative action variable and another substituting attitudes toward public accommodations for the affirmative action measure. As with the affirmative action model, while the individual path coefficients were relatively congruent with the PP perspective, neither of these models was found to give a satisfactory fit to the empirical data as a whole (redistributive government policy model: $\chi^2 = 62.19$, df $= 9$, $p < .0001$; AGFI $= 0.72$; public accommodations model: $\chi^2 = 43.69$, df $= 9$, $p < .0001$; AGFI $= 0.79$; see table 7.1).

Thus, while the principled politics models are certainly correct in stressing the importance of political conservatism and the Protestant work ethic as important determinants of people's racial policy attitudes across all three racial policy domains (see table 7.1), these models are clearly not adequate descriptions of the interrelationships among these attitude variables as a whole. Inspection of the standardized residuals for each of the three variations of PP model reveals that the covariances between SDO, on the one hand, and political conservatism, the work ethic, and affirmative action opposition, on the other, are poorly captured by the general principled politics model, suggesting a more substantial causal role for SDO than PP theorists are willing to tolerate. This, of course, points toward the SD model as an alternative.

THE SOCIAL DOMINANCE MODEL   The results for the model suggested by the SD perspective are shown in figure 7.3. In this model, SDO rather than political conservatism and the Protestant work ethic is given the pivotal role; it is assumed to directly drive political conservatism, work ethic endorsement, antiblack affect, and affirmative action opposition. Social dominance orientation in turn is assumed to be influenced by gender and SES. As in the principled politics model, conservatism and work ethic endorsement are also assumed to drive affirmative action opposition. Rather than being seen as the principal antecedents of opposition to affirmative action, however, they are also assumed to *mediate* the effects of a more important underlying variable, namely, SDO. Most important, and consistent with the spirit of

TABLE 7.1 Total and Indirect Effects of Political Conservatism, Protestant Work Ethic, and SDO on Attitudes toward Redistributive Government Policy According to Principled Conservatism and Social Dominance Theoretical Path Models (UCLA Student Sample, Whites Only)

Variables	PRINCIPLED CONSERVATISM MODELS			SOCIAL DOMINANCE MODELS		
	Redistributive Govt. Policy	Public Accommodations Policy	Affirmative Action Policy	Redistributive Govt. Policy	Public Accommodations Policy	Affirmative Action Policy
Political conservatism	.43°°	.21°°	.37°°	.37°°	.16°°	.32°°
Protestant work ethic	.29°°	.14	.14°	.26°°	.14	.11
SDO	N.A.	N.A.	N.A.	.55°°	.29°°	.35°°
(indirect effect)				**.21°°**	**.11°°**	**.16°°**
Antiblack affect	.19°°	.17°°	.00	N.A.	N.A.	N.A.
Total model fit						
χ²	62.19	43.69	43.93	10.80	12.09	7.63
df	9	9	8	9	9	8
p <	.0001	.0001	.0001	.29	.21	.47
Adjusted goodness of fit index	.72	.79	.76	.94	.93	.95
R²	.43	.13	.25	.54	.15	.27

Note: Bold figures indicate indirect effect.

° p < .05.   °° p < .01.

SD theory, antiblack affect is given *no role* in predicting racial policy attitudes.

The standardized parameter estimates displayed in figure 7.3 are in general quite consistent with the suggestions of SD theory. Social dominance orientation significantly and strongly predicted (1) political conservatism ($\beta = 0.39, p < .05$), (2) endorsement of the Protestant work ethic ($\beta = 0.31, p < .05$), and (3) antiblack affect ($\beta = 0.41, p < .05$). In addition, SDO was found to have a direct effect on affirmative action opposition ($\beta = 0.19, p < .05$). Also consistent with SD theory (and a great deal of other research) was the finding that women had consistently lower levels of SDO than men ($\gamma = -.23, p < .05$; for other examples, see Altemeyer 1998; Sidanius and Pratto 1999; Sidanius, Pratto, and Bobo 1994; Sidanius, Pratto, and Brief 1995). SDO also increased with SES ($\gamma = 0.22, p < .05$). Consistent with both the PP and the SD positions, political conservatism did make a substantial direct contribution to affirmative action opposition ($\beta = 0.32, p < .05$). However, endorsement of the work ethic did not make a significant independent contribution to affirmative action opposition ($\beta = .11$).

Consistent with the claims of SD theory, SDO was also found to make a significant *indirect* contribution to affirmative action opposition via the legitimizing ideologies of political conservatism and the Protestant work ethic (indirect effect [IE] = 0.16, $p < .01$).[4] Most important, and contrary to the claims of the PP theorists, when one considers the total effect (TE) of SDO on affirmative action opposition among whites (i.e., direct and indirect effects), we see that this effect is at least as powerful as that exerted by "principled" objections (i.e., political conservatism; TE = .35 versus TE = .32).

SDO not only exhibited a significant indirect effect (via political conservatism) on affirmative action opposition, but significant indirect effects on the other two racial policy attitudes as well (i.e., redistributive government policy: IE = .21, $p < .01$; public accommodations: IE = .11, $p < .01$; see table 7.1). Even with respect to these two other models, the total effect of SDO on policy attitudes consistently surpassed that of either political conservatism or the Protestant work ethic (see table 7.1). Moreover, as one can see in table 7.1, the three SD models were always able to explain a larger proportion of the variance of the racial policy attitudes than the corresponding PP models (i.e., .52 versus 43, .15 versus .13, .27 versus .25), even using the same number of degrees of freedom.

It is also important to note that, net of the effects of the other variables, there was not a single case in which antiblack affect made a significant independent contribution to any of the racial policy attitudes; it is thus safe to say that it can be ignored. In addition, both political conservatism and SDO were always found to be strongly related to whites' racial policy attitudes regardless of the attitude domain in question.

AFFIRMATIVE ACTION SUPPORT AND EQUALITY OF OPPORTUNITY NORMS

It should also be pointed out that SDO is very closely associated with generalized group-based antiegalitarianism. However, in contrast to the expectations of the PP theorists, it is distinctly *not* the case that egalitarianism (i.e., SDO) is associated with opposition to affirmative action, but exactly the opposite. That is, whites reject affirmative action precisely because they reject the principles of egalitarianism. Once again, the same general differences were found even when restricting ourselves to the construct of "equality of opportunity" (using the same two items as above). Rather than being associated with rejection of affirmative action, endorsement of equality of opportunity was associated with support of affirmative action ($r = .29, p < 10^{-4}$).[5]

Finally, in contrast to all three of the models derived from the PP perspectives, the overall fit of the SD model to the data was excellent with respect to all three racial policy attitudes: affirmative action policy: $\chi^2 = 7.63$, df $= 8, p = 0.47$; AGFI $= 0.95$; redistributive government policy: $\chi^2 = 10.80$, df $= 9, p = 0.29$; AGFI $= 0.94$; public accommodations policy: $\chi^2 = 12.09$, df $= 9, p = 0.21$; AGFI $= 0.93$.

On the whole, the SD model provided a substantially better fit to the empirical data than the PP model. These results thus offer further support for the arguments that racial policy attitudes are not merely a function of ideology and traditional values, but are also very strongly driven by group-dominance motives; that ideology and traditional values are themselves influenced by group-dominance motives; and that opposition to affirmative action is driven not by devotion to the norm of equality of opportunity, but by its exact opposite.

Thus far, we have focused our attention on three issues: (1) Americans' commitment to the value of equality; (2) the essential irrelevance of antiblack affect to racial policy attitudes; and (3) the relative ability of the PP and SD models to account for the relationships among variables such as racism, political ideology, social dominance, and racial policy attitudes.

However, while the student data set did allow us to explore differ-

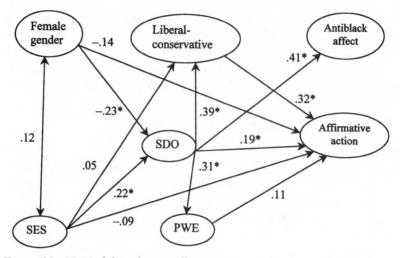

Figure 7.3. SD Model Predicting Affirmative Action (UCLA Student Sample, Whites Only). $\chi^2 = 7.63$, df $= 8, p < .47$, AGFI $= .95;$ °$p < .05$.

ent racial policy domains within a relatively well-educated population, it did not allow us to assess the significance of education in attenuating the impact of racial considerations or to test the effects of the specific target of affirmative action on opposition to affirmative action. Nor did it permit us to assess the role of perceived "unfairness" in opposition to such policies. To answer these additional questions, we now turn to an additional set of data.

STUDY II: METHOD

PARTICIPANTS AND PROCEDURE

The data for study II come from the 1996 Los Angeles County Social Survey (LACSS), conducted every year by the Institute for Social Science Research (ISSR) at the University of California, Los Angeles. The LACSS is an omnibus phone survey of the residents of Los Angeles County assessing approximately two hundred variables, including such things as standard demographics, feeling thermometers concerning numerous social groups, general ethnicity attitudes, political ideology, and support for policies targeted toward various social groups. The 1996 sample consisted of 697 randomly selected adults, contacted by phone using random-digit dialing, from Los Angeles County during the spring of 1996. Of these, 206 were white, 209 were black, 43 were Asian, 205 were Hispanic, and 34 were categorized as Others. The

Hispanic and black populations were oversampled. Since an experimental design was employed, in which separate portions of the sample were asked their attitudes toward support for government-sponsored policies for women, blacks, or the poor, the sample size was reduced for portions of the analyses. As in study I, the analyses in study II were performed with a combined sample of whites, Asians, and Hispanics.

INDEPENDENT VARIABLES

DEMOGRAPHICS This cluster consisted of the following variables: (1) estimated family income, (2) gender (men = 1, women = 2), and (3) participant's level of education (from 1 = "did not graduate from high school" to 6 = "graduate degree").

AFFECT TOWARD WOMEN, AFFECT TOWARD BLACKS, AND AFFECT TOWARD THE POOR These were measured using standard feeling thermometers. Respondents indicated their feelings about each group on a scale ranging from 1 = "cold/not favorable" to 100 = "warm/favorable."[6]

POLITICAL CONSERVATISM This was assessed using the following item: "Would you describe your political views in general as very conservative, somewhat conservative, neither conservative or liberal, somewhat liberal, very liberal."

PROTESTANT WORK ETHIC Protestant work ethic endorsement was assessed with two items (Cronbach's $\alpha = 0.56$): (1) "Although there was discrimination in the past, today members of all groups have an equal opportunity to succeed," and (2) "Success, or one's achievement in American society, depends primarily on individual merit." Both questions were answered on four-point scale, ranging from 1 = "strongly agree" to 4 = "strongly disagree."

SOCIAL DOMINANCE ORIENTATION This was again assessed using the complete sixteen-item Social Dominance Orientation Scale ($\alpha = 0.77$). All items used a four-point response scale, ranging from 1 = "strongly agree" to 4 = "strongly disagree."

PERCEIVED FAIRNESS OF AFFIRMATIVE ACTION Respondents were asked to indicate the degree to which their feelings about affirmative action were governed by the policy's perceived "unfairness." The specific question read: "People give many reasons for their position on affirmative action. I am going to read some of the reasons for each one. Please tell me how important this reason is for your position on affirmative action." The unfairness alternative read: "Affirmative action is basically unfair." Respondents gave their answers on a five-point scale, ranging from 1 = "not at all important reason" to 5 = "very important reason."

DEPENDENT VARIABLES

GENERAL SUPPORT FOR AFFIRMATIVE ACTION All respondents, regardless of the split-ballot group they were in, initially responded to a single item assessing their general (i.e., non-target-specific) attitude toward affirmative action: "In general, do you support or oppose affirmative action?" This question was answered on a scale ranging from 1 = "strongly support" to 4 = "strongly oppose."

ATTITUDES TOWARD TARGET-SPECIFIC AFFIRMATIVE ACTION As noted above, a split-ballot design was employed to experimentally manipulate the affirmative-action target group that respondents were asked about, such that separate subsamples of respondents were queried about their attitudes regarding affirmative action for women ($n = 151$), affirmative action for blacks ($n = 168$), and affirmative action for the poor ($n = 178$). All items used a four-point response scale, ranging from 1 = "strongly support" to 4 = "strongly oppose." Each of the three experimental groups responded only to questions specific to their particular target:

1. *Women as Target.* Respondents in this split-ballot group were asked about their attitudes toward affirmative action for women using three items $\alpha = 0.91$): (a) "Affirmative Action for women in university admissions," (b) "Affirmative Action for women in job hiring and promotion," and (c) "Affirmative Action for women in awarding government contracts."
2. *Blacks as Target.* Respondents in the split-ballot group were asked about their attitudes toward affirmative action for blacks using three items ($\alpha = 0.94$): (a) "Affirmative Action for blacks in university admissions," (b) "Affirmative Action for blacks in job hiring and promotion," and (c) "Affirmative Action for blacks in awarding government contracts."
3. *The Poor as Target.* Respondents in the split-ballot group were asked about their attitudes toward affirmative action for the poor using only two items ($\alpha = 0.89$): (a) "Affirmative

Action for the poor in university admissions" and (b) "Affirmative Action for the poor in hiring and promotion."

STUDY II: RESULTS

GROUP-BASED ANTIEGALITARIANISM AND ETHNIC STATUS

Once again, if, as the PP protagonists claim, commitment to equality is a basic and widely shared value in American society, then we should find no significant differences in antiegalitarianism among various ethnic groups. On the other hand, if the basic claim of SD theory is correct, we should find significant differences between groups in antiegalitarianism, with the traditionally subordinate American ethnic group (i.e., blacks) showing the lowest SDO scores and the traditionally dominant ethnic group (i.e., whites) exhibiting the highest SDO scores. To explore this issue, we conducted a one-way ANOVA on native-born American citizens from the four major ethnic groups (i.e., whites, Asians, Latinos, and blacks). Consistent with expectations, the mean logged antiegalitarianism scores for the two high-status groups were relatively high (i.e., whites and Asians: $M = .17$ for both groups), while the mean logged antiegalitarianism scores for the two low-status groups were relatively low (i.e., Latinos: $M = .13$; blacks: $M = .08$). As with the student sample, these mean differences were clearly significant ($F(3, 403) = 14.07$, $p < .001$, $\varepsilon = .31$). Similarly, the same general types of group differences were found even when using the equality of opportunity subscale ($F(3, 427) = 5.09, p < .002, \varepsilon = .19$).

PRINCIPLED OBJECTIONS, ANTIBLACK AFFECT, SOCIAL DOMINANCE ORIENTATION, INTELLECTUAL SOPHISTICATION, AND RACIAL POLICY ATTITUDES

A core claim of the PP theorists is that higher education attenuates the relationship between racism—which they, once again, define as antiblack affect—and both political conservatism and attitudes toward affirmative action. That is, the relationship between antiblack affect, on the one hand, and ideology and racial policy beliefs, on the other, should decrease in strength with increasing intellectual sophistication. In contrast, the SD perspective expects the opposite: that is, that education should strengthen the relationship between political conservatism and desires for group dominance.

To examine these questions, we first examined the relationship between political conservatism and the work ethic, on the one hand, and antiblack affect and SDO, on the other, at two different levels of intellectual sophistication. To create the education distinction, we divided the sample into those with some college education or less and those with a college degree. Given the strong association between ethnicity and education—as well as the fact that this aspect of the PP model was primarily framed in terms of American whites—we restricted these analyses to the Euro-American subsample. With respect to both low- and high-educated respondents, we performed two separate regression analyses where political conservatism and the work ethic were regressed on antiblack affect and SDO (see table 7.2).

The results of these analyses confirmed previous findings (see Sidanius et al. 1996) and were completely inconsistent with the claims of the PP position. Rather than SDO being more highly related to political conservatism and the work ethic at low levels of education, the exact opposite was the case. While neither antiblack affect nor SDO made significant contributions to either political conservatism or the work ethic among poorly educated whites, SDO in particular did make a significant net contribution to both political conservatism and the work ethic among highly educated whites (i.e., $\beta = .24$ and $\beta = .25$, respectively; see table 7.2).

Similarly, while both antiblack affect and SDO did make significant and independent contributions to opposition to affirmative action among poorly educated whites (B = .01 and B = 2.30, respectively; $R^2_{adj.} = .11$), this relationship, at least with respect to SDO, was even stronger rather than weaker among highly educated whites (B = 3.47, $R^2_{adj.} = .18$). Clearly, this implies that SDO is an even more important motive beyond white opposition to affirmative action among the well-educated than among those less well-educated.

DOES THE TARGET OF AFFIRMATIVE ACTION MATTER? IDEOLOGY, EDUCATION, AND THE PRACTICE OF A DOUBLE STANDARD IN PUBLIC OPPOSITION TO AFFIRMATIVE ACTION POLICIES

The above analyses suggest not that education attenuates the impact of group dominance motives on social attitudes, but rather that it has the exact opposite effect. These results were at such odds with the PP thesis that we undertook a more detailed examination of the effects of education by essentially replicating a prominent study conducted by the PP theorists (Sniderman et al. 1991). The purpose of this analysis was to examine the relationship between education and "racism," which, according to PP theorists, can be inferred by the practice of a racial double standard in public opposition to government-sponsored

TABLE 7.2 Political Conservatism, Protestant Work Ethic, and Opposition to Affirmative Action Regressed on Antiblack Affect and SDO for Low and High Levels of Education (LACSS Sample, White Adults Only)

Dependent variable	LOW EDUCATION		HIGH EDUCATION	
	Antiblack Affect	Social Dominance	Antiblack Affect	Social Dominance
Political conservatism				
N	87		97	
Product-moment r	.03	.03	.26°°	.32°°
Unstandardized B	−.003	.44	.01	2.32°°
Standardized β	−.03	.04	.15	.24
$R^2_{adj.}$	.00		.09°	
Work ethic				
N	86		98	
Product-moment r	.11	.04	.09	.21°°
Unstandardized B	.005	.05	−.002	1.93°
Standardized β	.11	.01	−.04	.25
$R^2_{adj.}$	.00		.04+	
Affirmative action				
N	84		95	
Product-moment r	.26°°	.31°°	.29°°	.43°°
Unstandardized B	.012+	2.30°°	.01	3.47°°
Standardized β	.19	.26	.13	.38
$R^2_{adj.}$	.11°°		.18°°	

$+p < 10.$ $°p < .05.$ $°°p < .01.$

policies, where poorly educated respondents reserve their strongest opposition to these policies for cases in which they are targeted specifically for blacks. More specifically, the PP theorists argue (1) that this double standard is restricted primarily to more poorly educated respondents, suggesting that racism is more prevalent in the policy reasoning of the less educated, and (2) that among the less sophisticated, both liberals and conservatives are equally likely to practice a double standard.

To examine these hypotheses, we conceptually replicated the Group Opportunity Experiment (Sniderman et al. 1991), experimentally varying the recipients of government assistance (specifically, affirmative action programs) such that one-third of the respondents in our analysis were asked their opinions about government-sponsored policies assisting women, one-third about policies assisting blacks, and one-third about policies assisting the poor. We then performed a series of two- and three-way analyses of variance to examine the effects of target group (i.e., women, blacks, or the poor), ideology, and education on opposition to affirmative action policies.[7]

The PP model contends that conservatives will uniformly oppose such policies, *regardless of the beneficiaries of the policies,* since conservative opposition to government-sponsored policies is grounded primarily in the principles of equity and fairness. Furthermore, such principle-driven opposition to affirmative action should be more evident among the well-educated than among the poorly educated. To test this claim, we performed two-way ANOVAs at two different levels of education: (1) a low education level indicating some college or less and (2) a high education level indicating a college degree or higher. Each of these analyses examined opposition to affirmative action as a function of (1) the beneficiary of the policies (i.e., women, blacks, or the poor) and (2) the ideological orientation of the respondent (i.e., liberals versus conservatives). In order to define the two ideological groups, the respondents were bifurcated into a conservative group ($n = 196$), consisting of those respondents who described themselves as "very conservative" or "somewhat conservative," and a liberal group ($n = 178$), consisting of those respondents who described themselves as "very liberal" or "somewhat liberal." Respondents who described themselves as "neither conservative or liberal" were excluded from the analyses. The results of these analyses are found in figure 7.4.

At first blush, the results appear to be consistent with the PP position in essentially three ways. First, conservatives were generally more opposed to affirmative action than liberals ($F(1, 362) = 11.15, p < .001; \beta = .16$).[8] Second, highly educated respondents were more opposed to affirmative action than poorly educated ones ($F(1, 326) = 16.01, p < .001; \beta = .20$).[9] Third, there was a significant education-by-ideology interaction effect. Well-educated conservatives were *particularly* opposed to affirmative action ($F(1, 362) = 7.10, p < .001$).

However, a closer inspection reveals that the data were clearly inconsistent with the core claims of the PP position. First and foremost, in complete contrast to the claims of the PP position, the nonblack public's attitudes about affirmative action were *not* independent of the beneficiaries of affirmative action. Rather, the nonblack respondents were least opposed to affirmative action when the beneficiaries were women ($m = 1.83$) and most opposed when the beneficiaries were blacks ($m = 2.30; F(1, 362) = 7.71, p < .001; \beta = .19$). This pattern was essentially the same for both male and female respondents. As one can see in figure 7.4, this target effect was found at both low and high levels of education (i.e., $F(1, 235) = 4.68, p < .01$; and $F(1,$

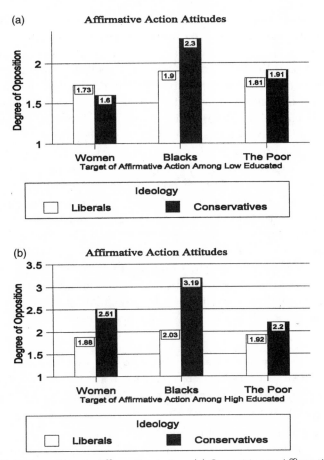

Figure 7.4. Opposition to Affirmative Action. (a) Opposition to Affirmative Action as a Function of the Target of Affirmative Action and the Political Ideology of the Respondents Among the Low Education Subsample (Los Angeles County Random Sample). (b) Affirmative Action Opposition as a Function of the Target of Affirmative Action and Political Ideology of the Respondents among the High Education Subsample (Los Angeles County Random Sample).

125) $= 3.63$, $p < .03$, respectively). Moreover, a comparison of the effect sizes associated with this target effect shows that discrimination against blacks was, if anything, even stronger among the relatively well-educated than among the relatively poorly educated (i.e., $\beta = .22$ versus $\beta = .19$, respectively).

The data were not kind to other core PP arguments regarding the relationship among ideology, education, and the practice of a double standard in opposition to affirmative action either. In particular, the data revealed a significant interaction between the target of affirmative action and the respondents' ideology, such that the target of affirmative action did not have a strong effect on the degree of affirmative action opposition among liberals (women: $m = 1.79$; the poor: $m = 1.86$; blacks: $m = 1.95$), while simultaneously having a substantial effect on affirmative action opposition among conservatives (women: $m = 1.87$; the poor: $m = 2.01$; blacks: $m = 2.62$; effect sizes: $\beta = .07$ versus $\beta = .31$, respectively).[10] Even more revealing, rather than being most pronounced among poorly educated conservatives, this tendency toward racial discrimination was most pronounced among well-educated conservatives (see figure 7.4). Thus, while conservatives are indeed more opposed to affirmative action than liberals, they are particularly opposed to affirmative action when blacks are the beneficiaries and are especially so when they are themselves well educated.[11] Furthermore, the same overall pattern was found even when restricting the analyses to whites. While these findings are clearly inconsistent with the PP model, they do support the contentions of the SD model.

SUPPORT FOR GOVERNMENT-SPONSORED POLICIES FOR WOMEN, BLACKS, AND THE POOR AS A FUNCTION OF AFFECT, POLITICAL CONSERVATISM, SDO, AND EDUCATIONAL ACHIEVEMENT

The above findings suggest (1) that public opposition to government-sponsored policies is greatest when these policies are targeted toward blacks, (2) that this differential pattern of opposition is especially strong among conservatives, and (3) that educational sophistication does not eliminate this double standard.

This alerts us to the possibilities that different motivations may shape policy positions toward different target groups and that different motivations may shape the policy positions of respondents across different categories of intellectual sophistication. In order to examine these issues, we performed separate regression analyses for each of the three target groups. In each case, attitudes toward affirmative action for the group in question were regressed on several relevant predictors, including demographics, affect toward the target group, conservatism, the Protestant work ethic, and SDO. Analyses were performed at both levels of educational sophistication. The results are found in table 7.3.

TABLE 7.3 Degree of Opposition to Affirmative Action as a Function of Affirmative Action Target, Education Level, and Predictor Variables (LACSS Sample 2: All Nonblack Adults)

Variables	Target: Women			Target: Blacks			Target: Poor People		
	TOTAL	LOW ED	HIGH ED	TOTAL	LOW ED	HIGH ED	TOTAL	LOW ED	HIGH ED
Female gender	-.05	-.06	-.04	.01	.00	.03	-.01	.04	-.10
	(-.10)	(-.13)	(-.07)	(.02)	(.00)	(.06)	(-.01)	(.09)	(-.16)
Education	.15°	N.A.	N.A.	.10°	N.A.	N.A.	.09	N.A.	N.A.
	(.28)			(.16)			(.04)		
SES	-.04	.15	-.25	.16	.18	.28	.07	.12	.30
	(-.03)	(.10)	(-.17)	(.11)	(.13)	(.17)	(.05)	(.08)	(.19)
"Whiteness"	.63°	.73°	.49°	.35°	.40°	.54°	.52°	.70°	.37°
	(.33)	(.38)	(.23)	(.17)	(.21)	(.24)	(.25)	(.33)	(.17)
Affect	-.05	.00	-.07	-.01	-.01	-.09	-.01	.00	-.01
	(-.07)	(-.05)	(-.28)	(-.11)	(-.17)	(-.11)	(-.10)	(-.01)	(-.17)
Protestant work ethic	.20°	-.02	.42°	.04	-.12	.33°	-.04	-.21	.07
	(.18)	(-.02)	(.40)	(.03)	(-.10)	(.25)	(-.03)	(-.15)	(.07)
Political conservatism	.07	-.04	.11	.22°	.18°	.22°	.05	-.07	.07
	(.03)	(-.05)	(.11)	(.27)	(.23)	(.25)	(.06)	(-.02)	(.06)
SDO	.82	.26	.38	2.46°	1.65	3.99°	1.04	.33	1.36
	(.10)	(.09)	(.04)	(.28)	(.19)	(.42)	(.12)	(.04)	(.14)
N	128	81	47	133	80	53	147	87	58
R^2_{adj}	.20°	.11°	.26°	.21°	.10°	.33°	.09°	.08	.09

Note: Entries are unstandardized regression coefficients (standardized regression coefficients).
°$p < .05$.   °°$p < .01$.

Looking first at the results for the total sample, negative affect toward the target group fails to make a significant independent contribution to affirmative action opposition in all three cases (i.e., women, blacks, or the poor; B = −.05, B = −.01, B = −.01, all n.s.).[12] Once again, this suggests that affect toward a particular group tells one relatively little about policy attitudes with respect to that group.

A second broad pattern emerged in analyses using a dummy "white ethnicity" variable, in which the effects of being white were contrasted with the effects of membership in all other ethnic categories (primarily Latino).[13] We should, first of all, note the relatively strong and consistent influence of "white" ethnic status. Even after considering all of the other demographic and ideological factors, being white was consistently and relatively strongly associated with opposition to affirmative action regardless of the target of such policies. Furthermore, there was no consistent trend showing that this "whiteness effect" was smaller among those with lower levels of education. However, it is best that these educational analyses be interpreted with some caution due to the relatively small sample sizes involved.

The third broad trend of note in these results is the finding that, besides white identity, no single factor seemed to have a uniform net effect on affirmative action opposition across all targets. Consistent with the PP position, among the highly educated the Protestant work ethic made an independent contribution to opposition to affirmative action for women (B = .42, $p < .05$) and blacks (B = .33, $p < .05$). However, this effect failed to appear with respect to the poor (B = .07, n.s.). Similarly, while political conservatism was related to opposition to government policies for blacks among both the low and the high education groups (B = .18, $p < .05$; and B = .22, $p < .05$, respectively), this variable failed to have any significant effect on support for affirmative action with respect to either women or the poor regardless of the respondent's educational sophistication.

The results also showed some support for the SD perspective. Even after controlling for all other variables, SDO still made a relatively strong contribution to affirmative action opposition with respect to blacks (B = 2.46, $p < .01$). Furthermore, in direct contradiction to the spirit of the PP perspective, SDO was a more powerful predictor of affirmative action opposition among the well-educated than among those less well-educated (B = 3.99 versus B = 1.65, respectively). However, SDO was not significantly related to affirmative action opposition for women or the poor (B = .82 and B = 1.04, n.s.).

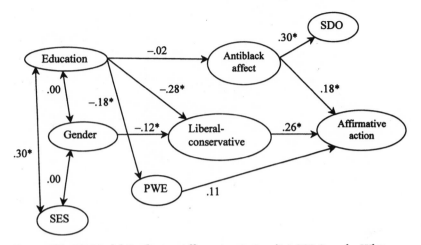

Figure 7.5. PP Model Predicting Affirmative Action (LACSS Sample, Whites Only). $\chi^2 = 38.34$, df $= 16$, $p < .001$, AGFI $= .87$; $^*p < .05$.

A COMPARISON OF CAUSAL MODELS: THE RELATIONSHIP AMONG GROUP DOMINANCE, POLITICAL IDEOLOGY, AND RACIAL POLICY ATTITUDES

As in study I, we estimated a series of path-analytic models in order to compare the predictions and overall adequacy of the general PP and SD models. Once again, these more detailed analyses used only the white respondents ($N = 148$). Maximum-likelihood estimates were once again used, and correlation matrices served as input for all models. In each model, seven variables were considered: gender, SES, SDO, antiblack affect, political conservatism, endorsement of the Protestant work ethic, and overall opposition to affirmative action.

THE PRINCIPLED POLITICS MODEL The results for the PP model are shown in figure 7.5; disturbances and error terms are not shown. The structure of this model is similar to the one tested in study I. In partial support of the PP perspective, conservatism was positively associated with opposition to affirmative action ($\beta = 0.26$, $p < .05$). However, while the work ethic (PWE) did have a positive net relationship with affirmative action attitudes, this relationship was not quite statistically significant ($\beta = 0.11$). Moreover, while antiblack affect did have a positive net relationship with affirmative action opposition ($\beta = 0.18$, $p < .05$), this effect was nonetheless smaller than that associated with

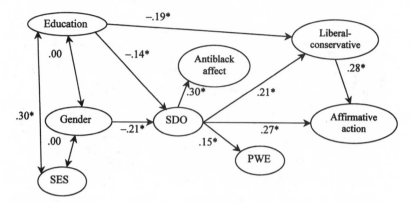

Figure 7.6. SD Model Predicting Affirmative Action (LACSS Sample, Whites Only). $\chi^2 = 21.77$, df = 16, $p < .15$, AGFI = .93; $°p < .05$.

political ideology. Finally, the overall fit of the model to the data was less than adequate ($\chi^2 = 38.34$, df = 16, $p < .001$; AGFI = 0.87). As was the case with the PP model in study I, an examination of the standardized residuals reveals that the covariances between SDO, on the one hand, and conservatism, the work ethic, and opposition to affirmative action, on the other, were not well accounted for by this model, again suggesting a set of relationships closer to those proposed by the SD model.

THE SOCIAL DOMINANCE MODEL The results for the SD model are displayed in figure 7.6. The overall structure of this model closely resembles the version examined in study I. Consistent with the expectations of SD theory, SDO was related to political conservatism ($\beta = 0.21$, $p < .05$), the work ethic ($\beta = 0.15$, $p < .05$), antiblack affect ($\beta = 0.30$, $p < .05$), and affirmative action opposition ($\beta = 0.27$, $p < .05$). Furthermore, SDO not only had a substantial direct effect on affirmative action opposition, but also had a statistically significant indirect effect on affirmative action opposition via its effect on conservatism (IE = .06, $p < .05$). This suggests that conservatism significantly mediates the relationship between social dominance and opposition to affirmative action. Furthermore, just as in study I, this also implies that, contrary to the PP perspective, group dominance motives are every bit as powerful as "political" and "principled" motives in determining whites' attitudes about affirmative action (TE = .33 versus TE = .28, respectively).

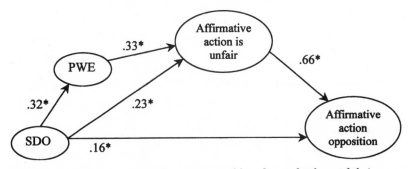

Figure 7.7. SD/Fairness Model (LACSS, Highly Educated White Adults). $\chi^2 = 1.23$, df $= 1$, $p < .27$, AGFI $= .94$; $^*p < .05$.

In contrast to the PP model, the overall fit of this model to the data was quite good ($\chi^2 = 21.77$, df $= 16$, $p < 0.15$; AGFI $= 0.93$), thus replicating the pattern found in study I.

AN ANALYSIS OF UNFAIRNESS

According to the PP perspective, the primary reason why whites oppose affirmative action is neither racial prejudice nor dominance drives, but the simple fact that they perceive these policies as "unfair." While there is certainly reason to believe that whites really do perceive affirmative action as "unfair," what the PP theorists fail to consider is where these perceptions of "unfairness" actually come from. We suggest that perceptions of unfairness are neither purely exogenous nor solely driven by some "objective" social condition of unfairness. Rather, we would suggest that perceptions of the unfairness of affirmative action will also be driven by the desire to maintain group superiority and group dominance. In other words, so long as the policy is not too blatantly at odds with accepted moral norms (e.g., slavery, apartheid), whites will feel that whatever helps to maintain their dominance is "fair," while whatever undermines this dominance is "unfair."

To demonstrate this "motivated fairness-perception effect," we tested a simple model in which perceptions of affirmative action as "unfair" were driven by factors such as the work ethic and SDO and in which overall opposition to affirmative action was in turn a function of all three factors (see figure 7.7). In exploring this question, we used only the highly educated white adults from Los Angeles County ($N = 96$). If the PP perspective is correct, fairness perceptions should have relatively little—if anything—to do with SDO among highly educated whites. On the other hand, if the SD perspective is correct, not only should perceptions of "fairness" be strongly associated with SDO, but even more important—since SD theory considers "fairness" perceptions and other such beliefs to be "legitimizing ideologies" (see Sidanius 1993; Sidanius and Pratto 1999)—they should serve a mediating role between SDO, on the one hand, and general opposition to affirmative action, on the other.

Rather than concentrating on whether or not the overall path model fit the data,[14] we will focus primarily on the question of whether perceptions of unfairness mediate the relationship between SDO and overall opposition to affirmative action. Inspection of figure 7.7 clearly shows support for this mediational hypothesis. First, the higher the SDO scores of highly educated whites were, the more they perceived affirmative action to be "unfair" ($\gamma = 0.23, p < .01$). Second, most of the correlation between SDO and general affirmative action opposition ($r = .38$) was mediated by the perception of affirmative action as "unfair" (i.e., IE $= .22, p < .001$).

Finally, PP advocates have claimed that even if white attitudes about affirmative action are in some cases driven by malevolence and/ or the desire to oppress others, such motives are largely restricted to the poorly educated. Once again, however, this claim is not borne out by the empirical data. The regression of "unfairness" on SDO among educationally unsophisticated whites was 2.81 ($N = 85, t = 2.72, r = .29, p < .008$), while the equivalent regression among educationally sophisticated whites was 4.11 ($N = 100, t = 4.11, r = .40, p < .00004$). Thus, if anything, SDO appears to have a stronger effect on perceptions of "unfairness" among the more sophisticated than among the less sophisticated.

AFFIRMATIVE ACTION SUPPORT AND EQUALITY OF OPPORTUNITY NORMS

We also repeated the "equality of opportunity" analysis conducted in study I. If the PP theorists and other advocates of the "end of discrimination" thesis (e.g, Thernstrom and Thernstrom 1997) are correct, *endorsement* of equality of opportunity should be associated with *rejection* of affirmative action. Once again, using the two "equality of opportunity" items from the SDO Scale (i.e., items 11 and 14 in the Appendix), we found the exact opposite pattern. The more whites *rejected* the equality of opportunity norm, the more they also *rejected* affirmative action ($r = .32, p < .0001$).

GENERAL DISCUSSION

The purpose of this chapter is to compare the relative adequacy of the PP and SD models of public opposition to race-targeted policies. While suggesting that the racial policy conflicts of the past were grounded in prejudice and antipathy toward blacks, PP theorists argue that current conflicts over racial issues are essentially disputes over political and ideological values. In contrast, while recognizing the importance of nonracial and political motives, SD theory also argues for the centrality of group-interested and antiegalitarian motives in the opposition to redistributive racial policies.

There are two major points on which both PP and SD theorists have always agreed. First, consistent with what SD theorists (e.g., Sidanius, Devereux, and Pratto 1992; Sidanius, Pratto, and Bobo 1996) have claimed for some time, we again find support for the claim that racial animus is *not* a particularly powerful source of public resistance to redistributive racial policies. Controlling for other factors, antiblack affect had virtually no independent effect on racial attitudes across different policy domains. The notion that affective evaluations have little or no influence on policy attitudes received additional support from our finding that negative affect toward women and the poor was also unrelated to support for policies specifically targeted toward these groups.

Second, SD theorists have never disputed the PP claim, again supported in the research here, that a substantial portion of opposition to redistributive racial policies is motivated by political and moral values having nothing at all to do with racism, antiblack affect, or social dominance drives. However, despite these two areas of agreement, our results are still fundamentally at odds with essentially *all of the other core predictions* of the PP perspective.

First, contrary to the claims of the PP theorists, the value of egalitarianism is distinctly *not* an uncontested and universally shared American value. Rather, one's endorsement of egalitarianism is systematically related to one's position in the "racial" hierarchy. The dominant "racial" group in American society (e.g., Euro-Americans) is distinctly less committed to the value of equality, while the traditionally subordinated groups in American society (i.e., blacks and Latinos) are distinctly more committed to the value of equality.

Second, there is no evidence that the association between political and moral ideologies (e.g., conservatism and the work ethic) and ideologies of dominance and submission become any weaker with increasing educational sophistication. Quite the opposite is true. The more highly educated whites are, the stronger the relationship is between political conservatism and the work ethic, on the one hand, and SDO, on the other.

Third, there is no evidence that dominance motives become any less important in determining racial policy at higher levels of educational sophistication. Again, quite the opposite is true. Fourth, rather than being a minor factor in the racial policy attitudes of white Americans, group identity and social dominance values are among the *most important* factors driving the racial policy attitudes of white Americans.

Fifth, contrary to the spirit of the PP theory, there is also evidence that these ostensibly "race-neutral" principles (e.g., political conservatism) serve to mediate the relationship between social dominance drives, on the one hand, and opposition to redistributive social policy, on the other. Thus, these "race-neutral" and "principled" belief systems become effective legitimizing foils for the masking of opposition to redistributive policy in terms that appear to be more morally and intellectually defensible. This masking function thus makes the task of preserving group-based hierarchy and dominance systems all the easier (Sidanius 1993; Sidanius and Pratto 1999).

Sixth, while concern about "fairness" is certainly a major factor influencing white public opinion concerning race-targeted policies, this concern with "fairness" is neither exogenous nor strictly "principled." Rather, whites' perceptions of what is "fair" are strongly influenced by a desire to maintain group dominance and a hierarchical social order.

A seventh area in which our results contradict the assumptions of the PP model relates to the claim that there is no longer one issue of race, but many. For example, Sniderman and Piazza give this contention a top spot in their list of principal findings: "It is no longer appropriate to speak of *the* issue of race. There are a variety of clashes, driven by different ideals, fears, and expectations of gain and loss. The politics of affirmative action is not the same as the politics of government spending, and both differ from the politics of fair housing" (1993, 12, emphasis in original). In fact, PP theorists are so certain of this position that they now simply assume that it is true (e.g., Sniderman and Carmines 1997a, 11). We strongly agree with the PP theorists that racial attitudes have multiple determinants and that racial policy attitudes do indeed factor into multiple and distinct policy domains. However, we strongly disagree that the determinants of these policy attitudes radically shift from one domain to another and from issue to issue. In particular, the evidence found in this and other studies shows that SDO has a powerful influence on policy attitudes not only across a number of different racial policy domains, but across a wide range of other and distinctly nonracial policy domains in the United States and several other nations as well (see Pratto et al. 1994; Sidanius, Pratto, and Bobo 1994; Sidanius and Pratto 1993b, 1999). Again, David Sears and his colleagues (Sears, Henry, and Kosterman this volume; Sears et al. 1997) provide converging evidence of a substantial uniformity in the strong predictive utility of symbolic racism across racial issues. Thus, the politics of race appears to still be about group hegemony and not strictly about some disembodied "politics."

The eighth, and perhaps the most absurd, claim of the PP and other "end of racism" theorists is the suggestion that opposition to race-targeted policies is actually motivated by the commitment to equality. Principled politics and other "end of racism" proponents (e.g., D'Souza 1995; Miller and Shanks 1996; Roth 1994; Thernstrom and Thernstrom 1997) have often suggested that one of the important reasons why whites oppose race-conscious policies, such as affirmative action, is that they have largely internalized the egalitarian message of the civil rights movement. For example, Sniderman and Carmines (1997a, 33) state, "A primary basis for the one-sided opposition to affirmative action which involves preferential treatment or explicit quotas is the belief that it is not fair to hire people for jobs or grant them admission to schools because they belong to a particular social group and not because they are the most qualified." That is, PP theorists and other members of the "end of racism" school suggest that the opposition to affirmative action stems primarily from the belief that affirmative action programs are racially inegalitarian. The empirical bankruptcy of this assertion not only is revealed by the data discussed in this chapter, but also should be obvious to anyone solidly familiar with the research literature. This literature shows quite unambiguously that resistance to race-targeted social policies is associated *not* with commitment to *equality*, but rather with its exact opposite. It is commitment to *antiegalitarianism* and racial *in*equality that is among the major sources of resistance to race-targeted policies (see Allen 1994; Flynn 1996; Pratto et al. 1994; Sidanius, Devereux, and Pratto 1992; Sidanius et al. 1999; Sidanius and Pratto 1993b, 1999; Sidanius et al. 1996; see also Feldman 1988; Rokeach 1973, 1979; Rokeach, Miller, and Snyder 1971). Even when we defined "egalitarianism" quite narrowly as "equality of opportunity" rather than as "equality of result," we found that opposition to affirmative action was associated with the rejection of egalitarianism and not its endorsement. Furthermore, the endorsement of antiegalitarian values by dominant social groups in the service of decidedly antiegalitarian political projects is not of recent vintage. Rather, this phenomenon has historical roots reaching back at least as far as the eighteenth century (see, e.g., Burke 1790). Since "end of racism" theorists (e.g., D'Souza 1995) tend not to be well acquainted with the empirical literature, it should be no surprise that this rather severe "egalitarianism" problem seems to have escaped them. If the "end of racism" theorists are to make a credible claim that opposition to affirmative action and similar policies among the average white is actually motivated by commitment to *egalitarian* rather than *antiegalitarian* values, the "proof by assertion" strategy they are presently pursuing will simply not do. Given the massive amount of empirical evidence contradicting their assertions, the burden is on them to actually produce credible empirical evidence in support of these assertions. Thus far, such evidence screams by its absence.

Altogether then, and consistent with the recent findings of Sidanius and his colleagues (Sidanius et al. 1996), the present results underscore the need to revise how we conceive of "racism" and what we consider to be "race-relevant" factors in public opposition to policies such as affirmative action. First and foremost, antiblack animus has little, if anything, to tell us about public resistance to redistributive racial policies. This fact notwithstanding, PP and "end of racism" theorists have gone on to draw the erroneous conclusion that ideologies of group superiority-inferiority are of no substantial consequence to American political discourse.

By confining themselves to animus (and in some cases, stereotypes), PP theorists and their "end of racism" allies are looking in the wrong place altogether and are in fact very busy slaying the proverbial straw man. Not only does racial inequality in contemporary America have little to do with negative animus, antiblack affect, or "prejudice," but also there is no real evidence that the American racial hierarchy has *ever* been centrally connected to antiblack affect (see especially van den Berghe 1967). Rather, there is strong evidence that the contemporary American racial hierarchy remains driven by what it has always been driven by, namely, the establishment and maintenance of the dominion, superiority, and power of the collective "US" over the collective "THEM." The central feature of racism—a belief in the moral, intellectual, or cultural superiority of one group over another—

need not be associated with negative affect toward the group in question (see also Jackman 1994). In fact, prior to the Civil War, positive affect toward blacks quite often accompanied the absolute certainty of black inferiority. This "paternalistic racism" persisted well into the 1960s. For example, when the Southern segregationist of the 1960s declared that he had no ill will toward and was actually quite fond of "Niggras," he was really not lying. There *really was* fondness between the "races," a fondness that would have continued so long as "Niggras kept their place." The simple fact of the matter is that the desire for group-based social hierarchy rather than mere racial animus lies at the heart of white opposition to redistributive social policies in general— and to race-targeted policies in particular.

Given the fact that the bulk of their arguments are directly contradicted by an impressive and consistent amount of data, how have the PP theorists chosen to respond? Thus far, their responses fall into three categories (see Sniderman et al. this volume). First, and perhaps most disappointingly, rather than engaging the real arguments that SD theory is making, the PP theorists have chosen instead to respond to what can only be regarded as a theoretical caricature. Rather than trying to *prove* the obvious (i.e., that human societies tend to be organized as group-based hierarchies), SD theory is actually concerned with trying to understand the *mechanisms and forces* that both produce and sustain these hierarchies. Second, PP theorists imply that the Los Angeles data used in this chapter, which contradict much of their own position, are either peculiar to this region or incompetently analyzed. However, the fact that large data sets taken from other parts of the United States (e.g., Texas) are also essentially inconsistent with PP arguments is simply ignored (see especially the results of Sidanius, Pratto, and Bobo 1996). Finally, rather than engaging the analyses of several large data sets from different populations showing the powerful effects of SDO on both the political attitudes and the racial policy positions of white Americans (see also Altemeyer 1998; McFarland and Adelson 1996), the PP theorists have simply chosen to be silent, thereby implying that (1) this evidence does not actually exist, (2) the evidence is somehow irrelevant to the arguments they are trying to make, or (3) they do not think that familiarizing themselves with the research literature is worth their efforts. Whatever the case may be, while silence is certainly a tactic, it is not an easily interpreted argument (for similar points, see Dawson this volume). By completely ignoring the powerful associations of SDO to both political ideology and racial policy attitudes, by failing to even seriously consider issues of relative group power, and by focusing instead on the anemic and impotent issue of racial animus, not only are the PP theorists fundamentally misunderstanding the dynamics of race relations in America, but also they are helping to actually *mask* these dynamics.

SOCIAL DOMINANCE THEORY AND SYMBOLIC RACISM

The careful reader will have noticed a few places in which SD theory and symbolic racism theory take complementary positions in refuting some of the PP assertions. First, both the SD and the symbolic racism theories find that education increases the association between racial considerations and opposition to racial policy as well as the relationship between racial considerations and ideology, contrary to the PP position. Both theories also agree that attitudes toward racial issues display substantial uniformity in their determinants (though they disagree as to exactly what these determinants are) and that these determinants involve racial considerations, again strongly contrary to the PP model. Finally, both theories take the position that, in America, blacks will face higher levels of discrimination than other ethnic groups and will inspire the greatest degree of white opposition to policies designed to help them (see also Bobo and Kluegel 1993).

However, despite this apparent convergence, the two models are still fundamentally different. First, SD theory holds that symbolic racism is only an indirect determinant of attitudes toward racial policy. Like political ideology, belief in the work ethic, norms of individualism, and old-fashioned racism, SD theorists view symbolic racism primarily as another "legitimizing ideology" (Sidanius, Devereux, and Pratto 1992). That is, symbolic racism can be seen as one of several ideologies that mediate between the desire for group-based hierarchy (i.e., SDO) and the opposition to redistributive social policies (e.g., Sidanius, Devereux, and Pratto 1992; Sidanius et al. 1999; Sidanius and Pratto 1999).

Second, SD theory argues that symbolic racism theory is too theoretically parochial (Sidanius 1993). By limiting its perspective to American race relations, symbolic racism theory fails to appreciate the degree to which opposition to policies designed to aid subordinates is driven by very similar forces and dynamics across a number of different social systems. Furthermore, these forces have little, if anything, to do with symbolic racism, a distinctly American phenomenon. That is, there is mounting cross-cultural evidence that group-based anti-egalitarianism and SDO are not simply driving social policy attitudes about blacks among white Americans, but also are critically important sources of opposition to group-relevant social policy attitudes across a wide variety of other cultures as well (e.g., Pratto et al. 1998; Sidanius et al. 1997; for a review, see Sidanius and Pratto 1999).

Just like PP theorists, the symbolic racism theorists make the fundamental error of assuming that, at least at one point in history, antiblack affect was actually at the heart of American racism (Kinder and Sanders 1996; Sears 1988; Sears, Henry, and Kosterman this volume; Sears et al. 1997). Not only do symbolic racism theorists assume that antiblack affect was important in the past, but also they insist on arguing that it remains important in the present. Like the PP theorists, the symbolic racism theorists also fail to appreciate the hierarchical nature of intergroup relations or how their central construct (e.g., symbolic racism/racial resentment) may serve as a legitimizing ideology mediating the relationship between dominance motives and attitudes toward hierarchy-enhancing and -attenuating social policies. Furthermore, their most recent attempt to conceptualize antiegalitarianism as simply a special case of symbolic racism (see Sears, Henry, and Kosterman this volume) is accomplished by the use of what are most likely poorly specified models in which the indirect effects of antiegalitarianism on symbolic racism and racial policy attitudes are never considered.[15]

THE BOTTOM LINE

In sum, we concur with the PP theorists that there are multiple and complex sources of American public opinion concerning issues of "race" and multiple domains of "racial" policy. There is a substantial body of evidence showing that truly race-neutral political and social values really do have a great deal to do with the public's attitudes toward race-targeted social policies. These policy attitudes cannot be simply or completely relegated to any form of racial prejudice or SDO. Even more sharply, we also agree that racial animus and classical "prejudice" have relatively little, if anything, to tell us about American public opinion concerning race-targeted social policies. Beyond this, however, we suggest that a careful inspection indicates that the empirical evidence is inconsistent with almost all of the other core claims of the PP position.

In short, while white public opinion regarding race-targeted social policies is not driven merely by group-interested, antiegalitarian motives, they are clearly centrally important. By ignoring or minimizing these motives, one is fundamentally misconstruing the nature of racial politics in America. Thus, not only have the PP theorists provided us with an incomplete, and substantially more sanitized, picture of the dynamics of racial politics in America than the data can support, but even more important, these theorists have presented us with a fundamentally flawed picture as well.

Finally, since so many of the core claims of the PP thesis have been shown to be unambiguously false, one is left to wonder why this thesis still enjoys such a wide and powerful following within contemporary American discourse. We suggest that a major reason for this popularity is to be found in the political psychology of denial and national conceit. Americans in general, and white Americans in particular, are strongly motivated to believe that the United States really has finally realized its promise of an open and equal opportunity structure and that all is fundamentally well in the land. It is clear that this denial and self-delusion affect not only the social perspicacity of very many lay citizens, but that of more than a few professional analysts and social scientists as well. Given the power of wishful thinking and the tendency for people to believe what they are truly motivated to believe, there is strong reason to doubt whether any amount of contradictory data will ever make a significant impact on the American discourse on "race." Most Americans will simply continue to believe what makes them most comfortable to believe.

APPENDIX: SDO$_6$ SCALE

INSTRUCTIONS

Below are a series of statements with which you may either agree or disagree. For each statement, please indicate the degree of your agreement/disagreement by circling the appropriate number from "1" to "7." Once again, remember that your first responses are usually the most accurate.

	STRONGLY DISAGREE/ DISAPPROVE				STRONGLY AGREE/ FAVOR		
1. Some groups of people are just more worthy than others	1	2	3	4	5	6	7
2. In getting what your group wants, it is sometimes necessary to use force against other groups	1	2	3	4	5	6	7
3. Superior groups should dominate inferior groups	1	2	3	4	5	6	7

4. To get ahead in life, it is sometimes neces- 1 2 3 4 5 6 7
   sary to step on other groups
5. If certain groups of people stayed in their   1 2 3 4 5 6 7
   place, we would have fewer problems
6. It's probably a good thing that certain   1 2 3 4 5 6 7
   groups are at the top and other groups are
   at the bottom
7. Inferior groups should stay in their place   1 2 3 4 5 6 7
8. Sometimes other groups must be kept in   1 2 3 4 5 6 7
   their place
9. It would be good if all groups could be   1 2 3 4 5 6 7
   equal
10. Group equality should be our ideal   1 2 3 4 5 6 7
11. All groups should be given an equal   1 2 3 4 5 6 7
    chance in life
12. We should do what we can to equalize   1 2 3 4 5 6 7
    conditions for different groups
13. Increased social equality   1 2 3 4 5 6 7
14. We would have fewer problems if we   1 2 3 4 5 6 7
    treated different groups more equally
15. We should strive to make incomes more   1 2 3 4 5 6 7
    equal
16. No one group should dominate in society   1 2 3 4 5 6 7

Note to users: Items 9–16 should be reverse coded.

EIGHT The Politics of Race

PAUL M. SNIDERMAN
GRETCHEN C. CROSBY
WILLIAM G. HOWELL

The argument over racial policy, we shall suggest, has become at its core an argument over politics. Remarkably, this is a controversial suggestion, as many of the chapters in this book make plain. But if it is not possible to escape controversy on so emotionally charged a subject as race, it is possible to minimize it, and we propose to do so by sketching what it means to offer a political—as opposed to, say, a more psychological or sociological—account of the clash over racial policy.[1]

Invoking politics naturally is not a magic elixir; there are aspects of the clash over race that can be plumbed only from other perspectives. But in casting an eye over the work of the last decade, we have been struck by how the actual political character of the contemporary argument over racial policies has been slighted. Citizens, it seems to us essential to recognize, get to choose only from among the choices on offer. How they go about making choices on public policy hinges on how these choices are organized by political institutions and presented by public leaders (for a systematic presentation of this institution-centered view of public choice, see Sniderman in press).

On an institution-oriented account of choice, the framing of public choices, particularly by the party system, defines the relevance of citizens' attitudes and orientations. By contrast, according to actor-centered accounts, the attitudes and orientations of citizens define the significance of their political choices. The two leading examples of actor-centered accounts, in the area of racial politics, are explanations centered on prejudice and group interest. On the first view, the driving force behind the opinions of white Americans about issues of race remains racism. It is not, to be sure, the naked prejudice of a half century ago. But it is racism all the same—irrational, categorical, malevolent. And racism is not merely one factor among many at work.

On the contrary, its tenets command the support of a clear majority of white Americans (see Kinder and Sanders 1996, 107, tab. 5.1), and it is, even taking account of an array of other influences, far and away the dominant force molding the thinking of white Americans on issues of race (Kinder and Sanders, 1996, 123). On the second view, the fundamental fault line in racial politics is race itself. Blacks, by virtue of their position as blacks, and whites, by virtue of their position as whites, have conflicting interests, and it is the reluctance of whites to surrender the privileges they enjoy merely by virtue of being white that is the defining rhythm of racial politics.

It is important to avoid false alternatives.[2] It is not a matter of dispute that racism and selfishness are part of the politics of race. Who would deny that in the world as it actually is there is mean-spiritedness, deep-rooted bigotry, and indifference to the plight of others, not to mention complacency and self-satisfaction and a desire to retain or increase the advantages of one's social position? Certainly, we never have. The task is to understand what the contemporary argument over racial politics is about. What are the considerations that citizens take into account, and what importance do they give them, in making up their minds about governmental policies dealing with race? How large a role does prejudice play, and is it sometimes of more consequence and sometimes of less? What part is played by citizens' broader political values? When do whites mean what they say about racial policies, and when are they saying what they think they should say? Is the politics of race essentially autonomous, or does it tend to conform to the larger contours of American politics? And what does it mean to speak of the politics of race? Is there one fundamental pattern, with specific policies merely representing different ways of putting the same question—Should blacks be helped or not?—in the minds of ordinary citizens? Or is the pattern of choices more complex, and the ways that citizens respond accordingly more complex?

These are the questions we think deserve consideration, and in getting a grip on them, we believe it is helpful to recognize that when citizens are grappling with public policies on race, they are making distinctly political choices. Specifically, our bedrock premise is that how citizens choose depends on the terms of their choices. For the politics of race, we are persuaded that two features of the terms of choice are pivotal. On the one side, policy alternatives come into focus under the pressure of competitive elections and the dynamics of the party system (see especially Huckfeld and Kohfeldt 1989 and Carmines and Stimson 1989). It follows that, given the ideological commitments of the two principal parties at the elite level, there is a natural tendency for policy alternatives to be posed within a liberal-conservative framework across issue domains, very much including racial policy. On the other side, there is not one problem of race, but a number—among them, the need to assure equal treatment under the law; to provide assistance to those who are poor; and to combat discrimination, which in itself can take different forms, as discrimination itself is differently defined. There is thus not one course of public action on race for citizens to accept or reject, but a number, and they differ in the goals that government is attempting to accomplish and the means by which it is attempting to accomplish them. It follows that, given the genuine variety of proposals falling under the overall tent of government actions dealing with race, citizens may, and likely will, take different positions as to what government should do regarding race, just so far as they are being asked to approve different courses of action.

We believe that these two features—ideological continuity and issue pluralism—define the terms of choice for issues of race and thus the process of choice. The first favors convergence across racial issues; the second, divergence. We obviously cannot give a complete account here of how each shapes the politics of race, but five points are worth mention.

• The fundamental lines of cleavage on issues of race, so far as they are defined by the party system, are not peculiar to issues of race. They belong, rather, to a larger pattern of division, defining the deeper-lying structure of American politics since the New Deal, centering on the clash of competing conceptions of the proper responsibilities of government and the appropriate obligations of citizens.[3]

• The lines of political cleavage, notwithstanding the sluggish attention the public characteristically pays to public affairs, differ according to the terms of choice of particular issues of race. Pursuing this notion of issue pluralism in the context of affirmative action politics, we shall suggest that a new fault line dividing liberalism is emerging not because of a resurgence of racism, but in response to competing conceptions of fairness.

• As against the common view that ideological orientations serve the interests of racial sentiment, we shall argue instead that citizens' political perspectives define the relevance of their racial prejudices in making choices about racial policy.

• We shall suggest that the gap between principle and implementation stressed in sociological accounts of racial politics is largely an illusion and arises precisely from the inclination of sociological accounts to omit the politics of racial policies.

• We shall call attention to the political ecology of issue arguments. Part of what underlies the politics of racial issues, we want to suggest, is the differential accessibility of arguments on opposing sides of particular issues. We propose to illustrate this notion of an ecology of arguments by considering the light it may throw on the politics of open housing.

We propose to proceed in three steps. First, we want to show how the notion of symbolic racism, conceptualized and measured just as the symbolic racism researchers wish it to be, collapses upon empirical examination. Second, we want to illustrate what we mean when we speak in behalf of a politics-centered account of the politics of race, though naturally our account will be selective rather than exhaustive.[4] Finally, given the adversarial character of much research on racial politics, we want to call attention to a number of points of agreement emerging across competing perspectives.

METHODS AND DATA

A decade ago the issue of race began to receive a fuller measure of the scholarly attention it merits. The flagship survey enterprises—the National Election Studies (NES) in political science and the General Social Survey (GSS) in sociology—have provided a rich array of expressly racial attitudes. A number of notable analyses of these data, particularly in their over-time dimension, have appeared (see especially Schuman et al. 1997). Yet if there incontrovertibly has been a concerted effort made to track Americans' attitudes toward race, it is not obvious that a comparable measure of progress has been made in understanding the sources and dynamics of American attitudes toward public policies dealing with race.

Doubtless, there are a variety of reasons for the limited progress that has been made, but as our own work got under way, one problem in particular has seemed to us especially crucial. It is the inferential limits of the conventional public opinion survey. For all the increased sophistication in estimation techniques over the last several decades, the standard opinion interview generates a fog over questions of causality that is next to impossible to dispel. And if this fog obscures public opinion in general, it blankets assessment and inference about attitudes toward race in particular.

For a decade, we and our colleagues have been working to develop a new approach to the study of public opinion. This approach capitalizes on the introduction of computer-assisted telephone interviewing (CATI) to integrate the internal validity strengths of experimental design with the external validity advantages of representative samples. Experiments had previously been incorporated in public opinion surveys, but always of the split-ballot variety, radically reducing the number of facets of an item that could randomly be manipulated—usually to one—while restricting the number of variations that could be introduced—usually to two (see Sniderman and Grob 1996). With CATI as a platform, multiple facets of multiple items, each capable of taking on multiple values, can be experimentally manipulated in a way that is invisible to respondents and effortless for interviewers.

Every application of any method is imperfect, any conclusion of every study provisional. But in this chapter, we will illustrate how experiment-centered analyses can illuminate aspects of the thinking of Americans about matters of race that have previously been invisible. We shall introduce some new findings as well as review some earlier ones. We do so not out of a belief that our approach is the last word, but, on the contrary, from a conviction that by furnishing examples of experiments we have devised, others will be encouraged to devise still better procedures.

FINDINGS

A POLITICS- OR A RACISM-CENTERED EXPLANATION

Over a quarter of a century ago, David Sears and Donald Kinder declared that a new form of racism had emerged (the concept of symbolic racism was proposed by Sears and Kinder in 1971). Surely, they argued, there must be some powerful force responsible for the persistent opposition of many whites to black candidates and to government policies to assist blacks. It could not be the old racism. An overwhelming number of white Americans, they acknowledged, now rejected the principle of biological inferiority and, at least in their public professions, accepted the principle of racial equality. So a new racism, more subtle, less blatantly offensive, must have taken the place of the old.

This racism was new, Sears and Kinder declared, in character as well as form. Opposition to public efforts to help blacks was mobilized around the values of individual effort, self-reliance, and achievement. This was not just a matter of window dressing. These values, they insisted, were a wellspring, in their own right, of racial animosity—indeed, so much so that they defined the new racism as a conjunction

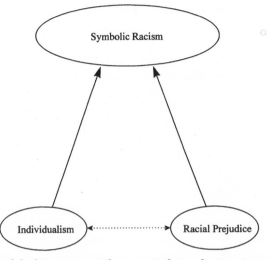

Figure 8.1. Model of Constituent Elements Defining the New Racism

or blending of antiblack affect and traditional American values, above all, individualism (e.g., Sears 1988; Kinder and Mendelberg this volume).

To make unmistakably clear Sears and Kinder's claim, figure 8.1 summarizes graphically their conceptual model. Two components—racial prejudice and individualism—constitute the new racism. They combine to produce "symbolic racism," "modern racism," "racial resentment"—the appellation has varied. They do so either working independently of one another or together—the formulation of a "conjunction" or "blend" is open to either additive or interactive interpretations—hence the dashed arrow between the two constituent elements in figure 8.1. But on either interpretation, Sears and Kinder have committed themselves to the view that the new racism *is* individualism plus antiblack affect.

If the new racism is a conjunction of antiblack affect and traditional American values, above all, individualism, then these two constituent elements should be powerful predictors of it. Indeed, they *must* be powerful predictors, since they literally constitute it. We have followed Sears and Kinder in the measurement of all the components—symbolic racism, individualism, and antiblack affect. Table 8.1 estimates their measurement model, taking advantage of the 1986 NES survey, the last of the NES surveys incorporating the particular measure they accept as a measure of individualism (the components of all measures are detailed in the Appendix).[5] We have biased this test in *favor* of the Sears and Kinder claim. Since the only variables that are explicitly taken into account are the two that they claim constitute symbolic racism, then these two will receive credit not only for the variation in the Sears-Kinder measure for which they are uniquely responsible, but also for the variation attributable to every other variable with which they are correlated.

If individualism and antiblack affect do indeed make up the new racism, then we should see in table 8.1 that they account for the largest part of variations in scores on the Sears-Kinder measure. The first column reports the standardized coefficients for the two measures. As a moment's inspection of the figures will show, although the coefficients for both are statistically significant, neither is overwhelmingly large, and that of individualism is embarrassingly small. Even if the contribution of both is taken into account, so far from explaining the overwhelming portion of the variation in the Sears-Kinder measure—or indeed even the largest part of it—they are responsible only for a relatively trivial fraction of it ($r^2 = .14$). In an effort to salvage the Sears-Kinder claim, the second column of table 8.1 takes account of not only the independent contributions of the two, but also their potential interaction. The interaction of the two is statistically significant and seems visually large, albeit with the wrong sign. Once you go through the arithmetic of calculating the impact of the interaction term netting out the impact of the two main effects, it is obvious that the interaction term adds nothing of consequence to the understanding of the variance in the Sears-Kinder measure, which shows up in a failure to account for substantially more variance ($r^2 = .14$).[6]

We do not wish to argue about words. A concept like individualism has more than one aspect, and the standard measure of it in the NES surveys cannot capture all of them. For that matter, it is very far from obvious that the "feeling thermometer" technique is a defensible measure of racial prejudice, let alone the best possible measure of it. Accordingly, turning to the 1992 NES, the third and fourth columns report a second test, examining a different facet of individualism, support for limited government, and a more direct indicator of racial prejudice, endorsement of negative racial stereotypes. The results are just as unsympathetic to the Sears and Kinder claim (r^2 is now .15) except that this alternative conception of individualism is even more remote from the measure of the "new racism" than the previous one. Our analysis, we would again underline, has been done on terms most favorable to Sears and Kinder's claim. If you look at Sears's own analy-

TABLE 8.1 Individualism and Racial Prejudice as Constituting Symbolic Racism

| | 1986 NES | | 1992 NES | |
	Model 1	Model 2	Model 1	Model 2
Measures of individualism				
Individualism	0.21°°	0.38°°		
Limited government			0.05	0.03
Measures of prejudice				
Antiblack affect	0.30°°	0.64°°		
Negative racial stereotypes			0.39°°	0.37°°
Interaction terms				
Indiv. ° antiblack affect		−0.41°°		
Lim. govt. ° racial stereotypes				0.04
Constant	0.35°°	0.23°°	0.51°°	0.51°°
Adjusted R^2	0.14	0.15	0.14	0.14
N	787	787	478	478

Note: On all models, the dependent variable is symbolic racism. Standardized coefficients reported from OLS regressions.
°$p < .05$.   °°$p < .01$.

sis in this book (see table 3.2, p. 90), you will see that merely by including other relevant factors, the contribution of individualism drops substantially, and so far from heading the list of predictors, it falls near the rear of the pack. In short, the two components that supposedly constitute the very heart of the new racism are, at the very best, only moderately related to it.

Nor is this surprising if you look carefully at the actual content of the questions that make up the Sears-Kinder measure (shown in figure 8.2). One reason for agreeing with an item like "Most blacks who receive money from welfare programs could get along without it if they tried" obviously is dislike of blacks. Just as obviously, though, it cannot be the only one reason, nor—given the results in table 8.1—the most important one. What is striking, however, is that most of the items have nothing to do with individualism. Four manifestly are about other matters. What does a belief that government officials treat blacks and whites pretty much alike (item 6) have to do with an ethic of self-reliance? How can disagreeing with the view that blacks get "less than they deserve" (item 1) or believing that the legacy of slavery no longer shackles blacks (item 4) be taken as defining elements of individualism? How exactly does a loose suspicion that blacks are taking advantage of welfare qualify one as an Emersonian individualist? All of these are politically interesting sentiments, and no doubt have

---

(1) Over the past few years, blacks have gotten less than they deserve.

(2) Irish, Italians, Jewish, and many other minorities overcame prejudice and worked their way up. Blacks should do the same without any special favors.

(3) It's really a matter of some people not trying hard enough; if blacks would only try harder they could be just as well off as whites.

(4) Generations of slavery and discrimination have created conditions that make it difficult for blacks to work their way out of the lower class.

(5) Most blacks who receive money from welfare programs could get along without it if they tried.°

(6) Government officials usually pay less attention to a request or complaint from a black person than from a white person.°

Figure 8.2. Components of the "New" Racism. *Sources:* 1986 and 1992 National Election Studies. *Note:* The 1986 and 1992 measures follow those used in Kinder and Sanders 1996, with the 1986 measure composed of variables 565–68, 579, and 580 and the 1992 measure composed of variables 6126–29.
°Question not asked in 1992.

a bearing on the positions whites take on racial issues, but none of them constitutes a defining idea of American individualism.

The remaining two can be interpreted to measure support for individualism. Indeed, as Kinder and Tali Mendelberg (chap. 2) point out, in a previous work one of us did precisely that (see Sniderman and Hagen 1985), and they present some interesting results suggesting that our conception was flawed. We agree. Indeed, we think the error is far more serious than they suggest, and since Kinder and Sears make exactly the same fatal mistake, there's something to recommend making plain how all three of us got things wrong.

Consider the item "It's really a matter of some people not trying hard enough; if blacks would only try harder they could be just as well off as whites."[7] The prototype of individualism, in the American context, is the individualism of Ralph Waldo Emerson, and when he spoke of it as an American value, he had in mind the commitment of Americans to an ethic of self-reliance in *their own* lives. Sears and Kinder's position is that whites, if they say that blacks should be self-reliant, are committed in their own lives to individualism as a value.

But this entirely overlooks the possibility of hypocrisy. It is simply a fallacy to suppose that because I say that you should stand on your own two feet and take care of your problems without help from others, I myself am willing to stand on my own two feet and take care of my problems without help from others.

Once commitment to the idea of self-reliance as a principle by which your life as well as the lives of others should be governed is distinguished from invoking the principle of self-reliance as a way to criticize and pass judgment on others, it should be obvious that the tack that we took in gauging individualism is indefensible. And it is equally indefensible for Sears and Kinder. They used exactly the same items and made exactly the same mistake as we. It is obviously a mistake—it seems embarrassingly so in retrospect—simply to assume that when a white tells blacks that they have to work hard, the white is himself willing to work hard.

It is not surprising, then, that we observed in table 8.1 that individualism standardly measured is only modestly related to these items that Sears and Kinder claim are measuring individualism. Both recognize there is a problem here in their chapters in this book. Their responses, however, take quite different forms. Sears mounts two lines of defense. The first is to expand the category of traditional values. So in his analysis in this book, he also folds under the umbrella of traditional American values inegalitarianism and personal morality (e.g., the breakdown of sexual morality), while in other work (see Sears et al. 1997), he includes authoritarianism as well. It is in terms of this enlarged conception of traditional values, and not on the basis of individualism alone or even predominantly, that Sears proposes to validate his conception of a new racism.

As a moment's thought will make clear, this line of defense cannot hold. To begin with, the key component of Sears's analysis in this book turns out to be (a racialized form of) inegalitarianism. But this result is exactly the wrong way around. In his conceptualization, Sears claims that the new form of racism is now buttressed by "the finest and proudest of traditional American values" (Sears 1988, 54). But under no description, racial or otherwise, has anyone suggested that inegalitarianism is an American ideal. It is, rather, a commitment to equality that is a defining component of the American Creed. What Sears has found, it follows, is that the values in which Americans distinctively have taken pride, rather than working in favor of racism, work against it. He is, in our view, on solid ground in suggesting that a variety of sentiments loosely labeled traditional values—authoritarianism and conventionality, among them—are somehow tied into racial prejudice. But since when is authoritarianism a traditional *American* value? At what point did opposition to sexual education or *in*tolerance of diverse lifestyles become a defining American ideal? Surely, it makes no sense to declare that a commitment to inequality, to authoritarianism, to intolerance is among "the finest and proudest of traditional American values."

Sears offers a second line of defense, however. Acknowledging that his measure of racism is rooted primarily in (a racialized form of) inegalitarianism rather than individualism, he claims that inegalitarianism in turn is rooted in individualistic beliefs (see table 3.6). But it turns out, upon inspection, that the principal items establishing that inegalitarianism is rooted in individualistic beliefs come from the Sears-Kinder measure itself. How, then, do we know that their measure is a measure of individualism? Because it is correlated with inegalitarianism, which is said to be an expression of individualism. And how do we know that inegalitarianism is a form of individualism? Because it is correlated with components of the original Sears-Kinder measure. Notice the structure of the argument. X is a measure of individualism. How do we know this? Not because it is predicted by Y, which is a measure of individualism, but because it is predicted by Z. And how do we know that Z, which appears to be a measure of egalitarianism and not of individualism, is a measure of individualism? Because it is predicted by X, which is (again) said to be a measure of individualism. The regress is infinite because the reasoning is circular.

Kinder, by contrast, treats the problem as conceptual rather than empirical. His argument takes an unusual shape because he starts by decrying the lack of attention in studies of racial politics to individualism as Emerson and James Bryce conceived it, but then devotes his principal critical energies to taking exception to a study attempting precisely that. This unusual bent in his argument illuminates what is distinctive in his concerns. It is not individualism standing on its own that strikes him as pivotal, but individualism fired in the crucible of racial politics. The sentiments making up the measure that he and Sears developed, he declares, tap "individualism-in-racism," and because they tap individualism-*in*-racism, it is a mistake to suppose that they should be directly connected to individualism taken on its own.

We characterize this as a conceptual rather than an empirical argument because it turns the research question of what the Sears-Kinder measure measures into a definitional exercise. It is not obvious to us what the concept of "individualism-in-racism" can mean, but if it means anything at all, it must mean that white Americans have a different response to the idea of individualism when it is invoked inside the context of race than outside it. To put the point as clearly as possible, if individualism takes on a distinct meaning in the context of race, and this surely must be what Kinder is contending, then it must be the case that whites are more likely to endorse it when it is applied to blacks having to deal with their problems on their own than to whites having to do the same.

The only way to tell whether this is so is to exploit the power of experimental randomization. We have accordingly focused on a core item that Kinder claims to be a measure of individualism-in-racism. We have chosen the "no special favors" item because it most clearly expresses on its face the obligation to get ahead on one's own, adopting exactly the wording that Sears and Kinder favor. One half of the time, it is asked just as Sears and Kinder ask it: "Irish, Italian, Jewish and many other minorities overcame prejudice and worked their way up. Blacks should do the same without any special favors." The other half of the time, however, rather than asking whether blacks should have to make it on their own, we ask instead whether "new immigrants from Europe" should have to work their way up without any special favors. Respondents may agree strongly or somewhat, disagree strongly or somewhat. Their scores have been scaled to run from 0 to 1: the higher the score, the greater the agreement that a group should work its way up without special favors.

If individualism takes a distinctive form in the context of race, as Kinder claims, then it necessarily follows that the ethic of self-reliance will enjoy a greater appeal when it is imposed on blacks. Table 8.2 shows the level of agreement with the proposition that a group should make its own way without special favors as a function of whether it is a group of blacks or a group of whites who must do so. As you can see, it is *not* the case that whites are distinctively, or especially, or even slightly more likely to approve of individualism when it is applied to blacks. On the contrary, they are just as likely to endorse standing on your own two feet when it comes to whites as when it comes to blacks. There is no evidence at all of a racial double standard.

It may, however, be objected that even if whites on average impose the obligation of self-reliance evenhandedly on blacks and fellow whites, a significant subset of whites conceives of individualism in dis-

TABLE 8.2   Racial Double Standards Hypothesis, by Ideology

	TARGET POPULATION		
Ideological Orientation	Blacks	New Immigrants from Europe	N
Liberal	58	65	273
Moderate	66	70	439
Conservative	75	79	448
All respondents	71	73	1,160

Source: 1991 Race and Politics Study.
Note: Values are calculated by taking the difference in the mean responses in the test and control conditions and multiplying by 100.

tinctively racial terms. Certainly, it is the case that the more conservative whites are, the more likely they are to believe that blacks should work their own way up without special favors. Accordingly, the body of table 8.2 presents, separately for conservatives, moderates, and liberals, the degree of agreement with the idea of having to make your own way without special favors as a function of whether it is blacks or fellow whites that must do so. Plainly, no one—neither conservatives nor liberals nor those in between—is more likely to impose an obligation of self-reliance on blacks than on whites. In short, quite contrary to Kinder's claim that his measure measures "individualism-*in*-racism," it instead embodies a proposition that commands wide agreement in the public as a whole quite independent of race.

We, therefore, conclude that neither Sears nor Kinder has as yet met his burden of proof. The absolute core of their argument is that a new racism has emerged made up of individualism and aversion to blacks. But there is still no compelling evidence that individualism is an integral component of racism *even if racism is measured exactly as they wish it to be measured.*

CLEAVAGES WITHIN LIBERALISM

In our previous work, one theme we have concentrated on is the ideological aspects of racial politics. As Edward Carmines and James Stimson (1989) demonstrated in their seminal work, the policy alternatives that citizens get to choose between are broadly shaped by the competing ideological trajectories of the two principal political parties. It no longer is a matter of serious dispute, certainly among political scientists, that the policy choices of the more articulate and politically aware citizens reflect currents of liberalism and conservatism that run through the larger domain of redistributive politics. Given this consensus, we now want to consider how taking account of the terms of choice for particular policies may expose not only the divide between liberalism and conservatism, but also cleavages within liberalism itself.

The standard account of the politics of race runs, briefly, like this. For a generation, the issue of race has served as a fulcrum of the American party system. In 1964, the Republican Party, which had been the champion of racial liberalism under Abraham Lincoln, became the advocate of racial conservatism under Barry Goldwater, while the Democratic Party, which had been the party of southern segregationists, became under Lyndon Johnson the party of racial liberalism. The consequence, according to the standard account, has been a steady defection of whites, particularly working-class whites and those who are less attached to the party's central principles, from the Democratic side of the political ledger to the Republican side in response to a series of racially divisive issues—above all, affirmative action.

And there is substantial backing for the standard account. Whether you draw on our own surveys or consult the usual series—the NES for political science and the GSS for sociology—there is a readily discernible ideological division over affirmative action. Conservatives are markedly more likely to oppose it, liberals comparatively more likely to support it.

Yet the standard account of the politics of race relies on measurement procedures that make it unmistakably clear what is being measured. It is a matter of asking straight out whether people support or oppose affirmative action. But surely it is reasonable to wonder whether, when it comes to matters of race, whites will say what they really think. Is it not more than possible that they instead will say what they think they should say?

There is no perfect measure of truth, in survey research or anywhere else. But we think that it is possible to come closer to the way things are, to reflect more accurately how people think about a controversial issue like affirmative action, by developing new methods of assessment. For our part, we have taken advantage of CATI to develop an array of methods centered on experimentation in order to determine more faithfully what people think about controversial and emotionally charged public issues. One of these is the "list" experiment.

Since the technique is elsewhere described in detail (see, e.g., Kuklinski et al. 1997; Sniderman and Carmines 1997a; Gilens, Sniderman, and Kuklinski 1998), we shall here say only a word about its underlying logic. Imagine that in the course of an extended public opinion interview, one-half of the time the interviewer presents respondents with the following task:

> Now I'm going to read you three things that sometimes make people angry or upset. After I read all three, just tell me HOW MANY of them upset you. I don't want to know which ones, just how many.

Then, the task having been defined, the interviewer goes on to read a list of three items:

1. "the federal government increasing the tax on gasoline";
2. "professional athletes getting million-dollar-plus salaries";
3. "large corporations polluting the environment."

and, having read the list, asks:

> How many, if any, of these things upset you?

Call this the baseline condition. In the test condition, except in one slight respect, everything is exactly the same. The question begins exactly as before. The request is exactly the same: "just tell me HOW MANY of them upset you. I don't want to know which ones, just how many." The only difference is that the list now has four items—the first three, plus

4. "black leaders asking for affirmative action."

Suppose, for the sake of illustrating the technique, that the person being interviewed randomly is assigned to the test condition and suppose further, for the sake of definiteness, that there are two things on the list that she cannot abide—all the money that baseball players make and affirmative action. Asked how many items make her angry, her response then is two. Notice that there is no way that the interviewer can tell that one of them is affirmative action, since the list is four items long, and, no less important, that the respondent knows that there is no way that the interviewer can tell that one of the items that upsets her is affirmative action. But although the interviewer cannot possibly tell the proportion of those who get angry at the mention of affirmative action, an analyst easily can simply subtract the mean number of angry responses in the baseline condition from the mean number of angry responses in the test condition and multiply by 100.

In table 8.3, we present an illustrative set of findings from one application of the list experiment. The logic of the hypothetical experiment we sketched and of the actual experiment we administered is

TABLE 8.3   The List Experiment: Overt and Covert Anger among Whites over Affirmative Action

By Ideology	Liberals (%)	Conservatives (%)	Difference (%)
A Overt measure of affirmative action attitudes	32.7	50.9	18.2°
B Covert measure of affirmative action attitudes	55.8	59.1	3.3
C Difference (B − A)	23.1°	8.2	
D Unacknowledged anger (C/B)	41.4	13.9	

By Partisanship	Democrats (%)	Republicans (%)	Difference (%)
A Overt measure of affirmative action attitudes	36.6	48.1	11.5°°
B Covert measure of affirmative action attitudes	52.0	43.5	−8.5
C Difference (B − A)	15.4°	n.s.	
D Unacknowledged anger (C/B)	29.6	n.s.	

Source: 1995 Multi-Investigator Study.

Note: Covert measure is the difference between the number of items that make respondents angry when affirmative action is on the list and when it is not, combining "black leaders" and "college scholarships" versions of the question.

Number of respondents: for liberals, 46 and 70 for the overt and covert measures, respectively; for conservatives, 101 and 76; for Democrats, 187 and 296; and for Republicans, 214 and 312.

°*p* < .05.   °°*p* < .01.

the same. The design of the actual experiment, however, is more complex in several ways. One of the ways that it is more complex is that in the course of the interview exactly the same test stimulus on affirmative action is presented—for one subset covertly, for another overtly—allowing us to compare and contrast reactions to race-conscious programs depending on whether respondents believe they can express how they feel without the interviewer being able to tell how they feel. Since our interest is in the politics of affirmative action, we compare and contrast the responses to affirmative action of liberals and conservatives and of Democrats and Republicans, depending on whether the measurement of their views on race-conscious programs is overt or covert. As a final word of introduction, notice that what is being assessed is not merely whether a person is opposed to affirmative action, but rather whether the mere mention of it *upsets* or *angers* him or her.

Consider first the responses of conservatives. A large proportion of them, about six in every ten, are angry at affirmative action, but what is interesting, comparing rows A and B, is that far and away most of them are willing to say so overtly. Consider, by contrast, the responses of liberals. When their attitudes toward affirmative action are assessed overtly, only about one-third of them express anger. When their attitudes are assessed covertly, however, more than one-half of them acknowledge they are angry at affirmative action—a number indistinguishable from that of conservatives.

The upper panel of table 8.3 thus reports two quite different pictures of the politics of affirmative action. When someone is listening, liberals and conservatives diverge; when they think they can say what they feel without anybody being able to tell, they converge. The lower panel of table 8.3, comparing and contrasting the overt and covert responses of Democrats and Republicans, corroborates the results of the upper panel in every crucial point. These findings, and they are only a selection from the series of national surveys we have conducted, suggest that the standard view of the ideological division over race misses precisely what is distinctive about the politics of affirmative action—namely, that the cleavage over race-conscious policies, rather than dividing liberals and conservatives, now is dividing liberals themselves.

It may be objected that although liberals and conservatives are equally likely to get angry over affirmative action, they do not get angry for the same reasons. Perhaps conservatives get angry because they believe that affirmative action is doing too much for blacks, but liberals get angry for just the opposite reason: because they believe too little is being done and the little that is being done now is in danger of being undone.

It cannot be said that this objection is compelling on its face, given the one-sided opposition to affirmative action evident in the NES time series. But it is at least logically possible, and so we have conducted a series of tests to assess its validity. First, if the greater anger expressed by liberals when their feelings toward affirmative action are expressed covertly is a function of *commitment* (rather than opposition) to affirmative action, then the difference should be especially large for liberals who support strong forms of affirmative action. In fact, the truth of the matter is just the other way around: the proportion of liberals who support strong forms of affirmative action who suppress their anger over it in the list experiment is indistinguishable from zero. Second, we put together an index measuring the degree to which respon-

dents get angry about "Giving blacks and other minorities special advantages in jobs and schools" and "Spokesmen for minorities who are
always complaining that blacks are being discriminated against." If the
liberal anger over affirmative action picked up by the covert measurement method of the list experiment represents anger at the frustration
of the goals of affirmative action, then the likelihood of expressing
anger in the test condition should, for liberals, be negatively correlated with the index of anger at blacks. In fact, instead of the correlation being negative, it is positive.

The suggestion that anger over affirmative action is driven, on the
left, by a frustration that too little is being done in behalf of blacks
thus fails. Liberals and Democrats, when free to express how they really feel, are just as likely to be angry and upset over affirmative action
as conservatives and Republicans.

PREJUDICE AND POLITICAL IDEOLOGY

In proposing that political considerations are integral to the positions
that white Americans take on racial policies, we have never suggested
that considerations of race in general, and racial prejudice in particular, do not matter. But from the start of our research program, we
could not escape observing the modesty of the correlation between
racial prejudice and racial policy preferences among white Americans,
whatever survey we analyzed and whatever measure of express prejudice we employed.[8] Prejudice certainly was one of the factors at work,
and for some areas of policy, such as welfare, its impact was substantial
(Sniderman and Piazza 1993). But rather than imprinting itself on the
positions that white Americans take on public policies dealing with
black Americans, correlation coefficients summarizing the covariation
between racial prejudice and racial policy preference typically were
squeezed around .1 and .2.

This result we cross-validated for surveys other than our own (see
Sniderman and Carmines 1997a, 72, tab. 4), but the findings, their
consistency notwithstanding, left us unsatisfied. The modesty of the
correlations between prejudice and racial policy preference, taken as
a whole, suggested that racial prejudice was largely a spent force. This
did not square with our own sense of the world. How could the empirical results and our own intuition both be right? The way out, it struck
us, was to take politics seriously. People, if they are politically engaged,
do not view public policies from nowhere. Just so far as they have
formed a coherent orientation, they have a point of view, and it is their
political point of view that determines which considerations are rele-

vant for them, and which not, in making a choice about an issue of public policy.

Consider a pair of citizens. Both are thorough-going conservatives in their political outlook, but one has distinctly negative feelings toward blacks; the other, distinctly positive ones. Suppose we ask each whether he or she supports or opposes a proposal to increase government expenditures on job-training programs for blacks. The answer of the first, the one who dislikes blacks, is obvious. But so, too, is the answer of the second. To support a policy because you like blacks, you must believe that it will help them. Naturally, if you are a liberal, you will think bigger government programs are going to help blacks. But just as naturally, if you are a conservative, you will think these programs will not in fact help blacks who need help; all they will do is waste money setting up a new government bureaucracy. In short, just so far as the second person genuinely is a conservative, she, too, will answer "opposed." Notice, less obviously, that in answering "opposed," it is not as though she is pulled in one direction, by her conservative views, to oppose the policy and in the opposite direction, by her feelings of regard for blacks, to support it. The policy choice presents no conflict, since the conclusion to draw, just so far as one is a conservative, is that another job-training program will not in fact help blacks.

Now imagine another pair of citizens. Both are thorough-going liberals in their political outlook, but one has distinctly negative feelings toward blacks; the other, distinctly positive ones. How should they go about deciding whether or not to support a job-training program for blacks or not? The answer for the second liberal is obvious. He has two reasons to support the program: his desire, as a person with a positive regard for blacks, to see them better off and his belief, as a liberal, that more government effort in the form of job-training programs will help blacks become better off. But what position will the first liberal take?

It is our hypothesis that his racial prejudice will trump his political principles. More exactly, we want to bet on a systematic interaction: the more liberal whites are, the more important racial prejudice should be in shaping their political thinking about race; conversely, the more conservative whites are, the less important racial prejudice should be in shaping their positions on issues of race. Prejudice, it should be underlined, is not less important for the political thinking of conservatives because conservatives are less prejudiced—on the contrary, they are more likely to be racially prejudiced than liberals.

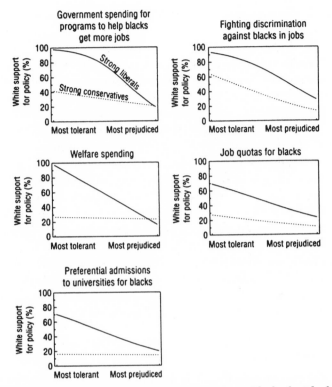

Figure 8.3. Support for Government Programs to Assist Blacks, by Ideology and Level of Prejudice. *Source:* 1991 Race and Politics Study. *Note:* Prejudice ranges from the most tolerant 1 percent to the most prejudiced 1 percent of whites.

But how conservatives feel toward blacks is a relatively unimportant factor in shaping their political thinking about issues of race because, just so far as they are conservative, they have a relevant and sufficient reason to oppose government programs to assist blacks. By contrast, the more liberal whites are, the more important racial prejudice should be as a factor shaping the positions they take on issues of race. And it should be more important because, just so far as they are prejudiced, they have a relevant and sufficient reason to oppose government-sponsored programs for blacks even though they are liberal. Measures of prejudice are described in detail in Sniderman and Carmines (1997a).

Drawing on the National Race and Politics Study, figure 8.3 reports a series of logistic regressions testing the hypothesis of an interaction of political ideology and racial prejudice. The solid lines summarize the impact of differences in feelings toward blacks on issue positions for liberals; the dotted lines, for conservatives.

As is readily apparent, on each of the issues shown from government job-training programs through preferential admissions, the influence of racial prejudice among liberals is striking. By contrast, though the impact of prejudice is not completely absent in every instance for conservatives—note particularly their responses to government-led efforts to fight racial discrimination in hiring—its impact characteristically is slight and often insignificant.

This is a finding worth close consideration, we think.[9] Here we want only to emphasize how this result fills out our larger argument on the centrality of politics. It is always a temptation, and usually a mistake, to ask whether the politics of race depends more heavily on racial or political factors. One reason that it is a mistake is because, as our findings illustrate, the former hinges on the latter. Hence the paradox of the interaction of racial prejudice and political ideology is this: where prejudice is more common—namely, on the political right—it is less important; where it is less common—namely, on the political left—it is more important.

THE "PRINCIPLE-POLICY" PUZZLE

In gauging one perspective, it is useful to lay it alongside another to see what distinctively recommends each. We, therefore, want to contrast the political perspective we are advocating with a sociological one that Howard Schuman and his colleagues have advanced.[10]

Racial norms are the fundamental factor in their account—so much so that they suggest that their book would better have been titled *Racial Norms*, not *Racial Attitudes* (Schuman et al. 1997, 3). Norms, they declare, reflect a social (or cultural) agreement on what is appropriate; racial norms accordingly define the appropriate relationship between black and white Americans in the larger society (p. 311). Beginning around World War II, they go on to argue, the racial norms in America began to change, and from the mid-1960s on, they have unambiguously called for equal treatment of blacks and whites. Norms are not the same as personal preferences: a person may recognize that he ought to be in favor of equal treatment for blacks—indeed may even publicly favor it—even though he privately opposes it (p. 3). But a fundamental reason why people think what they think and do what they do is societal norms. Just because they represent societal agreement on what is appropriate, they tend to be internalized or, at

any rate, complied with (p. 5). So viewed, the politics of race represents centrally a process of normative conformity. American society
now has committed itself to the norm of racial equality. A number of
public policies have been developed to work toward racial equality. It
follows that just so far as white Americans are genuinely committed
to the norm of racial equality, they should be motivated to implement
it by supporting policies to achieve it.

Schuman and his colleagues, of course, recognize that large numbers of Americans in fact oppose an array of public policies advanced
to achieve racial equality. Hence the principle-policy gap: why do so
many white Americans accept the value of racial equality at the level
of principle, but not at the level of policy? The gap between principle
and implementation arises from a variety of reasons—they point to,
among other factors, differing degrees of commitment to the norm of
equality in the first place, the intrusion of individual and group interests, competing values, and, naturally, racial prejudice—but the bedrock premise of their argument is that so far as white Americans
support the norm of racial equality, then they—logically and causally—should support governmental policies to achieve it.

We believe that this is a point of view that offers an important insight into some aspects of the politics of race and, more particularly,
issues on the equal treatment agenda.[11] Indeed, that is why we ourselves introduced the hypothesis of multiple agendas in racial politics,
distinguishing the equal treatment agenda from the social welfare
and the race-conscious agendas, respectively (Sniderman and Piazza
1993). But having underlined this point of agreement, we want also
to suggest that their posing the problem of explanation in terms of
conformity to a societal norm of equal treatment has led Schuman
and his colleagues to mistake the principal thrust of the contemporary
politics of race.

Think of the policy issues that have been at the center of debate
over racial policy over the last thirty years. Selecting from their own
list, there is, for example, the issue of whether the liberal government
has a special obligation to help improve the living standards of African
Americans, of whether it is important to correct the problems of poverty and unemployment, of whether federal spending on programs
that assist blacks should be increased.[12] On the normative conformity
interpretation, just so far as one supports the norm of equal treatment,
one should support these policy efforts to implement it.[13] But as a
moment's thought will make plain, this mistakes the fact that what we
are attempting to understand is a process not of societal conformity,

but of political choice. Viewed from a liberal perspective, it follows that if you support the norm of equal treatment, you should support more federal spending to assist blacks. But to view it only from a liberal perspective begs the question. It misses what is crucial—that there is a political debate as to whether bigger government is a good idea even for promoting the welfare of blacks. On the contrary, governmental activism of a liberal stripe on behalf of the disadvantaged, so far from being part of a solution to the problem of racial equality, is part of the problem from a conservative perspective. Schuman's conception of normative conformity presupposes that conservatives, to be consistent, must support liberal policies.

Our own views of these policies, let us emphasize, are quite beside the point. The point is instead that it is necessary to acknowledge the differing points of view of citizens in deciding whether to support or oppose, say, more government job-training programs for blacks—because if one wants to take the argument of norms seriously, what distinguishes politics as a domain of choice is that it is socially legitimate to disagree about policies like this. Not to put too fine a point on it, but it is, we think, impossible to understand the character of American politics over this century without understanding that it has been definitively shaped by a continuing debate between liberal and conservative conceptions of the obligations of government and the responsibilities of citizens.

Schuman and his colleagues, concentrating on processes of societal conformity, overlook the clash of competing political orientations. Remarkably, there is no attention in the whole of their empirical analysis given to the role of liberalism and conservatism as political perspectives that inform the positions that Americans take on racial policies. Indeed, their conception of ideology in American politics is a perplexing one. They characterize our argument on the centrality of the clash between liberal and conservative outlooks, for example, as an attempt "to explain differences between principle and implementation items by identifying a general rejection by many whites of government intervention, quite apart from racial issues" (Schuman et al. 1997, 308), equating this rejection with a reluctance "to accept constraints of *any* kind on behavior" (p. 309, emphasis in original). They then go on to show that opposition to government intrusion or coercion is, at most, of marginal importance in accounting for the positions white Americans take on racial issues by demonstrating, for example, that opposition to open housing laws is only slightly related to opposition to mandatory seat belts. But this misses what it means to say that politics matters. We certainly have never invoked the idea that whites who oppose more government support for job-training programs for blacks do so out of aversion to government coercion. We have instead argued that a large part of the clash, particularly over policies on the social welfare agenda, is driven by colliding views of the responsibilities of government and the obligations of citizens. Purely as a matter of fact we do not know the empirical relationship between liberalism-conservatism, on the one side, and support or opposition to mandatory seat belts, on the other. But people's views on seat belts are no indicator of their overall ideological orientations. Slighting politics, Schuman and his colleagues have mistaken libertarianism for conservatism.

The framework in which issues of race are fought out, if we are right, is defined by the American party system and the clash of competing ideological commitments embodied in the two principal parties. By way of offering a concrete example of what we have in mind, we shall draw on the Equal Opportunity Experiment, which was carried out in our first study of the politics of race.[14] We want to revisit this experiment not only because it illustrates, dramatically we believe, the imprint of ideology on the politics of race, but also because it drives home the mistake of false antitheses. As we have maintained from the start, the clash over a racial policy can have a quite different character for different strata of the public at large.

The Equal Opportunity Experiment is designed to examine the extent to which the willingness among white Americans to support a claim to government assistance is conditioned on whether the beneficiaries of the assistance are black or not. Accordingly, in carrying out the Equal Opportunity Experiment, every respondent was asked whether government should guarantee people an equal opportunity to succeed, but one-half of the time the people to benefit were blacks; the other half of the time, women. It can be argued that women, just as much as blacks, are entitled to government assurances of an equal opportunity to succeed—not equal outcomes, notice, but equal opportunities. It cannot be argued—at any rate, we know of no one who does argue—that women are entitled to such assurances, but blacks are not. It follows that to favor assurances of equal opportunity for women, but not for blacks, is evidence of a discriminatory double standard.

Our interest in the experiment is thus twofold. We mean to show, first, that racial discrimination still persists and, second, that to act as though one side to a political argument must accept the policies of the other—or expose itself as hypocritical—is to miss what political

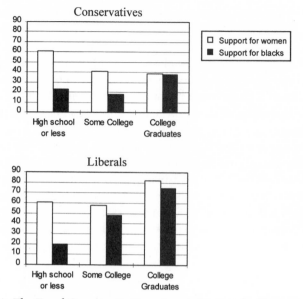

Figure 8.4. The Equal Opportunity Experiment: Support for Governmental Assurance of Equal Opportunity, by Ideology and Education. $N = 456$, minimum base $N = 20$. *Source:* Bay Area Regional Race and Politics Study.

argument is about. Figure 8.4 accordingly summarizes levels of support for government assurance of equal opportunity to succeed for a group as a function of three factors—the group to benefit, blacks or women; the respondents' political point of view, liberal or conservative; and the likelihood of their understanding the position appropriate to their political point of view, as indexed by formal education.

Focusing on those with the least education, one sees clear evidence of discriminatory double standards. Whites with a high school diploma or less are markedly less likely to support a claim to government assurance of equal opportunity to succeed when made in behalf of blacks than they are to support exactly the same claim when made in behalf of women. What is more, this discriminatory double standard holds as strongly for self-identified liberals as conservatives.

Now consider liberals and conservatives in a position to understand what their political philosophies require of them. Well-educated liberals, in the largest number, support government assurances of equal opportunity to succeed, and it makes no difference to them who benefits—women or blacks. Well-educated conservatives, in the largest number, oppose government assurances of an equal opportunity to succeed, and it makes no difference to them who is to benefit—women or blacks.

Both liberals and conservatives thus make their choice on the basis of their principles. Both liberals and conservatives thus are impartial in applying their principles. But contrary to the suggestion of the principle-policy puzzle, just insofar as their choice is principled, they diverge, not converge, on public policies proposed to assist minorities.

In this volume, Jim Sidanius and his colleagues report quite different results from a "replication" of the Equal Opportunity Experiment. But their suggestion that they have replicated our experiment is perplexing. Replication involves repeating the same procedures in an effort to see if one obtains the same results. But they have done something quite different from what we had done. We analyzed attitudes toward equal opportunity; they examine attitudes toward affirmative action; and there is a library chock-full of studies showing that the two are quite different. Just as puzzling, we analyzed a sample of white Americans; they analyze a sample half of whom are Hispanics.

Ordinarily, it would suffice to observe that if different investigators do different things, it should not be surprising that they observe different results. The Sidanius results, though, deserve consideration in their own right. Looking at their figure 7.4, we were taken aback, first, by the overall level of support that they observe for affirmative action. In their study, affirmative action is a relatively popular policy, with a clear majority opposed to it only among well-educated conservatives, and then only when blacks are its beneficiaries.[15] The finer grain of their findings is still more perplexing. It does not, for example, fit anyone's expectations on any side of the debate over racial politics to observe, as they do, that those who are better able to understand what liberalism asks of them are *more* likely to oppose affirmative action than are those who are less able to do so. Yet, according to Sidanius's results, well-educated liberals are *more* likely to oppose affirmative action than are less-educated liberals. And it seems positively perverse to take seriously a suggestion that conservatism has now thrown its weight behind affirmative action. Yet, again according to Sidanius's results, a majority of conservatives—including well-educated conservatives—are in favor of affirmative action for the poor.

We are not sufficiently familiar with the politics of Los Angeles County, where their sample was drawn, to judge whether these results ring true there. But the larger cautionary conclusion to draw is straightforward. Sidanius and his colleagues suggest that the problem is that our results do not match theirs. The problem is instead that their results do not match anyone else's, including ours. And turning from cautionary to substantive conclusions, we think the Equal Opportunity Experiment captures instructively the cross-currents of racial politics—the persistence of racial double standards, particularly among the less-educated strata of the public, and the clash of competing ideas of fairness, particularly among the more-educated strata.

THE ECOLOGY OF ISSUE ARGUMENTS: DISTINGUISHING BETWEEN THE ATTRIBUTES OF CITIZENS AND THE CHARACTERISTICS OF POLITICAL ENVIRONMENTS

Politics is not about choosing positions in a world where no pressure is brought to bear on citizens to favor one or the other side of a public issue. It is about the choice of positions that citizens make in the face of arguments crafted to win their support for one side of an issue—or at the least to qualify their allegiance to the other.

The standard public opinion interview is too tightly corsetted, we want to suggest, to accommodate the dynamics of political argumentation. The interview situation is deliberately designed to put respondents at their ease; to persuade them that there is no right or wrong answer to the questions asked of them; to minimize pressures on them, whether by virtue of the wording of a question or the reading of it by a questioner, to favor one rather than another side of an issue. By contrast, the politics of race, just so far as it really is politics, aims to persuade citizens, to call on their loyalties, to disarm their suspicions—in short, to win their support.

A principal aim of our effort to integrate experimental designs and public opinion interviews has been to explore the rhythms of political argument—to understand the reactions of citizens to issues of public policy as they confront the play of argument and counterargument as it occurs in the world of politics. One experiment designed to accomplish this is the Competing Values Experiment. But, and this is worth underlining, what we anticipated the experiment would teach us and what it did were two different things.

The Competing Values Experiment focuses on the issue of open housing—whether it should be against the law to refuse to sell a house to a buyer on the grounds of race. In the "neutral" condition, the GSS question is administered. In the second condition, respondents' attention is called to the value of "property rights" and, in the third, to the role of government in helping those in need. The experiment was thus designed to compare and contrast whites' reactions to the issue of open housing when it is isolated from other considerations and when it is put into play politically, once with an appeal to a value favoring the political right and once with an appeal to a value favoring the left. In the first condition, the issue is framed as follows:

> Suppose there were a community-wide vote on a general housing issue and that there were two possible laws to vote on. One law says that homeowners can decide for themselves who to sell their houses to, even if they prefer NOT to sell to blacks. The other law says that homeowners cannot refuse to sell to someone because of their race or color.

> Which law would you vote for?

This first condition we characterize as a "neutral" treatment. Following the GSS model, respondents are offered a choice between a pair of alternatives that stand on the same footing: one is a "law" that says "homeowners can decide for themselves"; the other, a "law" that "homeowners cannot refuse to sell to some because of their race or color."

So far as citizens choose on the basis of their political outlook, we should naturally expect an ideological division over the issue. And so there is. As table 8.4 shows, liberals are significantly more likely to support open housing than conservatives.

Liberals are significantly more likely than conservatives to support open housing, so formulated. But, of course, part of the point of public argument is precisely to move people from one side of an issue to the other by invoking competing values. What we should aim to understand is the politics of issues when they are put into play. Accordingly, in the second experimental condition, the competing consideration of property values was invoked.

> Some people believe that homeowners should be free to decide for themselves who to sell their house to, even if they prefer not to sell it to blacks. For example, some people might say it isn't that they don't want to sell to blacks; it's just that they don't want to be told what to do with their own property. In other words, they feel that because it's their property, they should have the right to sell to anyone they want to.

> How do you feel about this? Do you think homeowners should be able to decide for themselves who to sell their houses to, even if they prefer not to sell to blacks, or do you think homeowners should not be allowed to refuse to sell to someone because of their race or color?

Notice the contrast between the middle panel of table 8.4, which shows the politics of open housing when the issue is put into play by

TABLE 8.4   The Competing Values Experiment, by Education and Ideology

(A) OPEN HOUSING CONDITION		

	Ideological Orientation		
	Liberal	Moderate	Conservative
High school	67%	45%	45%
Some college	61%	51%	39%
College plus	67%	60%	57%
N	91	175	154

(B) PROPERTY VALUES CONDITION		

	Ideological Orientation		
	Liberal	Moderate	Conservative
High school	26%	17%	15%
Some college	48%	49%	31%
College plus	62%	31%	30%
N	102	156	141

(C) EQUAL TREATMENT CONDITION		

	Ideological Orientation		
	Liberal	Moderate	Conservative
High school	48%	37%	27%
Some college	32%	26%	30%
College plus	74%	31%	16%
N	79	108	150

Source: 1991 Race and Politics Study.

raising the competing value of property rights, and the top panel, which shows division over the issue in an artificially neutral condition. Support plummets. When open housing is considered in isolation from other considerations, a slight majority favors it; when the competing value of property rights is invoked, less than one-third do. As instructively, though support for open housing falls precipitously when the value of property rights is invoked, it does not fall equally everywhere. Liberalism as a political outlook helps immunize citizens against the appeal of competing values—provided, that is, that they have the awareness and intellectual training to appreciate what liberalism requires of them. And if they do, they are as likely to support open housing when the issue is brought into play as when they confront it on its own.

In the third experimental condition, we called attention to the role that government should play in assuring equal treatment.

> Some people believe that the government should make an active effort to see that blacks can live anywhere they choose, including white neighborhoods. Others believe that this is not the government's business and it should stay out of this.

> How do you feel? Is this an area the government should stay out of or should the government make an active effort to see that blacks can live anywhere they can afford to—including white neighborhoods?

We did this deliberately in order to provide a condition in which liberals would have an opportunity to respond to an appeal from their side of the aisle. The results, set out in the bottom panel of table 8.4, could not have been farther from our expectations. The idea that blacks should be able to live where they wished was no more popular in the third condition than in the second. Moreover, essentially the same pattern of defection (contrasted with the neutral condition) is evident, with only liberals, provided they are well enough educated to appreciate what liberalism requires of them, maintaining support for equal opportunity for blacks to live where they wish.

It is precisely in the upsetting of our expectations that a lesson deeper than the one we had anticipated is to be drawn. In designing the Competing Values Experiment, we had supposed the second and third conditions were collectively symmetrical—one intended to appeal to the right, the other to the left. But the politics of the issue turns out the same regardless of which is put into play: one-sided in opposition to equal opportunity in housing. There is, this suggests, something to be said for mapping the ecology of issue arguments.

An issue like open housing, as it seems to us in retrospect, may be distinguished by the asymmetry of accessible arguments. It is not that the positions taken in a neutral condition are a sham. They reflect, within the usual margin of error, the response that people believe correct to the problem posed to them. In the hurly-burly of real politics, however, their attention is called to a welter of competing arguments and counterarguments. But just because arguments may be found on both sides of an issue, it does not follow that they are equally distributed on both sides. On the contrary, open housing seems to be a specimen example of an issue of race for which the distribution of arguments is skewed.

We invoke the notion of an ecology of issue arguments in order to underline the need to take account of the rhetorical environments of issues. They, quite as much as the preferences of individuals, are an integral part of the politics of race. Some issues of race may have a distribution of arguments favoring proponents of government assistance, or at any rate not handicapping them. The issue of open housing, however, is not one of these. Opponents have more, or at any rate more readily accessible, arguments to invoke than proponents. And the one-sided politics of the issue—when it actually comes into play—is a consequence.

DISSENSUS AND CONSENSUS

Research on racial politics has been, to an unusual and a regrettable degree, adversarial. The issues, to be sure, are complex and emotionally charged, but the rhetoric has been extreme even so. Recognizing that offense has been given on all sides, it sometimes seems as if people are turning somersaults in order to disagree. Lawrence Bobo, for example, claims that our view is without evidentiary support and should be laid "to rest with finality" (this volume, p. 163). This seems a little extreme, not least because Bobo himself has offered support for our views at many points[16] and even those who disagree with some of our views acknowledge they have received enough support to be part of the mainstream view (Kinder and Sanders 1996, 269 ff). We have a sense of Bobo straining after a conclusion.[17] Then again, Sidanius and his colleagues charge us with not only "fundamentally misunderstanding the dynamics of race relations in America, but also . . . helping to actually *mask* these dynamics" (Sidanius et al. this volume, p. 232, emphasis in original). Race as a subject of research is obviously a thorny thicket, but although some of the thorns are genuine, others seem synthetic, fabricated for the purpose of turning differences of opinion over evidence into differences of opinion over politics.

For our part, we propose to review the competing perspectives in an effort to point to emerging areas of agreement. Agreement on each point, needless to say, is far from complete, and the parties in agreement shift from point to point. Our list, moreover, is illustrative, not exhaustive, and we apologize in advance if, in order to locate some points of consensus, we have read the views of others expansively rather than narrowly. We have striven, when criticizing other perspectives—and our own—to do so with an eye to pinpointing questions future research should address. No doubt we have not gotten the balance of things altogether right, but we do want to emphasize that our review of what is being done and how it is being done has left us with a conviction that progress is being made, the gnashing of teeth and the rending of veils notwithstanding.

Proceeding from the more specific to the more abstract, we start with the role of values.

THE ROLE OF VALUES IN SHAPING PUBLIC OPINION ON ISSUES OF RACE

There seems to be convergence on two points in particular. The first has to do with agreement on the relevance of values bearing on the broadly political issue of what government ought to do in behalf of those who are poor, particularly those who are economically disadvantaged or who historically have been disadvantaged by discrimination. We read Sears, Sidanius, and Kinder as concurring in this, as obviously, given our politics-oriented perspective, do we.

This agreement admittedly carries us only a modest distance. The value of equality surely is bound up with this complex of beliefs as to what government should and should not do in behalf of the disadvantaged. But it is not the whole of it, and as Sears's and Bobo's chapters in this volume make plain, the meaning of equality and its measurement are far from agreed. In this respect, Sidanius's chapter conveys an unfortunately close-cropped conception of equality, presupposing that it presents itself under only one description. It would seem preferable to be guided by Douglas Rae's (1981) classic analysis, which drove home the fundamental truth that not only does equality inevitably clash with competing values, such as liberty, but also competing conceptions of equality itself inescapably come into conflict with one another.[18]

Acknowledging these issues, there nonetheless seems to be broad agreement on an important point. Simply put, a significant part of the explanation over why Americans disagree about the politics of race is that they disagree about the politics of equality. And without wishing to nag a theme, once one acknowledges the central role of equality in the politics of race, one acknowledges in the bargain the continuity between racial politics and the larger politics of social welfare, which has been a defining feature of the American party system certainly since the New Deal. In saying this, we are far from denying that racial politics has a distinctive component. But we are contending that some of its deepest and most enduring cleavages are defined by the clash between competing conceptions of the obligations of government and the responsibilities of citizens.

The second point of agreement is that whatever values are centrally involved, individualism as standardly conceived is not one of them. We read Sidanius, Bobo, and even (on occasion) Sears (see, e.g., Sears 1988) as agreeing on this,[19] and we obviously concur. We should like, however, to make this point in a nonpartisan way. Kinder and Sears obviously continue to believe that individualism is integrally implicated in the politics of race. All that we should like to remark is that what they mean by and take to be a sign of individualism is equally obviously not what others mean by it, and the burden is, therefore, on them to establish by evidence that their usage is warranted. It does seem to us that any fair reading of Sears's and Kinder's chapters will conclude that they have not yet met this burden.

The liberal understanding of race, first formulated by Gunnar Myrdal (1944), stood on the premise that the strongest weapon against racial discrimination and inequality was the American Creed. Sears and Kinder have aimed to stand the liberal understanding on its head. It is their claim that, so far from racism being at odds with American ideals, it is inspired by "the finest and proudest of traditional American values" (Sears 1988, 54). If they are right, rather than looking to the American Creed for support in the effort to overcome racial inequality, it is the very values at the heart of the American experience that must be either transformed or transcended. In order for their revisionist claim to be right, it must be the case that these values actually are a wellspring for racism, new or old. But there is now agreement, by them as well as by everyone else, on the pillars of the American Creed. On the one side, individualism as it has customarily been understood and assessed is not integrally related to racism, while, on the other, inegalitarianism is deeply implicated. Since it is equality, not elitism, that is a defining element of the American Creed and since political toleration is a source of racial tolerance (for supporting evidence, see Sniderman, Brody, and Tetlock 1991, chap. 7), we think the liberal understanding of race better grounded than the revisionist.

THE AUTONOMOUS ROLE OF RACIAL PREJUDICE IN SHAPING PUBLIC OPINION ON ISSUES OF RACE

On every account, racial prejudice still colors the thinking of many white Americans about the responsibility of government to assist black Americans. But, considered as a factor operating in its own right, there is a sharp difference of opinion over the extent of its continuing power. We read all participants to the debate, with one very important exception, as agreeing that racial prejudice is no longer the paramount factor dominating the positions that white Americans take on issues of race. Sidanius and his colleagues make this point here as elsewhere (see Sidanius et al. this volume, p. 227). Bobo does the same, also here as elsewhere (see Bobo this volume, tab. 5.2, model 4). And we have done the same (Sniderman and Piazza 1993; Sniderman and Carmines 1997a). It is perhaps worth noting that this conclusion follows from analyses using a number of measures of prejudice—including feeling thermometers and negative stereotype indices calculated both absolutely and relatively—and drawing on a large variety of survey sources—including the NES surveys, the GSS, and the National Race and Politics Survey.

The one exception, of course, is the symbolic racism researchers. It is the distinctive contention of the new racism researchers that racism is the paramount factor defining the choices that white Americans make about matters of race. They have nailed their flag to this mast, asserting that racism is "the primary ingredient in white opinion on racial affairs" (Kinder and Sanders 1996, 301) and charging that those who suggest otherwise "participate in the demotion of prejudice as an explanation for political conflict" (p. 271) and are guilty of "whitewashing racism" (p. 269). Obviously, we do not agree, but our aim here is not to register our disagreement, but to highlight its basis. Everything hinges on the symbolic racism researchers' unique measure of racism. No other measure of racism—whether it makes use of indirect forms of assessment stereotypes or feeling thermometers (scored relatively or absolutely) or is conceived as affective, aversive, ambivalent, or stereotypical or in any other way—has even a remotely comparable power to predict the racial policy preferences of white Americans. The question, then, is why the connection between their unique measure of racism and measures of racial policy preferences is uniquely close. They would maintain that the closeness of the connection demonstrates the continuing power of racism. We strongly believe that it is instead a warning flag. We cannot see that it carries understanding very far to explain opposition to welfare for blacks in terms of a belief that those on welfare "can get along without it if they tried" (Kinder and Sanders 1996, 107, tab. 5.1). An analogy we think is apt is purporting to explain the vote for a presidential candidate on the basis of a belief that he is the better person for the job. What is supposed to be doing the job of explanation seems, to our eyes, to be difficult to distinguish from what it is supposed to be explaining. We leave this question to future research.

THE ROLE OF GROUP INTERESTS

Two of the contributors to this volume, Sidanius and Bobo, have argued that the positions of white Americans reflect in part group interests. We should like to explain, first, why the argument of Sidanius, because it is operationally more developed, is empirically vulnerable, while that of Bobo, precisely because it is underidentified, is protected against empirical assessment. Then, since group interests seem to us part of a rounded account of racial politics, we want to say a word about the logical shape these interests must take.

To begin with the first point, Sidanius does what Bobo fails to do—advance a direct indicator of whether, when a difference between the issue positions of two groups is observed, the reason for the difference is group interest. That, after all, is the job of the social dominance measure—to assess the strength of the desire of some to enjoy the benefits of dominance over others. Bobo, by contrast, takes the fact that a difference remains in the positions of the two groups after a number of plausibly relevant factors are taken into account to be his measure of the impact of group interest. Sidanius's procedure, of course, is superior because it allows his claims to be falsifiable. By way of supporting his conception that his measure of social dominance measures what it is supposed to measure, Sidanius presents evidence showing roughly that the more dominant the social position of a group, the higher its score on the social dominance measure.[20] This carries his argument forward, but not, however, very far. On exactly the same logic, it should be the case that the more dominant the social position of individuals within the socially dominant group is, the higher their scores on the social dominance measure should be. For if it is true that whites on average are better off than blacks, it also is true that there is a great range of variation in dominance among whites. This is true both when comparing individuals with one another and when comparing one class with another. It follows, if Sidanius's account is correct, that (taken as individuals or as groups) the better off and better educated whites are, the higher their scores on the social dominance measure will be. We lack the data to decide ourselves the validity of this prediction, but it will take braver people than we to bet, as Sidanius must, that the middle class (or the well-educated) will score higher on his measure of social dominance than the underclass (or the poorly educated). It is harder, just because Bobo lacks a direct indicator, to test the strength of his particular conception of a group interest hypothesis. A more rigorous treatment seems preferable, not least because this way of proceeding is particularly vulnerable to oscillations of semantic characterization, with Bobo referring at one point to "the powerfully robust racial difference in opinion that separates the views of blacks and of Latinos from those of whites" and yet at another remarking on "quite real, but muted racial differences" (see Bobo, pp. 160 and 149, respectively).

Taking the two together, the way in which both Bobo and Sidanius conceive of a group interest analysis has an odd logical shape and seems frankly preliminary. Consider their odd logical shape first. How do differences in group position play into the politics of affirmative action? According to Bobo, "[M]uch of the white opposition to affirmative action springs from a desire to maintain a privileged position in the American racial hierarchy" (p. 145), or as he also puts it, whites oppose affirmative action "because they perceive blacks as competitive threats for valued social resources, status, and privileges" (pp. 142–43). Sidanius sees the matter the same way, asserting that "one's commitment to equality is likely to be related to the social status of one's group, with members of [higher status] groups being more resistant to the redistribution of resources and less likely to endorse principles of equality" (Sidanius, p. 196). Both their formulations are, it would appear as a matter of principle, asymmetrical. It is whites who do the resisting, in an effort to hold onto what they have, not blacks or Hispanics who do the striving, in an effort to see that they are more fairly treated and better off, though the one matches the facts as well as the other. It has puzzled us why both Bobo and Sidanius have favored an asymmetrical formulation, accenting only the resisting of whites and passing over the striving of minorities. Treating minorities as passive must lead analytically to an overestimate of the opposition of whites and normatively to a slighting of the agency of the minorities.[21] Searching for an answer, we have found a clue in the (to us, odd) way that they characterize our approach. We are, Bobo declares, proponents of the principled objection hypothesis. This is an eccentrically truncated characterization. In our view, one of the principal factors shaping Americans' positions on issues of race is their political values and ideology, and this, consistent with ordinary usage, is a way of claiming *both* that those who are broadly conservative will favor a narrower view of the obligations of government to the less-well-off *and* that those who are broadly liberal will favor a more expansive one (for the record, we should also note that the reasoning behind the use of the term "principled" altogether eludes us). We think it essential to recognize also the role of liberalism, and the only reason for their restricting attention to conservativism, as best we can see, is an unacknowledged assumption in their argument: namely, that all that needs to be explained is opposition to affirmative action because in the absence of ill-will or self-interest people would naturally support it. Perhaps we may say that a justification for treating support for affirmative action as the default condition is not obvious.

The presentations of both Bobo and Sidanius also strike us as frankly preliminary and, by comparison with earlier work, curiously hollowed out.[22] Speaking in the spirit of people who believe that this line of work is promising, we want to say that it probably is time to go beyond observing that the political orientations of groups differ even after taking account of plausibly relevant factors. It would certainly be helpful to develop direct indicators of the clash of group interests, to examine some of the diverse forms (e.g., economic versus cultural) that these clashes may take, and to specify some of the conditions under which group interests play a more important, or a less important, role as an explanatory factor.

There is a final point about the limits of group interests as a basis for understanding the dynamics of racial politics. Recognizing that groups may have different interests, concentrating on the cleavage between blacks and whites misses the heart of the politics of race. There is a political contest over racial policy because white Americans themselves differ as to what should be done. If the cleavage over racial politics were fundamentally racial, it would not be possible to assemble a winning majority in behalf of policies to assist blacks. On the contrary, just so far as a coalition is formed across racial lines, racial policies are effectively contestable. The nub of the analytic problem, it follows, is to understand why some whites favor and others oppose an array of different policies to assist blacks, and if we read rightly the evidence, particularly that of Sears and Kinder (see, e.g., Kinder and Sears 1981), the role of interests in accounting for differences among whites is a comparatively minor one.

ISSUE PLURALISM

In his seminal work on mass belief systems, Philip Converse (1964) crystallized the hypothesis of issue commonality. On their face, he acknowledged, racial policies appeared diverse, some dealing with matters of education, others with the assurance of equal treatment under the law, and still others with employment or subsidies for housing and food. But this appearance of diversity, he suggested, was misleading. In the minds of white Americans, these different issues boiled down to different ways of asking the same question—how do you feel about black Americans? Just so far as white Americans disliked them, they would oppose policies designed to assist blacks across the board. There are common elements to government policies to assist blacks and accordingly an element of commonality in the responses of citizens to them. In order to capture the lines of political division, however, and no less important, the sources underlying them, there is increasing evidence of the need to attend to the diversity of racial politics.

To call attention to the variety of racial politics, we introduced the concept of issue pluralism (see Sniderman et al. 1993). It has seemed to us for a while that the Conversian perspective yields a misleadingly homogenized impression of the variety of clashes over racial policy, as though the profound differences in what the government actually proposes to do across the range of racial policies really are of no account to citizens. By contrast, we think that the actual terms of policy choice may matter in at least three distinct ways: (1) in the political balance of support and opposition for government programs, (2) in the comparative balance of underlying factors encouraging support or opposition, and (3) in the relative pliability or fixity of the positions that citizens take (for supporting evidence on all three aspects, see Sniderman and Piazza 1993).

The concept of issue pluralism is intended to underline the hypothesis that the actual terms of the choices that citizens are asked to make have something to do with the process by which they make these choices. The hypothesis, if not the term, has gained general acceptance.

To point to the most striking example, the issue of affirmative action has itself become nearly a poster issue for the notion of issue pluralism. In one of our studies, we carried out the Two Meaning Experiment, demonstrating the profoundly different reactions of white Americans depending on whether the issue of affirmative action is cast in terms of giving preferential treatment or of making an extra effort to assure equal treatment (Sniderman and Carmines 1997a, 23–27), Schuman et al. report similar results from a similar experiment (1997, 297–98), and the findings from the NES surveys solidly support the results of both experiments.

To say that a point is widely agreed on is not to say it is entirely uncontested. The whole premise of Bobo's chapter in this very volume is that it is sensible to speak of affirmative action without qualification. This difference in approach is less troubling than it may at first seem because Bobo's position is self-contradictory. Here he writes as though it is appropriate to treat affirmative action without distinguishing kinds of affirmative action; but elsewhere he and Schuman et al. (1997, 298) declare that "[w]hen speaking of support for 'affirmative action,' it is always important to specify exactly what kind of affirmative action policy is intended." More broadly, a belief—sometimes justified, sometimes not—that preferential treatment or racial quotas are in play transforms the clash over affirmative action—the evidence for this now is indisputable. And it equally is indisputable that there is a world of difference politically between an issue in which more than eight in every ten whites line up on the side of assistance for blacks and one in which one out of every two—or more—favor help for blacks. What conceivably is to be gained analytically by pretending that affirmative action is a foam rubber notion, embracing virtually any and all policies—from job-training programs to explicit quota systems for admission to law schools—intended to assist blacks (in addition to Bobo this volume, see Steeh and Krysan 1996)? Without meaning to be unkind, to overlook the rancor and turmoil that distinctively surround the politics of affirmative action—understood to involve preferential treatment or racial quotas—is to be politically tone-deaf.

In trying to account for why citizens may or may not support a proposal for government action, it is, we think, necessary to take account of what they actually are being asked to support. Whatever your personal view of the merits of different racial policies, in a democratic society it should be heartening that it makes a difference to citizens what they are specifically asked to approve in the way of government action. On the evidence at hand, it seems to us undeniable that the actual nature of the policy dealing with race—and not merely the fact that it deals with race—can affect the level of support for it, the sources of support, and, finally, the relative fixity (or pliability) of the positions that citizens take. Unchecked, however, the concept of issue pluralism turns into an argument that the politics of every issue is distinctive, idiosyncratic. But there is a structure to the politics of race, and to pick out its pattern of organization there is increasing agreement that a theory of the politics of race requires a hypothesis of multiple agendas.

THE POLICY AGENDA HYPOTHESIS

What is a useful way to think about linkages across racial policy issues? Just so far as the process of citizen choice is a function of the actual terms of choice, it is natural to think in terms of issue agendas. Issues so conceived fall on a common agenda just so far as the alternatives they pose—what government proposes to do and how it proposes to go about doing it—are similar.

More specifically, we proposed that three distinguishable agendas comprise the contemporary politics of race—the social welfare agenda, the race-conscious agenda, and the equal treatment agenda (see Sniderman and Piazza 1993). There is nothing magic about the number three, and the structure of racial politics is not fixed forever. On the contrary, so far as it is defined by the actual substance of public policy, it surely will change over time. But given the will to disagree about racial politics, the agreement achieved on the agenda structure of the politics of race, across data analysts and data sets, is impressive. Drawing on the NES surveys, Kinder and Sanders present a three-factor description of racial issues, corroborating not merely the general shape, but also the specific details of our triple agenda hypothesis. And drawing on the GSS in addition to the NES surveys, Schuman and his colleagues, in the revised version of their work, now agree with our suggestion of a triple agenda.[23]

We do not wish to suggest that the consensus is complete. Sidanius and his colleagues, for example, strongly dissent (see pp. 228–29), and there certainly are versions of the symbolic racism argument that can be read as being at odds with the idea of multiple agendas. But there seems to our eyes to be an encouraging measure of agreement not only that it is useful, in order to take cognizance of the diversity of racial politics, to recognize that there are multiple agendas, but also that it is helpful, in order to identify the distinctive dynamics of contemporary racial politics, to think in terms of three distinguishable agendas.

In speaking of the triple-agenda hypothesis as analytically useful, we do not mean merely that it is taxonomically tidy. The right test of classification schemes is whether, if they are imposed, the causes of the behavior under examination or its consequences are illuminated. Our core proposition is that the process of choice is a function in part of the terms of choice. We want to illustrate accordingly how the idea of multiple agendas helps expose the play of causal factors.

We take as our first example the contingency of the role of racial prejudice. If it is true that the structure of choice defines the relevance of explanatory factors for the process of choice, then the all-too-familiar debate over whether the impact of prejudice in shaping the political thinking of white Americans continues to be large is sterile. On the one side, racial prejudice—assessed by any conventional method—is a minor factor driving opposition to affirmative action—understood to entail either preferential treatment or racial quotas—while there is an accumulation of evidence that it is a more powerful force in fueling opposition to welfare.[24] The argument here is general, by no means peculiar to prejudice. An instructively parallel example, highlighting the interplay of policy agendas and values as explanatory factors, has been offered by Kinder and Sanders. Focusing on egalitarianism, they underline the contingency of its impact. On the one side, equality looms large for issues on the equal treatment agenda, while it "simply disappears from public opinion" for issues on the race-conscious agenda (Kinder and Sanders 1996, 159).

The contingency of causal factors conditional on the terms of choice seems to us an analytic theme emerging with increasing clarity and potentially of uncommon importance in developing a genuinely insightful account of political reasoning, and not only about issues of race.

DYNAMICS OF REASONING ABOUT RACIAL POLICY

In suggesting that the contemporary argument over race is, at its core, a political argument, we are advancing three ideas for consideration. The first is that the contours of the argument over racial policies are given their fundamental shape by the institutions of the party system and the ideological contours of the larger American political landscape. The second is that, so far as the actual terms of choice shape the process of political choice for citizens, there is not simply one issue of race appearing in different guises. There are different issues, and it is a fundamental mistake to suppose that the politics of affirmative action, for example, and the politics of social welfare are interchangeable. The third is that the contemporary debate over race is very much a matter of political argument. It is this third idea that we wish to consider.

Even a few years ago the nearly exclusive concern in the politics of race was with standing decisions on racial policy. These standing decisions may be a product of early socialization, as Sears and Kinder and their colleagues claimed, or of the positions of groups in society, as Bobo and Sidanius and their colleagues claimed, or of the political orientations of citizens, as we and our colleagues claimed. The point that we wish to underline is that all of these accounts, ours as much as anyone's, so far as they gave an account of the positions that citizens took on matters of race, concentrated on the fixed, the long-term, the seemingly immutable. By contrast, in calling attention to the role of political argumentation, we mean to focus attention on the fact that there is an inherent contingency to the politics of race.

To insist on the inherent contingency of the politics of race is not to deny that long-term factors are at work. On the contrary, one of the aims of our analysis of political arguments has been to show that citizens respond to them in the light of their deeper-lying political orientations. What we do believe our experiments on political argument have helped to expose is the sense in which slack is a constitutive feature of the politics of race. Citizens can take quite different positions on issues of race depending on which arguments are made to them— and how ably; indeed, this is so much so that the political balance can be swung from one side of the issue to another by argument and leadership (see Sniderman and Carmines 1997a, chap. 4).

A FINAL COMMENT ON FATALISM

It is a reproach, from time to time, that in arriving at a conclusion that racism no longer plays a paramount role in molding the political thinking of white Americans about issues of race we are undercutting the campaign to achieve, finally and meaningfully, racial equality. For our part, we have always replied that our aim has been to understand things as they are, however they in fact are. But insofar as there is a connection between scholarship and politics, we would like to close with one observation.

The other approaches, by neglecting politics, wind up as arguments for fatalism. This is easiest to see in the social dominance perspective. It consists in a claim that in every society subordinate groups are oppressed by superordinate ones. The argument, so far as we can make out, is unclear on whether the bases for inequality—apart from gender (Sidanius and Pratto refer to "the iron law of andrancy" [1993a, 174])—are the same in every society or not; on whether there is one or more superordinate groups; on the conditions under which inequality tends to be maximized or minimized. Instead, the social dominance theory consists in the assertion that some groups are subordinate to others in every society, modern, medieval, or ancient, capitalist or communist, democratic or dictatorial. It is not obvious what to do with a social science cast in such unconditional terms—putatively true always and everywhere—except to observe that, if it is true, it implies that the effort to combat inequality is futile. We accept that Sidanius and his colleagues wish inequality to be reduced. Our point is that they cannot get out of their theory an account of the conditions or mechanisms of change.

Traveling on a different track, the symbolic racism argument arrives at a similar destination. Sears and Kinder claim that racism regained its dominance after the mid-1960s. Consider the implications of this claim. After World War II, America underwent a series of profound transformations. The economic boom brought unprecedented prosperity. The expansion of the school system at all levels carried with it an unparalleled revolution of educational opportunity, and all that follows in its train for the value of tolerance, political, religious, and racial; the ascension of the new mass media; the urbanization of America; the mobility, geographical and social, of the postwar years; and, of course, the extraordinary drama of the civil rights movement. If all of these together produced only a temporary loosening of the hold of racism, then the conclusion that follows is that no degree of change conceivable in a democratic society can break its hold. By contrast, in our studies (see Sniderman and Carmines 1997a, chap. 4), we see evidence that a winning coalition can be assembled in behalf of policies to assist those who are poor, very much including blacks, by taking advantage of arguments that appeal to liberal political values that reach beyond race. It is not the least irony of the symbolic racism approach that, by insisting on the seemingly ineradicable domination of racism, it may squelch the very possibility of combating racial inequality and intolerance.

The fatalism bred into the bones of the social dominance and the symbolic racism arguments follows from a limit common to both. Neither has a way, drawing on its own resources, to give an account of the dynamics of racial politics. This, we would suggest, is a contribution that a political theory of the politics of race is best positioned to make.

APPENDIX: TABLE 8.1 COMPONENTS

DEPENDENT VARIABLE

The *symbolic racism* measure was constructed following Kinder and Sanders (1996). This index consists of six NES variables in 1986 (V565–V568, V579, V580) and four NES variables in 1992 (V6126–V6129). See figure 8.1 for the question wording. The index was rescaled 0–1, with 1 indicating high symbolic racism.

INDEPENDENT VARIABLES

Antiblack affect (1986 NES only) refers to the respondent's rating of blacks on a feeling thermometer (V149), rescaled 0–1, with 1 as least favorable feelings. The *GSS measure of prejudice* (1992 NES only) is an index of three questions ("Would you rate blacks as hard working or lazy?" "As unintelligent or intelligent?" "As violent or peaceful?"). These were rescaled 0–1, with 1 as most prejudiced.

Individualism (1986 NES only) is the standard six-variable Feldman index (V508–V513). Respondents were asked to agree or disagree on a five-point scale with the following statements: "People who don't get ahead have only themselves to blame"; "Hard work offers little guarantee of success"; "If people work hard they usually get what they want"; "Most people who don't get ahead probably work as hard as those who do"; "Anyone willing to work hard has good chance of succeeding"; "Even if people try hard they often cannot reach their goals." The index was rescaled 0–1, with 1 indicating most individualistic.

NINE Systematizing the Predictors of Prejudice

THOMAS F. PETTIGREW

INTRODUCTION

Prejudice toward outgroups has been a central application of social psychology and sociology for more than seventy years.[1] A major finding of this extensive research literature is the remarkable consistency that emerges in the predictors of prejudice at the individual level of analysis. This consistency extends across a vast variety of measures, samples, ingroups, outgroups, cultures, and industrial nations.

A partial listing underscores the point. Among the positive correlates of outgroup prejudice among individuals are age, authoritarian personality traits, nationalism, political conservatism, and a sense of group-relative deprivation. Among the negative correlates of prejudice are education, left-wing politics, and such optimal forms of intergroup contact as friendship with outgroup members. Obviously, there is likely to be considerable multicollinearity among these predictors—an issue this chapter will address.

Despite this consistency of predictors, however, there are no definitive theories of outgroup prejudice (Duckitt 1992a, 1992b). Even Gordon Allport's (1954) classic work, *The Nature of Prejudice*, presents a broad, eclectic perspective without a systematic theory. Though it organized the field and supplied key conceptualizations, this book offers largely a listing of the principal correlates of prejudice.

We now have many mini-theories that emphasize one or more of the consistent correlates. And the mini-theories vary in the primary question they address—from intergroup dynamics and the social transmission of prejudice to individual differences (Duckitt 1992a,

1992b). The present effort concentrates on individual differences. These mini-theories of prejudice also vary in scope. The authoritarian personality theory (Adorno et al. 1950) and the social dominance theory (Pratto et al. 1994) are broad conceptualizations at the individual level of analysis that attempt to explain critical parts—but not all—of the phenomenon of prejudice.

Two previous attempts to evaluate diverse predictors focus primarily on right-wing authoritarianism and social dominance (Altemeyer 1998; McFarland and Adelson 1996). Both attempts found the social dominance orientation to be the most powerful predictor of prejudice, and both personality syndromes proved more predictive than social location variables. The latter finding is made suspect, however, by the fact that these studies used student and adult samples of convenience that had severely restricted variances in such variables as education, age, and residential location. The present effort differs by using probability national samples and a wider range of both political and social location predictors.

Another prominent research finding is that there are multiple components of prejudice. During the cognitive revolution, social psychology overemphasized stereotypes and neglected the affective side of prejudice. There is now a major correction taking place (Pettigrew 1997b; Smith 1993). Indeed, the emotional component proves more predictive than stereotypes. Charles Stangor, Linda Sullivan, and Thomas Ford (1991) compared the predictive value of emotional responses with that of stereotypes. For a range of groups, the emotional indicators proved stronger and more consistent predictors of both intergroup attitudes and social distance. Similarly, Victoria Esses, Geoffrey Haddock, and Mark Zanna (1993) had Canadian subjects report on the emotions they experienced when they saw, met, or thought about various minorities. These reports related more strongly than the subjects' stereotypes to their general favorability toward these outgroups.

Other work in both North America and Europe has shown that different forms of prejudice vary sharply in their subtlety. Best known is David Sears's (1988) work in the United States with "symbolic racism" as a more subtle form of prejudice. Other work with "modern racism" (McConahay 1983), "aversive racism" (Gaertner and Dovidio 1986; Kovel 1970), and "subtle prejudice" (Meertens and Pettigrew 1997; Pettigrew and Meertens 1995; Pettigrew et al. 1998) also contrasts with the traditional, blatant forms of prejudice. Varying levels of covertness characterize these subtle forms. Yet researchers have seldom tested the various predictors of prejudice with this variety of prejudice forms—another task of this chapter.

In short, we need to reduce the number of predictors (independent variables or IVs), while enlarging the range of prejudice measures (dependent variables or DVs). Such a manageable matrix of independent predictors with varied dependent measures would be useful as an initial step toward broader theories of individual differences in prejudice. Hence, this chapter attempts to systemize the array of correlates that persistently arise in the huge prejudice literature. Four interrelated hypotheses guide the analysis:

1. When entered together in exploratory factor analyses, the major correlates of individual prejudice will yield a small set of meaningful, orthogonal predictor factors. These results in turn will shape a confirmatory factor analysis of practical value.
2. These factorial predictors will differentially relate to contrasting measures and types of prejudice.
3. This general pattern of factors predicting prejudice will broadly replicate across samples, nations, and target groups.
4. The matrix formed by these factorial predictors and an enlarged set of prejudice measures will provide a more meaningful and manageable empirical platform from which we can formulate more detailed theories of prejudice.

METHOD

The Eurobarometer Survey Number 30, one of the most extensive studies ever conducted on prejudice, makes this effort possible. Its 4,000 respondents were drawn from seven national probability samples of four Western European nations. A variety of minorities served as the targets of a wide range of prejudice measures. Extensive as these measures are, however, several important predictors are missing. In particular, the survey has no direct assessment of the social dominance orientation and only one item measuring the authoritarian personality syndrome.

SAMPLES

Surveys during the fall of 1988 in France, the Netherlands, Great Britain, and then–West Germany formed part of the European Union's

Eurobarometer 30. Only one target outgroup served for the entire West German sample, while separate samples tested for two target outgroups each in the other nations. Removing all minority respondents left 455 French asked about North Africans, 475 French asked about Asians (largely Vietnamese and Cambodians), 462 Dutch asked about Surinamers, 476 Dutch asked about Turks, 471 British asked about West Indians, 482 British asked about Asians (largely Pakistanis and Indians), and 985 West Germans asked about Turks. I conducted initial analyses with the full sample of 3,806 respondents. Then I repeated the full-sample analyses with each of the seven subsamples to test hypothesis 3 concerning generalization. (Complete details of the sampling procedures and the full schedule of the Eurobarometer 30 survey are available in Reif and Melich 1991.)

SELECTING THE INDEPENDENT VARIABLES

I tested more than sixty possible predictor variables in a series of stepwise regressions with each of eight measures of prejudice. In addition to routine diagnostic checks for nonlinearity, outliers, and nonnormality (Cook and Weisberg 1982; Fox 1991; Norusis 1990, B69–B91), this screening employed cross-validation, as recommended by Frederick Mosteller and John Tukey (1977). The initial regressions were run with a random half-sample ($n = 1,902$) and then replicated with the other half-sample ($n = 1,904$). In slightly different order, the same predictors emerged from both analyses.

Stepwise procedures reduced the multicollinearity among the predictors, ensuring that each retained variable independently contributes to the variance explained by the prejudice measures. The aim at this stage of the analysis was less to maximize the prediction than to obtain a rich and varied set of independent predictors. Eleven predictors consistently emerged. INTERGROUP FRIENDS, EDUCATION, and EUROPEAN IDENTITY are the major negative predictors, and POLITICAL CONSERVATISM is the major positive predictor. These findings are consistent with past work (Bobo and Licari 1989; Hamberger and Hewstone 1997; Pettigrew 1997a, 1997b, 1998). Also important are AGE, GROUP RELATIVE DEPRIVATION, NATIONAL PRIDE, POLITICAL INEFFICACY, POLITICAL INTEREST, and VOTE INTENTION. For clarity, another measure—URBANITY—was added, though it reached significance on only three of the prejudice measures.

Note that three variables (EDUCATION, AGE, URBANITY) involve social location, another (INTERGROUP FRIENDS) taps the

interpersonal level of analysis, and the remaining seven are psychological and political indicators at the individual level. This variable array
was deliberately sought so as to crosscut the three domains discussed
in this volume—the political, social psychological, and sociological domains.

MEASURES OF THE INDEPENDENT VARIABLES

THREE SOCIAL LOCATION MEASURES EDUCATION reflects the respondents' reported age during their last year of schooling. AGE is
calculated from reported birth date. URBANITY refers to the respondents' subjective views of their residential area. It has three categories:
"rural area or village" (scored 1), "small and mid-sized towns" (2), and
"large towns and cities" (3). Though related to the actual size of the
locality ($r = .38, p < .001$), this variable proves to be a stronger predictor of prejudice than the objective measure of population size.

ONE CONTACT MEASURE INTERGROUP FRIENDS is a scale of five
items. Respondents were shown a list: "People of another nationality,"
"People of another race," "People of another religion," "People with
another culture," and "People belonging to another social class." For
each item, interviewers asked: "Are there many such people [scored
3], a few [scored 2], or none [plus no answer, scored 1] that count
among your friends?" The five items form a reliable scale; the median
α for the seven samples is .84 and for the full sample, .85.[2]

FOUR POLITICAL MEASURES Self-placement on a ten-point scale
ranging from the political left to the political right assessed POLITI-
CAL CONSERVATISM. High scorers are more conservative.[3] PO-
LITICAL INEFFICACY describes a scale of five items: "Do you
yourself ever happen to think that (1) . . . most people in positions of
power try to gain something out of people like you. (2) . . . people who
run the country are not really concerned with what happens to you.
(3) . . . you feel left out of what is happening around you. (4) . . . the
rich get richer and the poor get poorer. (5) . . . what you think doesn't
count very much." Scoring for each item is 1 for "disagree," 2 for
"don't know" or no answer, and 3 for "agree." The scale's reliability
proves only marginally adequate; the α for the full sample is .64.

Two POLITICAL INTEREST items asked respondents how interested they are in politics generally and in European Union politics
specifically. High scorers report keen interest in both. VOTE INTEN-

TION records responses to the question "Do you think you will . . . vote" in the elections for the European Parliament?" I scored "no" as 1, "probably not" as 2, "don't know" or no answer as 3, "probably" as 4, and "will" as 5.

THREE SOCIAL PSYCHOLOGICAL MEASURES GROUP RELATIVE DEPRIVATION is measured by a single item: "Would you say that over the last five years people like yourself in [nation] have been economically a lot better off [scored 1], better off [2], the same [plus "don't know" or no answer, scored 3], worse off [4], or a lot worse off [5] than most [outgroupers] living here." High scorers feel relatively deprived in group terms.

Two predictors record the respondents' social identities. EUROPEAN IDENTITY records responses to the query "Does the thought ever occur to you that you are not only [nationality] but also European?" Responses were scored as follows: "never" (1), "don't know" (2), "sometimes" (3), and "often" (4). To measure NATIONAL PRIDE, respondents told how "proud" they were to be British, Dutch, French, or German: "very proud" (scored 5), "quite proud" (4), no answer or "don't know" (3), "not very proud" (2), and "not at all proud" (1).

MEASURES OF THE DEPENDENT VARIABLES

The present study employs a broad range of dependent variables. It uses the ten-item Likert scales to measure BLATANT PREJUDICE and SUBTLE PREJUDICE developed with these data by Thomas Pettigrew and Roel Meertens (1995). Table 9.1 shows the scales in English. They use Likert-scale scoring, with item responses scored 0, 1, (no 2), 3, and 4 on a strongly disagree–somewhat disagree–somewhat agree–strongly agree dimension. Higher scores reveal greater prejudice. Five reverse items score disagreement in the prejudiced direction (items 2, 3, and 4 of the ANTI–INTIMACY subscale and both items of the AFFECTIVE PREJUDICE subscale).

From a pool of more than fifty items, Pettigrew and Meertens (1995) chose ten items to measure each type on the basis of their conceptualization of the two forms and factor analyses. Exploratory principal components analyses yielded strikingly similar results across the seven samples. For the BLATANT scale, two primary factors emerged after varimax rotation in each sample (eigenvalues > .98): the four INTIMACY items and six THREAT AND REJECTION items listed

TABLE 9.1   The Blatant and Subtle Prejudice Scales and Their Five Subscales

THREAT AND REJECTION FACTOR ITEMS: BLATANT SCALE

1. West Indians have jobs that the British should have.   (*strongly agree to strongly disagree*)
2. Most West Indians living here who receive support from welfare could get along without it if they tried.   (*strongly agree to strongly disagree*)
3. British people and West Indians can never be really comfortable with each other, even if they are close friends.   (*strongly agree to strongly disagree*)
4. Most politicians in Britain care too much about West Indians and not enough about the average British person.   (*strongly agree to strongly disagree*)
5. West Indians come from less able races and this explains why they are not as well off as most British people.   (*strongly agree to strongly disagree*)
6. How different or similar do you think West Indians living here are to other British people like yourself—in how honest they are?   (*very different, somewhat different, somewhat similar, or very similar*)

INTIMACY FACTOR ITEMS: BLATANT SCALE

1. Suppose that a child of yours had children with a person of very different color and physical characteristics than your own. Do you think you would be very bothered, bothered, bothered a little, or not bothered at all, if your grandchildren did not physically resemble the people on your side of the family?
2. I would be willing to have sexual relationships with a West Indian.   (*strongly agree to strongly disagree*)   (Reversed scoring)
3. I would not mind if a suitably qualified West Indian person was appointed as my boss.   (*strongly agree to strongly disagree*)   (Reversed scoring)
4. I would not mind if a West Indian person who had a similar economic background as mine joined my close family by marriage.   (*strongly agree to strongly disagree*)   (Reversed scoring)

TRADITIONAL VALUES FACTOR ITEMS: SUBTLE SCALE

1. West Indians living here should not push themselves where they are not wanted.   (*strongly agree to strongly disagree*)
2. Many other groups have come to Britain and overcome prejudice and worked their way up. West Indians should do the same without special favor.   (*strongly agree to strongly disagree*)
3. It is just a matter of some people not trying hard enough. If West Indians would only try harder they could be as well off as British people.   (*strongly agree to strongly disagree*)
4. West Indians living here teach their children values and skills different from those required to be successful in Britain.   (*strongly agree to strongly disagree*)

CULTURAL DIFFERENCES FACTOR ITEMS: SUBTLE SCALE

How different or similar do you think West Indians living here are to other British people like yourself . . . (*very different, somewhat different, somewhat similar, or very similar*)

1. in the values that they teach their children?
2. in their religious beliefs and practices?
3. in their sexual values or sexual practices?
4. in the language that they speak?

AFFECTIVE PREJUDICE FACTOR ITEMS: SUBTLE SCALE

Have you ever felt the following ways about West Indians and their families living here . . . (*very often, fairly often, not too often, or never*)

1. How often have you felt sympathy for West Indians living here?   (Reversed scoring)
2. How often have you felt admiration for West Indians living here?   (Reversed scoring)

in table 9.1 (the latter subscale will be called REJECT). For the SUB-TLE scale, three primary orthogonal factors emerged after varimax rotation in each sample (eigenvalues > 1): the four TRADITIONAL VALUES items, four CULTURAL DIFFERENCES items, and two AFFECTIVE PREJUDICE items listed in table 9.1. For the full sample, the BLATANT and SUBTLE scales correlate +.60.

A key finding of the authoritarian personality research inspired an additional measure of prejudice—namely, that those prejudiced against one outgroup are likely to be prejudiced against other outgroups as well (Adorno et al. 1950). The ETHNOCENTRISM scale sought favorability ratings on a 0-to-100 thermometer of three diverse outgroups not covered by the other measures: southern Europeans, black Africans, and Jews. This scale has the advantage of using a format, response categories, and target groups that are markedly different from the other prejudice scales. With ratings reversed, high scorers reflect high prejudice. This ETHNOCENTRISM measure correlates +.50 with the BLATANT scale and +.39 with the SUBTLE scale.[4]

RESULTS

FOUR PRIMARY FACTORS

Using the full sample, table 9.2 shows the results of a principal components analysis after varimax rotation (with factor loadings less than .25 removed).[5] In support of hypothesis 1, four primary orthogonal factors emerge. This solution is robust. The four factors account for 54 percent of the total variance, with eigenvalues ranging from 1.00 to 2.13. Moreover, an oblimin rotation replicates table 9.2; it yields four factors that approach orthogonality and are nearly identical to those of the orthogonal solution.

FACTOR I: POLITICAL ENGAGEMENT This factor combines VOTE IN-TENTION and POLITICAL INTEREST with EUROPEAN IDEN-TITY. Other factor loadings show a tendency for older respondents who feel little threat from minorities to be high on this factor. It correlates negatively with prejudice measures. Note the absence of NA-TIONAL PRIDE on this factor. Interestingly, having a European identity does not relate to less pride in your national identity. This factor is further defined by its positive correlations with family income ($r = +.22, p < .001$), subjective social status ($r = +.22, p < .001$), and frequent discussion of politics ($r = +.38, p < .001$).

TABLE 9.2 Four Principal Predictive Factors

VARIABLES	FACTOR I: POLITICAL ENGAGEMENT	FACTOR II: GENCLASS (AGE & CLASS)	FACTOR III: TRADITIONAL CONSERVATISM	FACTOR IV: COSMOPOLITAN
VOTE INTENTION	.771	—	—	—
POLITICAL INTEREST	.724	—	—	—
EUROPEAN IDENTITY	.637	—	—	—
AGE	.267	.698	—	—
EDUCATION	—	-.706	—	—
GROUP RELATIVE DEPRIVATION	-.308	.413	—	—
POLITICAL INEFFICACY	—	.469	-.540	—
NATIONAL PRIDE	—	.285	.616	—
POLITICAL CONSERVATISM	—	—	.777	—
INTERGROUP FRIENDS	—	-.304	—	.537
URBANITY	—	—	—	.866

Note: All factor loadings below .25 are omitted for clarity.

FACTOR II: AGE AND SOCIAL CLASS (GENCLASS) EDUCATION, AGE, POLITICAL EFFICACY, and GROUP RELATIVE DEPRI-VATION load heavily on this factor. Older, poorly educated respondents anchor this factor. They are economically threatened by minorities and feel politically powerless. They also are less likely to have friends from diverse groups. Inflected, this factor involves younger, well-educated respondents who are unthreatened by minorities and feel politically efficacious. This factor is further delineated by its relationships with low economic expectations for the future ($r = -.25$, $p < .001$) and low subjective social class ratings ($r = -.30, p < .001$). This factor relates positively with prejudice, and since it taps both generation and social class, I shall call it "genclass."

FACTOR III: TRADITIONAL CONSERVATISM This factor loads principally on POLITICAL CONSERVATISM, NATIONAL PRIDE, and PO-LITICAL INEFFICACY. Respondents who anchor this factor are conservative in their politics, are very proud of their nation, and feel politically effectual. This factor correlates positively with prejudice. Inflected, the factor involves the political left who express less pride in their nation without a sense of political power. The traditionalism underlying this factor is revealed by its associations with the survey's religious variables. Respondents high on this factor rate themselves as quite religious ($r = +.29$, $p < .001$) and frequent attenders of religious services ($r = +.26, p < .001$).

FACTOR IV: COSMOPOLITAN This factor correlates negatively with prejudice. It is, however, the least sturdy of the four factors and has large loadings on only two variables. It represents urbanites who have highly diverse friends or, alternatively, rural and small town residents without such friends. This result reflects the fact that most of the new minorities of Western Europe reside in cities, where job opportunities exist. Hence, the link between URBANITY and INTERGROUP FRIENDS is in large part demographically determined.

PREDICTING PREJUDICE WITH THE FACTORS

Figure 9.1 depicts the correlations among the four factors and five of the prejudice scales. The genclass factor, featuring high loadings on AGE, EDUCATION, POLITICAL INEFFICACY, and GROUP RELATIVE DEPRIVATION, is the dominant predictor for the BLA-TANT PREJUDICE measure as well as its two subscales (not shown). The political engagement factor is also important for all the depen-

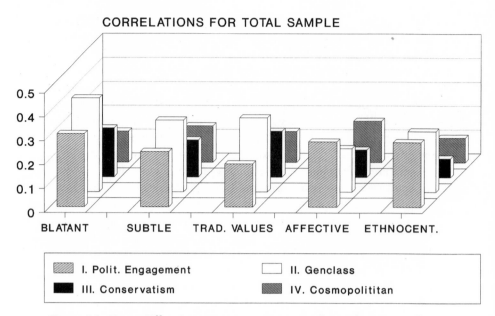

Figure 9.1. Factor Effect Sizes on Various Measures of Prejudice. *Note:* All correlations significant at $p < .001$.

dent variables. As figure 9.1 illustrates, political engagement is especially dominant for the AFFECTIVE PREJUDICE and ETHNOCENTRISM scales—two measures tapping affect. Since EUROPEAN IDENTITY has a strong weight on this factor, it suggests that this factor entails an emotional openness to outgroups of many types.[6] The traditional conservatism factor also predicts all the prejudice measures, but, as expected, it is especially related to the TRADITIONAL VALUES subscale of the SUBTLE PREJUDICE measure.

The cosmopolitan factor, combining urban residence with outgroup friends, is less predictive, though its relationships are highly significant for all but the CULTURAL DIFFERENCES scale (not shown). It, like the political engagement factor, strongly and negatively relates to AFFECTIVE PREJUDICE. Thus, the differential effects of the factors for the cognitive and affective measures, as shown in figure 9.1, lend support to hypothesis 2.

Another analysis is prompted by an interesting finding of Howard Schuman, Lawrence Bobo, and Maria Krysan (1992). With General Social Survey data, these investigators found that the relationship be-

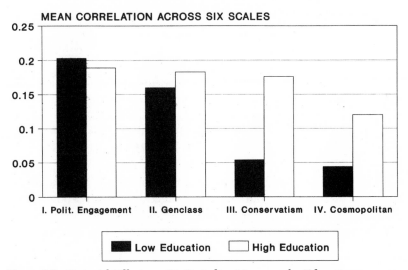

Figure 9.2. Factorial Effects on Six Prejudice Measures, by Education

tween authoritarianism and racial attitudes was strongest among well-educated respondents. Testing this finding, I again regressed the prejudice measures on the four factors with separate analyses for the poorly educated (education ended before seventeen years of age) and the well-educated (ended after sixteen years of age).

Figure 9.2 shows the average correlations across the six independent prejudice scales for the four factors by education (ignoring signs). As expected, the conservative factor, which most resembles the authoritarian syndrome, is significantly *stronger* among the well-educated. The cosmopolitan factor also predicts somewhat better for the well-educated respondents, but the political engagement and genclass factors do equally well for both educational groups. The principal result, then, is that the power of the conservatism factor to predict prejudice is concentrated among the well-educated. This finding is directly opposite from that predicted by Paul Sniderman, Gretchen Crosby, and William Howell in this volume—a point considered in later analyses.

AUTHORITARIANISM AND PREJUDICE

Speculations about the role of personality derive from the only item available that approximates right-wing authoritarianism. Three statements were read to respondents, and they were to choose "the one which best describes your own opinion." One statement called for revolutionary action and another for change by reform. I combined these responses, together with "don't know" responses, and scored them 1 in a dichotomous measure labeled ALTER SOCIETY. The key statement, scored 2, read "Our present society must be valiantly defended against all subversive forces." This simple dichotomous variable was then added to the standard eleven-variable regressions described earlier. ALTER SOCIETY strongly and significantly adds to the predictions of seven of the prejudice measures (ETHNOCENTRISM is the lone exception). When entered into the factor analysis, it loads heavily, positively, and only on the conservatism factor. Hence, a measure that approximates the authoritarian dimension adds predictive power even after the eleven basic predictors had been entered. Moreover, this result shows that the basic predictive factors capture this dimension.

DO THESE RESULTS GENERALIZE?

Hypothesis 3 held that the general factorial pattern of the entire sample would largely replicate across the study's seven samples. Although these samples are subsets of the entire sample, this test remains a rigorous one. The seven samples involve six highly diverse target groups, ranging from West Indians to Turks, and four European nations with disparate political systems and histories.

Despite this variety, the results typically support the generalization hypothesis. The patterns of the entire sample tend to be repeated for each subsample. There are, of course, deviations. Consider the major findings of the full sample tested across the seven subsamples.

VARIABLE PREDICTORS As with the full sample, INTERGROUP FRIENDS and EDUCATION prove to be robust negative predictors and POLITICAL CONSERVATISM a strong positive predictor of all eight prejudice scales across all seven subsamples. Some predictors provide stronger predictions in some nations than others. Hence, EUROPEAN IDENTITY, NATIONAL PRIDE, VOTE INTENTION, and EDUCATION are most predictive in the German and British samples and least predictive in those from the Netherlands. Several variables correlate with particular prejudice scales best across all samples. AGE, for instance, relates strongly and positively with the INTIMACY prejudice measure. Thus, the predominant trend is the similarity of relationships across the samples, with virtually no changing of signs between the predictors and prejudice.

FACTOR STRUCTURES   The three dominant factors of table 9.2 reappear in all seven subsamples. Thus, the political engagement, genclass, and conservatism factors account for roughly half or more of the variances of the subsamples' matrices. Even the fragile cosmopolitan factor emerges in five samples. Only minor deviations arise. INTERGROUP FRIENDS migrates in one sample to be a major positive component of the political engagement factor. In another sample, INTERGROUP FRIENDS is a negative component of the genclass factor.

FACTOR PREDICTIONS   The generalization hypothesis receives further support when the total sample's factor scores are used to predict the various prejudice measures across the four Western European countries. Combining samples within nations, there are 96 correlations (4 nations × 4 factors × 6 independent scales). Of these, 93 (97 percent) have the predicted sign, and 78 (81 percent) are statistically significant.[7] In short, the factorial predictions for the entire sample also predict the various types of prejudice within each nation—despite their widely varying cultures, histories, and target outgroups.

STRUCTURAL EQUATION MODELS

Confirmatory factor analysis both strengthens and clarifies our attempt to consolidate the predictors of prejudice. Figure 9.3 presents the confirmatory model. Several informative results emerge. First, the four-factorial solution provides an adequate fit for the eleven-variable matrix of predictors.[8] Second, the four factors are no longer orthogonal; indeed, three variables are now shared (GROUP RELATIVE DEPRIVATION and AGE with factors I and II, POLITICAL INEFFICACY with factors II and III). These crossover variables revealed these relationships in the original factor analysis in table 9.2. Strikingly, however, the two political factors, political engagement and traditional conservatism, remain unrelated.

Path models suggested by these factors test the claim that this approach provides a platform for more detailed theories of prejudice. Moreover, by selecting predictors from social psychology, sociology, and political science, the factors suggest possible cross-level and cross-disciplinary models. Figure 9.4 illustrates two such path models for BLATANT PREJUDICE.[9] Figure 9.4(a), drawn from the political engagement factor, begins with two uncorrelated variables, AGE and EUROPEAN IDENTITY, and has two political variables as mediators. EUROPEAN IDENTITY has a direct and negative effect on

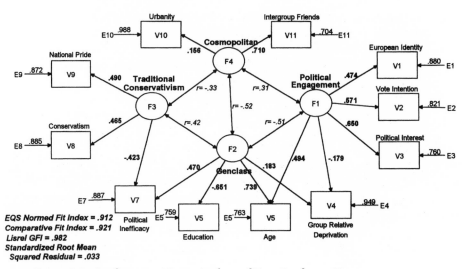

Figure 9.3. Confirmatory Factor Analysis of Four Predictive Factors

BLATANT PREJUDICE as well as being mediated by both VOTE INTENTION and POLITICAL INTEREST. AGE is unrelated to POLITICAL INTEREST. But AGE has two diverse effects on BLA-TANT PREJUDICE—a strong positive direct effect and a negative effect through VOTE INTENTION.

Figure 9.4(b), based on the genclass factor, begins with two inter-correlated social location factors, AGE and EDUCATION, and uses two subjective states as mediators. AGE has only an unmediated direct effect on BLATANT PREJUDICE. By contrast, EDUCATION is mediated by both POLITICAL INEFFICACY and GROUP REL-ATIVE DEPRIVATION as well as having a direct effect on BLATANT PREJUDICE.

TESTING THE PRINCIPLED OPPOSITION THESIS

Now we can apply this approach to a recurrent theme of this volume. Some chapters argue that prejudice and racial resentment are the principal determinants of resistance to such intergroup policies as af-firmative action. Sniderman, Crosby, and Howell disagree. They main-tain that this resistance simply reflects principled opposition of politi-cal conservatives and not prejudice. Several key predictions that flow from the Sniderman-Crosby-Howell contention are directly testable with the variables and data from the rich 1988 Eurobarometer study.

Sniderman and Philip Tetlock (1986a, 1986b; Sniderman et al.

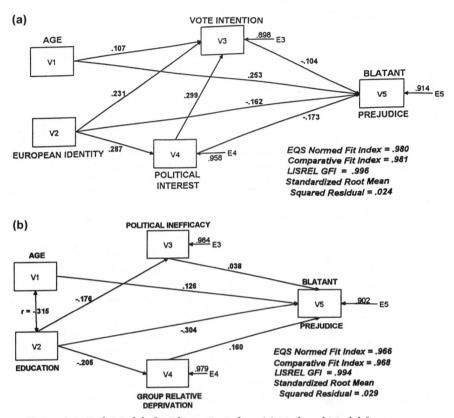

Figure 9.4. Path Models for Blatant Prejudice. (a) Mediated Model from Political Engagement Factor. (b) Mediated Model from Genclass Factor

1991; Tetlock 1994) question whether such measures as symbolic racism and subtle prejudice are distinct from traditional forms or even whether they represent prejudice at all. Central to their host of criticisms is their concern that these subtle prejudice measures are confounded by political conservatism and thus unfairly indict conservatives as prejudiced.

Using these same European data, Meertens and Pettigrew (1997) challenged this corollary of the principled opposition thesis. They showed that the self-report indicator of conservatism and the SUBTLE PREJUDICE scale are sharply different measures. Thus, they do not share the same predictors. Indeed, political conservatism in these data relates equally with or more positively to blatant than subtle prejudice in all seven national samples. In addition, the two-factor models required by the blatant-subtle distinction proved superior to the one-factor model in confirmatory factor analyses in all seven samples (Pettigrew and Meertens 1995).

Another corollary is that resistance to pro-minority policies is especially "principled" for those conservatives who are well educated and "politically engaged."[10] Earlier analyses have already cast doubt on this contention. Conservatism emerged as a separate, predictive factor. Moreover, figure 9.2 revealed that the power of the conservatism factor to predict prejudice was greater, not weaker, among the well-educated. In addition, figure 9.3 found that the conservatism factor was unrelated to the political engagement factor.

Here we explore these results further. The chief intergroup policy issues in Europe concern immigration and the treatment of immigrants. So I constructed a three-item immigration policy measure. High scorers support immigration. They favor allowing all immigrants to remain, enhancing their rights, and making it easier for them to gain citizenship.[11] These are the issues that generate even more heat in Western Europe than affirmative action in the United States.

Figure 9.5 is restricted to the 1,174 respondents who are among both the well-educated (the top half whose education extended beyond sixteen years of age) and the more politically engaged (the top half of scorers on the political engagement factor). These are the Europeans who, according to Sniderman, Crosby, and Howell's contentions, should show the least influence of prejudice in their attitudes toward immigration policy. But figure 9.5's path analysis reveals that much of the opposition of self-identified conservatives to pro-immigration policies is in fact channeled through both blatant and subtle prejudice. In fact, this educated, politically engaged subsample shows the effects of prejudice considerably more, not less, than the poorly educated, less politically engaged remainder of the sample (not shown).

Why do these results so consistently reject key corollaries of the principled opposition position? Could it be a continental difference: that North Americans reveal the phenomenon, but Europeans do not? This seems unlikely, given the fact that the results of this extensive European survey are so consistent with North American findings generally (Pettigrew et al. 1998). More likely, different measures are involved. For example, Sniderman, Crosby, and Howell employ the type of stereotype measure of prejudice that has proven least predictive in other research (Esses, Haddock, and Zanna 1993; Stangor, Sullivan, and Ford 1991).

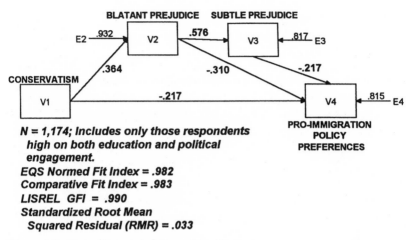

Figure 9.5. Test of Principled Opposition Conjecture

THEORETICAL IMPLICATIONS

"There is no master key," wrote Allport (1954, 208, 218). "Rather, what we have at our disposal is a ring of keys, each of which opens one gate of understanding. . . . We may lay it down as a general law applying to all social phenomena that *multiple causation* is invariably at work and nowhere is the law more clearly applicable than to prejudice." This chapter's findings affirm Allport's contention.

Various mini-theories concerning individual differences in prejudice derived largely in the United States receive support in these European results—with the exception of the principled opposition conjectures concerning political conservatism. Authoritarian personality contentions characterize the conservatism factor and the ALTER SOCIETY findings (Adorno et al. 1950). The power of INTERGROUP FRIENDS is consistent with intergroup contact theory (Allport 1954; Pettigrew 1997a, 1998). The EUROPEAN IDENTITY findings bolster the common ingroup identity model's emphasis on recategorization (Anastasio et al. 1997; Gaertner et al. 1993; Gaertner et al. 1994). The importance of group threat and group position is borne out by the role of GROUP RELATIVE DEPRIVATION (Blumer 1958; Bobo and Hutchings 1996; Smith and Pettigrew 1999). And the predictive power of AGE and EDUCATION concurs with a host of sociological contentions concerning prejudice. More important, the consistent factorial structure of these predictive variables indicates how these mini-theories of prejudice relate to each other.

Table 9.2 suggests that there exist at least three basic families of explanations for prejudice. They are tentatively labeled as political engagement, genclass, and traditional conservatism. The first family has two facets. Political engagement is obviously involved in the heavy positive loadings on VOTE INTENTION and POLITICAL INTEREST. Yet the high loading on EUROPEAN IDENTITY shows that this factor also includes a broad personal orientation.

The genclass factor includes not only EDUCATION and AGE, but also such class-linked phenomena as political inefficacy, group threat, and relative deprivation. Here low status and threat link with heightened prejudice and high status and lack of threat with reduced prejudice. Conservatives who are proud of their country and feel politically efficacious anchor the third family of explanations. Here fit the many mini-theories involving ingroup favoritism, nationalism, traditionalism, and conservative ideologies.

A fourth family of prejudice predictors revolves around the urban-rural dimension. It is the least developed and the most unstable factor across the subsamples. As a variable, URBANISM relates positively with prejudice in the eleven-variable regressions. In two national subsamples, it factorially joins with GROUP RELATIVE DEPRIVATION and POLITICAL INEFFICACY and is a strongly positive predictor of prejudice. Yet in five samples, when coupled with INTERGROUP FRIENDSHIP, it becomes a factor with a strong negative association with prejudice. Europe's new minorities live in cities, so friendship with minorities is limited to urban residents. And such friendships are a powerful counter to prejudice. URBANISM, then, acts as a distal variable, with its influence on prejudice subject to the mediation of proximal psychological variables.

Two measures of social identity operate differentially in these data. Consistent with recent emphases on the importance of ingroup identity for prejudice (Duckitt 1992b; Pettigrew 1997b; Smith 1993), NATIONAL PRIDE loads most heavily on the conservatism factor—a positive predictor of prejudice. Consistent with other emphases on inclusive group identities (Allport 1954; Anastasio et al. 1997; Gaertner et al. 1993; Gaertner et al. 1994), EUROPEAN IDENTITY loads heavily and exclusively on the political engagement factor—a negative predictor of prejudice.

These findings raise a long-standing issue regarding the relationship between ingroup and outgroup attitudes. William Graham Sumner (1906), in his concept of ethnocentrism, assumed that intense ingroup identification necessarily meant outgroup rejection. By extension, Sumner's reasoning leads to the prediction of a strongly negative relation between NATIONAL PRIDE and EUROPEAN IDENTITY. If I am a highly identified Scot who is proud to be Scottish, then I should rarely think of myself as a European.

Yet these data falsify this extension of Sumner's argument. The two identity measures are essentially unrelated ($-.01$ in the full sample and from $-.11$ to $+.10$ in the subsamples). One-third of the 3,806 respondents report pride in their nation *and* often think of themselves as Europeans. Thus, national and continental identities operate at separate levels of abstraction. I can easily regard myself as both a Scot and a European.

This partial rejection of Sumnerian theory fits with a growing literature on the subject. In their innovative study of tribal attitudes in East Africa, Marilynn Brewer and Donald Campbell (1976) found that ingroup and outgroup attitudes varied widely across tribes as well as attitude and behavioral domains. They called for a new perspective on ethnocentrism. In an ingenious laboratory experiment, David Wilder and John Thompson (1980) found that increased optimal contact with an outgroup improved attitudes toward the outgroup without altering attitudes toward the ingroup. Hence, these results suggest that even those highly identified with their ingroup can assume superordinate identities, as called for by the common ingroup identity model (Anastasio et al. 1997; Gaertner et al. 1993; Gaertner et al. 1994).

Another theoretical point involves differential effects for diverse types of prejudice (figure 9.1). The prediction patterns of BLATANT PREJUDICE and SUBTLE PREJUDICE are similar. Yet different patterns emerge between belief measures, such as the TRADITIONAL VALUES scale, and feeling measures, such as the AFFECTIVE scale. The genclass and conservatism dimensions relate most heavily to the belief measure, while the political engagement factor relates more to the feelings measure.

Another point involves how different contexts invoke different predictors. Figure 9.2's pattern of maximal predictions from the conservatism and cosmopolitan factors among the well-educated underlines further the need to employ multiple-level models of prejudice. Predicting prejudice among the poorly educated is best done with the political engagement and genclass factors.

A FINAL NOTE

American sociology often labels tentative explorations as "approaches." The late Harvard sociologist George Homans took a dim view of such work. "Approaches, approaches!" he would grumble. "What we need in social science are some *arrivals!*"

This chapter does not meet Homans's stricture. It is simply an approach, not an arrival, for its methods and the available data constrain the effort. The results of such analyses perforce are strictly limited to the variables supplied. And the Eurobarometer 30, extensive as it is, does not contain all the principal predictors of prejudice. Thus, the survey lacks a social dominance orientation measure, while its emphasis on political variables led to a surprisingly potent political engagement factor.

Yet support for the study's hypotheses offers encouragement for the strategy of systematizing and narrowing the number of predictor variables, while increasing the variety of prejudice measures. The resulting matrix from the extensive European data under test suggests several points of theoretical significance.

Many mini-theories of prejudice received support from individual predictor variables. And the analysis suggests that they can be parsimoniously classified under a few basic families of explanations. Robust factors representing political engagement, genclass, and conservatism emerged in the full sample and, with minor deviations, in each of the seven independent subsamples. A fourth, the cosmopolitan factor, combining URBANISM with INTERGROUP FRIENDS, was the least stable of the factors. This solution was found in orthogonal and oblique exploratory analyses as well as in a confirmatory factor analysis.

Future theorizing in prejudice must combine the many mini-theories within the context of both larger families of explanations and multiple levels of analysis that span social science disciplines. One indicated form consists of structural path models. These models can use social variables as distal predictors and individual variables as proximal predictors (Pettigrew et al. 1998). By including variables from different levels, the factors of this analysis suggest promising possibilities for further models. Figure 9.4 illustrates two such path models. Such work could clear the current underbrush and lead to more definitive theories of prejudice.

A final point concerns the remarkable parallel between these Western European findings and those uncovered in North America. Discussions of American racial opinions often unwittingly imply that much of the phenomenon is somehow unique to the United States. Increasingly, headlines from around the world underscore the fact that the values, ideologies, and prejudice of racialized politics in the

United States are not unique. To be sure, each nation's culture and social structure shape its intergroup conflict in distinctive ways. But many of the basic phenomena—political, psychological, and sociological—are shared across nations and groups. Looking closely at this rich data set from Western Europe offers a broader perspective on the American scene described in this volume's other chapters.

TEN

The Perils of
Correlation, the
Lure of Labels,
and the Beauty of
Negative Results

HOWARD SCHUMAN

All of the authors of the eight primary chapters in this volume wish
to understand the sources of present-day racial attitudes. Each
chapter pursues a different line of explanation, and each brings to bear
considerable evidence from survey data, mainly data on the U.S. white
population. Whether explicitly or not, causality is typically sought: the
variation in one variable is thought to be a cause of variation in another. My discussion considers some of the concrete problems and
possibilities that arise when the authors attempt to connect survey
variables in order to provide a satisfactory explanation about what Arthur Stinchcombe (1998) calls "underlying generative processes." Because of this singular focus, I leave out much that readers will find
interesting and valuable in the eight chapters. Nor do I consider at all
the extensive and valuable introductory chapter prepared by the editors.

To aid in reading eight data-intensive chapters on attitudes, the ac-
companying table shows a few of the main variables employed by the
various authors and the causal directions claimed or implied. The
headings of the columns should be self-explanatory, at least as starting
points; within each column, variables are ordered alphabetically. Only
some of the more important variables from the eight chapters are included, lest the table become overwhelming. Marylee Taylor's chapter
alone refers to more than thirty different variables, many represented
by more than one survey item, and several of the other authors are
almost as prolific.

TABLE 10.1   Selected Major Variables in This Volume

Demographic Context	Individual Attributes	Nonracial Attitudes	Racial Attitudes	Racial Policies
% Black	Education	Alter society	Affect toward blacks	Affirmative action (ranging from weak to strong forms)
Region	Ethnicity	Authoritarianism	Denial of discrimination	Equal opportunity
	Nationality	European identity	Personal threat	Federal assistance to blacks
	Race	Individualism	Symbolic racism; racial resentment; blatant/subtle prejudice	
	Religion	Inefficacy	Stereotypes	
		Inegalitarianism (we've gone too far)	Stratification beliefs	
		Liberal/conservative		
		Social dominance orientation		

   I have not attempted to draw arrows indicating causal direction, since these would differ by author and the table would become hopelessly complex, but generally the assumption is that causality flows from left to right. For example, Taylor focuses on Percent Black in metropolitan areas and seems to treat it as causal in relation to many, though not all, variables in the last three columns. She is not much concerned with accounting for variables in the second column, although she includes some as controls. It is also not practical to include all the variations in variable names employed in the different chapters, except in special cases (e.g., Donald Kinder and Tali Mendelberg refer in their chapter to what they consider their main causal variable as "prejudice," "racism," or "racial resentment" without distinguishing among these terms). Nor is any attempt made to tie variable names to specific measures. More generally, the table is intended simply as a very rough initial aid, and by no means as a rigorous sifting, listing, or organization of all the variables in the eight chapters.

CORRELATIONS AND THEIR PERILS

All of the chapters report correlational analysis in the broad sense of that term, which includes cross-tabulation, regression, and some fancier modes of analysis, and all are based on data collected by surveys. Since in most cases the authors wish to treat one variable as causal in relation to another, they invariably confront the classic problem of identifying as clearly as possible the extent to which *A* causes *B*, *B* causes *A*, or *A* and *B* are related because of some third variable, *C*, which may or may not have been measured. (Path analyses, such as those presented in the chapters by Thomas Pettigrew and by Jim Sidanius et al. can clarify an author's preferred causal model, but as O. D. Duncan [1966] stated when introducing path analysis into sociology, it cannot provide proof of a unique model.)

However, beyond or beneath this logical issue is the still more basic problem that occurs in most of the chapters when one attitude is related to another attitude. Attitudes are mental entities or constructs based on verbalizations, and they all swim around in the same heads, with no temporal or other labels to conveniently indicate causal order. Any correlation between two attitudes, therefore, starts off with the burden of proof on the investigator to show that the two are not just somewhat different ways of asking about the same construct, or at least about constructs that overlap greatly in meaning. Indeed, the stronger the correlation is, the more the issue of circularity arises: survey investigators experienced in analyzing individual-level data soon discover that the most likely interpretation of a very high correlation is that one has measured much the same thing under two different labels. In some cases, of course, this is acknowledged by an approach emphasizing factor analysis or some other method of sorting through items believed to operationalize the same general construct.[1]

The most difficult correlations to treat as causal in table 10.1 are those between the two right-hand columns, both of which deal with survey questions that are explicitly racial and explicitly intended to vary in positive/negative terms toward blacks. For example, the following question appears in the chapter by Kinder and Mendelberg as an item measuring prejudice (or racism or racial resentment); in the chapter by David Sears, P. J. Henry, and Rick Kosterman as a "symbolic racism" item; and, with wording changed to fit European settings, in Pettigrew's chapter as a "subtle prejudice" item:

It's really a matter of some people not trying hard enough; *if blacks would only try harder* they could be just as well off as whites. (emphasis added)

According to Kinder and Mendelberg, this and similar items, when used to create an index of prejudice, are "powerful [predictors of] white opinion on issues of race, nothing [else] works as well" (p. 62). Further, the authors state: "On the role of the federal government in providing assistance to blacks, on whether the government should intervene to ensure that blacks are not discriminated against at work, and on affirmative action for blacks in college admissions, the effects [of this measure of] prejudice are huge" (p. 62). I read such words to imply causality.

Yet one of these policy items reads:

Some people feel that the government in Washington should make every effort to improve the social and economic position of blacks. . . . Others feel that the government should not make any special effort to help blacks *because they should help themselves.* (A seven-point scale is presented; emphasis added.)

These two questions are not identical—for example, the second explicitly brings in help from the federal government—but they are so close in essential substance that they might conceivably be part of the same scale of racial attitudes. A second policy question on college quotas is not quite as close to the prejudice item as the above example, but if someone believes that blacks could do as well as whites simply by working harder, it is difficult to see why they would favor reserving college openings for blacks that, in the words of the question, "they haven't earned."[2] More generally, the two types of items labeled "prejudice" and "racial policy"—are so close in implication that a strong association between them might be thought of as indicating somewhat different aspects of the same general construct, negative attitudes toward the need to help blacks, rather than as distinguishing cause from effect.[3]

A related step in the Kinder and Mendelberg analysis draws on a survey-based experiment that seemed to me at first an illuminating interaction of the type discussed below. The authors use open-ended questions to compare how whites react to federal help for black advancement and how they react to federal help for people in general, the two questions having been asked of a national sample. The coded answers to the version that had been put in terms of federal help to blacks fall mainly (50 percent) into a category labeled "racial resentment," with examples indicating "that blacks should help themselves or try harder to make it on their own, that they should stop complaining and do a little bit of work for a change, that they should work like the rest of us, or that they are doing pretty well these days and do not need help" (p. 67). The version about people in general yields an even larger proportion (67 percent) categorized under the label "individualism," with examples indicating "that people should make it on their own, that people must be responsible for themselves, that welfare breeds dependency, that the poor deserve their poverty, that some people are just naturally lazy, that work gives people pride and self-esteem, or that government assistance is unfair to those who do work" (p. 68).

On reflection, the difference between these two types of responses seems to me less clear-cut than it does to Kinder and Mendelberg. Apart from the claim "that blacks are doing pretty well these days and don't need help," the main difference is that the question *asking explicitly* about help to blacks prompts responses that are *answered explicitly* in terms of helping blacks, yet the characterizations of *why* help should be denied do not seem all that different. It is certainly possible that the two sets of answers differ more sharply in other ways when examined closely, but the broad labels "racial resentment" and "individualism" do not tell readers what the categories contain or how much they differ other than in referencing or not referencing African Americans. A more detailed set of codes is needed (and may be available, according to a footnote in the chapter), with the coding itself having been organized to avoid influence from simply the mention of "blacks" or "people" in the answers.[4] In addition, it would be useful to know whether the two versions of the question produce different associations with background variables like education and with racial attitudes dissimilar to the code categories (e.g., negative affect toward blacks or hostility to intermarriage) that can help further in distinguishing the two sets of responses.

I do not mean to argue against exploring correlations between different measures of racial attitudes, but where it is likely that the correlations reflect aspects of the same basic construct or of somewhat overlapping constructs, an approach through or similar to factor analysis is appropriate for the exploration. In doing so, however, one must keep in mind that what comes out of a factor analysis is largely determined by what goes in. Thus, Michael Hughes and Steven Tuch produce a "structural" factor from their data that includes items measuring discrimination and lack of educational opportunities. Although reasonable in terms of the data they start from, these items offer different explanations for "economic and social problems," have some noticeably different correlates, and, in a different total set of items, might yield separate factors. An additional complication occurs where there are format differences within a set of items, as is the case with Pettigrew's several Blatant and Subtle Prejudice scales, for there is always the possibility that the separate factors may be based as much or more on the method of asking than on the constructs named.

Even in cases where causality seems likely, a modest correlation can imply no more than that one variable plays some role in determining variation in another. Sears, Henry, and Kosterman test the hypothesis that overt antiblack animus is *one* source of white opposition to a set of racial policies. Their evidence is convincing, but it tells us something that is probably not in great doubt. There clearly is still a nontrivial amount of open animus by whites toward blacks, as indicated by casual observation, by newspaper accounts, and by survey data (e.g., 13 percent of a national sample in 1996 wished to retain laws against racial intermarriage [Schuman et al. 1997, 107]). Since virtually all of these people should line up in opposition to policies that appear to them to be favorable to blacks, we should expect every correlation involving such policies to include overt antiblack animus as *one* component. Only if that component is so large as to dominate other sources of variation do we learn something appreciable when the correlation is presented. Since the correlations reported by Sears, Henry, and Kosterman of antiblack affect with both policy issues and symbolic racism are all under .30, it is difficult to agree with their characterization of them as "strong" (p. 89).[5]

The relation of the two right-hand columns in the table to the middle column is less vulnerable to problems of circularity, since the latter does not mention race at all. The chapter by Sidanius et al. fits this model, and Bob Altemeyer (1998) makes a strong case that social dominance orientation (SDO) can be thought of as one form of authoritarianism, a form that relates well to overt antiminority attitudes and other extreme views, as is also suggested by Sears, Henry, and Kosterman. We need more evidence of how SDO relates to less extreme racial items, and it would be especially helpful to see such relations at a more detailed level than summary coefficients provide.[6]

ASSOCIATIONS BETWEEN NONATTITUDINAL AND ATTITUDINAL VARIABLES

The most obvious way to guard against the danger of circularity in associations is to correlate variables that are indisputably different in character from one another. This approach is well represented by Taylor's chapter. Clearly significant relations are reported, but in this case, the key variables are conceptually and even methodologically quite distinct: Percent Black is based on government census data and is of a "factual" character, while Taylor's measures of racial and nonracial attitudes are derived from surveys in which people expressed a variety of opinions, including their views of other groups. We can be pretty confident that the main correlated measures are not being influenced by questions with a considerable overlap in meaning to respondents. We can also be fairly sure that if the variables are related causally, it is because Percent Black (of geographic units) somehow influences attitudes rather than attitudes affecting migration, though the latter possibility cannot be completely dismissed.

The main challenge presented by Taylor's approach is exactly opposite to that raised by interattitude correlations: the "distance" between the two types of measures is so great as to make it unclear why and how the one can influence the other. Apparently, some of the more obvious explanations do not hold, since in other analysis Taylor (1998) assessed concrete economic and political threats in several different ways and found no connecting link. She suggests that "the voices of local media, politicians, and other opinion leaders" may hold promise, but how that might work without showing up as threat is not indicated. Possibly more promising are white perceptions of physical threat or of cultural dominance, as noted in Taylor (1998), though no measures of these are introduced. She raises still another possibility by quoting Gordon Allport's (1954) observation that white perceptions of increased threat from a larger black population may be contingent on preexisting negative sentiments, which would point to an interaction calling for over-time measurements. For now, we have a finding that seems solid in statistical and measurement senses, but lacks an interpretation.

How to solve these problems is unclear at present, but an advantage of the type of analysis pursued by Taylor is that it discourages us from thinking too quickly that we understand a discovered relationship and spurs researchers to continue searching for interpretations that can be investigated. This assumes, of course, that we do not simply leap from the basic correlation to an interpretation that we have no way of testing. There is a touch of such residual stretching in Taylor's repeated insistence that her data are clearly inconsistent with the arguments of Paul Sniderman and his colleagues, since at this point we really don't know what has generated the relationships she has documented so carefully.

Another basic attempt to draw conclusions from variables that are fundamentally distinct appears in Lawrence Bobo's chapter. He shows that even with a variety of social background and attitudinal controls, race remains a very important determinant of attitudes toward affirmative action, and one can hardly argue that racial classification and affirmative action attitudes are circular measures. (Bobo's conclusion is supported by analyses provided by Hughes and Tuch and by Sidanius et al.) From this fundamental finding, Bobo draws the conclusion that "race matters!" (p. 152) and argues that it shows the most basic determinant of attitudes toward affirmative action to be "'realistic' or meaningful struggle over group interests defined along racial lines" (p. 142). This thesis, which Bobo has been a pioneer in urging, seems to me quite plausible, but several issues arising from his analysis need to be confronted.

First, as Bobo emphasizes, neither whites nor blacks are monolithic in their attitudes toward affirmative action, and it is necessary to account for why a fair number of whites endorse affirmative action if indeed the basic feature of black-white relations in the United States is conflict over group interests. The problem is a little like the one Karl Marx faced in trying to explain how, if class conflict is so fundamental, nonproletarians like himself and Friedrich Engels were so keen to join the revolution. The same issue arises in the conversion by Sidanius et al. of social dominance orientation from a universal motive supposedly influencing just about everyone everywhere into a measure of individual differences. Given basic assumptions about conflict over scarce resources, why should there be more than a trivial number of whites who believe in advancing racial equality, no matter the difficulties it causes their own racial group?

Second, Bobo created a direct measure of perceived threat by whites, but when he included it as a predictor of his main dependent variable, perceived negative effects of affirmative action attitudes, it runs into the problem of circularity that we considered earlier. For example, one item in the perceived threat index states "More good jobs for blacks means fewer good jobs for members of other groups," and that is not very different from one of his affirmative action items that reads "Affirmative action for blacks is unfair to whites." These are both reasonable items, but do we really have two substantially different measures?

Third and most basic, it becomes necessary to address the question of why group interests in the United States at this point in time are "defined along [these] racial lines" so strongly. This is indeed close to the heart of the question of race in America, and it is not simple to answer. Whites apparently do not feel the same kind or degree of realistic group conflict with all other racial groups—for example, with Japanese Americans, despite the history of extremely racist definitions of both Japanese and Japanese Americans before and during World War II as well as the success of Japanese Americans in "competing" with whites in occupational and other terms. Thus, something more must be involved in black-white relations than "realistic or meaningful struggle over group interests defined along racial lines." An effort to address this issue goes beyond the purview of the present chapter, but Bobo begins in his later pages to consider the factors that increase or decrease the salience of group interests and the conflict that results from them. Such inquiry seems essential if the problem is to be addressed clearly, with recourse to Taylor's approach in terms of percentages as one possible line to pursue.

STEERING BETWEEN SCYLLA AND CHARYBDIS

Although in principle one might search for variables to correlate that are neither too far apart nor too close together, it is not easy to find such variables. The classic example of such an attempt was that by T. W. Adorno et al. (1950). Thus, it is difficult to see circularity when one variable is based on an item like this:

> When a person has a problem or worry, it is best for him not to think about it, but to keep busy with more cheerful things.

and the other is based on an item like this:

> It would be a mistake ever to have Negroes for foremen and leaders over whites.

Hence, if the two variables are positively correlated, we learn something new and unexpected about the organization of attitudes, even though causal direction may remain a little murky. However, the Adorno et al. correlations ran into other serious problems, such as acquiescence response set, and in addition, Altemeyer (1988) found it necessary to drop some of the less "obvious" items in his revision of the F-scale.

The analysis presented by Sears, Henry, and Kosterman avoids the problem of circularity by focusing on egalitarian items not as a *cause* of symbolic racism, but as an essential component. In fact, most of their analysis is of equalitarian values as such, providing a useful example of an attempt to probe the meaning of a measure previously taken for granted. They distinguish two main constructs hidden under the general label of "equalitarian": one form, which they call "less equal treatment," essentially affirms the desirability of giving everyone an equal opportunity; the other form, which they call "we've gone too far," asserts that too much attention has been given to pushing "equal rights." It is the second and not the first that shows a substantial relation to symbolic racism measures and also to a specific measure of individualistic attribution. This effort to unpack a larger scale seems quite worthwhile, and their use of univariate item distributions as an initial clue to the distinction is instructive.[7]

So far so good. But Sears, Henry, and Kosterman attempt to salvage the theoretical expectation that individualism plays a major role in symbolic racism by claiming that the "we've gone too far" items are effective because they contain "individualistic" content: "Many whites may believe that 'we've gone too far' because . . . they may see any remaining racial inequalities as primarily attributable to blacks themselves, to their lack of work ethic . . ." (p. 103). It is difficult to see the rationale for this interpretation in the case of the three "we've gone too far" items presented in the authors' table 3.4, and their report of a high correlation with one individualistic attribution item (in table 3.6) provides evidence only when race is mentioned. At this point, we need to know more about the thinking behind answers to the "we've gone too far" items, and open-ended follow-up questions to respondents might be helpful. In any case, other than preserving the original claim that symbolic racism involves individualism joined to negative affect, there is no particular advantage to emphasis on individualism as a *key* element, especially with nonracial individualism having pretty much fallen out of the picture.[8] The authors make a stronger case that respondents who agree with these items have what Kinder and Lynn Sanders (1996) call resentment toward direct or indirect concerns about black disadvantage. More generally, the Sears, Henry, and Kosterman results might well lead to a rethinking of the assumption that symbolic racism is a combination of antiblack affect and individualism.

A different approach that can be useful for going beyond correlational analysis is exemplified in several of the chapters. First, in the spirit of discriminant validity, it can be helpful to produce negative findings, along with positive ones, in order to gain insight into the distinct meaning of variables—or if not negative results, then results that go in different directions or are at quite different levels of magnitude. Such combinations of findings imply some form of three-way interaction where one's key independent variable is positively related to one putative dependent variable and negatively related (or unrelated or little related) to another in a way that distinguishes the two correlations and sharpens our understanding of the focal variable.[9] Moreover, in pursuing these steps, it is desirable to keep an open mind about one's favorite variables, hoping to learn more fully what it is one has measured, even if this is different from what had been intended or assumed. Every analysis is in part, and often in good part, a form of construct validation, a discovery of what it is that we have actually been measuring.

One example of a useful interaction is Pettigrew's finding that his variable "conservatism" has much greater power as a predictor of prejudice measure among more-educated respondents than among less-educated respondents and moreover that this difference is not visible for his other two main independent variables, "political engagement" and "genclass." Although other chapters also report stronger correlations at higher educational levels, Pettigrew's finding goes beyond this by having the relation occur more for one dependent variable than for others, and he is able to link this finding to earlier results about how an authoritarianism measure works at different levels of education. Whether the interpretation is correct or not—and if we treat the Sidanius et al. social dominance orientation as a form of authoritarianism, a similar interaction they report provides further evidence—Pettigrew's empirical results should stimulate us to rethink what it is we are measuring when we ask such questions of less-educated respondents.

Another example of assessing discriminant validity occurs at the end of the Sidanius et al. chapter, where the authors report that their primary independent variable, social dominance orientation, is related in an experimental comparison to opposing affirmative action for blacks, but very little to opposing affirmative action for women or poor people. (There may or may not be a further interaction with education when blacks are the target, but if so, it does not alter the present point, though it creates an additional complication.) If we take seriously the authors' basic assumption that what is crucial in intergroup relations is "competition over scarce material and symbolic resources" (p. 196), the rapidly increasing entry of women into business and professional occupations previously closed to them should seem at least as great a threat to men as blacks are to whites. After all, women represent more than half the American population, while blacks represent only about 13 percent. Particularly striking, therefore, is the finding (p. 218) that men and women do not differ in attitudes toward affirmative action for women. Such results call for further clarification of what it is that SDO—or possibly the several dependent variables—measures, and for this purpose, such negative findings can be valuable.

There is also a reverse way of making use of an interactive approach implicit in the dependent variables that Sears, Henry, and Kosterman employ under the overall heading of racial policies. Although these authors often appear to view their three types of policies as more or less similar, why not accept initially, if only for the sake of testing more thoroughly, the possibility that there is a sharp distinction between support for government action that is limited to preventing discrimination (which they call equal opportunity) and support for government action that provides special help to blacks (federal assistance and affirmative action)? The hypothesis to be tested (and presumably *dis*confirmed if the authors are correct) is that symbolic racism will predict the latter two variables (especially the second, which is usually interpreted to call for preferential treatment) much more strongly than equal opportunity because the belief that blacks no longer face much discrimination or lowered opportunities is especially relevant to rejecting federal assistance and affirmative action. Even if one believes that discrimination has been largely eliminated, one should not oppose use of government action where the question itself actually states that discrimination is taking place or might well take place.

If this distinction between types of racial policies is to be tested rigorously, however, it is important that the equal opportunity set of questions be revised to avoid their present ambiguities. The question used by Sears, Henry, and Kosterman (and by Kinder and Mendelberg) about "black people not getting fair treatment in jobs" is seriously outdated. When first asked in the 1960s, "fair treatment" implied "equal treatment," but today some whites are quite likely to interpret it as calling for "preferential treatment" (Krysan 1999; Schuman et al. 1997).[10] If existing questions from major surveys are desired, the General Social Survey (GSS) question on open housing is much closer to the basic concept of equal opportunity, and it also continues to show considerable variation in response. Furthermore, the strategic group of respondents to focus on consists of those who unequivocally support equal treatment in terms of open housing, but oppose preferential treatment: their racial resentment scores should be compared with those of respondents who are consistently negative on both items (oppose open housing and oppose preferential treatment) as well as with those who are consistently positive on both items (support both policies).

I am not at all sure that the distinction just made will lead to a difference in results, and perhaps Sears and his colleagues will regard what is raised here as minor, even trivial, quibbling. But the point of focusing on the distinction is both theoretical and then some. On the theoretical side, if symbolic racism/racial resentment questions predict in essentially the same way and in the same degree to both equal opportunity and affirmative action variables, this will considerably strengthen the case that Sears, Kinder, and their colleagues wish to make about racial antipathy or sympathy underlying virtually all policy issues involving race today. In such an analysis, their expectation is to demonstrate the *absence* of a kind of interaction—that symbolic racism items are just as useful for classic issues of equal opportunity as for more recent issues of affirmative action. If so, so be it. But let's not build that into our measures from the very beginning.

The "then some" reason for clarifying the questions on equal opportunity is also important. That neither Sears, Henry, and Kosterman nor Kinder and Mendelberg note the glaring problem with the "fair job treatment" question is consistent with the way in which the term "racist" is implied for those who do not accept preferential treatment as an obviously appropriate approach to promoting racial equality. "Racist" is a vastly invidious label today, regardless of the modifier added ("symbolic") or its redefinition away from an assumption of belief in innate racial differences, and it should be used with some caution. Although I personally support some types and degrees of preferential treatment at present, I also believe that it is possible for someone to oppose preferential treatment on what are genuinely equalitarian grounds and at the same time to support vigorous efforts against all forms of discrimination, though I don't claim to know how many such people there are. For this reason, the renaming of symbolic racism as racial resentment by Kinder and Sanders (1996) might be seen as a helpful terminological change, regardless of why it was taken, though it does lose the useful theoretical connection to Sears's more general ideas on "symbolic politics" (e.g., Sears and Funk 1991).

Survey-based experiments offer still another way of testing for a difference in results that can clarify measures. Both the considerable strengths and the limitations of this approach are illustrated in the chapter by Sniderman, Crosby, and Howell. First, they show experimentally that the National Election Studies (NES) "no special favors" item about past ethnic minorities having "worked their way up" is answered in essentially the same way regardless of whether "blacks" or "new immigrants" are targeted. This result offers a strong challenge to the assumption that the question is aimed only at blacks, and it supports the authors' stress on the importance of nonracial values. A possible counterargument is that the finding simply expands the target of the item from blacks to minorities more generally, as happened when the Adorno et al. (1950) research five decades ago expanded its focus from anti-Semitism to ethnocentrism. We are thus stimulated to try to think of ways to distinguish between the two quite different interpretations.

A second experimental pair of questions asks whether it is the government's job to guarantee an "equal opportunity to succeed," with one version referring to blacks and the other version to women. Finding little difference, the authors conclude that they have additional evidence that a general (nonracial) attitude toward the role of government is directly involved. Fair enough in theory, but despite the authors' intention, the phrase "equal opportunity to succeed" may blur the distinction between "opportunity" and "outcome," with some respondents failing to emphasize "opportunity" in their thinking and changing "succeed" into outcome as they answer the question. This ambiguity of question framing calls for further clarification and is not met simply because the same question is asked about both blacks and women.

Both of the experiments just considered have the desirable characteristic of holding question wording constant except for varying one key word, consistent with an ideal experimental paradigm. But it seems to me that Sniderman, Crosby, and Howell go astray when they attempt more substantial variations in wording in another experiment. They start from a slight adaptation of the well-known GSS open housing question, which is carefully balanced to provide rationales both for supporting and for opposing an open housing law. They then deliberately try in another version to tip the balance in the direction of allowing discrimination, primarily by restating twice more that the reason for opposing an open housing law is simply the right of owners to sell or not sell to anyone they wish. In this condition, the authors find, as they expected, that opposition to open housing increases. (An additional important finding that seemed to me to deserve greater emphasis is that among the college-educated it is self-identified conservatives, not liberals, who are shown to be easily shifted from support for open housing to opposition once they are given some encouragement, which suggests that such conservatives are influenced more by redundant reassurance than by principled beliefs.)

Sniderman, Crosby, and Howell then seek to tip the balance in the opposite direction, toward supporting open housing, by altering the wording of the question to refer to active government effort on behalf of blacks to be able to "live anywhere they choose, including white neighborhoods." To the authors' surprise, this manipulation fails, or rather it succeeds again in moving conservatives—but not liberals— in the direction of opposing government intervention. The authors immediately conclude that it must be because there is an "asymmetry" in arguments on the two sides of the issue: "Opponents have more, or at any rate more readily accessible, arguments to invoke than proponents" (p. 266). But this assumes that their attempt to write the "reversal" item was an appropriate one. I have little doubt that it would be possible to revise the open housing question to move people in the support direction, but it would probably not be by emphasizing the activity of government beyond the fact of an open housing law already clearly built into the question. Even less appropriate is having the question postulate the existence of "white neighborhoods." The more likely rewording would be to reiterate in slightly different words the principle that an owner's rights do *not* include the right to discriminate on the grounds of race or color. It might well take some pilot work to arrive at a suitable variation of the original question, but that is true of all survey questions, and experiments do not free us from all the uncertainties of question writing.[11]

More generally, I wonder if it is plausible to assume, as Sniderman, Crosby, and Howell seem to do throughout their chapter, that virtually the entire white population shares uniform meanings for the words "liberal" and "conservative." Here, again, is where open-ended follow-up questions could be asked in order to discover and then use analytically the varied meanings that respondents give to these abstract terms.

SOME PERSONAL CONCLUDING CLARIFICATIONS, QUALIFICATIONS, AND RECOMMENDATIONS

BASIC ASSUMPTIONS

I agree with the position that Sidanius has emphasized in much of his writing (e.g., Sidanius and Pratto 1993a): racial and other forms of intergroup hostility and conflict are so common around the world as to be plausibly treated as the normal state of the human condition. Often such conflict seems to be based, as Sidanius et al. assert, on defense of hierarchical positions, though sometimes it is not entirely clear who has superiority when political power and economic power are distributed quite differently (for example, today in South Africa). Thus, although white Americans are sometimes characterized as peculiarly bigoted, a world map that highlights names like Bosnia, Northern Ireland, Palestine, and Rwanda points up the much greater intensity of racial and ethnic hostilities elsewhere these days. Moreover, these are simply names of places that make headlines at present, for there is hardly a nation or region where some substantial intergroup conflict is absent.

What makes the United States unusual has been the development of norms over the past half century that encourage the elimination from the public sphere of expressions of racial disparagement and practices of antiblack discrimination that were largely taken for granted in the first half of the century. The new norms, like all norms, have been internalized unevenly by the white American public. Some people accept them quite genuinely, and they become personal attitudes; others accept them at least in terms of outward behavior when observed, as, of course, occurs to some extent in survey interviews, but also in important parts of public life as well; and still others continue to reject them partly or entirely.

The basic thrust of the initial change was toward the removal of most forms of explicit discrimination and overt prejudice, and steps beyond these changes were never incorporated into the new norms. Despite some vague support for the notion that greater racial equality in outcomes is desirable, most of the programs that fall under the heading of affirmative action were never part of the new normative development. Much of the disagreement that runs through this volume, with Sniderman and his colleagues on one side and most of the other authors on the other side, turns mainly on how to characterize supporters and opponents of affirmative action programs.

SOME CLARIFICATIONS

Before offering thoughts on this fundamental issue, I would like to clarify the emphasis in my own book (Schuman et al. 1997), since Sniderman, Crosby, and Howell appear to misinterpret it in some important respects. The primary aims of the book were relatively modest: to locate as many as practical of the survey questions that have been used to track racial attitudes and beliefs over time, to categorize the questions in a way that is true to their content and at the same time connected to contemporary social issues, and to present and interpret the evidence of change or lack of change in the responses as well as other relevant demographic correlates that can help in understanding change.

The book makes a sharp distinction between questions dealing with equal treatment of blacks and whites (in tables 3.1 and 3.2) and questions dealing with issues that fall under the broad rubric of "affirmative action," which in turn is subdivided into two parts: federal assistance to blacks as a group (table 3.5A) and compensatory preferential treatment in education and employment (table 3.5B).[12] However, the book never claims and I do not believe that, in the words of Sniderman, Crosby, and Howell (p. 257), "so far as white Americans support the norm of racial equality, then they . . . should support [such] governmental policies to achieve it" as "whether the liberal government has a special obligation to help improve the living standards of African Americans, of whether it is important to correct the problems of poverty and unemployment, of whether federal spending on programs that assist blacks should be increased." Those may be very desirable steps to take—I personally think they are—but they do *not* follow from the norm of equal treatment. The distinction between equalizing treatment and equalizing outcomes is a basic one that has been made by many authors, and while it can sometimes be blurred when actual attitude items are examined, the conceptual distinction itself is generally clear.

The "principle-implementation gap" that my book investigates relates entirely to issues of equal treatment, and all the comparisons made (figures 3.8, 3.9, and 3.10) were limited to such issues. We were interested in the extent to which those who supported principles of equal treatment also supported the implementation of equal treatment by the government, though we found this difficult to investigate because, when looked at closely, there are only a very small number of trend questions that deal unambiguously with such implementation.

However, to the extent that investigation was possible, we found a moderate-sized gap between support for the principles and support for their implementation, and we provided some evidence that this gap is due to respondents whose support for the principles is weak in terms of an intensity measure in the first place (figure 3.10).

Moreover, consistent with this focus on equal treatment, we report an experiment on open housing that deals entirely with equal treatment in buying a home. The experiment contrasts an open housing law to be created by a local referendum with the same kind of law promulgated through federal legislation, testing the hypothesis that such a law is more acceptable when accomplished by personal voting at a local level than by imposition from Washington. Finding little difference, however, between the two question formulations, we then focused on what seemed to us a major rationale for opposing open housing: resistance to government intrusion into the right of individuals (in this case, homeowners) to make their own decision about whom to sell to. For this reason, the association of attitudes toward open housing (in either experimental form) and attitudes toward a "mandatory seat belt law" posed a useful (though hardly definitive) theoretical test, since both involve the issue of a societal rule that limits individual autonomy. There is indeed some association, but it is not great, and there are many people who object to government intrusion where racial discrimination may be at issue, but who are willing to accept such intrusion with regard to mandating the wearing of seat belts.

BEYOND EQUAL TREATMENT

What about affirmative action and the argument over whether opposition draws largely from nonracial political principles or largely from some form of racial prejudice? This question can be usefully connected to the issue of whether there is indeed a new form of prejudice, whether called symbolic racism, racial resentment, or some other name, and, if so, when it arose.

Kinder and Mendelberg seem to believe that this new form of prejudice "can be traced back to transformations set in motion during the racial crisis of the 1960s, as civil disobedience gave way to an epidemic of violence in American cities" (p. 60). Yet the first Herbert Hyman and Paul Sheatsley report in 1956 showed clearly that white support for segregation was crumbling, with the turning point probably having been shortly after the end of World War II.[13] Belief in racial differences in intelligence also declined sharply over that period, though how much this was because whites had genuinely changed on that score and how much because such assertions had become taboo is an open question.[14] But it is hardly the case that the stereotype of blacks as not trying hard enough—as lazy, in common parlance—was new even in the 1940s. The first published study of group stereotypes in America by Daniel Katz and Kenneth Braly (1933) found that 75 percent of their sample of Princeton students selected "lazy" from a list of eighty-four adjectives to characterize "Negroes," whereas the same adjective was not applied by more than 12 percent of the same students to any of nine other ethnic groups rated. No doubt the stereotype itself is much older, dating from well before there were any social psychologists around to obtain quantitative measures of popular beliefs. Thus, the explanation of black disadvantage in terms of lack of effort did not require that anything new be created, just a slight reformulation of an old stereotype.

I suspect, however, that the more general point made by Sears, Kinder, and others is correct: as support for all forms of discrimination became increasingly counternormative, many of those who had supported discrimination openly now moved increasingly to oppose the continued pressure for changes in race relations more generally. The urban riots of the late 1960s may or may not have accelerated this new kind of opposition, but it was already well under way by that time. Although none of the Kinder and Sanders (1996) racial resentment items appears to have been asked early enough to explore the issue of time of inception, Sears et al. (1997, 25–26) include as part of a symbolic racism measure the item "Are civil rights leaders trying to push too fast, going too slowly, or are they moving at about the right speed?" Data on this item go back to 1964 and indicate that "too fast" was chosen more often *before* than after the riots (Schuman et al. 1997, tab. 3.6). (It is interesting to note that the word "push," which occurs in this item, is the same word that appears in one of the three "we've gone too far" items of Sears, Henry, and Kosterman: "We have gone too far in pushing equal rights in this country.") Thus, resistance to equal treatment was manifested in the call to slow down the pressure for change, even when discrimination itself could no longer be justified. Perhaps in this sense only, there was a new form of antiblack attitudes, one that could continue to apply as times changed, almost irrespective of current issues.

More recently entirely new issues arose—especially issues of compensatory preferential treatment—and the picture became more complicated. It seems likely that most of those who agree with the vague statement that "civil rights leaders are trying to push too fast" will oppose preferential treatment, and a cross-tabulation using 1992 NES data on whites shows this to be the case: 82 percent of the "too fast" respondents were strongly opposed to preferential treatment in hiring and promotion, and another 11 percent were opposed less strongly ($N = 483$). A few of these people would probably show up as overtly prejudiced by any definition, but probably most would be captured by other "new racism" measures. However, it is also the case that of those who take the opposite position and say that civil rights leaders "are going too *slowly*" ($N = 219$), some 52 percent are strongly opposed to preferential treatment, and another 20 percent are opposed less strongly.[15] It seems reasonable to hypothesize that many of these people are opposed on grounds that preferential treatment—unless it can be shown necessary to overcome a specific pattern of discrimination—clashes with the norm of equal treatment and not because such people fit well under a new racism rubric. More generally, in the most recent year for which we have data (1996), 88 percent of all white respondents opposed preferential treatment in employment, and I find it implausible to assume that essentially all of these people do so out of prejudice.[16]

Thus, I believe that there is reason to see the opposition to affirmative action as reflecting *both* some continuing prejudice and some genuine concern that affirmative action goes against norms of equal treatment. I do not pretend to know what the relative proportions are or whether they can be distinguished in any simple way, but I am reluctant to treat opposition to preferential treatment per se as a sign of a "new racism." A better indicator is probably the complete denial that there is some continuing significant discrimination against blacks, though that also has its limitations.

ANOTHER APPROACH

The terms that most authors of these chapters use show that their focus is mainly on those whites who express negative attitudes toward blacks: "prejudice" (blatant and subtle), "racial resentment," "symbolic racism," "social dominance," "inegalitarianism." These terms are in keeping with a long tradition in research on race and ethnicity that has viewed negative attitudes as a type of irrationality (prejudice = prejudgment) or a form of deviance or in some other sense an aberration. We might well shift some of our attention from racial antipathies to what Allport (1954) called "love prejudice" (though the term itself may sound a little too irrational or too sentimental for easy use today) in order to understand better the minority of whites who support strong affirmative action steps, especially those outside academic settings. This includes a willingness to put aside to some extent one's own group and personal interests and to support government or other help directed toward those seen as handicapped by past or present obstacles of whatever kind that are related to race as well as a strong desire to increase what has come to be known as "diversity" throughout the society.

More than three decades ago John Harding and I tried to measure something of this sort with a set of questions that we called "sympathetic identification" (Schuman and Harding 1963). It dealt with several different minorities, and here is a slight adaptation of one item:

> Two black women get jobs in a large American business office. The white women in the office are courteous, but seem not to want to become too friendly with them. What is the reaction of the black women likely to be?
>
> _____ (a) They might prefer it this way, since they have each other as friends and would rather not mix a lot with white people.
>
> _____ (b) If the white women are polite, it probably makes little difference as long as the job is good in all other ways.
>
> _____ (c) Blacks are different in some of their beliefs and it would be difficult without more information for a white person to figure out what they would think in this case.
>
> _____ (d) They would almost certainly feel sad or angry or both.

Each alternative was intended to represent a not entirely unreasonable stance. One alternative interprets the incident as really a good thing from the minority members' point of view because it prevents trouble or fits their own ethnocentrism. Another alternative assumes that members of subordinate groups are sometimes indifferent to minor instances of rejection. A third alternative takes a reasonable agnostic position by indicating that not enough information is provided on which to judge the particular matter. And the fourth alternative (though the order of alternatives changed from one item to the next) assumed that members of minority groups in the United States are likely to be hurt or angered by such instances of prejudice. We did not claim to have the "right" answer to the vignette and could imagine there being minority members for whom each alternative might be correct. But we were interested in those white respondents who by choosing the fourth alternative expressed what could be called "sympathetic identification" with the minority member, and we tried to learn more about these people by additional quantitative and qualitative analysis.

Whether or not anything like this approach would be useful today, I do think that more effort should be put into focusing on those white Americans who manifest feelings that go beyond acceptance of formal equality of opportunity. They probably represent a relatively uncommon type of individual and deserve to be studied as more than a reference category. Based on results noted earlier, they may show up also as having highly intense feelings on traditional questions on principles of equal opportunity, even though on logical grounds one might well predict the opposite. That is an issue it would be useful to investigate and one to which I do not know the answer.

ELEVEN Lumpers and
Splitters, Individuals
and Structures

Comments on
Racialized Politics

JENNIFER L. HOCHSCHILD

y initial reaction upon reading these chapters, in conjunction
with other recent writings of these scholars, was the same as it
has been for a decade or more: I was convinced by each in turn that
proponents of principled conservatism, symbolic racism, and social
structural approaches were correctly analyzing white Americans' racial views. But according to all three sets of authors, the arguments of
the other two sets are less correct than their own, if not simply wrong.
It is not possible, of course, for all three to be correct if they set their
arguments up in opposition to the others. Yet each set of proponents
presents elegant theoretical arguments, strong evidence, sophisticated
methodological dissections of that evidence, and moral commitments
to racial justice and social scientific truth. Furthermore, in many cases
they are analyzing precisely the same data sets. What is going on?

I see two kinds of explanations for my (and others'?) inability or unwillingness to accept one of these approaches at the expense of the
other two. The first cluster of explanations lies within the paradigm of
survey research in which these authors work; the second explanation
puts that paradigm into a broader structural context. My goal in these
comments is not to come down in favor of one or another approach,
but rather to explore the commitments one makes by accepting one
or another of them. I will also argue for approaches that move outside
all three of the positions featured in *Racialized Politics* and conclude
with a sketch of my own view of the puzzles presented by racialized
politics in the United States.

EXPLANATIONS OF RACIAL POLITICS WITHIN THE SURVEY RESEARCH PARADIGM

LUMPERS AND SPLITTERS

For several centuries, taxonomists of the natural world have been divided into lumpers, who seek to merge a larger number of proposed species or genera into a smaller number, and splitters, who seek to move in the opposite direction. Some of the debate among the three basic approaches on display in *Racialized Politics* has the flavor of this difference in taste (or in epistemological starting point, to be more formal).

Paul Sniderman and his colleagues believe that one must separate out characteristics of individuals that are often associated with racial animus from that racial animus itself in order to determine how much effect prejudice has on political views. Thus, in their chapter, Sniderman, Gretchen Crosby, and William Howell carefully distinguish values such as individualism or egalitarianism, ideologies such as political conservatism or liberalism, levels of education, and so on from negative racial affect. Once the affect is isolated, they argue, one can examine its influence on policy views and other dependent variables, either alone or in conjunction with some of the characteristics from which it was first isolated. But only when the concept of racial prejudice is purified from other concepts can we see what real work it does in individuals' psyches and political stances. As they put it, "[L]evels of support for government assurance of equal opportunity to succeed for a group . . . [are] a function of three factors—the group to benefit, blacks or women [that is, prejudice]; the respondents' political point of view, liberal or conservative [that is, political ideology or principles]; and . . . formal education" (p. 260).[1]

Donald Kinder and his colleagues, in contrast, believe that splitting more and more characteristics away from racial prejudice artificially shrivels it into irrelevance-by-definition; racial affect must be lumped together with certain other values and emotions with which it is closely associated in order to see its real force. Those values and emotions may well change over time, so that racism in the 1990s involves a slightly different set of elements than racism did in the 1950s. Thus, "for reasons of history individualism and prejudice have become entangled: properly conceived, individualism is *in* prejudice" (Kinder and Mendelberg this volume, pp. 44–45). In their chapter, David Sears, P. J. Henry, and Rick Kosterman (p. 112) concur, concluding after examination that "individualism does indeed have an important role in the racial resentments captured in the symbolic racism belief system—*when individualism is racialized*."[2]

As with a taxonomy of species and genera, this debate seems to me more a matter of preference, or of usefulness for a particular purpose, than of correct or incorrect theorizing. If one narrows the definition of racial prejudice, one is likely to find less of it or to find that it is less influential in comparison with other motivators than if one includes those motivators within one's definition of racial prejudice. That is a matter of simple arithmetic logic. Whether one *should* narrow the definition of racial prejudice in this way or conversely broaden it to include various other values and beliefs is a matter of theoretical purpose. One should narrow it if the question is how and how much whites' feelings about African Americans, as distinguished from other feelings and values, affect what they think should be done by or for African Americans. One should broaden it if the question is whether and why whites react differently to African Americans than to other groups or differently to policy issues that are racially inflected than to policy issues that are not. They are different questions; they are both legitimate.

Choosing to be a lumper or a splitter also has political implications, if not political motivations. Splitters are likely to give comfort, whether intentionally or not, to those who see racial divisions as simply one among many equally important social differences in a complex society. Lumpers are likely to give comfort, whether intentionally or not, to those who see racial divisions as more important than, or even causing, most other social differences. Much of the animus in this research arena derives, so far as I can tell, from normative disputes between those who see racial inequality as *the* central issue and study public opinion in order to alleviate it and those who see the role of public opinion in governance as *the* central issue and study racial attitudes in order to understand that link.

Of course, one can go too far in lumping or splitting, as none of the authors in this volume does, to a point where the enterprise loses intellectual legitimacy. Dinesh D'Souza defines racism very narrowly—as a belief in the biological inferiority of the subordinated race[3]—and thereby can claim that illegitimate racism has practically disappeared in the United States. Conversely, some proponents of affirmative action claim that any opposition to even its strongest forms is evidence of racism.[4] Both arguments are wrong, largely because most of the work is done by choosing a particular definition of "racism." Thus, it is not silly to worry about whether an author is taking everything meaningful out of a concept or is stuffing too much into it. But within the range of arguments represented by the authors in *Racialized Politics* and the writers to whom they are responding, different operationalizations of key terms are appropriate to different research questions and different normative starting points.

FIGURE AND GROUND

A different metaphor from a different craft also helps to explain why each approach seems convincing on its own terms, yet all insist that they cannot all be correct. What is a central theoretical or empirical concern to one set of authors often is a relatively trivial or unproblematic fragment of the analysis to another. One must, of course, simplify some questions in order to focus detailed attention on others, but what one chooses to set in the center of the picture or relegate to the background can be (and here is) subject to dispute.

Consider the concept of affirmative action, for example. Jim Sidanius and his colleagues measure "respondent reactions to a single item: 'Affirmative Action.'" (this volume, p. 204; they do not provide question wording). Sniderman, Crosby, and Howell use the series of National Election Studies (NES) questions, which include the word "preference" for the query about jobs and (in some years) the word "quota" for the query about college admissions.[5] Sniderman's 1986 Race and Politics Survey (Sniderman and Piazza 1993) also uses the word "quota" in the question about admissions and the phrase "law to ensure that a certain number of federal contracts go to minority contractors" in the question about set-asides. His 1991 Race and Politics Study (Sniderman and Carmines 1997a) asks if "companies should be required to give a certain number of jobs to blacks."[6]

And yet Lawrence Bobo (this volume, p. 138), building on the work of Charlotte Steeh and Maria Krysan (1996) and his own previous work, correctly castigates "the distorted view that opposition to affirmative action among whites is monolithic." It is not just that whites oppose some forms of affirmative action less than they oppose other forms. In fact, they consistently *support* some forms, such as educational outreach programs or job-training and outreach programs. Furthermore, although most whites vehemently oppose "quotas" and "preferences," so do many (sometimes most) blacks, Latinos, and Asians. So do the courts; except in very specific circumstances, quotas have been held to be illegal. In fact, "quotas are a rarity in all affirmative action programs focused on employers" (Reskin 1998, 5). Thus, to ask survey respondents about "support for affirmative action" (as in Sidanius et al. and in Sniderman, Crosby, and Howell, both in this volume) is to leave indeterminate what the respondent is in fact responding to. Similarly, to assume (as in Sniderman's, Sears's, and Kinder's work) that one has captured views on affirmative action through responses to questions referring to "preferences" or "quotas" is probably to exaggerate the amount of opposition and possibly to distort the relationship between political ideology and views of affirmative action.[7]

Whether a more careful treatment of the concept of affirmative action would change Sniderman and his colleagues' results—or Kinder and his colleagues' results—or lead either group to reformulate its theoretical approach remains unknown. It might not, but I can imagine how it could. In the list experiment, for example, Sniderman, Crosby, and Howell might find less covert anger at "black leaders asking for educational outreach and job training for blacks" than at "black leaders asking for affirmative action." Would those people who are less angry as a consequence of the new wording be more liberal? More conservative? More individualistic? We do not know, but several hypotheses are plausible, and it would be worthwhile to find out which, if any, obtains. Similarly, in the section of chapter 8 that analyzes liberals' and conservatives' views of governmental intervention, the relationship between political ideology and racial prejudice might be different if affirmative action were defined as "outreach and training programs" rather than as preferences and quotas. That new result could in turn significantly affect the conclusions in their core argument about the importance of the specific political choices that citizens face.

Kinder and his colleagues have a slightly different problem of figure and ground in their treatment of individualism. As Sniderman and others have pointed out, most of the canonical measures of individualism (in the NES) invoke the idea of hard work. That set of wording choices probably says a lot about academics who write survey questions. But it does not necessarily say a lot about individualism—which could encompass a sense of individual autonomy, pride in one's uniqueness, fear of entangling alliances, political independence, rejection of ascriptive labeling, or other conceptions that have little to do with hard work. Might measures of individualism have more effect on racial politics if they were operationalized more broadly or differently? And if so, would that change Kinder's claim that individualism has no effect on racial policy views because "individualism is *in* prejudice"?

We do not know because Kinder and other authors of the NES have seen the *individual*ness of the NES questions as the figure and the *hard work* connotations as the background.[8]

For a third example, consider the value of equality. Many writers within the tradition of survey research have treated the concept of egalitarianism as relatively simple and one-dimensional. But, as Sears, Henry, and Kosterman show in this volume, it is not. They report on one distinction within the global concept of egalitarianism—"consensual support" for "the general principle of equality" for both individuals and groups versus the "highly contested" "assertion that our society continues to have insufficient equality and repairing that flaw would improve the society" (p. 94). That distinction helps to bring the vague background more sharply into focus as the central figure with texture and shadings. But in making that distinction clearer, they allow other meanings of equality, at least as important, to remain muddled.

Equality means many different things, some of which appear distinctly *in*egalitarian to proponents of some other definition of equality.[9] The simplest division is between equal opportunity and equal results—most people prefer one to the other, and it seems pointless to assert that one or the other is the "real" egalitarian preference. Furthermore, the NES/Los Angeles County Social Survey (LACSS) egalitarianism items are ambiguous even if one is prepared to assert that a particular understanding of equality is the "real" one. Consider "If people [or "blacks and whites" or "men and women"] were treated more equally in this country we would have many fewer problems." I could agree with that as a strong proponent of equal opportunity or as a strong proponent of equal results. (After all, the term "treated equally" can be understood as "giving the same treatment" as in the same medicine or the same amount of schooling, as "treating with the same amount of respect," or perhaps as "giving the same outcome.") It is impossible, therefore, to know if the contestation that Sears, Henry, and Kosterman report over this question results from citizens' real disagreement about the value of equal results, or from their real disagreement about the value of strong forms of equal opportunity, or from their varying interpretations about what the question is asking. And yet Sears, Henry, and Kosterman interpret the contestation as evidence that the questions "involve a mixture of inegalitarian . . . and individualistic beliefs"; they interpret only the items on which most Americans agree to be "egalitarian" (p. 108). Neither philosophically nor empirically does that conclusion seem warranted at this point.

One could continue this discussion for a long list of concepts used in these studies. For example, how settled are social groups in Sidanius et al.'s study, given that 11 percent of their student respondents identified themselves as "other" rather than as white, black, Hispanic, or Asian?[10] If a substantial fraction of respondents is unwilling to classify themselves racially or ethnically, might those respondents also envision very different entities, either within a single person's set of survey responses or across respondents, when they consider undefined "groups" in the sixteen-item social dominance orientation (SDO) index? And might these fluid and changeable understandings of "groups" affect the robustness of the underlying theory about social dominance of one group over others? We do not know.

As before, my point is not to specify which concepts should be the figure and which should be relegated to the background. Also as before, the "right" choice depends on what one most urgently needs to know to answer a particular question. Sniderman does not need to worry as much as Sidanius et al. about what respondents mean by a social group, whether in their self-identification or in their answers to survey questions. But Sniderman, Crosby, and Howell (as well as Sears, Henry, and Kosterman and Kinder and Mendelberg) should worry much more than they have up to this point, and probably more than Sidanius and his colleagues need to worry, about the various meanings of affirmative action. That issue, after all, is crucial to understanding how liberal and conservative ideologies function in racial policy preferences.

There is a broad silver lining to this cloud. My claim about the need to bring vague background concepts into the sharply etched foreground gains credence from the results of what these scholars have discovered by beginning to do precisely that. Researchers realized only recently that egalitarianism has much more impact on racial policy views than does individualism, at least as both values are commonly measured. Given that newly clear pattern, we now know that it is important both to deconstruct the various meanings of equality and to broaden the operational definitions of individualism. Similarly, only within the past few years have enough surveys cumulated on evaluations of different affirmative action practices for us to realize just how systematic and meaningful are the public's varied responses to it. New research on the social construction of group identity (as well as the social fact of an increasing number of mixed-race children) is sensitizing us to the permeability of group boundaries and the fluidity of individual self-identification.

This discussion could be formulated as a variation on the theme of lumping and splitting. Disparate meanings of concepts such as affirmative action or equality are lumped together when the concept remains in the background and are split apart when the concept is brought into the glaring spotlight of the foreground. Unlike with the first form of lumping and splitting, in this case I have a starting premise: the concepts discussed here, among others, need to be treated to a more subtle array of measures and more sophisticated philosophical discussion before one can make broad claims about their causes and effects.

Many analysts agree; that proposition is insufficiently implemented more often for practical than for substantive reasons. Whether one can be sufficiently subtle in one's treatment of egalitarianism, individualism, affirmative action, group identity, and other concepts in the same piece of work that is already seeking to parse meanings of racism and race-related policy preferences, without drowning in complexity, remains to be seen. Probably not, given the evidence of the analyses already before us. That suggests the need for intellectual approaches beyond survey research to parse what people mean when they identify themselves as individualistic, supportive of equality, hesitant about affirmative action, or a member of an "other" racial or ethnic group.

One candidate is focus groups, which could ask people to discuss what they mean by these and other concepts and how they use them to make policy choices. Some research is beginning to integrate results of focus groups with results of survey research or to blend the two techniques in order to attain the richness of the former along with the generalizability of the latter (e.g., Sigel 1996; Lamont 1992; Conover and Searing 1998; Conover, Searing, and Crewe 1998; Fried 1997; Hibbing and Theiss-Morse 1995). Another strategy is intensive interviews, either with randomly selected individuals across an array of social locations or with people specifically selected because of their particular social location. Here, too, interviews could be combined with surveys to get the best of both worlds (e.g., Krysan 1995; Hochschild 1981). Yet another strategy is to follow the path blazed by Sniderman and his colleagues and make surveys themselves much more interactive and attentive to individual nuances (see also Kinder and Sanders 1996). Or one could do more imaginative work with open-ended responses embedded in conventional surveys (Kelley 1983; Knight 1998).

In short, these authors appropriately criticize each other for not paying sufficient attention to the many meanings of concepts that they have found to be crucial to their own research. They might instead, or in addition, devote their energy to developing new ways to bring more of these concepts into the foreground, where they can be carefully analyzed without drowning themselves and their readers in endless detail.

EITHER/OR OR BOTH/AND

We see another epistemological choice in the way that authors in *Racialized Politics* handle alternative hypotheses. None rejects out of hand the legitimacy of competitors to his or her favorite argument. How could one? All of the research traditions are too robust to be completely dismissed by a responsible analyst. But some of the authors in *Racialized Politics* admit the partial correctness of competing views mainly in order to show thereafter the superiority of their preferred view, whereas others set out to see how many views can plausibly be supported under specified conditions.

Compare, for example, the strategies of Sidanius et al. and Thomas Pettigrew. The former seek to "compare the relative adequacy of the PP [principled-politics] and SD [social dominance] models of public opposition to race-targeted policies." They find "two major points on which both PP and SD theorists have always agreed," but conclude that "our results are still fundamentally at odds with essentially *all of the other* core predictions of the PP perspective" (p. 227, emphasis in original). Similarly, despite "a few places in which SD theory and symbolic racism theory take complementary positions . . . , the two models are still fundamentally different" (p. 232).

Pettigrew, in contrast, seeks "to systematize the array of correlates that persistently arise in the huge prejudice literature" in order to move "toward broader theories of individual differences in prejudice" (p. 282).[11] Thus, he spends most of his chapter examining as many possible explanations for prejudice as he can find, across as many nations and objects of prejudice as are available. He seeks not to show that one explanation (or a small set) works better than others, but rather to winnow all the plausible explanations down to a manageable set that covers as much conceptual territory as possible.

Most contributors to *Racialized Politics* organize their work in terms of "either/or" rather than "both/and" because that is how the debate among the symbolic racism, principled conservatism, and social structural views has been constructed. In my view, that logical structure is unfortunate.[12] The arena of racial and ethnic politics is so complex and survey research (like other methods) is so far from being able to capture all racial attitudes that the effort to find a single best explanation for racial views seems not only impossible, but also misguided.[13] As I read the evidence on the recent history of Americans' racial attitudes, most citizens do not have simple or settled affects, perceptions, or policy preferences with regard to race that lead them actually to exclude other logically antithetical affects, perceptions, or preferences. John Zaller's (1992) portrayal of people who carry around a basket of views and feelings, which are sampled (randomly or systematically) to produce a given survey response, seems more appropriate in the intricate world of racial politics than any of the fixed theoretical constructs we are offered in *Racialized Politics*. Alternatively, Robert Lane's (1962) concept of morselization—in which people hold distinct and even contradictory views in separate "parts" of their mind—suggests that respondents could be simultaneously principled conservatives (or liberals) *and* symbolic racists. Alternatively, people are ambivalent about racial matters (Hochschild 1993; Smelser 1998), so they knowingly hold contradictory views. At a minimum, the both/ and construction provides some sort of resolution to the dilemma with which I began these reflections—the fact that I find each of these theories about equally persuasive.

I am *not* claiming that there is no structure to American racial politics—far from it, as I shall argue in the next section. I *am* claiming that white Americans' racial views are so multifaceted or contingent that a "both/and" strategy for making sense of them is a more promising premise on which to build a research program than is an "either/ or" strategy.

A BIFOCAL OR MULTIFOCAL PARADIGM

Some contributors to *Racialized Politics* focus exclusively on the relationship between European Americans and African Americans (or between whites and minorities).[14] That is the case for Sears, Henry, and Kosterman; Kinder and Mendelberg; Sidanius et al.; and Taylor. (It is also the case for Sniderman and his various colleagues; in this, at least, most contenders among the three basic approaches concur.) For some such as Sniderman, it is an unspoken starting premise of their research. For others, it is both a starting premise and a research result. Sidanius et al., for example, find that "SDO . . . made a relatively strong contribution to affirmative action opposition with respect to blacks. . . . However, SDO was not significantly related to affirmative action opposition for women or the poor" (p. 222). This finding accords with their theoretical expectations, since, "in America, blacks will face higher levels of discrimination than other ethnic groups and will inspire the greatest degree of white opposition to policies designed to help them" (p. 232).

Kinder and Mendelberg also focus exclusively on the binary relationship between blacks and whites because of both their reading of American history and their empirical findings. They find that "[t]he impact of prejudice is most pronounced on policies that deal explicitly and unambiguously with race . . . ; is modest, though still sizeable, on what might be called 'covert' racial issues . . . ; and vanishes altogether on broad social programs" (p. 72).[15] Kinder furthermore agrees with Sidanius et al. that "divisions by race are nothing new to American politics, but if anything, they are more prominent now than they were a generation ago" (Kinder and Sanders 1996, 288). Sears and his co-authors are perhaps a touch more optimistic (they do not argue that racism is *worse* than it was a generation ago), but they, too, keep their focus on the fact that "blacks and whites remain severely polarized over racial issues" (p. 76).

Sniderman and his colleagues see greater declines in racial prejudice and its effects than do the other scholars discussed here. As they put it, "[A] quarter century ago, what counted was who a policy would benefit, blacks or whites; now, what counts as much, or more, is what the policy aims to accomplish and how it proposes to go about accomplishing it" (Sniderman and Piazza 1993, 4–5).[16] But they agree with the others that "race has not receded into the background of American life. On the contrary, . . . race remains as divisive as ever" (Sniderman and Carmines 1997a, 1). And more important at the moment, by "race" they share the bifocal attention to the relationship between white and black Americans.[17] Finally, Marylee Taylor also focuses in her chapter on the relationship between whites and blacks.[18] She seeks to "assess the impact of black population share on racial policy opinion, racial policy–related beliefs, and ostensibly nonracial views often taken as alternative explanations of racial policy opinion"— by which she means whites' views about blacks and about policies that directly or disproportionately affect blacks (p. 120).

In contrast with these scholars, some contributors to *Racialized Politics* have a multifocal framework. Pettigrew eschews any discussion of white and black Americans—in fact, of Americans of any race or ethnicity. His purpose is to understand the causes of prejudice among people of many nationalities aimed at people of many other nationalities. Explanations that are specific to one nation's political ideology (e.g., the American Creed) or one nation's distinctive outgroup (black slaves rather than Native Americans or non-Anglo immigrants) do not fit into his search for a systematic or broad theory of prejudice. Thus, he focuses on the Eurobarometer, which surveyed people in four Western European nations, asking them about six "target groups." He devotes most of his attention to analyses that hold across all of the nations, all of the nationalities, and all of the disparaged groups. He concludes with a note of encouragement to scholars (if not to activists fighting racist practices): "mini-theories of prejudice . . . can be parsimoniously classified under a few basic families of explanations. . . . [M]any of the basic phenomena—political, psychological, and sociological—are shared across nations and groups" (pp. 300–301).

Unfortunately, the Eurobarometer does not include a survey of Americans (who are not, after all, Europeans). An obvious next step in Pettigrew's research program would be to see if white American prejudice against blacks or immigrants analytically resembles French, British, or German prejudice against Turks or Asians. If not, that leaves space for arguments about American exceptionalism, the unique effects of slavery, and so on. If so, studies (including my own, Hochschild 1995) that are entirely focused on the United States could usefully be reformulated in a more broadly comparative framework. In short, we have here another case of lumping or splitting—in this case, of nations or nationalities rather than of concepts or theoretical frameworks. Most American scholars of race split the American case away from other possibly analogous cases; it would be worthwhile to devote more attention to the implications of lumping the American case into a comparative framework in order to see what is in fact distinctive or shared across nations (as in Gilroy 1993; Fredrickson 1995; Marx 1998; Parikh 1997).

Bobo and Michael Hughes and Steven Tuch are multifocal in a different way. Like most of the other authors in *Racialized Politics*, they focus on the United States, and they include within their analyses factors that are specific to American history and practice. But unlike most of the others, they start from the premise that it is "unfortunate" that "nearly all past research on racial and ethnic differences . . . has focused exclusively on whites and blacks" (Hughes and Tuch, p. 165). Bobo's goals include a systematic (and rare) comparison of attitudes among blacks, whites, Latinos, and Asian Americans on affirmative action for blacks. Hughes and Tuch carry the multifocal framework a step further by looking at variations in all four groups' explanations for poverty among the three minority groups.

At this point, the story gets very complicated in a way that should yield research agendas for generations of graduate students to come. Bobo shows that racial and ethnic groups differ in their support for affirmative action for blacks; that result opens up the question of why Latinos (who are likely to be "white") resemble blacks in their views on this issue, whereas Asians (who are racially not "white") resemble whites in their views. If Bobo's pattern holds across other policy domains (as it sometimes does, Hochschild and Rogers 1999), then we can no longer talk about racial division in the United States as we have been wont to do. It appears that two distinct races, one of which is disproportionately comprised of recent immigrants (i.e., whites and Asians), resemble each other; a third race and a predominantly white ethnicity that is disproportionately comprised of recent immigrants (i.e., blacks and Latinos) sometimes resemble each other.

Why is this: Skin color? Location in the economy? Culture, family practices, and values? The divergent trajectories of Latinos and Asian Americans are not due to historical differences in the scope of white prejudice and discrimination; whites treated Asians at least as badly as Latinos for most of the nineteenth and twentieth centuries. We know too little about whites' views of people who are neither white nor black, as well as too little about the views of Latinos and Asians themselves, to do much more than suggest the nature, causes, and consequences of interracial and interethnic attitudes.[19] But as the demography of the United States changes over the next few decades, so will its politics and social practices (and hopefully its research agendas). The possibilities for racial/ethnic coalitions and contestations could well move to the center of the study of racialized politics.

Hughes and Tuch point to the complications inherent in the study and practice of interracial and interethnic politics, since their research indicates that all four racial/ethnic groups have different views of all four racial/ethnic groups.[20] They find that groups differ somewhat in their attributions for the poverty of other groups and in the effect of those attributions on their preferences for racial policy. They also find, intriguingly, that "minority resentment . . . emerges . . . as an important determinant of racial policy attitudes" among minority groups as well as among whites (pp. 186–87, quotation on p. 189). If this finding holds up, it calls into question theories based on the social dominance of whites or on the unacknowledged benefits of whiteness.

A further hint of the complexities to come in multiracial and multiethnic interactions appears in one of the only other national surveys

TABLE 11.1   Racial and Ethnic Groups' Affinity for One Another

"Of these groups, if you had to say, which one do you feel you have the most in common with/least in common with?" (% choosing each group)

RESPONDENTS

Feel most in common with	White N = 1,093	Black N = 1,006	Latino N = 502	Asian N = 154
Whites	—	34	55	50
Blacks	38	—	25	12
Latinos	28	45	—	27
Asians	19	19	6	—
D.K./N.A.	15	2	14	11

RESPONDENTS

Feel least in common with	White	Black	Latino	Asian
Whites	—	36	21	21
Blacks	24	—	36	53
Latinos	24	19	—	13
Asians	36	36	32	—
D.K./N.A.	16	9	11	13

Source: National Conference of Christians and Jews 1994, 32.

with substantial numbers of respondents from all four racial/ethnic groups. In 1994, members of the four groups were asked which of the other three they felt they had the most and least in common with. As table 11.1 shows, the responses were almost perfectly unstable. Whites feel they have the most in common with blacks, who feel they have little in common with whites. Blacks feel they have the most in common with Latinos, who feel they have the least in common with blacks. Latinos feel they have the most in common with whites, who do not feel they have much in common with Latinos. Asians feel they have the most in common with whites, who feel they have the least in common with Asians. Each group is chasing another, which is running from it.

If this pattern of results obtains across a broad array of political and policy views, American politics in the twenty-first century is going to be interesting, to say the least. Most of our standard theories about the nature of racial prejudice and the direction of racial discrimination may become *bouleversé*.

THE FIRST CAUSE

We come finally to the core dispute between Sniderman and his co-authors, on the one hand, and most contributors to *Racialized Politics*, on the other. The former claim that "the fundamental lines of cleavage on issues of race... are not peculiar to issues of race. They belong, rather, to a larger pattern of division, defining the deeper-lying structure of American politics since the New Deal, centering on the clash of competing conceptions of the proper responsibilities of government and the appropriate obligations of citizens" (p. 238).[21] Sniderman and his various co-authors begin from the reasonable premise that one must take conservatives at their word as much as, although no more than, one must take liberals, whites, African Americans, or members of any other group at *their* word. Thus, when conservatives claim that their opposition to government programs to aid African Americans stems from their general opposition to governmental intervention in the society and economy, not from hostility to African Americans or a desire to keep them in their place, Sniderman and his colleagues believe those claims unless and until they can demonstrate their falsity.

Kinder and Mendelberg; Sears, Henry, and Kosterman; Sidanius et al.; and Bobo (to name only the most explicit members of the opposite cluster included in this volume) start from the opposite premise and argue that the results of their research support that premise. As Sidanius et al. (p. 228, emphasis in original) put it, "[G]roup identity and social dominance values are among the *most important* factors driving the racial policy attitudes of white Americans. . . . '[R]ace-neutral' and 'principled' belief systems become effective legitimizing foils for the masking of opposition to redistributive policy in terms that appear to be more morally and intellectually defensible." Bobo rejects the claim that principled conservative opposition to affirmative action is merely rationalization for racism. But he insists that "[racially based group] interests are a necessary element of our thinking about the politics of affirmative action. . . . [I]t has been easy to overplay the argument from principles. Those on the right who wish to don the armor of moral innocence in their war against affirmative action are ready to accept this view" (pp. 158, 161). The scholars in this cluster, to put it mildly, do not accept at face value conservative justifications of opposition to government programs to aid blacks because they do not think it possible for an American to have a political ideology that is neutral on the question of race.

Here we have the core of all of the other disagreements and the explanation for much of the intensity that has permeated this debate for decades. And here we have the ultimate question of lumping and splitting: can Americans split political ideologies from their racial history, presumptions, and practices or not? To put the debate in the terms that I employed over a decade ago (Hochschild 1984), are racial views *anomalous* to Americans' typical political values and ideologies, such that they can be separated from them and changed without doing violence to those values and ideologies? Or are they *symbiotic* with most Americans' core values and ideologies, such that the latter are largely created and driven by racial affect, racial position, or racial commitments?

Here I will remain perched firmly on the top of the fence for two reasons. First, I am less certain that there is a single correct answer than I used to be. Until the 1960s, the model of symbiosis seemed incontrovertibly correct. But the evidence suggests that something deep and broad has happened to whites' racial attitudes over the past three decades. Many, perhaps even most, white Americans now believe in the legitimacy of basic racial equality in rights and opportunities. One must query how many whites hold that belief, what costs—if any—they are prepared to pay to put the belief into practice, what contradictory beliefs they hold, and so on. But I see little reason to predict that citizens of the United States would allow our nation to return to a Jim Crow system of segregation and degradation.

Thus far, most of the authors in *Racialized Politics* agree.[22] And if that point is granted, it follows that the basic values of egalitarianism (defined as equal opportunity and equality of core rights), individualism (defined as self-ownership and autonomy of all persons), and liberalism (defined as the legitimacy of governmental intervention to protect core rights, provide equal opportunity, and ensure autonomy) are now substantially independent of racial affect and group commitments—even though they once were not (E. Morgan 1975; Smith 1997; P. Morgan 1998). That conclusion implies nothing about the best policies to create, sustain, or enhance the practice of these values. Americans will surely continue to debate this question, but that is a different and somewhat more superficial debate.

However, the relationship between racial hierarchy and American values has not fully shifted from symbiosis to anomaly, and I do not believe that it ever will. Compelling evidence, ranging from psychological experiments to audits of housing and job opportunities to individual testimony to, yes, even survey research, shows that many white (and perhaps nonwhite) Americans harbor hostility to or seek dominance over black Americans. The point holds for liberals as well as for conservatives, although the ways in which racial hierarchy entwines with ostensibly nonracial values may be different across the two ideologies. What Charles Silberman (1964, 819) wrote decades ago remains partly true:

> The tragedy of race relations in the United States is that there is no American dilemma. White Americans are not torn and tortured by the conflict between their devotion to the American creed and their actual behavior. They are upset by the current state of race relations, to be sure. But what troubles them is not that justice is being denied but that their peace is being shattered and their business interrupted.

Thus, one reason that I will not take sides on the dispute over the First Cause is that in my view the best analysis of white Americans' racial attitudes should have a "both/and" rather than an "either/or" framing. I think, in short, that the debate among proponents of principled conservatism, symbolic racism, and social structural approaches has gone as far as it can for the present.

The other reason for my agnosticism on the First Cause is that I would like to shift our attention away from it regardless of what position one holds. The contributors to *Racialized Politics* implicitly, if not explicitly, agree that "the most complicated aspect of race relations in America today concerns attitude" (Kinder and Sanders 1996, 6). I disagree. In my view, structural features of American racial politics are at least as important as attitudes. How people behave and how their behavior is constrained or encouraged by phenomena outside their or anyone else's volition matter as much as, or arguably more than, what people feel or want in determining our (or any nation's) racial future.

This claim takes me back to the opening paragraph of this commentary, in which I proposed two types of explanation for my (and others'?) inability or unwillingness to reject two of the three basic approaches articulated in *Racialized Politics*. I turn briefly to the second explanation now.

AN EXPLANATION OF RACIAL POLITICS OUTSIDE THE SURVEY RESEARCH PARADIGM

Taylor's contribution to *Racialized Politics* comes closest to my assertion that the structure of constraints and opportunities has more impact on racial politics than do attitudes about race and racial policy.

She examines the effects of the proportion of blacks in their community on white respondents' racial attitudes and generates impressive results. Traditional prejudice, opinions about race policy, racial resentment, beliefs underlying policy preferences, and even some views that are ostensibly not related to race are all affected by the proportion of blacks living in the communities of white respondents. "Altogether, examining the sensitivity of white public opinion to the local racial context seems a promising means of detecting the role of racial sentiment in shaping public opinion . . ." (p. 136). Whites may not know the racial composition of their communities—Taylor gives us no evidence on this point—but it deeply influences their views, for the worst from the perspective of African Americans.

This line of argument begins to move the research agenda in a useful direction, toward a focus on the ways in which structures, institutions, circumstances, and practices differentially affect the life chances of people of different races (and ethnicities?) without anyone necessarily intending it or even recognizing it. Following this path would lead us away from survey research (as well as focus groups and intensive interviews) and toward analyses of such things as the economic impact of a given level of education, the political effect of electoral laws and metropolitan boundaries, the impact on health and longevity of living in a particular location, the social consequences of demographic dynamics, the trajectory of cultural influences across groups, and so on. There are, of course, huge literatures on these and other subjects that I cannot begin to review here. I will conclude instead with something of an obiter dictum about what they tell us.

Race matters. The contributors to *Racialized Politics* and almost all Americans agree. But race matters in complicated ways about which there is plenty of disagreement. In my view, four features stand out from the welter of conflicting evidence and assertions:[23]

- African Americans are and will continue to be at a disadvantage compared with all other Americans (except Native Americans) on most dimensions that affect a person's life chances— the range of plausible marriage partners, the prospect of living in any community that one chooses, the opportunity to reach the top of one's profession, the chance of attaining a high political office, the simple option of disappearing in a crowd when one wants to. Most Asian Americans are close to attaining "the honorific of 'white,'" in Andrew Hacker's (1992, 15) inimitable phrase, and within a few decades, the trajectory of Latinos will come to resemble the trajectory of white ethnic immigrants after the turn of the century.

- Class matters deeply among African Americans, but not in the same way that it matters for people of other races and ethnicities. To begin with, there is greater economic and social disparity between wealthy and poor blacks than between wealthy and poor whites, and that disparity is growing. A nontrivial proportion of poor blacks live in circumstances that are worse than those of all other groups, and I see no evidence that most Americans are willing to do what would be necessary to improve those circumstances. Nevertheless, it is the relatively well-off African Americans who are most alienated from American society and most likely to despair about the eventual attainment of racial equality and justice. That is historically unprecedented for a recently upwardly mobile group, and it augurs very badly for American politics and society unless something changes soon.

- Regardless of their racially oriented intentions, nonblacks behave in ways that reinforce disparities between blacks—especially poor blacks—and all other groups. Conservatives are content to leave too many outcomes to be determined by markets, which are as likely to reinforce as to offset initial economic inequalities; they fail to see how social structures and practices benefit those who were born lucky and harm those who were not. Liberals allow too many decisions to be made by political forces, which are as likely to reinforce as to offset initial political inequalities; they fail to see ways in which their own behavior benefits people like themselves who are mobilized into politics at the expense of people unlike themselves who are not. Possessors of both viewpoints are more inclined to blame the other side than to make painful ideological and behavioral changes in order to ameliorate America's racial and class problems (Hochschild 1991).

- In short, inequality between black Americans and all other Americans is embedded in our history, economic processes, political institutions, unexamined assumptions, and norms. Pejorative racial attitudes, the desire for dominance, or opposition to liberal racial policy proposals—none is necessary to maintain this inequality, and probably none would suffice to keep it in place if structures and processes somehow shifted to provide disproportionate benefits in the opposite direction (Mills 1997).

I will conclude this contentious list of assertions with one that moves in the opposite direction—and one that might help to keep all of us working as hard as the authors in *Racialized Politics* do to foster racial justice:

- Real movement toward racial equality has occurred in all of these features of the American polity as well as in individuals' attitudes. That movement was enhanced, if not created, by extraordinary efforts of identifiable individuals, ranging from Civil War soldiers to Supreme Court justices to civil rights activists to corporate leaders seeking profit from diversity. Racial inequality is deeply embedded in Americans' practices, and possibly in their views and values, but it is not immovably so. We did move for the better at various points in our history, and we can do so again. Attitudes will matter for that effort, although they will not be all that will matter.

TWELVE Slowly Coming
to Grips with
the Effects of the
American Racial
Order on American
Policy Preferences

MICHAEL C. DAWSON

INTRODUCTION

A hierarchical racial order continues to shape all aspects of American life and, as the chapters in this volume make clear, American public opinion as well. Sociologists have definitively shown that wealth holding, residential housing patterns, and work itself are all profoundly shaped by race. Political scientists have shown how the party system and electoral outcomes are also fundamentally shaped by the racialization of American politics. Urban economists have conducted meticulous real-world experiments to show how racial bias shapes loan, housing, consumer, and labor markets in this nation's cities. Less powerfully than half a century ago, nevertheless, race continues to profoundly shape American citizens' life chances.

Some public opinion specialists and fewer historians have stubbornly insisted, however, that race plays an increasingly insignificant role in shaping white preferences. On the whole, the research presented in this volume makes a powerful, if incomplete, case for finally laying that set of views to rest. The continued existence of a hierarchical American racial order is a phenomenon with which many researchers are loathe to deal. This volume demonstrates what should be a growing consensus in the arena of race and public opinion. This consensus would include recognition that racial considerations remain critical for shaping Americans' attitudes and policy preferences. Further, not only does this remain the case for whites, but also whites' particular antipathy toward blacks on average leads to different and more negative responses when policies are targeted toward blacks as opposed to Asians or Latinos. A consensus would also include recognition that politics and ideology matter, not as much as some have argued, but consistently they have an independent effect on racial attitudes and policy preferences. This is perhaps the politically least controversial component of a developing consensus. Why shouldn't we expect political and ideological orientations to matter in the highly contentious field of American racial policy? The evidence also seems to suggest, but is not overwhelming, that education does not consistently act as a mediator of white racial attitudes. Indeed, it appears across a number of studies to play the opposite role. The picture that emerges is of an America where a number of considerations matter for the shaping of policy preferences, but to borrow from Lawrence Bobo (who borrowed from his colleague Cornell West), race matters.

But what this volume also makes clear is that there is much work that remains to be done. In this chapter, I will outline what I see as a developing consensus in the realm of race and public opinion and sketch areas where there are both problems and promising opportunities for future research, but then move to a discussion of the politics of racial research and the political obstacles to forging the most productive research agenda.

SUMMARY AND JUDGMENTS

The overwhelming weight of evidence across most of the chapters is that racial considerations shape white policy preferences. Jim Sidanius and his colleagues (chap. 7) present convincing evidence, as do several authors, that white judgments are tied to perceptions of their racial group interests. Bobo goes further and argues that Americans' policy preferences mirror those of what he calls the American racial hierarchy, a concept that I have referred to in my work as the "racial order" (a phrase that Bobo also uses in chapter 5). This racial order's structure, Bobo suggests, is reflected in public opinion. Specifically, the degree to which each racial and ethnic group has been incorporated within American society predicts the level of support for racially oriented public policies, such as affirmative action. Bobo used the Los Angeles County Social Survey of 1992 to draw these conclusions, and a similar pattern can be found in the 1995 *Washington Post* poll on racial attitudes (see chapter 6 for Hughes and Tuch's more detailed

TABLE 12.1   Perception of Racism in American Society

How big a problem is racism in our society today?
Is it a big problem, somewhat of a problem, a small problem, or not a
problem at all?

GROUP	% RESPONDING "BIG PROBLEM"
Asians	33
Black	70
Hispanic	49
White	38

Source: Compiled from the 1995 *Washington Post* Racial Attitudes Study.

TABLE 12.2   Perception of Who Loses More Due to Unfair Racial Policies

Which do you see as the bigger national problem: whites losing out
to minorities in the workplace due to unfair preferences in hiring or
promotion, or minorities facing discrimination and lack of opportunity
for an advancement?

GROUP	% RESPONDING "WHITES LOSING OUT"
Asians	21
Black	04
Hispanic	16
White	40

Source: Compiled from the 1995 *Washington Post* Racial Attitudes Study.

discussion of this study). Tables 12.1 and 12.2 suggest that the general perception of the severity of racism as an American problem, as well as the perceptions of who loses as a result of unfair racial policies, follows the same pattern that Bobo identifies.

These tables also suggest the complexity contained within the modern racial order. Blacks, whites, and Latinos are in the same relative position to each other, but Asians flip positions with whites depending on whether the question references racism as a general American problem or the specific problems caused by unfair racial policies. Indeed, on the issue of unfair racial policies, Asians, Latinos, and blacks are closer to each other when compared to whites, but there is considerably more spread on the question of how pervasive racism is, with blacks being the isolated group. These complex patterns, which we see in public opinion, are also to be found, not surprisingly, in the rough and tumble world of real-life racial politics. In California, we have seen very fluid coalitions form and reform around racially oriented referendums on issues such as immigration and affirmative action. While the evidence increasingly suggests an established racial order, this order does not force coalitions into any predetermined patterns. What coalitions form depends on the complex interplay between the content and framing of any given issue and the involved racial groups. Further, Paul Sniderman, Gretchen Crosby, and William Howell (chap. 8) are absolutely right when they argue that on matters of race the nature of political leadership around these issues is critical for framing political debate and shaping public opinion. The American racial order provides the terrain on which American racial politics occurs. There is still plenty of room for political agency and leadership within this terrain.

Michael Hughes and Steven Tuch (chap. 6) come to a similar conclusion about the importance of racial hierarchy for shaping public opinion in their analyses of the *Washington Post* data. They show, for example, that blacks are most supportive of egalitarian policies, whites are least supportive, and Asian Americans and Latinos fall in between. Further, they argue that because of whites' "dominant position," whites both are unsympathetic to the plight of minorities and do not see it as being in their interest to support racial policies, which a large minority of whites explicitly perceive as most harmful to whites. Marylee Taylor (chap. 4), on the other hand, argues that whites have their own internalized conception of a racial order (my term again), which leads whites to be sensitive to the size of the local black population, but not to the size of either the local Asian-American population or the local Latino population. She speculates that whites feel more threatened by blacks even though Asian Americans and Latinos present more of an economic, social, and political threat (on the last point I disagree; blacks are much more entrenched and unified politically than either Asian Americans or Latinos). Sidanius and his colleagues also reach similar conclusions about the importance of group interests for structuring racial attitudes. They report that "the desire for group-based social hierarchy rather than mere racial animus lies at the heart of white opposition to redistributive social policies in general—and to race-targeted policies in particular" (p. 231).

All of these authors, and several others as well, ground "inter-group attitudes in social structure," to use Kinder's phrase. This is a welcome trend in the study of American public opinion. For example, the idea that Americans' racial attitudes across racial groups reflect the nation's racial order and that white attitudes bear their own racial order, one that has blacks on the bottom, is a promising one, but one that needs much further research. Bobo's comments about a racial hierarchy are intriguing, but only suggestive at this point. There is sociological evidence that parallels the attitudinal data. Douglas Massey and Nancy Denton's (1993) work on patterns of residential segregation also emphasizes whites' widespread propensity to avoid even upper-income blacks more than they do Latinos or Asian Americans. The work of Melvin Oliver and Thomas Shapiro (1995) extends this type of work into the important, if understudied, realm of racial differences in wealth. A tighter grounding of public opinion work in both sociological and historical research about the nature and evolution of racial hierarchies within the United States would help us to better explore the effects of the racial social structures that shape American opinion.

There is one area where the principled conservatism claims are largely confirmed. Politics matter. Education, however, does not consistently serve as a mediator of racial attitudes. Context also matters—and helps shape which racial antagonisms get triggered. Indeed, work by Lynn Sanders demonstrates how white considerations change; the actual model by which whites produce racial preferences changes depending on the racial context. Taylor's work shows how much more needs to be done if we are to understand how context shapes racial attitudes. There is at least as much evidence that the highly educated show more antiblack resentment. To summarize, race matters much more than general "race neutral principles," but what type of model best serves to show how race influences policy preferences and racial attitudes is not yet clear.

WHAT NEEDS TO BE DONE

Now that principled conservatism has been shown to play at best a meaningful, but limited role in the shaping of white racial attitudes, what is the next step? Much theoretical work needs to be done. Particularly disappointing is the lack of direct comparison between the group conflict and social dominance models, on one hand, and the racial resentment/symbolic racism models, on the other. It is inexcusable that Kinder and Mendelberg and Sniderman, Crosby, and Howell, for example, cite Mary Jackman's excellent work, which is now significantly over a decade old, without directly confronting the powerful models of Bobo and of Sidanius and his various co-authors. This volume unfortunately does not help us determine whether these two sets of models are competitive with or, as I (and perhaps Bobo) suspect, complementary to each other.

And while strong versions of principled conservatism theories of ideology and racial attitudes can be laid to rest, are we done with investigating the effect of political ideologies on American racial attitudes and policy preferences? Not at all. We need to think more specifically about the relationship between racial group interests and ideologies that are specifically relevant to racial issues. Traditional "liberal-conservative" scales are best at capturing orientations toward redistributive politics and policies. This ideological cleavage is the familiar one in Western democracies; for example, the swing from a left-of-center New Deal/Great Society majority to a rightist Reagan/Gingrich politics has defined much of this country's politics over the last thirty years. That there is a racial component to redistributive politics is clear from the symbolic racism literature, and the work on welfare and racial politics by Marty Gilens (1999) drives this home. But the traditional left-right divide does not capture the entire range of effects of ideological thinking on the politics of race. There are both intra- and intergroup racial ideologies that shape opinion and behavior.

There is a conceptual paucity to our understanding of ideology within public opinion as well as an appalling lack of actual research. The conceptual paucity is reflected in the limitation of our study of ideology to mainly the left-right split. Yet we know historically that ideologies such as nationalism continue to shape American politics. White, black, and Latino nationalisms, for example, have all been prominent in twentieth-century racial politics within the United States. My own work, as well as that of several colleagues around the country using the 1993–94 National Black Politics Study, shows not only that ideologies such as black feminism, black Marxism, and black nationalism (in addition to liberal ideologies) shape black public opinion, but also that black nationalism, not the various black liberal ideologies, is the most important ideological determinant of black public opinion.

As Hughes and Taylor suggest, research that is more generally focused on the relationship between interests and racial attitudes is still needed. For example, we know from the work of Michael Dawson and many others that black racial attitudes, and black public opinion more generally, are profoundly shaped by perceptions of racial group interests. Research efforts into Latino and black racial attitudes have generally taken different paths, while scholars such as Bruce Cain and

Wendy Tam are pioneering the largely unexplored realm of Asian-American public opinion. The work in this volume reinforces the suggestion found in conference papers, unpublished manuscripts, dissertations, and other cutting-edge research that (1) racial attitudes are structured across racial groups, (2) perceptions of group interests significantly shape racial attitudes for most racial and ethnic groups within the United States (most solidly established for blacks, the case is also now very strong for whites as well), (3) the actual mechanism and models differ between groups, and (4) there is an enormous amount of variation within groups, but still less in general than the between-group variation.

This last point stresses the importance of incorporating context within our models. To present one small example, I report that during the 1980s class cleavages significantly divided black support for nationalism, yet in the 1990s class cleavages almost disappeared and were replaced by significant generational effects. Robert Brown and his colleagues have confirmed the important role that generational cleavages play within the arena of black ideologies. In this example, temporal context makes a significant difference in our models (as Bobo has also shown in his work using Los Angeles data), just as Cohen and I have shown that spatial context is also an important determinant of black (and in unpublished work, white) racial attitudes. Our understanding of the determinants of Americans' racial attitudes would be considerably deepened if our work incorporated and built on the analyses of the preferences and orientations of all Americans and did not limit the concept of "Americans" to whites, as some authors in this volume have a propensity to do.

Much of what is needed is a combination of more of the causal modeling that David Sears, P. J. Henry, and Rick Kosterman (chap. 3) as well as Sidanius and his colleagues engage in, with the direct tests between particularly the principled conservatism and the social dominance models found in Sidanius's work. A couple of methodological extensions would help further our research efforts. As Taylor proposes for her future modeling, the use of hierarchical linear and nonlinear models is an obvious next step for modeling the within- and between-group differences in racial attitudes. This family of estimators would allow us to estimate parameters at the level of the entire population, while simultaneously modeling racial- and ethnic-group-specific effects.

These models seem particularly appropriate now that we are beginning to acquire data that have an adequate number of respondents from two or more racial groups. Another extension that might prove useful is the wider, but cautious, adoption of auxiliary least squares models. These models allow one to create instrumental variables to model indicators that are present in one data set, but not another. While these models have built in some fairly heroic assumptions, they are most appropriate for creating instruments where the target populations are the same and measurement error is likely to be similar across data sets. These estimators might be useful, for example, if one wanted to create the recent stereotype items from the General Social Survey for years in which they were not asked. Similarly, another use might be to create government spending items from the National Black Elections Studies for use in the very similar National Black Politics Study. Like any other estimation technique, these newer estimators have to be applied with care, but given the increasingly formidable challenges that our data confront us with and the opportunities for greatly expanding our understanding of race and public opinion, we should vigorously explore the utility of these and other new estimation tools.

Causal modeling with new data sets would also help us determine the institutional context for racial attitude formation; more integrated media studies, such as the ones performed by Shanto Iyengar and Frank Gilliam, would serve to further pin down the relationship between the short-term triggering of racial stereotypes and frames and the more settled racial attitudes and racial policy preferences. Following Sniderman, Crosby, and Howell as well as many others, we need future studies that help delineate the role of political leadership and racial entrepreneurs.

More intensive historical work would provide a firmer foundation for both the modeling and the various empirical and normative claims that are made. For example, claims by Sniderman, Crosby, and Howell about the fairness of the American Creed are based on, as political philosopher Charles Mills shows in *The Racial Contract* (1997), a false and ahistorical misreading of the history of the American Creed, which indeed contains within its canon racist impulses. Ironically, whether one prefers Mills's reading of the history of American political thought (as I do) or the empirically stunning work of Rogers Smith (1997) (which claims correctly that there are multiple American traditions, some of which are blatantly racist and chauvinist), a sound historical reading of the record would suggest that a correct understanding of the American Creed(s) would be more consistent with the story of proponents of symbolic racism theory than with that told by those oriented around a principled conservative line of argumentation. Smith's historical work also provides a foundation for our understanding of Sidanius and his colleagues' statement that "higher levels of education are associated with an increase in the relationship between racism and SDO [social dominance orientation], on the one hand, and with affirmative action opposition, on the other, even after controlling for political conservatism" (p. 199). The historical record clearly shows that there are numerous episodes within American history where it is white elites who are at the forefront of chauvinist social and political movements.

Additional misconceptions, or at least a lack of consideration of different perspectives, about the history of modern racial strife also drive public opinion research to an unfortunate degree. African Americans in the middle 1960s were overwhelmingly of the opinion that Northern and Western whites perceived that the enforcement of residential antidiscrimination ordinances, as well as their economic dominance, would be threatened by black insurgency, an opinion that led blacks to believe that whites, not blacks, had switched course midstream. By this narrative, it was whites who had abandoned the egalitarian tenets of the American Creed. A different interpretation than Kinder's might note that blacks hardly lost interest in race matters, though whites may well have. No less a personage than Martin Luther King, Jr., came to adopt this view. By 1967, he was arguing that white Americans never wanted true racial equality:

> These are the deepest causes for contemporary abrasions between the races. Loose and easy language about equality, resonant resolutions about brotherhood fall pleasantly on the ear, but for the Negro there is a credibility gap he cannot overlook. He remembers that with each modest advance the white population promptly raises the argument that the Negro has come far enough. Each step forward accents an ever-present tendency to backlash. This characterization is necessarily general. It would be grossly unfair to omit recognition of a minority of whites who genuinely want authentic equality. Their commitment is real, sincere, and is expressed in a thousand deeds. But they are balanced at the other end of the pole by the unregenerate segregationists who have declared that democracy is not worth having if it involves equality.... The great majority of Americans are suspended between these opposing attitudes. They are uneasy with injustice but unwillingly yet to pay a significant price to eradicate it. The persistence of racism in depth and the dawning awareness that Negro demands will necessitate

structural changes in society have generated a new phase of white resistance in North and South. Based on the cruel judgment that Negroes have come far enough, there is a strong mood to bring the civil rights movement to a halt or reduce it to a crawl. Negro demands that yesterday evoked admiration and support, today—to many—have become tiresome, unwarranted and a disturbance to the enjoyment of life. Cries of Black Power and riots are not the causes of white resistance, they are the consequences of it. (King 1967, 11–12)

The findings from many authors that suggest a strong antiegalitarian strain among whites are more consistent with this historical narrative than are the findings of those who advocate a principled conservatism interpretation of modern racial history and attitudes.

The growing use of experimental work in this field makes a welcome contribution to this volume. The researchers associated with Sniderman's research agenda have contributed a number of experimental innovations that have enhanced our understanding of racial attitude formation. Sniderman, Crosby, and Howell's chapter makes excellent use, for example, of a baseline experiment to be able to disentangle the effects of anger toward affirmative action policy. Kinder's analyses of experimental data from the 1987 National Election Studies pilot study are extremely useful for determining that indeed, as other researchers in this volume find, the presence of blacks as the target group mobilizes white racial resentment, while the absence of blacks means that racial resentment becomes a nonfactor in determining white support for various social programs. Sears and Kosterman's (1991) experimental work reinforces this general result. They conclude that adding explicit references to blacks and whites in the wording of traditional values added enormously to their influence over racial policy preferences. In all of these cases, the use of experiments has usefully expanded our understanding of the determinants of racial policy preferences.

Bobo makes the important point in his chapter that we must understand the political significance of what have been at times treated as merely technical difficulties or "simple methodological artifact[s]" (p. 139). Bobo shows that differences in question wording can help reveal important substantive differences for level of support of affirmative action. Papers outside of this volume make similar contributions. Maria Krysan (in press) demonstrates that in-depth cognitive interviews are an important tool for determining the meaning respondents assign seemingly similar questions about racial policies and principles. Sanders has pursued a research agenda over a number of data sets and studies that further highlights the importance of context for survey research. For example, she shows not only that means shift for blacks and whites depending on the race of the interviewer, but also that under some conditions the actual considerations that whites bring to bear in forming racial attitudes shift with the race of the interviewer. Over a decade of research by Sanders and many others conclusively attests to the need to treat survey studies on race as contextually shaped by the racial context (and this applies to qualitative research as well, as Sanders shows). While racial attitudes do not vary all over the map, if one varies the racial context (and my work shows that the race of interviewer is not the only contextual factor that can influence results), they vary enough that one needs to be quite precise in specifying both the racial context and the substantive content under investigation.

The research contained within this volume attests to the significant progress that has been made in our quest to better understand the antecedents and consequences of racial policy preferences. As this section has tried to suggest, much work remains to be done. But progress on all of these fronts will be limited as long as the consequences of racialization of the research process itself are not confronted.

RACIALIZATION OF RESEARCH

The effects of the racialization of both the research process and the subject matter (obviously) must be taken into account when evaluating research on racial attitudes and racial policy preferences. That the subject of our investigations is racialized has been an important theme of this chapter. I have argued at length that the existing racial order structures American public opinion. In addition, race shapes the weight of normative opinion in different ethnic and racial communities. For example, in the 1960s and 1970s, large majorities of blacks and whites had exactly opposite evaluations of the Black Panther Party and the Bernard Goetz subway shooting incident. In the 1990s, the weight of normative opinion remains split about whether too much or not nearly enough attention/progress has been received by the quest for racial equality. The different normative weights attached to events such as the urban disturbances in Los Angeles, the O. J. Simpson trial, and the evaluations of Ronald Reagan and Jesse Jackson make the act of interpretation of public opinion a more difficult one for public opinion specialists.

On the psychological level, racially structured schemas facilitate the selective filtering, recall, and interpretation of the "same" political events. The result is that the same events have different meanings, as in the examples cited above. But this is even more true linguistically. King is not the only member of the African-American elite or black grassroots to bitterly comment on the different meanings that blacks and whites assign to the concept of "equality." In the 1970s, Joel Aberbach and Jack Walker (1973) systematically studied a similar phenomenon. They found that while whites overwhelmingly opposed the concept of black power and opinion was divided among blacks, there were enormous racial differences in what meaning was assigned to the term. Whites by and large interpreted the phrase to mean black over white, while blacks overwhelmingly interpreted the phrase to mean either black pride or blacks having their fair share. Aberbach and Walker did not comment on the irony of whites interpreting the term to mean "black supremacy" when less than a decade earlier the Alabama state Democratic Party had the term "white supremacy" as part of its official slogan.

The racial structuring of the research communities also affects our research no less profoundly, but in ways that we are much less willing to admit. Ernest Wilson III and I (Dawson and Wilson 1991) argued several years ago that our discipline of political science was significantly divided along racial lines. This is true as well, I would argue, of the research community that studies the contemporary effects of race within the United States (historians assure me this is true of historians as well). By and large, there are racially separate research communities with some, but not abundant crossover. Black researchers are concentrated in the study of blacks; whites relatively rarely study black opinion, and when they do, they do not normally use the extensive and excellent black-pioneered research studies. Latino scholars have pioneered the study of Latino public opinion. Even within single disciplinary gatherings, such as the American Political Science Association annual meetings, these research communities are usually found at different panels. Different questions, norms, and priors are often found embedded within the respective research traditions. Formal modeling, for example, is viewed with a great deal of distrust among those who study African Americans, while urban case studies are often belittled among "mainstream" political scientists. Historically, researchers such as Sanders have documented, for example, a tendency for black researchers to cite structural reasons to explain group conflict and racial difference, while whites have been more willing to adopt psychological theories for explaining the same phenomenon.

Some of what I have just described is an expected and relatively benign sorting of scholars based on their interests and backgrounds. Debilitating and more sinister, I argue, are the following tendencies. For some scholars, such as Stephan and Abigail Thernstrom (1997), there is a normalizing of white viewpoints and opinion as the only valid viewpoints and opinion. Thus, if blacks and whites disagree about the nature of equality and egalitarian initiatives, whites are the ones that must have the correct perspectives. Closely tied to this is the unfortunate tendency for some scholars to label, often inadvertently, I suspect (or, more correctly perhaps, hope), white responses as representing those of "citizens," "Americans," or some similarly general category. This practice can be found (as it was in some of the early drafts of this volume's chapters) in tables that are misleadingly labeled, leading to grander pronouncements about what "Americans" believe when in fact the data are exclusively from whites. The result, once again, is to normalize and raise the status of white opinion over that of other Americans.

One pernicious and all too common variant on this set of practices is the systematic and willful ignoring of the work of minority scholars. Minority scholars are claimed to be "biased" and "self-interested" when it comes to affairs of race. The research from this volume should drive home the facts not only that all groups of Americans have firm opinions on race, but also that opinion is shaped by perceptions of group self-interest. Minority scholars often complain about having to be at least "bilingual." They must know not only the major work produced by minority scholars, but also that of whites. The complaint is not about knowing what is necessary to do decent work in one's field; that is a reasonable minimum expectation. The complaint is about the systematic refusal of some white scholars to confront the work of established minority scholars within their fields. The Thernstroms, I have written, provide one particularly egregious example of this practice, but within the field of race and public opinion, it is no longer professional, for example, not to confront the serious challenge provided by the excellent work of Bobo or of Sidanius and his various co-authors. Jackman's work on education and group interest is of fundamental importance and provided an excellent contribution at the time. Discussing her work two decades later does not provide an adequate alternative for directly confronting the powerful challenges presented by realistic group conflict and social dominance theories.

CONCLUSION

Where does this leave us? The major task is to reintegrate public opinion research on race into larger research agendas that allow us to forge a richer understanding of the interaction of public opinion, the institutions of state and civil society, social movements, and intra- as well as intergroup conflict and cooperation. To move to this stage necessitates that we openly confront the difficulties of conducting research on racial policy and opinion within a society that remains bitterly divided by race. What this volume alludes to, but rarely directly addresses, is the research and political problem of trying to evaluate public opinion when major groups in society not only strongly disagree with each other about both specific policies and what constitutes the good life, but also hold different concepts of what key ideas such as equality mean. This makes public opinion research on race simultaneously more difficult and more important. It is more difficult because, as the work of Aberbach and Walker demonstrated explicitly in the early 1970s and the work of Krysan implicitly demonstrates today, we cannot take for granted that respondents from different racial and ethnic groups mean the same thing when using politically charged concepts, such as "equality." It is more important because without such a shared understanding, as Jürgen Habermas reminds us, no progress is possible toward resolving the increasingly bitter and occasionally violent racial conflicts that afflict this nation.

CHAPTER ONE

1. See, among many others, Key 1949; Williamson 1997; Woodward 1957.

2. Sears and McConahay 1973; Aberbach and Walker 1973. See Hagen 1995; Kinder and Sanders 1996; Schuman et al. 1997.

3. For more comprehensive summaries of this literature, see Farley 1996; Thernstrom and Thernstrom 1997; Jaynes and Williams 1989.

4. For men, the racial gap in longevity dropped only from ten years to nine years from 1940 to 1994. As with some other indicators, black women have fared better than black men. Over the same period, the racial gap in longevity dropped from thirteen years to six years for women (Farley 1996, 225; also see Thernstrom and Thernstrom 1997, 264–65).

5. For example, in 1979, the unemployment rate for those twenty years old or older was 5 percent for whites and 10 percent for blacks. In 1995, it was 4.5 percent and 9.5 percent, respectively. In this case, the racial differences were similar for men and women (Farley 1996, 241).

6. See Farley 1996; Thernstrom and Thernstrom 1997, 185, 187. For example, in 1990, 12 percent of the general population was black, but fewer than 5 percent of all college professors were.

7. Another example is that blacks are only 65 percent as likely to own their own homes as whites are. These shortfalls are reduced, but remain substantial with income controlled (Oliver and Shapiro 1995).

8. In 1960, 4 percent of all college students were black, whereas 10 percent were in 1980. Indeed, in 1976, a slightly higher percentage of black high school graduates were attending college than were whites. But in 1992, only 80 percent as many blacks as whites were (Farley 1996, 233; Thernstrom and Thernstrom 1997, 36, 191, 391).

9. Indeed, one-third of African Americans lived under conditions of such intense segregation that there were no whites in their immediate neighborhood, in the adjacent neighborhoods, or even in the neighborhoods adjacent to those, a condition Massey and Denton (1993, 2) describe as "hypersegregation."

10. Newer metropolitan areas in the West and South fit that pattern less well, since they have undergone significant expansion since federal fair housing legisla-

tion was passed. And black suburbanization does include some, albeit often token, movement of affluent blacks into previously all-white suburbs. See Farley 1996.

11. By comparison, about 40 percent of young native-born Hispanics and about 66 percent of young native-born Asian Americans had married outside their own ethnic group. Still, even this minimal rate of black-white marriage reflects a substantial change. In 1963, only 1 percent of all new marriages by African Americans were interracial. See Farley 1996; Thernstrom and Thernstrom 1997, 524–26. Partly this increase reflects radically changed attitudes among whites. In 1963, only 10 percent of whites thought it was all right for whites and blacks to date each other, while 65 percent did in 1994 and, perhaps even more relevant, 85 percent of whites aged 18 to 24 did.

12. In the South, only 3 percent of adult blacks had been registered to vote in 1940, but by 1970, 67 percent were. Racial differences in registration and turnout are usually minimal or nonexistent after the effects of their lesser education and income are controlled (Thernstrom and Thernstrom 1997, 152, 291–92).

13. Only a relatively small minority typically supports black nationalist or black separatist politics. See, for example, Gurin, Hatchett, and Jackson 1989; Dawson 1994; Tate 1993. For similar data from earlier eras, see Marx 1967; Sears and McConahay 1973; Aberbach and Walker 1973; Campbell and Schuman 1968.

14. One estimate has them increasing from 103 in 1964 to 8,406 in 1994. See Thernstrom and Thernstrom 1997, 289.

15. Jesse Jackson's 1984 and 1988 bids for the Democratic presidential nomination are good cases in point. On the former, see Sears, Citrin, and Kosterman 1987.

16. Important exceptions include one election for governor of Virginia and mayoralty elections in Los Angeles, Seattle, San Francisco, and New York City. Two blacks have even been elected as Republican congressmen in virtually all-white districts, in Connecticut and Oklahoma, though that was obviously highly unusual.

17. Considering only those with college degrees, blacks had only 23 percent as much net worth as did whites in the late 1980s. See Oliver and Shapiro 1995, 93.

18. In 1994, 70 percent of black children and 25 percent of white children were born out of wedlock. In 1995, 52 percent and 18 percent, respectively, were living in female-headed households. Both racial gaps are of long standing; even in 1970, 30 percent of all black children lived in female-headed households. But these problems have gotten much worse in recent years. And they have clear, and serious, economic consequences: 62 percent of all children in female-headed families lived under the poverty line in 1995, whereas only 13 percent of those in traditional nuclear families did (Thernstrom and Thernstrom 1997, 236, 238, 240).

19. Moreover, there is reason to believe that blacks' situations might be worsened still further by the great expansion in immigration that began in 1965. By most socioeconomic indicators, blacks are worse off than all other major ethnic groups other than the immigrant Hispanic population (Farley 1996, 245–67).

20. Sears and Citrin (1985) found a significant effect of racial prejudice in whites' votes for tax reductions during the California tax revolt two decades ago.

And Carnoy (1994) views recent conservative political regimes as particularly responsible for the stagnation in blacks' progress over the past two decades.

21. Finally, still others combine these explanations, arguing that the remaining racial gaps cannot be explained by exclusive reference to either cultural deficits or racial discrimination. Rather, they are better understood in terms of the mutually reinforcing effects of both sets of forces. See Sidanius and Pratto 1999.

22. This in fact triggered a gradual long-term realignment of white Southerners to the Republican Party. By 1994, the Republicans held a majority of Southern congressional and senatorial seats. For these historical developments, see especially Key 1949; Kousser 1974; Carmines and Stimson 1989. The influence of racial attitudes over whites' partisan attitudes today is a matter of considerable controversy. Some researchers view them as having been quite central since the 1960s, while others see them as subsidiary to other issues. For the former, see Carmines and Stimson 1989 and Kinder and Sanders 1996. Miller and Shanks (1996) are more uncertain about the role of race, and Abramowitz (1994) is downright skeptical. However, there is no debate about the continuing polarization of the parties over racial issues.

23. The initial busing plan involved Charlotte, North Carolina. The Detroit decision came in *Milliken v. Bradley.* For public opinion on busing, see Sears, Hensler, and Speer 1979; McConahay 1982; Sears and Allen 1984; Armor 1980.

24. This plan, modeled on the Nixon administration's 1969 "Philadelphia Plan," provided quotas for blacks in each of the skilled trades in the construction industry. Such hiring targets were sustained in 1971 by the Supreme Court in *Griggs v. Duke Power Co.*

25. The disparate-impact standard in employment began to be rejected by the Supreme Court in 1989 in *Wards Cove Packing Co. v. Atonio.* In *Adarand Constructors v. Pena* in 1995, the Court extended to all federal programs the requirement that race-based action meet the demanding test of "strict scrutiny," showing that it had been narrowly tailored to serve a compelling state interest. See Thernstrom and Thernstrom 1997.

26. The state of Washington passed a similar initiative in 1998. The Regents of the University of California had already eliminated racial and gender preferences in admissions and employment in 1995. Nationally, blacks' rate of college graduation had already been slipping, as noted earlier, and reducing the number of affirmative action programs in public universities would seem likely to exacerbate that trend.

27. Interestingly enough, dire predictions that this decision would produce a massive reduction in minority representation in Congress have not to date come true, as incumbent black congressional representatives have almost all been reelected even when post-*Shaw* redistricting has reduced the number of their black constituents.

28. Also see, e.g., Taylor 1994; Walzer 1994.

29. For this history, see Fredrickson 1971; Roth 1994.

30. For this history, see Degler 1991; Roth 1994.

31. In the 1990 GSS, whites' negative stereotypes of blacks' intelligence outnumbered positive ones by a small margin (31 percent rated blacks as "unintelli-

gent" and 21 percent as "intelligent"), while 49 percent declined to evaluate blacks in general as either "intelligent" or "unintelligent" (Bobo and Kluegel 1997).

32. Similar findings were reported in most other national surveys of the day. See Hyman and Sheatsley 1964; Sheatsley 1966; Campbell 1971; Schwartz 1967; Stember 1961.

33. Hochschild (1995) also presents a wealth of valuable data on this and related points.

34. See Schuman et al. 1997. It is important to note, however, that in both cases a majority of blacks believed that the races had equal opportunity (63 percent and 58 percent, respectively). These latter cases suggest that blacks tend to perceive greater equality of opportunity when queried about their own local community than when asked about the obstacles blacks in general face. Compare the last two entries in the right-hand column of table 1.1.

35. The exact wordings of the two items shown at the top of table 1.2 were "the government in Washington should see to it that white and colored children should go to the same schools. . . . Do you agree that the government should do this or do you think the government should not do it?" A second question involved guaranteeing equal opportunity in jobs: "Some people feel that if black people are not getting fair treatment in jobs, the government in Washington ought to see to it that they do. Others feel that this is not the federal government's business. . . . How do you feel?" These item wordings and survey results are from Schuman et al. 1997, 104–6, 123–25). And 73 percent (in 1963) said that "Negroes should have the right to use the same parks, restaurants, and hotels as white people," while only 49 percent (in 1964) said that the government in Washington should support a bill passed by Congress "that says that black people should have the right to go to any hotel or restaurant they can afford, just like anybody else." There were some slight changes in wording over the years.

36. Also see Sniderman et al. 1996.

37. To be sure, it seems likely that after the 1960s such items were increasingly interpreted as referring to more outcome-oriented policies, such as busing and affirmative action, rather than to the eradication of vestigial Southern Jim Crow practices that had limited opportunities for blacks.

38. These relationships have not yet been explored in sufficient detail for us to be confident of the reasons for these departures from the patterns that held on the older, pre–civil rights issues. But depart they do. Also see Glaser and Gilens 1997; Tuch and Martin 1997.

39. Racial differences in "implicit" racial issues—those that implicate blacks more than other groups, but that are not explicitly race-targeted—show similar, but smaller differences. In various surveys from 1986 to 1992, blacks were far more likely to support increased spending on food stamps (51 percent to 18 percent) or a generally expanded level of government service (72 percent to 42 percent) (Kinder and Sanders 1996, 30). This is what Bobo (1997b) has called "the racial subtext of the politics of crime and welfare" (p. 51).

40. For symbolic racism, see Kinder and Sears 1981; McConahay and Hough 1976; Sears 1988; Sears and Kinder 1971; Sears and McConahay 1973; Sears, Henry, and Kosterman this volume; Sears et al. 1997; for modern racism, see

McConahay 1982, 1986; for racial resentment, see Kinder and Sanders 1996; Kinder and Mendelberg this volume. Other than nomenclature, there are only minor disagreements among these theories, mainly concerning the relative susceptibility of modern and old-fashioned racism to social desirability biases in the interview situation.

41. In the original study, Jim Crow racism was labeled "generalized inegalitarianism." In later studies, it was labeled "old-fashioned" or "redneck" racism. See McConahay and Hough 1976; McConahay, Hardee, and Batts 1981; McConahay 1982.

42. Also see Kinder and Sanders 1996; Citrin and Green 1990.

43. For critiques, also see, inter alia, Fazio et al. 1995; Raden 1994; Roth 1990; Sidanius, Devereux, and Pratto 1992; Tetlock 1994; Weigel and Howes 1985. For responses, see especially Kinder 1986; Sears 1988, 1994; Sears et al. 1997.

44. Hughes 1997; Sears 1988; Sears et al. 1997; Sears, Henry, and Kosterman this volume; Sidanius, Devereux, and Pratto 1992; Sniderman, Crosby, and Howell this volume; Kinder and Mendelberg this volume.

45. See Bobo and Hutchings 1996; Bobo and Kluegel 1997; Hughes 1997; Sears and Jessor 1996; Tuch and Hughes 1996; Sears and Kinder 1985.

46. There have been a few tests. Some find little to no effect of such variables (e.g., Alvarez and Brehm 1997; Sears et al. 1997), while others find positive evidence of their impact (e.g., Sniderman and Piazza 1993).

47. For other examples of this approach applied to racial issues, see Gaertner and McLaughlin 1983; von Hippel, Sekaquaptewa, and Vargas 1997; Wittenbrink, Judd, and Park 1997. For reviews, see Bargh 1997; Greenwald and Banaji 1995.

48. Also see Gilbert and Hixon 1991; Macrae et al. 1997.

49. Also see LeVine and Campbell 1972. For application to white public opinion, see Bobo 1983, 1988b.

50. Blalock (1967) followed with a more formalized theory, distinguishing between economic and political threats to whites' racially advantaged position.

51. There are questions about the size of the effects in the Duke cases; see Voss 1996. Also see Giles and Hertz 1994; Taylor 1998, this volume.

52. For reviews, see Brewer 1979; Mullen, Brown, and Smith 1992. The presumed motive is to attain a positive social identity, whether serving global self-esteem (Tajfel and Turner 1986; Wills 1981), consistency (Hogg and Abrams 1993), or specific, collective self-esteem needs (Rubin and Hewstone 1998). Evidence on the esteem-enhancing effects of ingroup favoritism is less convincing than demonstrations of the effect itself.

53. However, some studies (Sears and Jessor 1996; Sears et al. 1999) have examined the influence of affect toward whites (the ingroup) as a predictor of attitudes toward racial policy and found that it had no discernible effect.

54. Kluegel and Smith 1982; Bobo 1988b; Sears and Jessor 1996; though see Tuch and Hughes 1996.

55. Also see Blumer 1958; Bobo and Hutchings 1996.

56. Bobo and Kluegel 1993, 1997; Bobo this volume; Hughes and Tuch this volume; Sidanius et al. this volume.

57. Bobo and Hutchings 1996; Kinder and Sanders 1996; Tuch and Hughes

1996; Sears and Jessor 1996. The other cognitive elements of the model have generally not been tested in these studies, however.

58. Significant work remains to be done on the more appropriate conceptualization and operationalization of racial threat (or group interest) and symbolic racism as distinct from each other.

For part of this debate, see Bobo 1983, 1988b, this volume; Kinder and Sanders 1996; Sears and Kinder 1985; Sears and Jessor 1996.

59. Bobo 1997a; Bobo and Kluegel 1997; Bobo, Kluegel, and Smith 1997. For work leading to the development of this position, also see Bobo and Kluegel 1993; Kluegel and Bobo 1993.

60. Distinguishing between these two positions will clearly require further research and may require the inclusion of blacks and other nonwhites in the analyses (Bobo this volume; Jackman 1994).

61. See Pratto et al. 1994; Sidanius 1993; Sidanius and Pratto 1999. For similar arguments, see Campbell 1965; Fiske 1991; Hamilton 1964; van den Berghe 1978a; Reynolds, Falger, and Vine 1987.

62. Sidanius et al. 1994; Sidanius et al. 1996; van Laar et al. 1999; Sidanius and Pratto 1999.

63. For similar perspectives regarding ideological justification of inequality, also see Huber and Form 1973; Kluegel and Smith 1986.

64. One could draw additional evidence for Jackman's argument from the evidence of covert racism in whites' responses to blacks previously discussed. Jackman also suspects that whites' commitment to principles of racial equality is largely illusory; for example, when given the opportunity, whites are far more likely to support something in between racial integration and racial segregation than one or the other. For similar arguments, see Jost 1995; Jost and Banaji 1994.

65. For their initial critique of the new racism research, see Sniderman and Tetlock 1986a, 1986b. The major theorizing and research findings are presented by Sniderman and Piazza (1993) and Sniderman and Carmines (1997a), though much of it has also appeared in numerous journal articles in recent years. Most recently, see Gilens, Sniderman, and Kuklinski 1998; Kuklinski et al. 1997; Sniderman et al. 1996. For similar perspectives, see D'Souza 1995; Roth 1994.

66. The data on the greater effects of prejudice among liberals than conservatives are not uniform throughout this research, however. Compare Sniderman and Carmines 1997a, 79–81, with Sniderman et al. 1991; Sniderman and Piazza 1993, chap. 3; or Sniderman and Carmines 1997a, 95.

67. They also make a plea for switching aid to the poor (regardless of race) from programs benefiting the black middle class, who "are now decisively better off," though they provide no evidence on the relative appeal of policies that are targeted for different social classes.

68. One exception is a measure of judgments of "fairness" based on items often used to measure the new racisms; see Sniderman and Piazza 1993, 114–17.

69. The weak effects reported by Sniderman and Carmines (1997a, 72) from three surveys occur irrespective of issue area. The stronger effects emerge on the social welfare and race-conscious policy agendas, but with respect to crime as well (Hurwitz and Peffley 1997; Peffley, Hurwitz, and Sniderman 1997; Snider-

man and Piazza 1993). For the racial equality data, see Sniderman and Carmines 1997a, 52, 128.

70. Also see Peffley, Hurwitz, and Sniderman 1997, 47, 50.

71. Bobo this volume; Kinder and Mendelberg this volume; Meertens and Pettigrew 1997; Rabinowitz 1999; Sears et al. 1997; Sidanius, Pratto, and Bobo 1996; Sidanius et al. this volume; Tarman and Sears 1998.

72. Even its definition is contested. As applied to the system of Jim Crow racism or old-fashioned racism, the term was used to describe a belief system that incorporates both an ideology of racial domination and a justification in terms of the innate inferiority of one particular race. As applied to more contemporary beliefs, some argue its appropriateness because the residues of slavery and Jim Crow continue to place blacks in a position of structural disadvantage and because whites' explanations for that position often appeal to a belief in black cultural inferiority. Others use "racism" to describe any animus or negative attitudes and discrimination against blacks as a group, much as "anti-Semitism" describes negative attitudes and behavior toward Jews because they are Jews. For discussions of these definitional issues, see Bobo, Kluegel, and Smith 1997; Sears et al. 1997.

73. The yeasayers include Sniderman and Piazza (1993), Sidanius et al. (1996), Kinder and Sanders (1996), and Pettigrew and Meertens (1995); and the naysayers, McConahay (1986), Sears et al. (1997), Sears, Henry, and Kosterman (this volume).

74. See Sears et al. 1997, as opposed to Roth 1994; Sniderman and Piazza 1993.

75. As it turns out, as also indicated earlier, these issue categories also distinguish attitudes that typically show age, education, and regional differences from attitudes that do not. See Schuman et al. 1997.

76. Sears et al. (1997; also see Sears, Henry, and Kosterman this volume) find considerable consistency across racial policy issues, whereas Kinder and Sanders (1996) find more profile.

77. They do avoid making claims that racism and conservatism are synonymous, a point that is sometimes misunderstood.

78. Bobo, Kluegel, and Smith 1997; Kluegel and Bobo 1993; Kluegel and Smith 1986; also see Sigelman and Welch 1994; Tuch and Taylor 1986.

79. Indeed, the two values are often seen as trade-offs, as in the "racial ambivalence" thesis described earlier. Lipset and Schneider (1978b) suggest that the nation cycles through periods in which one or the other value dominates, with egalitarianism and egalitarian politics dominating in the 1960s and early 1970s, and individualistic values and market-based politics since then.

80. For example, see Hughes 1997; Kinder and Sanders 1996; Sears 1988; Sears, Henry, and Kosterman this volume; Sniderman, Crosby, and Howell this volume; Tuch and Hughes 1996.

81. For social dominance orientation, see Pratto at al. 1994; Sidanius et al. this volume. For a similar conceptualization framed instead as "social responsibility," see Bobo 1991.

82. Pole's (1993) historical treatment of the idea of equality in America or, more properly, the several quite different domains and ideas of equality would be a useful starting point. Also see Rae 1981.

83. As pointed out earlier, though, black public opinion is scarcely monolithic, and this assumption is largely unexamined (see Bobo 1997b; Hochschild 1995; Kinder and Sanders 1996).

CHAPTER TWO

We are grateful to Larry Bartels, Lisa D'Ambrosio, Nancy Burns, Stanley Feldman, Kim Gross, Leonie Huddy, Andy Koppelman, Lynn Sanders, Jim Sidanius, Janet Weiss, and the Press's anonymous reviewers for helpful suggestions on earlier versions of our chapter and to Adam Berinsky and Nicholas Winter for splendid technical assistance. The data we analyze here were collected by the National Election Studies at the Center for Political Studies, University of Michigan, and are available through the Inter-University Consortium for Political and Social Research.

1. For additional claims promoting the prominence of individualism in American political life, see Gans 1988; Lukes 1973; Markus 1993; Miller 1967; Wills 1987.

2. All quotations are from Rodgers (1978, 231, 217, 220, 212).

3. *Progressives* endorse the claim that racial differences in achieving the good life in America are due to white exploitation and deny the claim that racial differences can be explained by failures of character on the part of blacks; *fundamentalists* believe that racial differences are part of God's divine plan and not traceable to white exploitation or black shiftlessness; *historicists* pin current racial differences on generations of slavery and discrimination, not on any of the other three. The core items used in *Race and Inequality* and in our analysis appear as V606–V609 in the 1972 NES Codebook.

4. Despite the assistance generously provided by Michael Hagen, we have been unable to exactly reproduce *Race and Inequality*'s results. Sniderman and Hagen defined their typology with admirable clarity (at pages 35–37 and in footnotes 13, 14, 16, and 19 following chapter 2). But as it was actually created, the typology contains two mistakes: *Race and Inequality* discovered too many fundamentalists and a few too many historicists.

Correcting these errors does not materially alter Sniderman and Hagen's conclusions, however. We know this because we did a series of parallel analyses, comparing the results reported by Sniderman and Hagen with those they would have reported had they created their typology correctly. Such comparisons show little difference between the reported and the corrected results. The only systematic difference, and it is a small one, is that historicists are a bit more liberal than *Race and Inequality* reported them to be. Naturally, all the results and reanalysis we present here are based on the corrected version of the typology. Percentages are calculated on a base of all white respondents classified into one of the four types (the percentages sum to 100).

5. Sniderman and Hagen are persuaded to take this position at least in part because of the evidence they report indicating that individualism, as they operationalize it, is associated with views on class and gender inequality as well as racial inequality. Thus, individualists, they conclude, "judge everyone in the same terms" (1985, 111).

In fact, individualists do *not* "judge everyone in the same terms." Figures 4.6 and 4.7 (pp. 92, 94) in *Race and Inequality* display the relationship between individualism and what Sniderman and Hagen call equal opportunity for blacks, equal opportunity for the poor, and equal opportunity for women. The figures make it appear that the relationship is as strong in the case of equal opportunity for blacks—with individualists taking the position that blacks do not face discrimination and that blacks are held back because of their own deficiencies—as it is in the cases of equal opportunity for women and for the poor. But this result is an appearance only, traceable to the fact that the three measures of equal opportunity are scaled on very different ranges. In this form, the figures cannot be compared. When adjustments are made to make the results comparable (by scaling each of the three dependent variables to range from a hypothetical minimum of 0 to a hypothetical maximum of 1), a different pattern emerges. Now the effect of individualism appears to be substantial and roughly equal on perceptions of equal opportunity for blacks and for the poor ($B = .21$, se $= .03$; $B = .24$, se $= .03$, respectively), in support for Sniderman and Hagen's claim for the generality of their measure of individualism, but smaller by half on perceptions of equal opportunity for women ($B = .09$, se $= .03$). These mixed results make individualism look less like a "master idea."

6. The variable numbers for the race question are V118, V115, V104, V110, V106, V202, and V605. Participants interviewed in the 1972 NES survey were questioned again in 1974 and once more in 1976. The 1976 installment included the questions on government health insurance and the ERA. We made use of responses to these two questions in order to broaden our coverage on policy relevant to class and gender. Following the order they were introduced in the text, the full set of class and gender policy variables are V613, V178, V3273, V232, V251, V239, and V3787. In the analysis that follows, "don't know" responses were recoded to the middle position.

7. In our specification, "historicists" serves as the omitted reference group, and all opinion variables are coded for convenience on the 0–1 interval. Ordinary least squares regression is not really appropriate here, given the form of the dependent variables, but in this part of the analysis, we wanted to replicate closely the analysis carried out and reported in *Race and Inequality*. Again, following Sniderman and Hagen's usual example, our regression equations also included a measure of education (V300, coded into five categories).

8. Additional problems with the analysis and interpretation presented in *Race and Inequality* are spelled out in chapter 5 of Kinder 1999. These add to the case against Sniderman and Hagen's conclusion that individualism accounts for white opposition to racial inequality.

9. Sniderman now appears to agree with this conclusion. In *The Scar of Race*, Sniderman and Piazza (1993) conclude that "over a wide range of different conceptions of individualism, and regardless of whether the focus is on white attitudes toward blacks or on *white attitudes toward public policies dealing with blacks*, the suggestion that the classic American value of individualism is at the heart of the contemporary problem of race is simply, and flatly, wrong" (p. 63, emphasis added).

Sniderman repeats this rejection of individualism in chapter 8, with Crosby and Howell, in this volume. We are glad to welcome him on board, but we would be happier still if we agreed with the reason he provides for the shift in his position. We do not.

Here Sniderman seems to be arguing that to measure political principles—individualism, conservatism, equality, whatever—one must ask people not whether such principles apply to society as a whole, but only whether such principles apply to their own lives (chap. 8, p. 244). Sniderman makes this point first, as far we can tell, in Sniderman and Piazza 1993, 60. So, evidently, looking back on it, the empirical analysis in *Race and Inequality* was misguided because it depended on survey questions that asked whites to say how hard blacks try, not how hard they themselves try:

> It is obviously a mistake—it seems embarrassingly so in retrospect—simply to assume that when a white tells blacks that they have to work hard, the white is himself willing to work hard. (Chap. 8, p. 245)

There is a difference between the two, of course, but the question is what should be made of it. We find Sniderman's solution—that commitment to individualism comes only when people are prepared to say that they themselves abide by its dictates—ill-advised.

First of all, Sniderman's solution leaves us without anything to say about the positive results presented in *Race and Inequality.* Indeed, from Sniderman's new perspective on the measurement of political principles, shouldn't we be surprised that *Race and Inequality* turned up any positive findings at all? Put another way, if these findings are not about individualism, as Sniderman now concedes, what are they about? Another problem is that Sniderman's solution closes off inquiry on what we take to be an open and extremely interesting question: namely, do people apply principles consistently across different realms of experience? Under Sniderman's recommendation, we would never have learned of the fascinating and intelligible discontinuities that Hochschild (1981) traces across home, work, and politics in Americans' conceptions of fairness. Finally, to confine the assessment of principles to an individual's private experience seems needlessly and destructively restrictive. Principles are partly about how people choose to live and interpret their own lives, certainly, but political principles are important in part precisely because they are also claims about how *all* members of a political community should behave, about how *entire* societies should be organized. It is principles conceived of in this way that animate the work of Feldman (1988), Inglehart (1977), McCloskey and Zaller (1984), and Verba and Orren (1985), among others, and indeed seem to be what Sniderman has in mind when he says that the politics of race is primarily about principled and abiding disputes over the proper scope and authority of the federal government.

None of this should distract us from the conclusion, now virtually unanimous, that individualism is irrelevant to white Americans' views on issues of race.

10. Notable and illuminating exceptions to this generalization are provided by Feldman (1988) and McCloskey and Zaller (1984).

11. For white Americans questioned as part of the 1986 NES survey, the aver-

age interitem Pearson *r* is .20, the item-total correlations (corrected) are relatively homogeneous (they range from .22 to .43), and Cronbach's α for the linear composite scale is .59. For black Americans from the same study, the average interitem Pearson *r* is .21, the item-total correlations (corrected) are also reasonably homogeneous (they range from .26 to .45), and Cronbach's α for the scale is .62. These reliability estimates are not exactly exhilarating, but they are not awful either. And they are almost certainly underestimates of the real reliabilities because the individualism items were written to be balanced against the intrusions of acquiescence (three of the items are worded so that agreement means support for individualism, while the other three are worded so that agreement means opposition to individualism), which depresses Cronbach's α (Bollen 1989).

12. Including structural equation estimates that take into account errors of measurement (details presented in Kinder 1999).

13. Variables V508–V513 in the 1986 NES Codebook.

14. To measure prejudice, we averaged responses to six separate questions into an overall linear composite scale. These questions share the sense that blacks have been handed advantages and that hard work no longer counts for much (V565–V568, V579, and V580 in the 1986 NES Codebook). For the scale as a whole, Cronbach's α is .77. We will have more to say about this measure later in the chapter.

To assess views on equality, we created a composite scale, based on a simple linear combination of answers to six questions (variables V364–V369 in the 1986 NES Codebook). The questions, developed by Feldman (1988), are preoccupied for the most part with equality of opportunity in the abstract (e.g., "Our society should do whatever is necessary to make sure that everyone has an equal opportunity to succeed" and "We have gone too far in pushing equal rights in this country"). A scale is justified empirically because whites (and blacks) respond to these questions quite consistently. For white Americans, the average interitem Pearson *r* is .22, the item-total correlations (corrected) range from .33 to .39, and Cronbach's α for the entire scale is .63.

15. In the 1986 NES Codebook, the race policies are V506, V426, and V478; the social welfare policies are V332, V330, and V448.

16. Black and white Americans differ enormously in their views on race policy (Jackman 1994; Kinder and Sanders 1996), and this is generally consistent with Jackman's argument. But direct tests suggest that only a modest portion of this huge racial divide in opinion can actually be explained by group interest (Kinder and Winter 1997).

17. According to Kinder and Sanders (1996, 98–106). Explaining the origins of the "new" prejudice is one place where the differences among the various theorists is more than terminological. In particular, Bobo and Smith's (1998) account emphasizes macro changes in material conditions more and micro mechanisms less than do Kinder and Sanders (1996). These are real differences, though they seem largely complementary rather than competitive, and in any case, testing between them seems nearly impossible, given the unavailability of the requisite data.

18. The careful reader will note that two of these questions, the first and the third, come directly from the battery originally developed by Glock and his associ-

ates (Apostle et al. 1983) and employed by Sniderman and Hagen (1985)—incorrectly, we have argued and shown here—as measures of individualism. For additional empirical support for this move, see Kinder 1999.

19. Compared to other efforts to measure prejudice, these questions are rather subtle. They do not require whites to declare in straightforward fashion that blacks are stupid or lazy or promiscuous. Their approach is more roundabout. It might be said that these questions do for race prejudice what Adorno's *The Authoritarian Personality* (1950) did for anti-Semitism. The famous "F-scale" that Adorno and his research team employed to measure authoritarianism was composed of questions that resemble ours, in that they were carefully formulated, as Roger Brown once put it, "to express a subtle hostility without seeming to offend the democratic values that most subjects would feel bound to support. Each question has a kind of fair-minded and reasonable veneer. It is sometimes rather difficult to find the sting" (Brown 1965, 483).

The subtlety of these questions probably diminishes the problem posed by "social desirability": the tendency for people to present themselves as "well adjusted, unprejudiced, rational, open minded, and democratic" (Cook and Seltiz 1964, 39).

20. The 1987 interviews were carried out by Institute for Social Research (ISR) professional staff who recorded verbalizations verbatim. These responses were then subjected to elaborate analysis, involving some 150 separate codes. The coding scheme was developed by Feldman and Zaller in consultation with a senior member of the coding section of ISR and carried out under close supervision by experienced members of the ISR coding section.

Respondents were actually questioned twice: first in May ($n = 457$) and then again in June ($n = 360$). The results presented here come from the first interview, in the interest of maximizing quality of sample and number of cases, though we find essentially the identical results using the second.

21. Differences between the two forms of eliciting verbalizations turn out to be unimportant for our purposes, so table 2.4 combines results across the two procedures.

22. In the vocabulary of the 1987 NES Pilot Study Codebook, the "frame of reference codes" are racial resentment: 171, 237, 238, and 241; biological racism: 239 and 247; individualism: 120, 136, 140, 141, 142, 143, 145, and 148; limited government: 152, 153, 156, 157, 158, 159, 165, and 166; and equality: 130, 131, 132, 133, 134, 135 and 172.

23. Indeed, at several points in the presentation of his theory, Sidanius acknowledges that social dominance orientation is either equivalent to or a close cousin of antiegalitarianism (e.g., Sidanius, Devereux, and Pratto 1992, 380).

24. In this respect, notice the striking resemblance between our analysis of opinion on hate speech (Gross and Kinder 1998), where arguments in the political environment seem to tip heavily in the direction of protecting speech, and Sniderman, Crosby, and Howell's analysis of fair housing, where arguments in the political environment seem to favor property rights.

25. See note 9.

CHAPTER THREE

Portions of this chapter were presented at the annual meeting of the Midwest Political Science Association, Chicago, Illinois, April 19, 1991, and at the Summer Institute in Political Psychology, The Ohio State University, July 19, 1991. The National Election Studies survey data were made available by the Inter-University Consortium for Political and Social Research, with the help of Elizabeth Stephenson. We owe thanks to Professors Frank Gilliam, John Petrocik, and Jim Sidanius and to Michael Greenwell of the UCLA Institute for Social Science Research for assistance with obtaining the Los Angeles County Social Survey data. We owe thanks to Lawrence Bobo, Leonie Huddy, George Marcus, Joshua Rabinowitz, Howard Schuman, Jim Sidanius, and Marilynn Brewer for their helpful comments about the manuscript.

1. Others have offered similar views, though describing contemporary racism variously as "modern racism" (McConahay 1986), "racial resentments" (Kinder and Sanders 1996), and "subtle prejudice" (Pettigrew and Meertens 1995). These have similar conceptual and operational definitions, and we do not attempt to address the distinctions among them here.

2. The main original sources for this theory include Sears and Kinder 1971; McConahay and Hough 1976; Kinder and Sears 1981; Kinder 1986; Sears 1988; Sears and McConahay 1973; and McConahay 1986. The question has been raised about whether or not the content of symbolic racism has been described in consistent terms over this long period of time (e.g., Schuman et al. 1997). Further, Bobo (chap. 5) suggests that some conceptual ambiguity still surrounds the concept of symbolic racism. In our view, while the description of this belief system has often been somewhat general, and sometimes limited to the dimensions measured in a particular study, there has been substantial continuity in describing its basic themes over time. Measurement of symbolic racism originally involved three of the four dimensions cited here: antagonisms toward blacks' demands, resentments about special favors given them, and denial of continuing discrimination (Sears 1988). In recognition of the presumed origins of symbolic racism in individualism, the focus on blacks' failure to work hard enough was later explicitly added (see Kinder and Sanders 1996; Sears et al. 1997). In one recent article (Sears et al. 1997), items measuring the absence of positive emotions toward blacks were used as a fifth dimension of symbolic racism in an effort to represent the antiblack affect component of its presumed origins as well as to take into account findings by those working with "aversive racism" and "subtle prejudice" (e.g., Dovidio and Gaertner 1986; Pettigrew and Meertens 1995). That may simply have generated more confusion, however.

3. In this usage, "racism" does not necessarily include beliefs in biological or constitutional bases for racial inferiority or a desire to control and oppress a racial minority, as in most definitions of "racialism," although, of course, it may include those elements as well. We would agree with Schuman (chap. 10) that "racism" is quite an invidious term and sympathize with Bobo's concern (chap. 5) about hurling "the brickbats of moral superiority," donning "the armor of moral superiority," or staking out a "claim to moral virtue." Bobo quotes from an earlier article (Sears

1988) on this point, and perhaps it would be helpful to add the quote that soon follows in that context (p. 79): "[I]f there is a single individual in the United States, black, white, red, yellow, or brown, who is not somewhat racist and prejudiced against blacks, this condition strikes me as a remarkable feat of resistance to a quite overwhelming saturation of centuries of cultural socialization. . . . It is hard for me to see why individuals should hold themselves morally responsible for reflecting some rudiments of a nearly universal cultural socialization. . . ." We use it rather than changing the label of a construct that is still measured in substantially the same terms as it was originally. Others have chosen to change that usage nonetheless (see Kinder and Sanders 1996; McConahay 1986), and we acknowledge that our decision is open to reasonable debate. We also want to emphasize that we argue only that there is a significant component of racial animus motivating whites' racial policy preferences, averaging over many respondents and amidst other motivations. We do not intend the term "racist" to be applied to any specific individual. There is no obvious legitimate way to convert an ordinal scale of symbolic racism into a nominal scale with an absolute dividing line between "racists" and "nonracists." Nor can we determine the extent to which any individual is motivated by racism; the underlying measurement theory is probabilistic. And while an early article (Kinder and Sears 1981) did treat opposition to affirmative action as prima facie evidence of symbolic racism, that has not been true in subsequent work. That change, made more than a decade and a half ago, seems not to be recognized in some quarters (e.g., Hurwitz and Peffley 1998a; Stoker 1998; Tetlock 1994; Thernstrom and Thernstrom 1997).

4. See Kinder and Sanders 1996; Sears, Hensler, and Speer 1979; Sears et al. 1997; Kinder and Sears 1981; Sears, Citrin, and Kosterman 1987; Howell 1991; Gilens 1998a, 1998b; Sears and Citrin 1985; Sears et al. 1980; Sears and van Laar 1999; Smith 1987.

5. See Fazio et al. 1995; Sniderman and Tetlock 1986b; Sniderman and Piazza 1993; Tetlock 1994.

6. See especially Hughes 1997; Sears and Citrin 1985; Sears et al. 1997; Sears and van Laar 1999; also see Sears 1994 for a review.

7. See Bobo 1991; Hughes 1997; Kinder and Sanders 1996; Sears 1988; Sears and Huddy 1992; Kluegel and Smith 1986; Kinder and Mendelberg, chap. 2; Sniderman, Crosby, and Howell, chap. 8.

8. Sniderman and his colleagues make the puzzling observation about the racial resentment scale used by Kinder and Sanders (1996) that "most of the items have nothing to do with individualism" (chap. 8, p. 243). Two of the items focus specifically on blacks and work (blacks working their way up without special favors and blacks being unable to work their way out of the lower class), two on the extent to which blacks are trying hard (they could get along without welfare if they tried, and they would be as well off as whites if they would only try harder), and a fifth on whether or not they have gotten as much as they have earned (have they gotten as much as they deserve). The sixth item is less obviously individualistic (blacks get less attention from government officials). It is easier to accept Kinder and Mendelberg's (chap. 2, p. 61) interpretation that they reflect "individ-

ualistic resentments." Their scale contains six of the seven items we use in this chapter in analyzing the 1986 NES survey.

9. These values have most often been indexed with either the egalitarianism scale used in the National Election Studies (NES) surveys (Feldman 1988) or social dominance orientation (Pratto et al. 1994). These effects of inegalitarian beliefs have been reported by Hughes (1997), Kinder and Sanders (1996), Sears (1988), Sears and Kosterman (1991), Sidanius et al. (1996), Sidanius, Devereux, and Pratto (1992), Sniderman et al. (1997), and Wong and Bowers (1997). Related findings have been reported from studies of stratification beliefs (Bobo 1991; Kluegel and Smith 1986), though these studies do not measure beliefs about equality as directly.

10. A further question about the origins of symbolic racism concerns the psychological dynamic by which antiblack affect might mix with perceived violations of traditional values (Hughes 1997; Sears and Kosterman 1991; Sniderman and Tetlock 1986b; Wood 1994). We do not address that issue here.

11. The African Americans were not the only groups to be treated in a formally inegalitarian manner, of course. Native Americans and women also were restricted in many ways. But neither was treated as heritable property for life.

12. It should be noted though that a longer process of education and generational replacement was required before that came to pass (Schuman et al. 1997).

13. This view appears to be shared by Sniderman and his colleagues: "Though there are elements of the [American] Creed that can be deployed in favor of affirmative action, the fundamental ideas of fairness and equal treatment, for ordinary citizens, thrust in exactly the opposite direction. . . . [T]he principle of preferential treatment runs *against* the Creed" (Sniderman and Piazza 1993, 177); "in the name of achieving racial equality and tolerance . . . the ideals of equality and tolerance have been upended" (Sniderman and Carmines 1997a, 3).

14. The fact that some, but not all, egalitarian values may be dependent on beliefs about individualism is suggested by the moderate correlation usually found between them (e.g., Feldman 1988).

15. The symbolic racism perspective is by no means the only approach to racial politics that features conflicts between individualism and egalitarianism. Lipset (1996; Lipset and Schneider 1978b) has long viewed their relative political impacts as varying consequentially over time, and the Katz and Hass (1988) theory of "racial ambivalence" centers on a related trade-off between humanitarianism and the Protestant ethic. Also see Monteith and Walters 1998.

16. Use of a weight variable was necessary for all analyses of the 1985 NES pilot study (to account for an oversample of respondents over sixty years of age). The 1986 NES survey used a split-form design with two independent samples; only one was employed in the analyses, since it contained most of the racial variables. Similarly, the 1983 and 1985 NES pilot studies used a split-form design, and some variables (noted in the text) were included on only one form of the surveys, administered to approximately half the samples.

17. We are grateful to Jim Sidanius for providing us with these data analyses.

18. These latter two items had varied wording, framed in terms of either dis-

crimination against whites (1985, form A) or giving blacks advantages they have not earned (1985, form B; 1986). Dealing with this distinction is beyond the scope of this chapter, though it is of some consequence; see Kinder and Sanders 1990, 1996.

19. The *individualism* scale was not included in the 1990 and 1992 NES surveys. The exact wording of the egalitarianism items is given in table 3.4.

20. Specifically, respondents were asked "why there are poor people in this country." The attributions offered were (a) "lack of effort by the poor themselves," (b) "lack of thrift and proper money management skills by poor people," (c) "loose morals and drunkenness," (d) "low wages in some businesses and industries," (e) "failure of society to provide good schools for many Americans," (f) "failure of private industry to provide enough jobs," and (g) "being taken advantage of by rich people." Agree-disagree response scales were provided for each.

21. The specific individualistic questions included (a) "failure of some groups in society to instill proper morals and values in their children," (b) "breakdown of the family structure," (c) "enforcement of the death penalty for persons convicted of murder," and (d) "three strikes and you're out legislation." The specific structuralist questions included (a) "not enough decent-paying jobs," (b) "lack of good schools," (c) "reducing poverty," and (d) "providing prison inmates with education and job training." Agree-disagree response alternatives were provided for each.

22. The specific questions used in the NES were as follows: "Why [do] white people seem to get more of the good things in life in America—such as better jobs and money—than black people do?" (a) "The differences are brought about by God; God made the races different as part of his divine plan." (b) "It's really only a matter of some people not trying hard enough; if blacks would only try harder they could be just as well off as whites." (c) "Generations of slavery and discrimination have created conditions that make it difficult for blacks to work their way out of the lower class." (d) "Blacks come from a less able race and this explains why blacks are not as well off as whites in America." In the LACSS, the questions were (e) "People in these groups suffer from a lack of jobs and inadequate education" and (f) "People in these groups are less intellectually able than other groups." Agree-disagree response alternatives were supplied for each.

23. The seven-point ideology scale used in the 1985 NES survey was the summary variable based on the branching format. In all others, the single seven-point item was used.

24. Questions have been raised about the internal consistency of the symbolic racism belief system (e.g., Colleau et al. 1990; Sniderman and Tetlock 1986b). To test this, we carried out exploratory principal axis factor analyses, with oblique (oblimin) rotations, in the three surveys we here most rely on. The 1985 NES survey contained seven symbolic racism items. The initial analysis yielded two factors, with the first factor explaining 34 percent of the variance, while the eigenvalue for the second fell below the usual threshold (0.54) and explained little additional variance (8 percent). All variables loaded highly ($>$ .30) on both factors. With an oblique rotation, however, two highly correlated factors emerged (ϕ = .57). The 1986 NES survey also contained seven symbolic racism items. In the initial analysis, the first factor explained most of the variance (36 percent), while

the second was again relatively weak (eigenvalue = 0.46, explaining 7 percent of the variance). Again, the oblique rotation turned up two highly correlated factors (ϕ = .52), with all but one item loading highly (> .30) on both factors. The 1997 LACSS contained eleven symbolic racism items. Again, in the initial analysis, the first factor explained 35 percent of the variance, while the second had an eigenvalue of 0.65 and explained 6 percent of the variance. And, again, the oblique rotation yields two highly correlated factors (ϕ = .62). With one exception, the loadings all exceeded the .30 threshold.

In all three surveys, then, we initially find one strong factor and a second that fails the usual eigenvalue threshold in an initial single-factor solution. With an oblique rotation, we are able to distinguish two highly correlated factors, one focusing on the situation confronting blacks (amount of discrimination, requests to government go unheard, civil rights leaders push too fast, blacks have gotten less than they deserve, they get too much attention from government, slavery and discrimination have held them down) and the other focusing on their own dispositions and behavior (they should work their way up like other minorities, they don't need welfare, they are too demanding, they should just try harder). Our conclusion is that this is a reasonable distinction that white Americans make within an overall belief system that is quite substantively meaningful and internally consistent by statistical criteria (also see Tarman and Sears 1998).

25. Research showing symbolic racism to be a powerful predictor of policy preferences is sometimes criticized as being merely tautological, charged with placing excessive government attention to blacks on both sides of the equation (e.g., Sniderman and Tetlock 1986b). In an earlier article, we addressed this point by substituting symbolic racism subscales that were purged of all items that refer to government, government programs (such as welfare), or "special favors," leaving only items on perceived discrimination and blacks' work ethic (Sears et al. 1997). Such scales had virtually the same effects on policy preferences as did the complete symbolic racism scales. We would conclude that the effects of symbolic racism are not such artifacts.

26. Egalitarian values were included in the models tested by Hughes (1997), but not in those tested by Sears et al. (1997). Here they have significant effects on preferences about both federal assistance to blacks and equal opportunity for them, but in all cases, these were considerably weaker than the effects of symbolic racism. The only demographic predictor with an important effect is education. It did have significant effects on support for affirmative action in 1985 (p < .01). However, elsewhere its effects are at best sporadic.

27. To be sure, group stereotypes about valued traits persist, if in diminished form (Bobo and Kluegel 1997; Schuman et al. 1997). But for the present purpose, it is crucial that items measuring those stereotypes do not add this second element by which group differences in capacity justify group differences in access, such as ". . . and therefore blacks should not be allowed to go to business school. . . ."

28. One possible methodological artifact needs to be addressed first. All six egalitarianism items use "agree" or "disagree" response alternatives. However, the items loading most heavily on one factor are keyed such that agreement reflects egalitarianism, whereas the items loading most heavily on the other factor are

keyed such that agreement reflects inegalitarianism. This two-factor solution could, therefore, be a mere byproduct of the familiar acquiescence response bias, masking what might otherwise be a truly single-dimensional scale (Green and Citrin 1994; Green, Goldman, and Salovey 1993).

We tested whether or not acquiescence bias was responsible for this two-factor solution in two ways. First, we created an independent measure of acquiescence response bias based on the six agree-disagree individualism items (in the three NES surveys that included both them and the egalitarianism items, 1984, 1985, and 1986). Half of the individualism items were also keyed in an "agree" direction and half in a "disagree" direction, so we generated an acquiescence score that was neutral with respect to individualism by simply adding the number of times a respondent selected "agree" to those six items. Each egalitarianism item was then regressed upon this score, yielding residual corrected scores for each egalitarianism item with acquiescence bias partialled out. Factor analysis of the corrected egalitarianism items yielded exactly the same two separate factors in each case. And they are no closer to each other. The correlation between the two factors increased only negligibly (the Pearson r increasing from .30 to .31 in 1984, from .25 to .27 in 1985, and from .27 to .29 in 1986).

The six individualism items were not available in the 1990 and 1992 NES surveys, so we turned to a second method for assessing acquiescence bias artifacts, using a structural modeling approach to confirmatory factor analysis (following Nelson 1998). We identified a single-factor solution and a two-factor solution for the six-item egalitarianism scale and included in both models a method factor to account for any measurement error. This method factor loaded onto all six egalitarianism items, and the paths were constrained to be equal. The variance of all latent factors was constrained to 1.0, and the correlations between the method factor and the egalitarianism factor(s) were constrained to 0. Additionally, in the two-factor solution, a two-way path was set between the two egalitarianism factors, allowing them to correlate. Using the EQS 5.3 statistical package (Bentler and Wu 1995), we obtained parameter estimates using the maximum likelihood method and compared the goodness-of-fit statistics of the single-factor solution with those of the two-factor solution. In particular, we examined the difference in χ^2 between the two solutions.

The results overwhelmingly favored the two-factor solution over the single-factor solution, even when accounting for the method factor. In every data set, the reduction in χ^2 from the single-factor solution to the two-factor solution, accounting for method variance, was statistically significant:

$\Delta\chi^2 (1) = 26.4, p < .001$ in 1984
$\Delta\chi^2 (1) = 10.3, p < .01$ in 1985
$\Delta\chi^2 (1) = 55.6, p < .001$ in 1986
$\Delta\chi^2 (1) = 2,480.0, p < .001$ in 1990
$\Delta\chi^2 (1) = 323.1, p < .001$ in 1992

Additionally, in all samples, the two-factor solution constituted an excellent fit to the data (comparative fit index (CFI) = .98, .99, 1.0, 1.0, and .99 in the five data sets, respectively).

Both methodological approaches, then, indicate that the two-factor egalitarianism solution is not merely a measurement artifact, such as an acquiescence response bias. Rather, the two factors reflect substantive differences that go beyond the mere direction of the wording of the items.

29. These subscales correlated only weakly ($r = .14$), but this particular survey included only a small portion of the full social dominance orientation scale (see Pratto et al. 1994; Sidanius et al. this volume). This factor analysis also cleaves the items that require agreement to be high in social dominance from those that require disagreement. To check that their separateness was not merely a function of that methodological difference, we created an acquiescence bias scale on the basis of a balanced set of agree-disagree items concerning attributions for the causes and solutions for crime, in the same manner as done earlier with the NES items. The correlation between the two subscales rose only to .16 when acquiescence bias was partialled out.

30. When we substitute the purged symbolic racism subscales (see note 25) for the full scales in testing for the origins of symbolic racism in the models shown in table 3.5, the findings are virtually unaffected. Contrary to the politics-centered theory that Sniderman proposes (chap. 8, p. 269), using the purged symbolic racism scale does not reduce the effect of antiblack affect and does not increase the impact of party identification and ideology. More relevant for our purposes, the relative effects of the two inegalitarianism subscales do not change either. However, the variance accounted for is somewhat reduced.

31. In the 1985 and 1986 NES surveys and in the 1997 LACSS, six of the symbolic racism items used agree-disagree response alternatives, three keyed in the "agree" direction and three in the "disagree" direction. The two-factor solution of the factor analyses presented earlier (see note 24) turns out in each case to separate items along this divide, raising the possibility of an acquiescence response bias artifact. To check this, we used the same technique of partialling out the acquiescence bias scale as used earlier for the egalitarianism items. When this is done, the two-factor solution collapses in all three studies into its more theoretically predictable single-factor solution, which was not the case for the egalitarianism and social dominance scales.

32. This difference is not merely an artifact of acquiescence bias; when it is controlled in the manner described earlier, the correlations of symbolic racism with "we've gone too far" are .42 in both NES surveys and with "less equal treatment" are .22 and .24, respectively.

33. The correlation between individualistic and structural attributions for poverty in 1985 was $-.21$; the same correlation for attributions about crime in 1997 was $-.08$.

34. It might be noted that these effects do not change when the acquiescence bias is partialled out.

35. Recall that two of the black-disadvantage items have been incorporated into the symbolic racism scale, and so they could not be used as predictors of symbolic racism in the analyses shown in table 3. 5. Sniderman, Crosby, and Howell (pp. 246–47) appear to misunderstand our purpose in these analyses as an attempt to present the link of symbolic racism to "we've gone too far" once again,

but with the new claim that it now shows "we've gone too far" to be a form of racialized individualism. Rather, it is to use the availability of attributions that vary orthogonally on two dimensions, explicit versus implicit racial content and individualism versus structuralism, as an opportunity for a quasi-experimental test of the racialized individualism of this subtype of inegalitarian values. The results seem quite clear.

36. The specific correlations were .08, .03, .19, and .18 for low ability and −.10 and −.07 for God's will.

37. There is further, though circumstantial, evidence that "we've gone too far" is racialized and "less equal treatment" is not. The only demographic variables that correlate significantly with "we've gone too far" in both NES surveys are age and education, two standard correlates of racial attitudes (see Schuman et al. 1997); older and less educated whites are more likely to feel "we've gone too far." In contrast, two of the three demographic variables that correlate significantly with "less equal treatment" are normally more closely linked to class: lower subjective social class and lower income (single marital status does as well). These several pieces of evidence suggest, then, that "less equal treatment" is not strongly racialized today. And it focuses more on structural impediments to equality than on the individual shortcomings of blacks.

38. This is exactly the opposite of the pattern for "we've gone too far," which has average correlations of .24 with old-fashioned racism and .45 with symbolic racism.

39. A more comprehensive causal model incorporating all these variables would be desirable, but would go beyond the scope of this chapter.

40. The politics-centered theory also emphasizes ideology and other nonracial values (e.g., Fazio et al. 1995; Sniderman and Piazza 1993), but in our work, these prove not to have much effect on policy preferences when symbolic racism is taken into account (also see Sears et al. 1997).

41. There is a long tradition of treating both egalitarianism and individualism as values that are acquired early in life, that are retained for many years, and that help to organize Americans' thinking about social and political issues. In that sense, they are thought to be more psychologically fundamental than are beliefs or opinions about transient matters of public life (Feldman 1988; Lipset 1996; Rokeach 1973). There is reasonable evidence that the "less equal treatment" dimension fits this description as a core value. Individual differences on this dimension have been shown to be highly stable over time and to have strong associations with a wide variety of social and political issues (Feldman 1988). However, we, like Schuman (chap. 10), would speculate that the beliefs we have summarized as "we've gone too far" represent ostensibly nonracial beliefs closely intertwined with the symbolic racism belief system rather than being sources of it, and we treat it as such in the remainder of the chapter.

42. That is the strategy adopted in our research on the effects of self-interest on political attitudes (Sears and Funk 1991). In fact, though, neither objective nor subjective indicators of self-interest had much effect, underlining Schuman's (chap. 10) point about the value of weak correlations.

43. Bobo and Kluegel 1993; Gilens 1998; Peffley and Hurwitz 1998; Peffley, Hurwitz, and Sniderman 1997; Sears and van Laar 1999. Also see Kuklinski et al. 1997; Sidanius et al. this volume, chap. 7; Sniderman et al. 1997; Sniderman et al. 1991.

44. One effort to do so, by Sidanius, Devereux, and Pratto (1992), emerged with very similar indices of fit for both causal orders.

45. Kinder and Sanders (1990) represent an exception, but they assess the effects of different framings of a single policy issue, not the effects on public opinion of substantive differences in policies.

46. Indeed, it was just such a comment by James Q. Wilson (1966) that stimulated our initial comparisons of interests with the racialized moral values entangled in symbolic racism (Sears and Kinder 1971).

CHAPTER FIVE

An earlier draft of this paper benefited from comments from Edward Carmines, Jack Citrin, Donald Kinder, David Sears, Jim Sidanius, and Paul Sniderman. I also wish to thank Vincent Kang Fu and Devon Johnson for their able research assistance. This research was partly supported by National Science Foundation grant SBR-9515183.

1. Some prominent analysts of public opinion do commit the error of interpreting whites' views on affirmative action as implacable and monolithic. For example, early in their book Sniderman and Carmines write: "opposition to affirmative action was and is intense, unvarying, and above all pervasive" (1997a, 30). In the concluding chapter, they return to this theme: "opposition to affirmative action is one-sided, intense, and remarkably invariant over time" (Sniderman and Carmines 1997a, 145). This interpretation is not consistent with the full body of public opinion data on the subject, which is considerably more complex than these statements allow (see Steeh and Krysan 1996; Schuman et al. 1997), including many of the results of their own surveys.

2. Kinder and Sanders (1996) provide one recent examination of race differences in opinion. Several African-American scholars have previously emphasized the necessity of conducting such analyses (see Tate 1993; Bobo and Smith 1994; Dawson 1994).

3. Group position theory holds that it is essential to understand individual-level attitudes as centrally concerned with relative group positions. At a macro-social, historical, and cultural level, it is surely legitimate to understand group position theory as speaking to the dynamics of racism (Bobo, Kluegel, and Smith 1997). Unlike symbolic racism theory, however, the group position argument does not hinge on the existence of a singular, individual-level attitudinal dimension best conceptualized as running from tolerance at one end to racism at the other. Instead, consistent with See and Wilson (1989), racism is best conceptualized as a property of social systems and prejudiced attitudes as a property of individuals.

4. A fuller discussion of the survey sample can be found in Bobo and Hutchings 1996 and Bobo and Zubrinsky 1996. The Ethnic Antagonism in LA survey had multiple objectives and piloted many new items. In order to accomplish this

multipurpose agenda, it had a split-ballot structure. One-third of the sample received questions on attitudes toward Asians and immigration involving Asians. One-third of the sample received questions on attitudes toward Latinos and immigration involving Latinos. This analysis centers on the one-third of the sample that received questions concerning blacks and affirmative action for blacks in particular.

5. The three items had a Likert response format and involved favoring or opposing "Preferential treatment in hiring and promotion for blacks," "Special job training and assistance programs for blacks," and "Special openings in colleges and universities for blacks." The scale is highly reliable, with a Cronbach's α of .78.

6. There may be other principled grounds of objection to affirmative action. These would include concern over limiting the coercive power of government, especially the federal government (Schuman and Bobo 1988), and an aversion to governmental policy recognition of "racial" distinctions among its citizenry (Patterson 1997), but as part of the affirmative action debate, the latter is a theme of quite recent emphasis.

CHAPTER SIX

We thank David O. Sears, Rachel Parker-Gwin, Jill K. Kiecolt, and Matthew O. Hunt for comments on a previous draft.

1. Feagin (1975) also identified what he called fatalistic explanations of poverty, such as bad luck or chance, but such explanations are not nearly as prominent as the others are.

2. Although the wording of the attribution items refers to "social and economic problems" rather than "poverty" per se, the items encourage respondents to interpret the questions in economic terms. Hence, we refer to attributions about poverty.

3. The positive correlation between these two variables, though consistent with other research (Hunt 1996), is counterintuitive and inconsistent with the presumption in the literature that these dimensions are polar opposites. One possible explanation for this correlation is that it is due to response behavior and is partly independent of the substance of people's structuralist and individualistic attitudes. Recall that people were asked to indicate which things in a list were important reasons for the social and economic problems faced by a particular group. People may vary in their tendency to cooperate in the interview and to think about and report that any factors are important. If so, there will be at least a weak tendency for the individual and structural indices to be positively correlated regardless of what people actually believe. We have no way to determine how much of the correlation between structural and individualistic beliefs in the present study is influenced by such response behavior. We are inclined to believe that, if it exists, this influence is relatively small. If so, our findings of modest, but significant correlations between structural and individual attributions may reflect the fact that these dimensions have a weak positive—or at worst, zero—correlation.

4. The finding of a significant effect of conservatism contradicts some earlier work, including our own (Tuch and Hughes 1996a). Further research is needed to sort out these inconsistent results.

CHAPTER SEVEN

1. These include the *group positions model* (Blumer 1961; Smith 1981; Wellman 1977), the *expectation states model* (Berger et al. 1977; Cohen 1982), the *realistic group conflict model* (Bobo 1983, 1988a, 1988b; Jackman 1994), the *racial oppression model* (Turner, Singleton, and Musick 1984), the *neoclassical hegemony models* (Gramsci 1976; Michels 1959; Mosca 1939; Pareto 1943; Scott 1990), and *social dominance theory* (see Sidanius 1993; Sidanius and Pratto 1999).

2. Due to the fact that the SDO Scale is highly skewed, we log-transform the SDO scores for all analyses (see Tabachnick and Fidell 1996).

3. For the sake of simplicity, the error terms are not displayed in the figure. Note also that in all models a correlation between the error terms for political conservatism and the Protestant work ethic was estimated (i.e., an element of the ι-matrix).

4. Note that the relationship between the work ethic and affirmative action opposition was not significant and, therefore, contributed little to this indirect effect.

5. Note again that this "equality of opportunity" subscale was also log-transformed.

6. Note that since we did not have access to relevant contrast variables for all attitude objects, the affect measures used in these initial analyses were the raw thermometer ratings for each group. However, in the path-analytic models to be discussed shortly and using whites only, the affect measure used the same affective difference score as used with the student data set.

7. Note that in order to have a sufficiently large sample size in each of the three experimental conditions, we used all nonblacks for these analyses.

8. Note that the β-coefficient is a net effect size coefficient taken from multiple classification analysis. It provides the importance of this main effect, net of the effects of the other main effects.

9. This education effect held even after controlling for the effects of "race" (i.e., the white versus Latino distinction).

10. Interaction effect: $F(2, 368) = 3.30, p < .04$.

11. Note that the data trended in the same direction, even when restricted to whites.

12. These Bs are the unstandardized regression coefficients.

13. Remember that blacks were excluded from these analyses.

14. However, the model fit the data very well indeed ($\chi^2(1) = 1.23, p < .27$; AGFI = .94).

15. Unfortunately, space does not permit a more thorough critique of the symbolic racism/racial resentment thesis. However, see Sidanius, Devereux, and Pratto 1992 and Sidanius et al. 1999.

CHAPTER EIGHT

1. We are offering here an account only of American politics. Things may well be otherwise in other places, not least because of the importance of politics itself.

2. Our two favorites, in this volume, are Kinder and Mendelberg's attributing

to us the claim that prejudice is "a spent force" (p. 71), when our contention is just the opposite—that "this did not square with our own sense of the world" (p. 253)—and Bobo's declamation that "race matters" (p. 152), as though we contend that it does not (see, for example, the finding of racial discrimination in our Equal Opportunity Experiment, pp. 260–61).

3. In highlighting the ideological framework of racial politics here, we are far from denying that issues of race can have a distinctively racial component, let alone that the expression of underlying ideological impulses can take on a distinct form in the context of race—for example, the exceptional sympathy of liberals for injustices of race.

4. Quite apart from Sniderman and Piazza 1993 and Sniderman and Carmines 1997a, we should like particularly to call attention to the independent analyses of our collaborators in the National Race and Politics Study. See Hurwitz and Peffley 1998b.

5. All of the surveys we draw on were funded by the National Science Foundation. Table 8.1 takes advantage of the 1986 and 1992 NES surveys; subsequent tables and figures utilize a series of surveys we have ourselves carried out: the National Race and Politics Study in 1991 (SES-8508937), the Multi-Investigator Study in 1995 (SBR93–9946), and the Regional Race and Politics Survey in 1986 (SES-8821575).

6. To our knowledge, Wong and Bowers (1997) were the first to observe and report this result.

7. We examine the other item, "work their way up," in detail below.

8. Obviously, we do not count the symbolic "racism" measure as an expression of prejudice. We do agree, and have ourselves shown, that one of its components is racial prejudice, albeit not the most important.

9. We have accordingly replicated it on every data set available and also identified and systematically tested an array of methodological counterinterpretations—among them, the possibility that the result is an artifact of ceiling effects or, more generally, of differential restrictions of variance. If the variance in the independent and/or dependent variables was drastically different for conservatives and liberals, then it could be this difference that accounts for the finding that prejudice has more impact on liberals than conservatives. This does not appear to be the case. What follows are the standard deviations for prejudice and for five racial policies, from the National Race and Politics Study, for liberals and conservatives, respectively: prejudice: 10.0 and 8.8; government spending: .48 and .47; fighting discrimination: .48 and .48; welfare spending: .42 and .35; job quotas: .50 and .46; and preferential admissions: .48 and .38. Although there is, sometimes, less variance on some of the variables among conservatives than liberals, the differences are too slight to account for our findings. Moreover, our measure of prejudice is just as reliable for conservatives ($\alpha = .80$) as for liberals ($\alpha = .79$). Finally, it is worth noting that the correlation between prejudice and ideological self-identification, though statistically significant, is modest ($r = .11$).

10. We shall concentrate on the claims of Schuman et al. (1997), though an earlier (and, in ways irrelevant to our concerns here, significantly different) version of the argument was offered by Jackman (1978).

11. We would speculate that for Schuman and his colleagues issues on the equal treatment agenda are the paradigmatic racial policies; certainly, they focus their most detailed and original analyses on open housing and desegregation.

12. These issues are taken as examples. See Schuman et al. 1997, 172–75, tab. 3.5A.

13. Sears, Hetts, Sidanius, and Bobo concur, declaring in their introductory chapter to this volume that "[a]lmost all whites support general principles of racial equality but are more divided about government action to ensure it" (p. 33)— government actions proposed by liberals, that is.

14. See Sniderman and Piazza 1993. The sample for the principal survey on which this study relies, we would underline, is drawn from the San Francisco–Oakland Bay area.

15. They report employing "a four-point response scale ranging from 1 = 'strongly support' to 4 = 'strongly oppose' " (this volume, p. 214).

16. For example, Bobo concurs that (1) racial prejudice is not the paramount factor in contemporary racial politics; (2) it is necessary to distinguish between types of affirmative action; (3) the measure of symbolic racism owes its predictive power to the fact that what is supposed to be doing the job of explanation is difficult to distinguish from what it is supposed to be explaining; and (4) contemporary racial politics is organized around three policy agendas—equal treatment, social welfare, and race-conscious. See his book with Schuman and colleagues (1997).

17. Sniderman and Carmines, *Reaching beyond Race* (1997a). It perhaps is also worth observing that Bobo himself, in his most comprehensive work on racial politics, makes a number of keystone contributions to the politics-oriented approach we are urging. We list some of these below.

18. See Rae 1981. It is Sidanius's apolitical conception of equality as a singular value that underlies his categorization as "absurd" our supposition that opposition to affirmative action in the form of preferential treatment or quotas can collide with a commitment to equality conceived in terms of equal commitment. See Sidanius et al. this volume, p. 229.

19. Bobo even contends that individualism, if involved, works in just the opposite direction to the one hypothesized by Sears, Kinder, and their colleagues in the symbolic racism research program. See Bobo this volume, p. 153. This seems to us to go one bridge too far.

20. Sidanius's two dimensions of group classification are ethnicity and gender.

21. Compare the accounts of Bobo and Sidanius with the classic work on ethnic politics by Wolfinger (1974), which places the agency of ethnic groups at the center of its account. See especially chapter 3.

22. Wolfinger (1974) presents a masterful account of the intergenerational dynamics of the contestation of groups for public influence and social resources. The accounts of both Bobo and Sidanius, by contrast, are starkly ahistorical.

23. Schuman et al. wish it to be noted that they have their own distinct grounds for agreement (1997, 300).

24. For evidence of racial prejudice's power in shaping white reactions to welfare, see especially Gilens 1999 and Sniderman and Piazza 1993. For evidence on

the weakness of the connection between racial prejudice and attitudes toward affirmative action, see Sniderman and Carmines 1997a.

CHAPTER NINE

I wish to thank the editors, Howard Schuman, Marylee Taylor, and Linda Tropp for their helpful comments.

1. Bogardus (1925, 1928) and Thurstone (1928) provide early examples of such work.

2. For independent analyses of this negative predictor of prejudice with these data, see Pettigrew 1997a, 1997b and Hamberger and Hewstone 1997. Since those who are prejudiced actively avoid having outgroup friends (Herek and Capitanio 1996; Pettigrew 1997a), the independent variable status of INTERGROUP FRIENDS can be questioned. But different methods agree that the causal path from INTERGROUP FRIENDS to less prejudice is significantly stronger than the path from fewer intergroup friends to prejudice (Pettigrew 1997a; Powers and Ellison 1995).

3. For detailed analyses with this variable, see Meertens and Pettigrew 1997.

4. For further details concerning these eight measures of prejudice, see Pettigrew and Meertens 1995.

5. This analysis was initially done on a random half-sample and then repeated on the other half-sample. Since there were no substantial differences in the results, table 9.2 provides the results for the full sample.

6. Further support for this interpretation is supplied by relating the factors to other dependent variables tapping affect. The political awareness factor consistently proves the most important predictor of negative emotions toward minorities. Respondents high on this factor are significantly less likely to report being fearful of, disturbed by, or irritated by minorities.

7. Half of the coefficients failing to reach significance involve CULTURAL DIFFERENCES—the least reliable of the prejudice scales.

8. For simplicity, the figure 9.3 solution does not consider correlated errors (E1 with E2, E9 with E7). When these are entered, the fit improves marginally: the EQS normed fit index rises to .912, the comparative fit index to .934, and the LISREL GFI to .986).

9. Comparable, though slightly weaker, EQS models can be established for SUBTLE PREJUDICE as well. It should be emphasized that these models are strictly illustrative; other plausible models are also possible with these variables.

10. To support this view, Sniderman, Crosby, and Howell show in their chapter that prejudice correlates more with policy preference among "strong liberals" than "strong conservatives." This phenomenon also occurs in these European data, but it is largely a statistical artifact. On both the prejudice and the policy preference measures, liberals possess larger variances. In short, strong conservatives have restricted variances on these measures from ceiling effects; their levels of prejudice and opposition to pro-immigration policies are so high that the correlation between them is attenuated. Variances are not provided by Sniderman, Crosby, and Howell to test this possible explanation for the U.S. data.

11. The three items are "The government should not send back to their own

country any of the [minority] now living in [the nation]" (only 14 percent chose this response); "Speaking of these people, do you think we should extend their rights, restrict their rights or leave things as they are?" (only 17 percent would expand immigrant rights); and "[W]ould it be a good idea or a bad idea to make naturalization easier?" (38 percent thought it would be a "good idea").

CHAPTER TEN

1. Pettigrew uses factor analysis for a somewhat different purpose: to build meta-concepts for a specific analytic purpose. I assume he does so without claiming that they (e.g., the conjunction of age and education) represent homogeneous constructs in other regards.

2. The third policy issue shown in Kinder and Mendelberg's table 2.2 concerns "fairness" in employment and raises a somewhat different problem, which I will address at a later point. These wordings are taken from the National Election Study (NES) Codebook, since Kinder and Mendelberg give only NES variable numbers, not the actual wording of the policy items they use. The absence of question wording presents readers with a still more serious problem in the Sniderman, Crosby, and Howell chapter, since the authors report data about the connection of "prejudice" to several policy issues, but give no indication of how prejudice was operationalized.

3. Sears, Henry, and Kosterman refer to this as the problem of content overlap and note that it was investigated by Sears et al. (1997). However, the overlap considered there had to do with purging references in items to government help, which is different from the issue of overlap raised here.

4. Such detailed empirical coding offers the additional benefit of bringing us a little closer to the thoughts and words of real respondents. The proliferation of attitude items by social scientists often sequestered on academic campuses and lacking much qualitative contact with the people they study has its limitations. Obtaining less-constrained answers to open questions reduces a little of the distance between investigators and those being investigated. (For these two questions, which were apparently asked of the same respondents, possible order effects also need to be considered.)

5. Evidence reported by Sidanius et al. and by Sniderman, Crosby, and Howell also points to low levels of association between affect toward blacks and racial policies.

6. It would also be useful to see the univariate distributions of the SDO items—some of which are quite extreme in wording—using reasonably representative general population samples, not college students. In addition, synthesizing different reports based on SDO is hampered by changes in the items; for example, most of the items used in this chapter are not in the scale that was employed by Altemeyer (1998).

7. Unfortunately, the items in this case differ systematically in the direction of agree-disagree wording, suggesting the possibility of acquiescence bias. Although the authors offer indirect evidence that the problem is not serious, I suspect that they have not eliminated it entirely and that it continues to affect some of their correlations, especially in table 3.6.

8. It remains perplexing that nonracial individualism is related to nonracial forms of government intervention, yet is not related to government intervention in support of blacks (see, e.g., Kinder and Mendelberg's table 2.2). There are a few clues worth noting. First, Bobo reports the interesting finding that "the more whites are committed to notions of reward for hard work, the *less* likely they are to hold negative beliefs about the effects of affirmative action for blacks" (p. 153, emphasis added). Second, Hughes and Tuch provide some evidence that individualism plays an interactive role with their measure of structuralism: "as individualism increases, the effect of structuralism in reducing opposition to egalitarian policies is reduced" (p. 187). Third, some analysis I have been doing with Maria Krysan has indicated that measures of individualism do affect affirmative action variables among those with a college education, but not at lower levels of schooling—another instance of focusing on interaction, as discussed below. These several findings suggest that there may still be something important to learn about the meaning of measures of "individualism" in surveys.

9. It is all the better if the interaction has a between-subjects component, as with survey-based randomized experiments, so as to prevent question order effects.

10. Even the wording of the question about school integration is a bit confusing (and the NES has asked it in confusing ways, as noted in Schuman et al. 1997), for the strict equal opportunity issue is to prevent actions, both de jure and de facto, that produce the segregation of black and white children, not for the government to "see to it" that black and white children go to the same schools, however desirable that may be in affirmative action terms.

11. Sniderman, Crosby, and Howell advocate going beyond simple split-ballot experiments that restrict question variations to two (p. 240). However, of the four experiments presented in their chapter, three can be characterized as split-ballot experiments with just two forms; the fourth experiment merely adds a third form, as others have done before when a hypothesis called for it and sample size was sufficiently large. (Factorial designs do point in a somewhat different direction, but none is included in this chapter.) The more important point, however, is that the extent to which an experiment addresses well a significant theoretical issue is what counts in the end, not the number of manipulations that can be performed in a CATI setting.

12. References to tables and figures in this and the next paragraph are to Schuman et al. 1997.

13. Although the reasons for this striking normative shift are not easy to demonstrate, my own belief is that there were two main forces at work on white Americans, in addition, of course, to the crucial fact of increasingly effective protest actions by black Americans. One force came out of World War II, but was not the war itself (which had a heavily racist component in the full sense of the word), but rather the victory by the United States and the way that victory became connected with the defeat of those responsible for death camps and other atrocities, so that one could not take pride in the victory without condemning what was said to be the ideology of the enemy. The other main force was the role of leadership that the United States took up once the Cold War got under way, which in turn

meant the full exposure of practices in this country to the eyes of a rapidly decolonizing world. As someone once observed, "Conscience is that still small voice within us that says: Someone may be watching!" This applies as much at the collective level as at the individual level, and it is exactly the sort of national vulnerability to which nine white Establishment Supreme Court justices would have been sensitive as they began to reach crucial legal decisions on racial issues.

14. This is a difficult issue to investigate in surveys, though there is now considerable evidence of continuing white stereotypes regarding racial differences in intelligence and other characteristics even when inquired into directly, and more so when some indirection is employed. See Jackman and Senter 1980; Kinder and Sanders 1996; Bobo and Kluegel 1997.

15. Omitted from the tabulations just presented is the bulk of the 1992 sample ($N = 991$), who chose "about right" to the civil rights push question. Some 86 percent of these respondents opposed preferential treatment strongly or not strongly.

16. The result in the text is based on an NES question that assumes past discrimination as a general justification. However, Stoker (1998) has recently reported results suggesting that if the question focuses directly on particular companies that are said to have discriminated, support for preferential treatment as a remedy goes up and its correlates in relation to prejudice measures also become sharper.

CHAPTER ELEVEN

1. Sniderman, Crosby, and Howell are splitters in the realm of policy choice as well as in the psychological realm: "there is not one problem of race, but a number—among them, the need to assure equal treatment under the law; to provide assistance to those who are poor; and to combat discrimination, which in itself can take different forms, as discrimination itself is differently defined" (p. 238).

2. Paralleling my observation in note 1, Sears, Henry, and Kosterman are lumpers in the realm of policy choices as well as in the psychological realm: antiblack affect's "effects . . . on policy preferences are quite similar across all three domains of racial issues. This further supports the notion that whites' attention is mostly captured by the racial content of these issues" (p. 89).

Sidanius et al. are also lumpers rather than splitters, although along somewhat different dimensions than the other two central models. For example, "opposition to policies designed to aid subordinates is driven by very similar forces and dynamics across a number of different social systems. . . . [G]roup-based antiegalitarianism and SDO [social dominance orientation] are not simply driving social policy attitudes about blacks among white Americans, but also are critically important sources of opposition to group-relevant social policy attitudes across a wide variety of other cultures as well [as the United States]" (pp. 232–33).

3. "Racism is an ideology of intellectual or moral superiority based upon the biological characteristics of race" (D'Souza 1995, 27).

4. "Those who resist [affirmative action programs] deny that they are racists, but the truth is that their real motivation is racism, a belief in the inherent inferi-

ority of African-Americans and people of mixed racial backgrounds" (Motley 1998, 61).

5. Kinder and Sanders use the same NES questions with the words "preference" and "quotas," despite their discussion of Stoker's finding that support for affirmative action increases when the question more carefully tracks Supreme Court rulings (1996, 174–82, 194–95). Sears, Henry, and Kosterman also use the NES questions, so their chapter is subject to the same critique.

6. In their chapter in *Racialized Politics*, Sniderman, Crosby, and Howell conduct a detailed analysis of whites' attitudes toward "black leaders asking for affirmative action." Although their interest centers on whether that phenomenon makes whites angry, they make no effort to discover what angry (or nonangry) whites mean by "affirmative action."

7. The problem in Sniderman and Carmines (1997a) is more subtle than the problem in Sniderman and Piazza (1993). In the later book, the authors elegantly demonstrate (pp. 22–27) just what Bobo points out—that a majority of whites support "extra effort," although a majority oppose "preferential treatment." Nevertheless, throughout the rest of the book, they equate affirmative action with quotas and preferences rather than with special efforts.

8. Kinder and Mendelberg discuss Jackman and Muha's (1984) rather different understanding of individualism in their chapter in this volume, but they focus more on relating it to their extant theory than on using it or other meanings as a fresh start in developing new theories.

9. Rae (1981) sorts out the many other meanings of equality and the ways in which some can directly offset others.

10. Page 203. "Other" might mean non-American; how should we locate them on a social dominance scale?

11. Pettigrew treats individual racial or ethnic prejudice as a dependent variable, whereas most of the other authors in *Racialized Politics* use it as an independent variable. I will not discuss that point, since it is simply a choice of research agenda rather than part of an ongoing dispute that these comments seek to understand and negotiate.

12. In this case, I am a lumper (I argue for combining theories as much as possible) rather than a splitter (who would argue for separating out the one best theory from the other, less effective alternatives).

13. Alternatively, one could argue that the three basic approaches in *Racialized Politics* are key conceptualizations that organize the field, but that we do not yet have a systematic or definitive theory of racial interactions that could integrate all of the relevant elements (Pettigrew this volume).

14. Surveyors, as well as survey analysts, vary greatly and unsystematically in how they deal with people who are neither white Americans nor African Americans. Some surveys and some theories distinguish between whites and minorities (which typically include Latinos, Asians, and "others"). In other surveys and theoretical frameworks, the focus is on whites and blacks (in which case Latinos, Asians, and "others" are excluded from the survey or from the analysis altogether). In still other surveys and frameworks, the distinction is between blacks and non-blacks (in which case Latinos, Asians, and "others" are included in the "white"

population). In this chapter, I am lumping all of these possibilities together into the category of bifocal analysis, to be distinguished from a multifocal analysis as described in the text.

15. It would be worthwhile for Kinder to reconcile this finding with that in Kinder and Sanders (1996, 272) that "our most striking result is the long reach of racial resentment into diverse aspects of American opinion. We found racial resentment to be implicated in whites' views not just on affirmative action or school desegregation, but on welfare, capital punishment, urban unrest, family leave, sexual harassment, gay rights, immigration, spending on defense, and more."

16. In an alternative phrasing, "the fundamental lines of cleavage on issues of race, so far as they are defined by the party system, are not peculiar to issues of race. They belong, rather, to a larger pattern of division, defining the deeper-lying structure of American politics since the New Deal, centering on the clash of competing conceptions of the proper responsibilities of government and the appropriate obligations of citizens" (Sniderman, Crosby, and Howell this volume, p. 238).

17. The terms "Asian," "Hispanic," and "Latino" and other related words do not appear in the index of either the 1993 or the 1997 book, and neither book discusses racial or ethnic groups other than blacks and whites. The same obtains for Kinder and Sanders 1996.

18. She differs from those just discussed in a crucial way, which I will address below, but for now, I am focusing on the resemblance.

19. There is no national survey of Asians; there are only two national surveys of Latinos, the most recent of which is a decade old.

20. The lack of national surveys in which all four groups are surveyed symmetrically about all four groups is intensely frustrating. Even the 1995 *Washington Post* survey, which Hughes and Tuch use and which is the best source of national data on the attitudes of all four groups, missed a major opportunity by not asking the four groups how they explained *white* poverty. Thus, the four-way comparison that we need in order to understand how poverty influences racial policy attitudes is unavailable.

This is an instance of a larger complaint I have about survey research—surveyors ask endless questions about the poor, but few about the rich; many questions about women, but very few about men; a multitude of questions about blacks (and increasingly about Latinos and Asians), but almost none about whites. Postmodernists write about "The Gaze"; surveyors seldom turn it onto people like themselves.

21. Or, more epigrammatically, "the contemporary debate over racial policy is driven primarily by conflict over what government should try to do, and only secondarily over what it should try to do *for blacks*" (Sniderman and Carmines 1997a, 4, emphasis in original).

22. With perhaps the crucial and disturbing exception of the two senior black contributors.

23. Much of the evidence for and analyses underlying the following claims is in Hochschild 1995.

REFERENCES

Aberbach, Joel A., and Jack L. Walker. 1973. *Race in the city*. Boston: Little, Brown.

Abramowitz, Alan I. 1994. Issue evolution reconsidered: Racial attitudes and partisanship in the U.S. electorate. *American Journal of Political Science* 38 (1): 1–24.

Adorno, T. W., Else Frankel-Brunswik, Daniel J. Levinson, and R. Nevitt Sanford. 1950. *The authoritarian personality*. New York: Harper & Row.

Allen, R. L. 1994. Structural equality in black and white. *Howard Journal of Communications* 5:69–91.

Allport, Gordon W. 1954. *The nature of prejudice*. Garden City, N.Y.: Doubleday Anchor.

Altemeyer, Bob. 1981. *Right-wing authoritarianism*. Winnipeg, Canada: University of Manitoba Press.

———. 1988. *Enemies of freedom: Understanding right-wing authoritarianism*. San Francisco: Jossey-Bass.

———. 1994. Reducing prejudice in right-wing authoritarians. In *The psychology of prejudice*, edited by Mark P. Zanna and James M. Olson, 131–48. Hillsdale, N.J.: Erlbaum.

———. 1998. The other "authoritarian personality." *Advances in Experimental Social Psychology* 30:47–92.

Alvarez, R. Michael, and John Brehm. 1997. Are Americans ambivalent towards racial policies? *American Journal of Political Science* 41:345–74.

Anastasio, Phyllis, Betty Bachman, Samuel Gaertner, and John Dovidio. 1997. Categorization, recategorization and common ingroup identity. In *The social psychology of stereotyping and group life*, edited by Russell Spears, Penelope J. Oakes, Naomi Ellemers, and S. Alexander Haslam, 236–56. Oxford, England: Blackwell.

Apostle, Richard A., Charles Y. Glock, Thomas Piazza, and Marijean Suelzle. 1983. *The anatomy of racial attitudes*. Berkeley: University of California Press.

Appiah, K. Anthony, and Amy Gutmann. 1996. *Color conscious: The political morality of race*. Princeton: Princeton University Press.

391

Armor, David J. 1980. White flight and the future of social desegregation. In *School desegregation: Past, present, and future,* edited by Walter G. Stephan and Joe R. Feagin, 187–226. New York: Plenum.

Bargh, John A. 1997. The automaticity of everyday life. In *Advances in social cognition,* edited by Robert S. Wyer, Jr., 1–61. Mahwah, N.J.: Erlbaum.

Bargh, John A., Mark Chen, and Lara Burrows. 1996. Automaticity of social behavior: Direct effects of trait construct and stereotype activation on action. *Journal of Personality & Social Psychology* 71:230–44.

Bell, Derrick. 1992. *Faces at the bottom of the well: The permanence of racism.* New York: Basic Books.

Bellah, Robert N., Richard Madsen, William N. Sullivan, Ann Swidler, and Steven M. Tipton. 1985. *Habits of the heart: Individualism and commitment in American life.* Berkeley: University of California Press.

Bentler, Peter M. 1989. *EQS structural equations program manual.* Los Angeles: BMDP Statistical Software.

Bentler, Peter M., and Eric J. C. Wu. 1995. *EQS for Windows user's guide.* Encino, Calif.: Multivariate Software.

Berger, Joseph, et al. 1977. *Status characteristics and social interaction: An expectation-states approach.* New York: Elsevier Scientific Publishing Co.

Blair, Irene V., and Mahzarin R. Banaji. 1996. Automatic and controlled processes in stereotype priming. *Journal of Personality & Social Psychology* 70:1142–63.

Blalock, Hubert M., Jr. 1967. *Toward a theory of minority-group relations.* New York: Wiley.

Blumer, Herbert. 1958. Race prejudice as a sense of group position. *Pacific Sociological Review* 1:3–7.

———. 1961. Race prejudice as a sense of group position. In *Race relations: Problems and theory,* edited by J. Masuoka and P. Valien, 217–27. Chapel Hill: University of North Carolina Press.

Bobo, Lawrence. 1983. Whites' opposition to busing: Symbolic racism or realistic group conflict? *Journal of Personality & Social Psychology* 45:1195–1210.

———. 1988a. Attitudes toward the black political movement: Trends, meaning and effects on racial policy preferences. *Social Psychology Quarterly* 51: 287–302.

———. 1988b. Group conflict, prejudice, and the paradox of contemporary racial attitudes. In *Eliminating racism: Profiles in controversy,* edited by Phyllis A. Katz and Dalmas A. Taylor, 85–114. New York: Plenum.

———. 1991. Social responsibility, individualism, and redistributive policies. *Sociological Forum* 6:71–92.

———. 1997a. The color line, the dilemma, and the dream: Race relations at the close of the twentieth century. In *Civil rights and social wrongs: Black-white relations since World War II,* edited by John Higham, 31–55. University Park: Pennsylvania State University Press.

———. 1997b. Race, public opinion, and the social sphere. *Public Opinion Quarterly* 61:1–15.

———. 1997c. Prejudice as group position. Under review.

———. 1998. Race, interests, and beliefs about affirmative action: Unanswered questions and new directions. *American Behavioral Scientist* 41:985–1003.

Bobo, Lawrence, and Vincent L. Hutchings. 1994a. Black and Latino conflict with Asians: Extending the theory of group position. Paper presented at the annual meeting of the Western Political Science Association, Albuquerque, N.M.

———. 1994b. Immigration politics, race, and the sense of group position. Paper presented at the annual meeting of American Political Science Association, New York.

———. 1996. Perceptions of racial group competition: Extending Blumer's theory of group position to a multiracial social context. *American Sociological Review* 61:951–72.

Bobo, Lawrence, and James R. Kluegel. 1993. Opposition to race-targeting: Self-interest, stratification ideology, or racial attitudes? *American Sociological Review* 58:443–64.

———. 1997. Status, ideology, and dimensions of whites' racial beliefs and attitudes: Progress and stagnation. In *Racial attitudes in the 1990s: Continuity and change,* edited by Steven A. Tuch and Jack K. Martin, 93–120. Westport, Conn.: Praeger.

Bobo, Lawrence, James R. Kluegel, and Ryan A. Smith. 1997. Laissez-faire racism: The crystallization of a kinder, gentler, antiblack ideology. In *Racial attitudes in the 1990s: Continuity and change,* edited by Steven A. Tuch and Jack K. Martin, 15–41. Westport, Conn.: Praeger.

Bobo, Lawrence, and Frederick C. Licari. 1989. Education and political tolerance: Testing the effects of cognitive sophistication and target group affect. *Public Opinion Quarterly* 53:285–308.

Bobo, Lawrence, and Ryan A. Smith. 1994. Antipoverty policy, affirmative action, and racial attitudes. In *Confronting poverty: Prescriptions for change,* edited by Sheldon Danziger, G. D. Sandefur, and Daniel H. Weinberg, 365–95. Cambridge: Harvard University Press.

———. 1998. From Jim Crow racism to laissez-faire racism: The transformation of racial attitudes. In *Beyond pluralism: The conception of groups and group identities in America,* edited by Wendy F. Katkin, Ned Landsman, and Andrea Tyree, 182–220. Urbana: University of Illinois Press.

Bobo, Lawrence, and Camille Zubrinsky. 1996. Attitudes on residential integration: Perceived status differences, mere in-group preference, or racial prejudice? *Social Forces* 74:883–909.

Bogardus, E. S. 1925. Measuring social distance. *Journal of Applied Sociology* 9:298–308.

———. 1928. *Immigration and race attitudes.* Boston: Heath.

Bollen, Kenneth A. 1989. *Structural equations with latent variables.* New York: Wiley.

Boston, Thomas D. 1988. *Race, class, and conservatism.* Boston: Unwin Hyman.

Bowen, William G., and Derek Bok. 1998. *The shape of the river: Long-term consequences of considering race in college and university admissions.* Princeton: Princeton University Press.

Brauer, Carl M. 1977. *John F. Kennedy and the second reconstruction.* New York; Columbia University Press.

Brewer, Marilynn B. 1979. In-group bias in the minimal intergroup situation: A cognitive-motivational analysis. *Psychological Bulletin* 86:307–24.

Brewer, Marilynn B., and Donald T. Campbell. 1976. *Ethnocentrism and intergroup attitudes: East African evidence.* New York: Sage.

Brigham, John C., John J. Woodmansee, and Stuart W. Cook. 1976. Dimensions of verbal racial attitudes: Interracial marriage and approaches to racial equality. *Journal of Social Issues* 32:9–21.

Brown, Roger. 1965. *Social psychology.* New York: Free Press.

Bryce, James B. 1900. *The American commonwealth.* London: Macmillan.

Bryk, Anthony S., Stephen W. Raudenbush, and Richard T. Congdon, Jr. 1994. *Hierarchical linear modeling with the HLM/2L and HLM/3L programs.* Chicago: Scientific Software International.

Burke, Edmund. [1790] 1955. *Reflections on the revolution in France.* Reprint, Chicago: Regnery.

Campbell, Angus. 1971. *White attitudes toward black people.* Ann Arbor, Mich.: Institute for Social Research.

Campbell, Angus, Philip E. Converse, Warren E. Miller, and Donald E. Stokes. 1960. *The American voter.* New York: Wiley.

Campbell, Angus, and Howard Schuman. 1968. Racial attitudes in fifteen American cities. In *Supplemental studies for the National Advisory Commission on Civil Disorders.* Washington, D.C.: U.S. Government Printing Office.

Campbell, Donald T. 1965. Ethnocentric and other altruistic motives. In *Nebraska symposium on motivation,* edited by Robert Levine. Lincoln: University of Nebraska Press.

Carmines, Edward G., and W. Richard Merriman, Jr. 1993. The changing American dilemma: Liberal values and racial policies. In *Prejudice, politics, and the American dilemma,* edited by Paul M. Sniderman, Philip E. Tetlock, and Edward G. Carmines, 237–55. Stanford: Stanford University Press.

Carmines, Edward G., and James A. Stimson. 1989. *Issue evolution: Race and the transformation of American politics.* Princeton: Princeton University Press.

Carnoy, Martin I. 1994. *Faded dreams: The politics and economics of race in America.* New York: Cambridge University Press.

Chen, M., and John A. Bargh. 1997. Nonconscious behavioral confirmation processes: The self-fulfilling consequences of automatic stereotype activation. *Journal of Experimental Social Psychology* 33:541–60.

Chermerinsky, Erwin. 1997. Making sense of the affirmative action debate. In *Civil rights and social wrongs: Black-white relations since World War II,* edited by John Higham, 86–101. University Park: Pennsylvania State University Press.

Citrin, Jack. 1996. Affirmative action in the people's court. *Public Interest* 122: 39–48.

Citrin, Jack, and Donald Philip Green. 1990. The self-interest motive in American public opinion. In *Research in micropolitics,* edited by S. Long. Vol. 3, 1–28. Greenwich, Conn.: JAI Press.

Citrin, Jack, Donald Philip Green, and David O. Sears. 1990. White reactions to black candidates: When does race matter? *Public Opinion Quarterly* 54:74–96.

Cohen, Cathy J., and Michael Dawson. 1993. Neighborhood politics and African-American politics. *American Political Science Review* 87:286–302.

Cohen, Elizabeth G. 1982. Expectation states and interracial interaction in school settings. *Annual Review of Sociology* 8:209–35.

Colleau, Sophie M., Kevin Glynn, Steve Lybrand, Richard M. Merelman, Paula Mohan, and James E. Wall. 1990. Symbolic racism in candidate evaluation: An experiment. *Political Behavior* 12:385–402.

Conover, Pamela, and Donald Searing. 1998. Political discussion and the politics of identity. Paper presented at the annual meeting of the Midwest Political Science Association, Chicago.

Conover, Pamela, Donald Searing, and Ivor Crewe. 1998. Tolerance and community in the United States and Great Britain. Paper presented at the annual meeting of the American Political Science Association, Boston.

Converse, Philip E. 1964. The nature of belief systems in mass publics. In *Ideology and discontent,* edited by David E. Apter, 206–61. New York: Free Press.

———. 1975. Public opinion and voting behavior. In *Handbook of political science,* edited by Fred I. Greenstein and Nelson W. Polsby. Vol. 4, 75–170. Reading, Mass.: Addison-Wesley.

Converse, Philip E., and Gregory B. Markus. 1979. Plus ça change . . . : The new CPS election study panel. *American Political Science Review* 73 (March): 32–49.

Cook, R. Dennis, and Sanford Weisberg. 1982. Criticism in regression. In *Sociological methodology,* edited by S. Leinhardt, 313–61. San Francisco: Jossey-Bass.

Cook, Stuart W., and Claire E. Seltiz. 1964. A multi-indicator approach to attitude measurement. *Psychological Bulletin* 62:36–55.

Crosby, Faye, S. Bromley, and Leonard Saxe. 1980. Recent unobtrusive studies of black and white discrimination and prejudice: A literature review. *Psychological Bulletin* 87:546–63.

Danziger, Sheldon, and Peter Gottschalk. 1996. *America unequal.* New York: Russell Sage.

Davis, Darren W. 1996. White Americans' opposition to racial policies: Where are the political explanations? *Social Science Quarterly* 77:746–50.

Davis, James A., and Tom W. Smith. 1990. *The General Social Survey: Cumulative codebook and data file.* Chicago: National Opinion Research Center and University of Chicago.

———. 1994. *General Social Surveys 1972–1994: Cumulative codebook.* Chicago: National Opinion Research Center and University of Chicago.

Dawson, Michael C. 1994. *Behind the mule: Race and class in African American politics.* Princeton: Princeton University Press.

Dawson, Michael C., and Ernest Wilson III. 1991. Paradigms and paradoxes: Political science and the study of African American politics. In *Political science: Looking to the future,* edited by William Crotty, Vol. 1, 189–234. Evanston, Ill.: Northwestern University Press.

Degler, Carl N. 1991. *In search of human nature*. New York: Oxford University Press.

Devine, Patricia G. 1989. Stereotypes and prejudice: Their automatic and controlled components. *Journal of Personality & Social Psychology* 56:5–18.

Devine, Patricia G., and Andrew J. Elliot. 1995. Are racial stereotypes really fading? The Princeton trilogy revisited. *Personality & Social Psychology Bulletin* 21:1139–50.

Dovidio, John F., Nancy Evans, and Richard B. Tyler. 1986. Racial stereotypes: The contents of their cognitive representations. *Journal of Experimental Social Psychology* 22:22–37.

Dovidio, John F., and Samuel L. Gaertner, eds. 1986. *Prejudice, discrimination and racism*. Orlando: Academic Press.

Dovidio, John F., Kerry Kawakami, Craig Johnson, Brenda Johnson, and Adaiah Howard. 1997. On the nature of prejudice: Automatic and controlled processes. *Journal of Experimental Social Psychology* 33:510–40.

D'Souza, Dinesh. 1995. *The end of racism: Principles for a multiracial society*. New York: Free Press.

Duckitt, John H. 1992a. Psychology and prejudice: A historical analysis and integrative framework. *American Psychologist* 47:1182–93.

———. 1992b. *The social psychology of prejudice*. New York: Praeger.

Duncan, Otis Dudley. 1966. Path analysis: Sociological examples. *American Journal of Sociology* 195 (December): 35–39.

Edley, Christopher. 1996. *Not all black and white: Affirmative action and American values*. New York: Hill and Wang.

Edsall, Thomas B., and Mary D. Edsall. 1991a. *Chain reaction: The impact of race, rights, and taxes on American politics*. New York: Norton.

———. 1991b. When the official subject is presidential politics, taxes, welfare, crime, rights, or values . . . the real subject is race. *Atlantic Monthly*, May, 53–86.

Entman, Robert M. (1997). Manufacturing discord: Media in the affirmative action debate. *Press/Politics* 2:32–51.

Ericsson, K. Anders, and Herbert A. Simon. 1993. *Protocol analysis*. Cambridge: MIT Press.

Esses, Victoria M., Geoffrey Haddock, and Mark P. Zanna. 1993. Values, stereotypes, and emotions as determinants of intergroup attitudes. In *Affect, cognition, and stereotyping: Interactive processes in group perception*, edited by Diane M. Mackie and David L. Hamilton, 137–66. San Diego: Academic Press.

Farley, Reynolds. 1996. *The new American reality: Who we are, how we got here, where we are going*. New York: Russell Sage Foundation.

Farley, Reynolds, Howard Schuman, Suzanne Bianchi, Diane Colasanto, and Shirley Hatchett. 1978. "Chocolate city, vanilla suburbs": Will the trend toward racially separate communities continue? *Social Science Research* 7:319–44.

Fazio, Russell H., and Bridget C. Dunton. 1997. Categorization by race: The impact of automatic and controlled components of racial prejudice. *Journal of Experimental Social Psychology* 33:451–70.

Fazio, Russell H., Joni R. Jackson, Bridget C. Dunton, and Carol J. Williams. 1995. Variability in automatic activation as an unobtrusive measure of racial attitudes: A bona fide pipeline? *Journal of Personality & Social Psychology* 69:1013–27.

Feagin, Joe. 1975. When it comes to poverty, it's still, "God helps those who help themselves." *Psychology Today* 6:101–29.

Feagin, Joe, and Melvin Sikes. 1994. *Living with racism: The black middle-class experience*. Boston: Beacon Press.

Feldman, Stanley. 1988. Structure and consistency in public opinion: The role of core beliefs and values. *American Journal of Political Science* 32:416–40.

Feldman, Stanley, and John Zaller. 1992. The political culture of ambivalence: Ideological responses to the welfare state. *American Journal of Political Science* 36:268–307.

Firebaugh, Glenn, and Kenneth E. Davis. 1988. Trends in antiblack prejudice, 1972–1984: Region and cohort effects. *American Journal of Sociology* 94: 251–72.

Fiske, Alan P. 1991. *Structures of social life: The four elementary forms of human relations: Communal sharing, authority ranking, equality matching, market pricing*. New York: Free Press.

Flynn, James R. 1996. Group differences: Is the good society impossible? *Journal of Biosocial Science* 28:573–85.

Fossett, Mark, and Jill Kiecolt. 1989. The relative size of minority populations and white racial attitudes. *Social Science Quarterly* 70:820–35.

Fox, John. 1991. *Regression diagnostics*. Newbury Park, Calif.: Sage.

Fredrickson, George M. 1971. *The black image in the white mind: The debate on Afro-American character and destiny, 1817–1914*. New York: Harper & Row.

———. 1995. *Black liberation: A comparative history of black ideologies in the United States and South Africa*. New York: Oxford University Press.

Frey, David L., and Samuel L. Gaertner. 1986. Helping and the avoidance of inappropriate interracial behavior: A strategy that perpetuates a nonprejudiced self-image. *Journal of Personality & Social Psychology* 50:1083–90.

Fried, Amy. 1997. *Muffled echoes: Oliver North and the politics of public opinion*. New York: Columbia University Press.

Gaertner, Samuel L., and John F. Dovidio. 1977. The subtlety of white racism, arousal, and helping behavior. *Journal of Personality & Social Psychology* 35: 691–707.

———. 1986. The aversive form of racism. In *Prejudice, discrimination, and racism*, edited by John F. Dovidio and Samuel L. Gaertner, 61–89. Orlando: Academic Press.

Gaertner, Samuel L., John F. Dovidio, Phyllis A. Anastasio, Betty A. Bachman, and Mary C. Rust. 1993. The common ingroup identity model: Recategorization and the reduction of intergroup bias. *European Review of Social Psychology* 4:1–26.

Gaertner, Samuel L., and John P. McLaughlin. 1983. Racial stereotypes: Associations and ascriptions of positive and negative characteristics. *Social Psychology Quarterly* 46:23–30.

Gaertner, Samuel L., Mary C. Rust, John F. Dovidio, Betty A. Bachman, and Phyllis A. Anastasio. 1994. The contact hypothesis: The role of a common ingroup identity on reducing intergroup bias. *Small Group Research* 25:224–49.

Gallup Poll Social Audit. 1997. Black/white relations in the United States. Princeton, N.J.: Gallup Organization.

Gans, Herbert J. 1988. *Middle American individualism.* New York: Free Press.

Geertz, Clifford. 1964. Ideology as a cultural system. In *Ideology and discontent,* edited by David E. Apter, 47–76. Glencoe, Ill.: Free Press.

Gilbert, Daniel T., and J. Gregory Hixon. 1991. The trouble of thinking: Activation and application of stereotypic beliefs. *Journal of Personality & Social Psychology* 60:509–17.

Gilens, Martin. 1996a. "Race coding" and white opposition to welfare. *American Political Science Review* 90:593–604.

———. 1996b. Race and poverty in America: Public misperceptions and the American news media. *Public Opinion Quarterly* 60:515–41.

———. 1998. Racial attitudes and race-neutral social policies: White opposition to welfare and the politics of racial inequality. In *Perception and prejudice: Race and politics in the United States,* edited by Jon Hurwitz and Mark Peffley, 171–201. New Haven: Yale University Press.

———. 1999. *Why Americans hate welfare: Race, media, and the politics of anti-poverty policy.* Chicago: University of Chicago Press.

Gilens, Martin, Paul M. Sniderman, and James H. Kuklinski. 1998. Affirmative action and the politics of realignment. *British Journal of Political Science* 28: 159–83.

Giles, Michael W., and Melanie A. Buckner. 1993. David Duke and black threat: An old hypothesis revisited. *Journal of Politics* 55:702–13.

———. David Duke and the electoral politics of racial threat. In *David Duke and the politics of race in the South,* edited by John C. Kuzenski, Charles S. Bullock III, and Ronald Keith Gaddie, 88–98. Nashville: Vanderbilt University Press.

Giles, Michael W., and Arthur S. Evans. 1986. The power approach to intergroup hostility. *Journal of Conflict Resolution* 30:469–86.

Giles, Michael W., and Kaenan Hertz. 1994. Racial threat and partisan identification. *American Political Science Review* 88:317–26.

Gilovich, Thomas, Victoria H. Medvec, and Daniel Kahneman. 1998. Varieties of regret: A debate and partial resolution. *Psychological Review* 105:602–05.

Gilroy, Paul. 1993. *The black Atlantic: Modernity and double consciousness.* Cambridge: Harvard University Press.

Glaser, James M., and Martin Gilens. 1997. Interregional migration and political resocialization: A study of racial attitudes under pressure. *Public Opinion Quarterly* 61:72–86.

Glazer, Nathan. 1975. *Affirmative discrimination, ethnic inequality and public policy.* New York: Basic Books.

———. 1997. *We are all multiculturalists now.* Cambridge: Harvard University Press.

Gramsci, Antonio. 1976. *Selections from the prison notebooks,* translated and edited by Q. Hoare and G. N. Smith. New York: International Publishers.

Gray D., A. Dymond, J. Towers, J. Petrocelli, and S. Rotheberger. 1997. A first examination of the simultaneous construct validation of belief in equality and social dominance orientation. Paper presented at the twentieth annual scientific meeting of the International Society of Political Psychology, Krakow, Poland.

Green, Donald Philip, and Jack Citrin. 1994. Measurement error and the structure of attitudes: Are positive and negative judgments opposites? *American Journal of Political Science* 38:256–81.

Green, Donald Philip, Susan Lee Goldman, and Peter Salovey. 1993. Measurement error masks bipolarity in affect ratings. *Journal of Personality & Social Psychology* 64:1029–41.

Greenberg, Jeff, Tom Pyszczynski, Sheldon Solomon, Abram Rosenblatt, Mitchell Veeder, Shari Kirkland, and Deborah Lyon. 1990. Evidence for terror management theory II: The effects of mortality salience on reactions to those who threaten or bolster the cultural worldview. *Journal of Personality & Social Psychology* 58:308–18.

Greenwald, Anthony G., and Mahzarin R. Banaji. 1995. Implicit social cognition: Attitudes, self-esteem, and stereotypes. *Psychological Review* 102:4–27.

Gross, Kimberly A., and Donald R. Kinder. 1998. A collision of principles? Free expression, racial equality, and the prohibition of racist speech. *British Journal of Political Science* 28:445–71.

Guinier, Lani. 1998. *Lift every voice: Turning a civil rights setback into a new vision of social justice.* New York: Simon & Schuster.

Gurin, Patricia, Shirley Hatchett, and James S. Jackson. 1989. *Hope and independence: Blacks' response to electoral and party politics.* New York: Russell Sage Foundation.

Hacker, Andrew. 1992. *Two nations: Black and white, separate, hostile, unequal.* New York: Scribner's.

Hagen, Michael G. 1995. References to racial issues. *Political Behavior* 17:49–88.

Hamberger, Juergen, and Miles Hewstone. 1997. Inter-ethnic contact as a predictor of blatant and subtle prejudice: Tests of a model in four West European nations. *British Journal of Social Psychology* 36:173–90.

Hamilton, William D. 1964. The genetical evolution of social behavior. *Journal of Theoretical Biology* 7:1–16, 17–52.

Harrison, Roderick J., and C. E. Bennett. 1995. Racial and ethnic diversity. In *Social trends.* Vol. 2 of *State of the union, America in the 1990s,* edited by Reynolds Farley, 141–210. New York: Russell Sage.

Hartz, Louis. 1955. *The liberal tradition in America.* New York: Harcourt, Brace.

Hass, R. Glen, Irwin Katz, Nina Rizzo, Joan Bailey, and Lynn Moore. 1991. Cross-racial appraisal as related to attitude ambivalence and cognitive complexity. *Personality & Social Psychology Bulletin* 17:83–92.

———. 1992. When racial ambivalence evokes negative affect, using a disguised measure of mood. *Personality & Social Psychology Bulletin* 18:786–97.

Hauser, Robert M. 1993. Trends in college entry among whites, blacks, and Hispanics. In *Studies of supply and demand in higher education,* edited by Charles T. Clotfelter and Michael Rothschild, 76–92. Chicago: University of Chicago Press.

Herek, Geoffrey M., and John P. Capitanio. 1996. Some of my best friends: Intergroup contact, concealable stigma, and heterosexuals' attitudes toward gay men and lesbians. *Personality & Social Psychology Bulletin* 22:412–24.

Hibbing, John, and Elizabeth Theiss-Morse. 1995. *Congress as public enemy: Public attitudes toward political institutions.* New York: Cambridge University Press.

Higham, John. 1997. Introduction: A historical perspective. In *Civil rights and social wrongs: Black-white relations since World War II,* edited by John Higham, 3–30. University Park: Pennsylvania State University Press.

Hochschild, Jennifer L. 1981. *What's fair? American beliefs about distributive justice.* Cambridge: Harvard University Press.

———. 1984. *The new American dilemma: Liberal democracy and school desegregation.* New Haven: Yale University Press.

———. 1991. The politics of the estranged poor. *Ethics* 101 (3): 560–78.

———. 1993. Disjunction and ambivalence in citizens' political outlooks. In *Reconsidering the democratic public,* edited by George Marcus and Russell Hanson, 187–210. University Park: Pennsylvania State University Press.

———. 1995. *Facing up to the American dream: Race, class, and the soul of the nation.* Princeton: Princeton University Press.

Hochschild, Jennifer L., and Reuel Rogers. In press. Race relations in a diversifying nation. *New directions: African Americans in a diversifying nation,* edited by J. Jackson. Washington, D.C.: National Planning Association.

Hofstadter, Richard. 1948. *The American political tradition.* New York: Vintage.

Hogg, Michael A., and Dominic Abrams. 1993. Towards a single-process uncertainty-reduction model of social motivation in groups. In *Group motivation: Social psychological perspectives,* edited by Michael A. Hogg and Dominic Abrams, 173–90. London: Harvester Wheatsheaf.

Hollinger, David A. 1995. *Postethnic America: Beyond multiculturalism.* New York: Basic Books.

Holzer, Harry J. 1996. *What employers want: Job prospects for less-educated workers.* New York: Russell Sage.

Howell, Susan E. 1991. Race, economics, trust and David Duke. Paper presented at the annual meeting of the American Association for Public Opinion Research, Phoenix.

Huber, Joan, and William H. Form. 1973. *Income and ideology: An analysis of the American political formula.* New York: Free Press.

Huckfeld, Robert, and Carol Weitzel Kohfeld. 1989. *Race and the decline of class in American politics.* Urbana: University of Illinois Press.

Hughes, Michael. 1997. Symbolic racism, old-fashioned racism, and whites' opposition to affirmative action. In *Racial attitudes in the 1990s: Continuity and change,* edited by Steven A. Tuch and Jack K. Martin, 45–75. Westport, Conn.: Praeger.

Hunt, Matthew O. 1996. The individual, society, or both? A comparison of black, Latino, and white beliefs about the causes of poverty. *Social Forces* 75:293–322.

Hurwitz, Jon, and Mark Peffley. 1997. Public perceptions of race and crime: The role of racial stereotypes. *American Journal of Political Science* 41:375.

————. 1998a. Introduction. In *Perception and prejudice: Race and politics in the United States,* edited by Jon Hurwitz and Mark Peffley, 1–16. New Haven: Yale University Press.

————, eds. 1998b. *Perception and prejudice: Race and politics in the United States.* New Haven: Yale University Press.

Hyman, Herbert H., and Paul B. Sheatsley. 1956. Attitudes toward desegregation. *Scientific American* 195:35–39.

————. 1964. Attitudes toward desegregation. *Scientific American* 211:16–23.

Inglehart, Ronald. 1977. *The silent revolution.* Princeton: Princeton University Press.

Jackman, Mary R. 1976. The relation between verbal attitude and overt behavior: A public opinion application. *Social Forces* 54:646–68.

————. 1978. General and applied tolerance: Does education increase commitment to racial integration? *American Journal of Political Science* 22:302–24.

————. 1994. *The velvet glove: Paternalism and conflict in gender, class, and race relations.* Berkeley: University of California Press.

————. 1996. Individualism, self-interest, and white racism. *Social Science Quarterly* 77:760–67.

Jackman, Mary R., and Robert Jackman. 1983. *Class awareness in the United States.* Berkeley: University of California Press.

Jackman, Mary R., and Michael J. Muha. 1984. Education and intergroup attitudes: Moral enlightenment, superficial democratic commitment, or ideological refinement? *American Sociological Review* 49:751–69.

Jackman, Mary R., and Mary Scheuer Senter. 1980. Images of social groups: Categorical or qualified? *Public Opinion Quarterly* 44:341–61.

Jaynes, Gerald D., and Robin M. Williams, Jr. 1989. *A common destiny: Blacks and American society.* Washington, D.C.: National Academy Press.

Jordan, Winthrop D. 1968. *White over black: American attitudes toward the negro, 1550–1812.* Chapel Hill: University of North Carolina Press.

Jöreskog, Karl G., and Dag Sörbom. 1993. LISREL 8. Chicago: Scientific Software International, Inc.

Jost, John T. 1995. Negative illusions: Conceptual clarification and psychological evidence concerning false consciousness. *Political Psychology* 16:397–424.

Jost, John T., and Mahzarin R. Banaji. 1994. The role of stereotyping in system-justification and the production of false consciousness. Special issue: Stereotypes: Structure, function and process. *British Journal of Social Psychology* 33:1–27.

Katz, Daniel, and Kenneth W. Braly. 1933. Racial stereotypes of 100 college students. *Journal of Abnormal & Social Psychology* 28:280–90.

Katz, Irwin, and R. Glen Hass. 1988. Racial ambivalence and American value conflict: Correlational and priming studies of dual cognitive structures. *Journal of Personality & Social Psychology* 55:893–905.

Katz, Irwin, Joyce Wackenhut, and R. Glen Hass. 1986. Racial ambivalence, value duality, and behavior. In *Prejudice, discrimination, and racism,* edited by John F. Dovidio and Samuel L. Gaertner, 35–59. Orlando: Academic Press.

Kelley, S. 1983. *Interpreting elections.* Princeton: Princeton University Press.

Kemmelmeier, Markus, Jessica Cameron, and Shelley Chaiken. 1998. An experimental test of social dominance theory: The power-prejudice hypothesis. Paper presented at the twenty-first annual scientific meeting of the International Society of Political Psychology, Montreal.

Key, V. O., Jr. 1949. *Southern politics in state and nation.* New York: Knopf.

Kinder, Donald R. 1983. Diversity and complexity in American public opinion. In *Political science: The state of the discipline,* edited by Ada Finifter, 389–425. Washington, D.C.: American Political Science Association.

———. 1986. The continuing American dilemma: White resistance to racial change forty years after Myrdal. *Journal of Social Issues* 42:151–71.

———. 1998a. Opinion and action in the realm of politics. In *Handbook of social psychology,* 4th ed., edited by Daniel T. Gilbert, Susan T. Fiske, and Gardner Lindzey, 778–867. Boston: McGraw-Hill.

———. 1998b. Belief systems after Converse. Paper delivered at a conference in honor of Philip E. Converse in conjunction with the annual meeting of the American Political Science Association, Boston.

———. 1999. Whitewashing racism. Manuscript. (Institute for Social Research, University of Michigan, Ann Arbor 48106–1248.)

Kinder, Donald R., and Adam Berinsky. 1998. Making sense of issues through frames. Paper delivered at the annual meeting of the American Political Science Association, Boston.

Kinder, Donald R., and Tali Mendelberg. 1995. Cracks in American apartheid: The political impact of prejudice among desegregated whites. *Journal of Politics* 57:401–24.

Kinder, Donald R., and Thomas E. Nelson. 1998. Democratic debate and real opinions. In *The dynamics of issue framing: Elite discourse and the formation of public opinion,* edited by Nayda Terkildsen and Frauke Schnell. Cambridge: Cambridge University Press. In press.

Kinder, Donald R., and Thomas R. Palfrey, eds. 1993. *Experimental foundations of political science.* Ann Arbor: University of Michigan Press.

Kinder, Donald R., and Lynn M. Sanders. 1990. Mimicking political debate with survey questions: The case of white opinion on affirmative action for blacks. *Social Cognition* 8:73–103.

———. 1996. *Divided by color: Racial politics and democratic ideals.* Chicago: University of Chicago Press.

Kinder, Donald R., and David O. Sears. 1981. Prejudice and politics: Symbolic racism versus racial threats to the good life. *Journal of Personality & Social Psychology* 40:414–31.

Kinder, Donald R., and Nicholas Winter. 1997. Explaining the racial divide. Paper delivered at the annual meeting of the American Political Science Association, Washington, D.C.

King, Martin Luther, Jr. 1967. *Where do we go from here: Chaos or community?* Boston: Beacon Hill Press.

Kirschenman, Joleen, and Kathryn Neckerman. 1991. "We'd love to hire them, but . . .": The meaning of race for employers. In *The urban underclass*. edited by Christopher Jencks and Paul E. Peterson, 203–32. Washington, D.C.: Brookings Institution.

Kleppner, Paul. 1985. *Chicago divided: The making of a black mayor.* DeKalb: Northern Illinois University Press.

Kluegel, James R. 1990. Trends in whites' explanations of the black-white gap in socioeconomic status, 1977–1989. *American Sociological Review* 55:512–25.

Kluegel, James R., and Lawrence Bobo. 1993. Dimensions of whites' beliefs about the black-white socioeconomic gap. In *Prejudice, politics, and the American dilemma,* edited by Paul M. Sniderman, Philip E. Tetlock, and Edward G. Carmines, 127–47. Stanford: Stanford University Press.

Kluegel, James R., and Eliot R. Smith. 1981. Beliefs about stratification. *Annual Review of Sociology* 7:29–56.

———. 1982. Whites' beliefs about blacks' opportunity. *American Sociological Review* 47:518–32.

———. 1983. Affirmative action attitudes: Effects of self-interest, racial affect, and stratification beliefs on whites' views. *Social Forces* 61:797–824.

———. 1986. *Beliefs about inequality: Americans' views of what is and what ought to be.* New York: Aldine de Gruyter.

Knight, Kathleen. 1998. In their own words: Citizens' explanations of inequality between the races. In *Perception and prejudice: Race and politics in the United States,* edited by Jon Hurwitz and Mark Peffley, 202–32. New Haven: Yale University Press.

Kousser, J. Morgan. 1974. *The shaping of Southern politics: Suffrage restriction and the establishment of the one-party South, 1880–1910.* New Haven: Yale University Press.

Kovel, John. 1970. *White racism: A psychohistory.* New York: Pantheon Books.

Krysan, Maria. 1995. White racial attitudes: Does it matter how we ask? Ph.D. diss., Department of Psychology, University of Michigan.

———. 1999. Qualifying a quantifying analysis on racial equality. *Social Psychology Quarterly* 62:211–18.

Kuklinski, James H., Michael D. Cobb, and Martin Gilens. 1997. Racial attitudes and the "New South." *Journal of Politics* 59:323–49.

Kuklinski, James H., and Wayne Parent. 1981. Race and big government: Contamination in measuring racial attitudes. *Political Methodology* 7:131–59.

Kuklinski, James H., Paul M. Sniderman, Kathleen Knight, Thomas Piazza, Philip E. Tetlock, Gordon R. Lawrence, and Barbara Mellers. 1997. Racial prejudice and attitudes toward affirmative action. *American Journal of Political Science* 41:402–19.

Kuzenski, John C., Charles S. Bullock III, and Ronald Keith Gaddie, eds. 1995. *David Duke and the politics of race in the South.* Nashville: Vanderbilt University Press.

Lamont, Michele. 1992. *Money, morals, and manners: The culture of the French and American upper-middle class.* Chicago: University of Chicago Press.

Lane, Robert E. 1962. *Political ideology: Why the American common man believes what he does.* Glencoe, Ill.: Free Press.

———. 1986. Market justice, political justice. *American Political Science Review* 80:383–402.

———. 1991. *The market experience.* Cambridge: Cambridge University Press.

LeVine, Robert A., and Donald T. Campbell. 1972. *Ethnocentrism: Theories of conflict, ethnic attitudes, and group behavior.* New York: Wiley.

Lipset, Seymour M. 1963. *The first new nation.* New York: Norton.

———. 1996. *American exceptionalism: A double-edged sword.* New York: Norton.

Lipset, Seymour M., and William Schneider. 1978a. Racial equality in America. *New Society* 44:128–31.

———. 1978b. The *Bakke* case: How would it be decided at the bar of public opinion? *Public Opinion* 1:38–44.

Lukes, Steven. 1973. *Individualism.* Oxford, England: Basil Blackwell.

Macrae, C. Neil, Galen V. Bodenhausen, Alan B. Milne, and Tania M. J. Thorn. 1997. On the activation of social stereotypes: The moderating role of processing objectives. *Journal of Experimental Social Psychology* 33:471–89.

Maier, Pauline. 1997. *American scripture: Making the Declaration of Independence.* New York: Knopf.

Mann, Michael. 1970. The social cohesion of liberal democracy. *American Sociological Review* 35:423–39.

Markus, Gregory B. 1993. American individualism reconsidered. Unpublished manuscript. (Center for Political Studies, Institute for Social Research, University of Michigan, Ann Arbor 48106–1248.)

Marx, Anthony. 1998. *Making race and nation: A comparison of South Africa, the United States, and Brazil.* New York: Cambridge University Press.

Marx, Gary T. 1967. *Protest and prejudice.* New York: Harper & Row.

Massey, Douglas S., and Nancy A. Denton. 1993. *American apartheid: Segregation and the making of the underclass.* Cambridge: Harvard University Press.

McClosky, Herbert, and John Zaller. 1984. *The American ethos: Public attitudes toward capitalism and democracy.* Cambridge: Harvard University Press.

McConahay, John B. 1982. Self-interest versus racial attitudes as correlates of anti-busing attitudes in Louisville: Is it the buses or the blacks? *Journal of Politics* 44:692–720.

———. 1983. Modern racism and modern discrimination: The effects of race, racial attitudes, and context on simulated hiring decisions. *Personality & Social Psychology Bulletin* 9:551–58.

———. 1986. Modern racism, ambivalence, and the modern racism scale. In *Prejudice, discrimination, and racism,* edited by John F. Dovidio and Samuel L. Gaertner, 91–125. Orlando: Academic Press.

McConahay, John B., Betty B. Hardee, and Valerie Batts. 1981. Has racism declined in America? It depends upon who is asking and what is asked. *Journal of Conflict Resolution* 25:563–79.

McConahay, John B., and Joseph C. Hough. 1976. Symbolic racism. *Journal of Social Issues* 32:23–45.

McFarland, Samuel G., and Sherman Adelson. 1996. An omnibus study of personality, values, and prejudice. Paper presented at the nineteenth annual meeting of the International Society for Political Psychology, Vancouver, Canada.

Meertens, Roel W., and Thomas F. Pettigrew. 1997. Is subtle prejudice really prejudice? *Public Opinion Quarterly* 61:54–71.

Mendelberg, Tali. 1997. Executing Hortons: Racial crime in the 1988 presidential campaign. *Public Opinion Quarterly* 61:134–57.

Michels, Robert. 1959. *Political parties: A sociological study of oligarchical tendencies in modern democracy,* translated by E. C. Paul. New York: Dover Press.

Miller, David L. 1967. *Individualism.* Austin: University of Texas Press.

Miller, Warren E., and J. Merrill Shanks. 1996. *The new American voter.* Cambridge: Harvard University Press.

Mills, Charles W. 1997. *The racial contract.* Ithaca: Cornell University Press.

Monteith, Margo J., and Gina L. Walters. 1998. Egalitarianism, moral obligation, and prejudice-related personal standards. *Personality & Social Psychology Bulletin* 24:186–99.

Morgan, Edmund. 1975. *American slavery, American freedom: The ordeal of colonial Virginia.* New York: Norton.

Morgan, Philip. 1998. *Slave counterpoint: Black culture in the eighteenth century Chesapeake and lowcountry.* Chapel Hill: University of North Carolina Press.

Mosca, Gaetano. 1939. *The ruling class,* translated by Hannah Kahn. New York: McGraw-Hill.

Mosteller, Frederick, and John W. Tukey. 1977. *Data analysis and regression: A second course in statistics.* Reading, Mass.: Addison-Wesley.

Motley, Constance Baker. 1998. *Equal justice under law.* New York: Farrar, Straus & Giroux.

Mullen, Brian, Rupert Brown, and Colleen Smith. 1992. Ingroup bias as a function of salience, relevance, and status: An integration. *European Journal of Social Psychology* 22:103–22.

Myrdal, Gunnar. 1944. *An American dilemma.* New York: Harper & Row.

National Conference of Christians and Jews. 1994. *Taking America's pulse: The full report of the National Conference survey on inter-group relations.* New York: National Conference of Christians and Jews.

Nelson, Thomas E. 1998. Group affect and attribution in social policy opinion. Unpublished manuscript. (Ohio State University.)

Nelson, Thomas E., and Donald R. Kinder. 1996. Issue frames and group-centrism in American public opinion. *Journal of Politics* 58:1055–78.

Newell, Allen A., and Herbert A. Simon. 1972. *Human problem solving.* Englewood Cliffs, N.J.: Prentice-Hall.

Norusis, Marija J. 1990. *SPSS statistical data analysis: SPSS/PC+ Statistics 4.0.* Chicago: SPSS.

Oliver, Melvin L., and Thomas M. Shapiro. 1995. *Black wealth/white wealth: A new perspective on racial inequality.* New York: Routledge.

Pareto, Vilfredo. 1943. *The mind and society,* translated by Andrew Bongiorno and Arthur Livingston. New York: Harcourt, Brace & World.

Parikh, Sunita. 1997. *The politics of preference: Democratic institutions and the politics of preference in the United States and India.* Ann Arbor: University of Michigan Press.

Patterson, Orlando. 1997. *The ordeal of integration: Progress and resentment in America's "racial" crisis.* Washington, D.C.: Civitas Counterpoint.

Peffley, Mark, and Jon Hurwitz. 1998. Whites' stereotypes of blacks: Sources and political consequences. In *Perception and prejudice: Race and politics in the United States,* edited by Jon Hurwitz and Mark Peffley, 58–99. New Haven: Yale University Press.

Peffley, Mark, Jon Hurwitz, and Paul M. Sniderman. 1997. Racial stereotypes and whites' political views of blacks in the context of welfare and crime. *American Journal of Political Science* 41 (1): 30–60.

Peterson, Paul E., ed. 1995. *Classifying by race.* Princeton: Princeton University Press.

Pettigrew, Thomas F. 1979. The ultimate attribution error: Extending Allport's cognitive analysis of prejudice. *Personality & Social Psychology Bulletin* 5: 461–76.

———. 1985. New black-white patterns: How best to conceptualize them? *Annual Review of Sociology* 11:329–46.

———. 1997a. Generalized intergroup contact effects on prejudice. *Personality & Social Psychology Bulletin* 23:173–85.

———. 1997b. The affective component of prejudice: Results from Western Europe. In *Racial attitudes in the 1990s: Continuity and change,* edited by Steven A. Tuch and Jack K. Martin, 76–90. Westport, Conn.: Praeger.

———. 1998. Intergroup contact theory. *Annual Review of Psychology* 49: 65–85.

Pettigrew, Thomas F., James Jackson, Jeanne Ben Brika, Gerard Lemain, Roel W. Meertens, Ulrich Wagner, and Andreas Zick. 1998. Outgroup prejudice in Western Europe. *European Review of Social Psychology* 8:241–73.

Pettigrew, Thomas F., and Roel W. Meertens. 1995. Subtle and blatant prejudice in Western Europe. *European Journal of Social Psychology* 25:57–75.

Pole, Jack Richon. 1978. *The pursuit of equality in American history.* Berkeley: University of California Press.

———. 1993. *The pursuit of equality in American history.* Rev. ed. Berkeley: University of California Press.

Powers, Daniel A., and Christopher G. Ellison. 1995. Interracial contact and black racial attitudes: The contact hypothesis and selectivity bias. *Social Forces* 74: 205–26.

Prager, Jeffrey. 1987. American political culture and the shifting meaning of race. *Ethnic & Racial Studies* 10:62–81.

Pratto, Felicia, James H. Liu, Shana Levin, Jim Sidanius, Margaret Shih, Hagit Bachrach, and Peter Hegarty. 1998. Social dominance orientation and legitimization of inequality across cultures. Unpublished manuscript.

Pratto, Felicia, Jim Sidanius, and Lisa M. Stallworth. 1993. Sexual selection and the sexual and ethnic basis of social hierarchy. In *Social stratification and socioeconomic inequality: A comparative biosocial analysis,* edited by L. Ellis, 111–37. New York: Praeger.

Pratto, Felicia, Jim Sidanius, Lisa M. Stallworth, and Bertrand F. Malle. 1994. Social dominance orientation: A personality variable predicting social and political attitudes. *Journal of Personality & Social Psychology* 67:741–63.

Pyszczynski, Tom, Jeff Greenberg, Sheldon Solomon, and James Hamilton. 1991. A terror management analysis of self-awareness and anxiety: The hierarchy of terror. In *Anxiety and self-focused attention,* edited by Ralf Schwarzer and Robert A. Wicklund, 67–85. New York: Harwood Academic Publishers.

Quillian, Lincoln. 1995. Prejudice as a response to perceived group threat: Population composition and anti-immigrant and racial prejudice in Europe. *American Sociological Review* 60:586–611.

———. 1996. Group threat and regional change in attitudes toward African Americans. *American Journal of Sociology* 102:816–60.

Rabinowitz, Joshua L. 1999. Interpreting the politics of race: The importance of equality beliefs and their implications for white Americans' attitudes toward racial policy. Ph.D. diss., Department of Psychology, University of California, Los Angeles.

Raden, David. 1994. Are symbolic racism and traditional prejudice part of a contemporary authoritarian attitude syndrome? *Political Behavior* 16:365–84.

Rae, Douglas. 1981. *Equalities.* Cambridge: Harvard University Press.

Reif, Karlheinz, and Anna Melich. 1991. *Euro-Barometer 30: Immigrants and out-groups in Western Europe, October–November 1988* (ICPSR 9321). Ann Arbor, Mich.: Inter-University Consortium for Political and Social Research.

Report of the National Advisory Commission on Civil Disorders. 1968. New York: Bantam Books.

Reskin, Barbara. 1998. *The realities of affirmative action in employment.* Washington, D.C.: American Sociological Association.

Reynolds, Vernon, Vincent S. E. Falger, and Ian Vine. 1987. *The sociobiology of ethnocentrism: Evolutionary dimensions of xenophobia, discrimination, racism, and nationalism.* London: Croom Helm.

Rodgers, Daniel T. 1978. *The work ethic in industrial America, 1850–1920.* Chicago: University of Chicago Press.

———. 1987. *Contested truths: Keywords in American politics since independence.* New York: Basic.

Rogers, Ronald W., and Steven Prentice-Dunn. 1981. Deindividuation and anger-mediated interracial aggression: Unmasking regressive racism. *Journal of Personality & Social Psychology* 41:63–73.

Rokeach, Milton. 1973. *The nature of human values.* New York: Free Press.

———. 1979. The two-value model of political ideology and British politics. *British Journal of Social & Clinical Psychology* 18:169–72.

Rokeach, Milton, M. G. Miller, and J. A. Snyder. 1971. The value gap between police and policed. *Journal of Social Issues* 27:155–71.

Roth, Byron M. 1990. Social psychology's racism. *Public Interest* 98:26–36.

———. 1994. *Prescription for failure: Race relations in the age of social science.* New Brunswick, N.J.: Transaction Publishers.

Rubin, Mark, and Miles Hewstone. 1998. Social identity theory's self-esteem hypothesis: A review and clarification. *Personality & Social Psychology Review* 2:40–62.

Runciman, W. G. 1966. *Relative deprivation and social justice.* Berkeley: University of California Press.

Ryan, William. 1971. *Blaming the victim.* New York: Vintage.

Salovey, Peter, Alexander Rothman, and Judith Rodin. 1998. Health behavior. In *Handbook of social psychology,* 4th ed., edited by Daniel T. Gilbert, Susan T. Fiske, and Gardner Lindzey, 633–83. Boston: McGraw-Hill.

Sanchez Jankowski, Martin. 1995. The rising significance of status in U.S. race relations. In *The bubbling cauldron: Race, ethnicity, and the urban crisis,* edited by Michael P. Smith and Joe R. Feagin, 77–98. Minneapolis: University of Minnesota Press.

Schlozman, Kay L., and Sidney Verba. 1979. *Injury to insult.* Cambridge: Harvard University Press.

Schuman, Howard, Lawrence Bobo, and Maria Krysan. 1992. Authoritarianism in the general population: The education interaction hypothesis. *Social Psychology Quarterly* 55:379–87.

Schuman, Howard, and John Harding. 1963. Sympathetic identification with the underdog. *Public Opinion Quarterly* 27:230–41.

———. 1964. Prejudice and the norm of rationality. *Sociometry* 27:353–71.

Schuman, Howard, Charlotte Steeh, and Lawrence Bobo. 1985. *Racial attitudes in America: Trends and interpretations.* Cambridge: Harvard University Press.

Schuman, Howard, Charlotte Steeh, Lawrence Bobo, and Maria Krysan. 1997. *Racial attitudes in America: Trends and interpretations.* Rev. ed. Cambridge: Harvard University Press.

Schwartz, Mildred A. 1967. *Trends in white attitudes toward Negroes.* Chicago: National Opinion Research Center.

Scott, James C. 1990. *Domination and the arts of resistance: Hidden transcripts.* New Haven: Yale University Press.

Sears, David O. 1981. Life stage effects upon attitude change, especially among the elderly. In *Aging: Social change,* edited by Sara B. Kiesler, James N. Morgan, and Valerie K. Oppenheimer, 183–204. New York: Academic Press.

———. 1988. Symbolic racism. In *Eliminating racism: Profiles in controversy,* edited by Phyllis A. Katz and Dalmas A. Taylor, 53–84. New York: Plenum Press.

———. 1993. Symbolic politics: A socio-psychological theory. In *Explorations in political psychology,* edited by Shanto Iyengar and William J. McGuire, 113–49. Durham, N.C.: Duke University Press.

———. 1994. Ideological bias in political psychology: The view from scientific hell. *Political Psychology* 15:547–56.

———. 1998. Racism and politics in the United States. In *Confronting racism: The problem and the response,* edited by Jennifer Eberhardt and Susan T. Fiske, 76–100. Thousand Oaks, Calif.: Sage.

Sears, David O., and Harris M. Allen, Jr. 1984. The trajectory of local desegregation controversies and whites' opposition to busing. In *Groups in contact: The psychology of desegregation,* edited by Norman Miller and Marilynn B. Brewer, 123–51. New York: Academic Press.

Sears, David O., and Jack Citrin. 1985. *Tax revolt: Something for nothing in California.* Enlarged ed. Cambridge: Harvard University Press.

Sears, David O., Jack Citrin, Sharmaine V. Cheleden, and Colette van Laar. 1999. Cultural diversity and multicultural politics: Is ethnic balkanization psychologically inevitable? In *Cultural divides: Understanding and overcoming group conflict,* edited by Deborah A. Prentice and Dale T. Miller, 35–79. New York: Russell Sage Foundation.

Sears, David O., Jack Citrin, and Richard Kosterman. 1987. Jesse Jackson and the Southern white electorate in 1984. In *Blacks in Southern politics,* edited by Robert P. Steed, Laurence W. Moreland, and Tod A. Baker, 209–25. New York: Praeger.

Sears, David O., and Carolyn L. Funk. 1991. The role of self-interest in social and political attitudes. *Advances in Experimental Social Psychology* 24:1–91.

———. 1999. Evidence of the long-term persistence of adults' political predispositions. *Journal of Politics* 61:1–28.

Sears, David O., Carl P. Hensler, and Leslie K. Speer. 1979. Whites' opposition to "busing": Self-interest or symbolic politics? *American Political Science Review* 73:369–84.

Sears, David O., and Leonie Huddy. 1992. The symbolic politics of opposition to bilingual education. In *Conflict between people and peoples,* edited by Jeffrey Simpson and Stephen Worchel, 145–69. Chicago: Nelson-Hall.

Sears, David O., Leonie Huddy, and Lynitta G. Schaffer. 1986. A schematic variant of symbolic politics theory, as applied to racial and gender equality. In *Political cognition,* edited by Richard R. Lau and David O. Sears, 159–202. Hillsdale, N.J.: Erlbaum.

Sears, David O., and Tom Jessor. 1996. Whites' racial policy attitudes: The role of white racism. *Social Science Quarterly* 77:751–59.

Sears, David O., and Donald R. Kinder. 1971. Racial tensions and voting in Los Angeles. In *Los Angeles: Viability and prospects for metropolitan leadership,* edited by Werner Z. Hirsch, 51–88. New York: Praeger.

———. 1985. Whites' opposition to busing: On conceptualizing and operationalizing group conflict. *Journal of Personality & Social Psychology* 48: 1148–61.

Sears, David O., and Richard Kosterman. 1991. Is it really racism? The origins and dynamics of symbolic racism. Paper presented at the annual meeting of the Midwest Political Science Association, Chicago.

Sears, David O., Richard R. Lau, Tom R. Tyler, and Harris M. Allen, Jr. 1980. Self-interest vs. symbolic politics in policy attitudes and presidential voting. *American Political Science Review* 74:670–84.

Sears, David O., and John B. McConahay. 1973. *The politics of violence: The new urban blacks and the Watts riot.* Boston: Houghton-Mifflin.

Sears, David O., and Colette van Laar. 1999. Black exceptionalism in a culturally diverse society. Unpublished manuscript. (University of California, Los Angeles.)

Sears, David O., Colette van Laar, Mary Carrillo, and Rick Kosterman. 1997. Is it really racism? The origins of white Americans' opposition to race-targeted policies. *Public Opinion Quarterly* 61:16–53.

See, Katherine O., and William J. Wilson. 1989. Race and ethnicity. In *Handbook of sociology,* edited by Neil Smelser, 233–42. Beverly Hills, Calif.: Sage.

Sennett, Richard, and Jonathan Cobb. 1972. *The hidden injuries of class.* New York: Knopf.

Sheatsley, Paul B. 1966. White attitudes toward the Negro. *Daedalus,* Winter, 217–38.

Sherif, Muzafer. 1966. *Group conflict and co-operation: Their social psychology.* London: Routledge and Kegan Paul.

Sidanius, Jim. 1993. The psychology of group conflict and the dynamics of oppression: A social dominance perspective. In *Explorations in political psychology,* edited by Shanto Iyengar and William J. McGuire, 183–219. Durham, N.C.: Duke University Press.

Sidanius, Jim, B. J. Cling, and Felicia Pratto. 1991. Ranking and linking as a function of sex and gender role attitudes. *Journal of Social Issues* 47:131–49.

Sidanius, Jim, Erik Devereux, and Felicia Pratto. 1992. A comparison of symbolic racism theory and social dominance theory as explanations for racial policy attitudes. *Journal of Social Psychology* 132:377–95.

Sidanius, Jim, Bo Ekehammar, and Michael Ross. 1979. Comparisons of sociopolitical attitudes between two democratic societies. *International Journal of Psychology* 14:225–40.

Sidanius, Jim, Seymour Feshbach, Shana Levin, and Felicia Pratto. 1997. The interface between ethnic and national attachment: Ethnic pluralism or ethnic dominance? *Public Opinion Quarterly* 61:103–33.

Sidanius, Jim, Shana Levin, Joshua Rabinowitz, Chris Federico, and Felicia Pratto. 1999. Peering into the jaws of the beast: The integrative dynamics of social identity, symbolic racism, and social dominance. In *Cultural divides: Understanding and overcoming group conflict,* edited by Deborah A. Prentice and Dale T. Miller, 80–132. New York: Russell Sage Foundation.

Sidanius, Jim, and James Liu. 1992. Racism, support for the Persian Gulf war, and the police beating of Rodney King: A social dominance perspective. *Journal of Social Psychology* 132:685–700.

Sidanius, Jim, James Liu, Felicia Pratto, and John Shaw. 1994. Social dominance orientation, hierarchy-attenuators and hierarchy-enhancers: Social dominance theory and the criminal justice system. *Journal of Applied Social Psychology* 24:338–66.

Sidanius, Jim, and Felicia Pratto. 1993a. The inevitability of oppression and the dynamics of social dominance. In *Prejudice, politics, and the American dilemma,* edited by Paul M. Sniderman, Philip E. Tetlock, and Edward G. Carmines, 173–211. Stanford: Stanford University Press.

———. 1993b. Racism and support of free-market capitalism: A cross-cultural analysis. *Political Psychology* 14:383–403.

———. 1999. *Social dominance: An intergroup theory of social hierarchy and oppression.* New York: Cambridge University Press.

Sidanius, Jim, Felicia Pratto, and Lawrence Bobo. 1994. Social dominance orientation and the political psychology of gender: A case of invariance? *Journal of Personality & Social Psychology* 67:998–1011.

———. 1996. Racism, conservatism, affirmative action and intellectual sophistication: A matter of principled conservatism or group dominance? *Journal of Personality & Social Psychology* 70:476–90.

Sidanius, Jim, Felicia Pratto, and Diana Brief. 1995. Group dominance and the political psychology of gender: A cross-cultural comparison. *Political Psychology* 16:381–96.

Sidanius, Jim, Felicia Pratto, Michael Martin, and Lisa Stallworth. 1991. Consensual racism and career track: Some implications of social dominance theory. *Political Psychology* 12:691–721.

Sidanius, Jim, Felicia Pratto, and Joshua Rabinowitz. 1994. Gender, ethnic status, ingroup attachment and social dominance orientation. *Journal of Cross-Cultural Psychology* 25:194–216.

Sidanius, Jim, Felicia Pratto, Stacey Sinclair, and Colette van Laar. 1996. Mother Teresa meets Genghis Khan: The dialectics of hierarchy-enhancing and hierarchy-attenuating career choices. *Social Justice Research* 9:145–70.

Siegel, Paul. 1971. Prestige in the American occupational structure. Ph.D. diss., Department of Sociology, University of Chicago.

Sigall, Harold, and Richard A. Page. 1971. Current stereotypes: A little fading, a little faking. *Journal of Personality & Social Psychology* 18:247–55.

Sigel, Roberta. 1996. *Ambition and accommodation: How women view gender relations.* Chicago: University of Chicago Press.

Sigelman, Lee, and Susan Welch. 1994. *Black Americans' views of racial inequality: The dream deferred.* 2nd ed. New York: Cambridge University Press.

Silberman, Charles. 1964. *Crisis in black and white.* New York: Random House.

Skrentny, John D. 1996. *The ironies of affirmative action.* Chicago: University of Chicago Press.

Smelser, Neil. 1998. The rational and the ambivalent in the social sciences. *American Sociological Review* 63:1–16.

Smith, A. Wade. 1981. Racial tolerance as a function of group position. *American Sociological Review* 46:558–73.

Smith, Eliot R. 1993. Social identity and social emotions: Toward new conceptions of prejudice. In *Affect, cognition, and stereotyping: Interactive processes in group perception,* edited by Diane M. Mackie and David L. Hamilton, 297–315. San Diego: Academic Press.

Smith, Eliot R., and James R. Kluegel. 1984. Beliefs and attitudes about women's opportunity: Comparisons with beliefs about blacks and a general perspective. *Social Psychology Quarterly* 47:81–95.

Smith, Heather J., and Thomas F. Pettigrew. 1999. Relative deprivation: A conceptual critique and meta-analysis. Unpublished manuscript. (University of California, Santa Cruz.)

Smith, Rogers. 1997. *Civic ideals: Conflicting visions of citizenship in U.S. history.* New Haven: Yale University Press.

Smith, Tom W. 1987. That which we call welfare by any other name would smell sweeter: An analysis of the impact of question wording on response patterns. *Public Opinion Quarterly* 51:75–83.

———. 1991. *What do Americans think about Jews? Working papers on contemporary anti-Semitism.* New York: American Jewish Committee, Institute of Human Relations.

Smith, Tom W., and Paul B. Sheatsley. 1984. American attitudes toward race relations. *Public Opinion* 6:14–15, 50–53.

Sniderman, Paul M. In press. Taking sides: A fixed choice theory of political reasoning. In *Elements of reason: Understanding and expanding the limits of political rationality,* edited by Arthur Lupia, Mathew D. McCubbins, and Samuel L. Popkin. New York: Cambridge University Press.

Sniderman, Paul M., Richard A. Brody, and James H. Kuklinski. 1984. Policy reasoning and political issues: The case of racial equality. *American Journal of Political Science* 28:75–94.

Sniderman, Paul M., Richard A. Brody, and Philip E. Tetlock. 1991. *Reasoning and choice.* New York: Cambridge University Press.

Sniderman, Paul M., and Edward G. Carmines. 1997a. *Reaching beyond race.* Cambridge: Harvard University Press.

———. 1997b. Reaching beyond race. *PS: Political Science & Politics* 30:466–71.

Sniderman, Paul M., Edward G. Carmines, William Howell, and Will Morgan. 1997. A test of alternative interpretations of the contemporary politics of race: A critical examination of *Divided by color.* Prepared for the annual meeting of the Midwest Political Science Association.

Sniderman, Paul M., Edward G. Carmines, Geoffrey C. Layman, and Michael Carter. 1996. Beyond race: Social justice as a race neutral ideal. *American Journal of Political Science* 40:33–55.

Sniderman, Paul M., and Douglas Grob. 1996. Innovations in experimental design in general population attitude surveys. *Annual Review of Sociology* 22:377–99.

Sniderman, Paul M., and Michael G. Hagen. 1985. *Race and inequality: A study in American values.* Chatham, N.J.: Chatham House.

Sniderman, Paul M., Michael G. Hagen, Philip E. Tetlock, and Henry D. Brady. 1986. Reasoning chains: Causal models of racial policy reasoning. *British Journal of Political Science* 16:405–30.

Sniderman, Paul M., and Thomas Piazza. 1993. *The scar of race.* Cambridge: Belknap Press/Harvard University Press.

Sniderman, Paul M., Thomas Piazza, Philip E. Tetlock, and Ann Kendrick. 1991. The new racism. *American Journal of Political Science* 35:423–47.

Sniderman, Paul M., and Philip E. Tetlock. 1986a. Reflections on American racism. *Journal of Social Issues* 42:173–87.

———. 1986b. Symbolic racism: Problems of motive attribution in political analysis. *Journal of Social Issues* 42:129–50.

Sniderman, Paul M., Philip E. Tetlock, Edward G. Carmines, and Randall S. Peterson. 1993. The politics of the American dilemma: Issue pluralism. In *Prejudice, politics, and the American dilemma,* edited by Paul M. Sniderman, Philip E. Tetlock, and Edward G. Carmines, 212–36. Stanford: Stanford University Press.

Sowell, Thomas. 1984. *Civil rights: Rhetoric or reality?* New York: William Morrow.

———. 1994. *Race and culture: A world view.* New York: Basic Books.

Stangor, Charles, Linda A. Sullivan, and Thomas E. Ford. 1991. Affective and cognitive determinants of prejudice. *Social Cognition* 9:359–80.

Steeh, Charlotte, and Maria Krysan. 1996. Trends: Affirmative action and the public, 1970–1995. *Public Opinion Quarterly* 60:128–58.

Steeh, Charlotte, and Howard Schuman. 1992. Young white adults: Did racial attitudes change in the 1980s? *American Journal of Sociology* 98:340–67.

Steinberg, Stephen. 1995. *Turning back: The retreat from racial justice in American thought and policy.* Boston: Beacon Press.

Stember, Charles H. 1961. *Education and attitude change.* New York: Institute of Human Relations Press.

Stinchcombe, Arthur L. 1988. Review of *Causality in crisis,* by Vaughn R. McKim and Stephen P. Turner. *Contemporary Sociology* 27:664–66.

Stoker, Laura. 1992. Interests and ethics in politics. *American Political Science Review* 86:369–80.

———. 1996. Understanding differences in whites' opinions across racial policies. *Social Science Quarterly* 77:768–77.

———. 1998. Understanding whites' resistance to affirmative action: The role of principled commitments and racial prejudice. In *Perception and prejudice: Race and politics in the United States,* edited by Jon Hurwitz and Mark Peffley, 135–70. New Haven: Yale University Press.

Stouffer, Samuel A. 1955. *Communism, conformity, and civil liberties: A cross-section of the nation speaks its mind.* Garden City, N.Y.: Doubleday.

Sturm, Susan, and Lani Guinier. 1996. The future of affirmative action: Reclaiming the innovative ideal. *California Law Review* 84:953–1036.

Sumner, William G. 1906. *Folkways.* Boston: Ginn.

Tabachnick, Barbara G., and Linda S. Fidell. 1996. *Using multivariate statistics.* 3rd ed. New York: Harper Collins.

Tajfel, Henri. 1982. *Social identity and intergroup relations.* Cambridge: Cambridge University Press.

Tajfel, Henri, and John C. Turner. 1986. The social identity theory of intergroup behavior. In *Psychology of intergroup relations,* edited by Stephen Worchel and William G. Austin, 7–24. Chicago: Nelson Hall.

Takaki, Ronald. 1994. Reflections on racial patterns in America. In *From different shores: Perspectives on race and ethnicity in America,* edited by Ronald Takaki, 24–36. New York: Oxford University Press.

Tarman, Christopher, and David O. Sears. 1998. The measurement of symbolic racism: A structural equations model. Paper presented at the annual meeting of the International Society of Political Psychology, Montreal.

Tate, Katherine. 1993. *From protest to politics.* New York: Russell Sage.

Taylor, Marylee C. 1979. Fraternal deprivation and competitive racism: A second look. *Sociology & Social Research* 65:37–55.

———. 1994. The impact of affirmative action on beneficiary groups: Evidence from the 1990 General Social Survey. *Basic & Applied Social Psychology* 25: 181–92.

———. 1997. Support for "safety net" programs among white Americans. Unpublished manuscript.

———. 1998. How white attitudes vary with the racial composition of local populations: Numbers count. *American Sociological Review* 63:512–35.

Tetlock, Philip E. 1994. Political psychology or politicized psychology: Is the road to scientific hell paved with good moral intentions? *Political Psychology* 15: 509–29.

Thernstrom, Stephan, and Abigail Thernstrom. 1997. *America in black and white: One nation, indivisible.* New York: Simon & Schuster.

Thurow, Lester. [1972] 1994. Affirmative action in a zero-sum society. In *From different shores: Perspectives on race and ethnicity in America,* edited by Ronald Takaki, 235–40. Reprint, New York: Oxford University Press.

Thurstone, L. L. 1928. An experimental study of nationality preferences. *Journal of Genetic Psychology* 1:405–25.

Tocqueville, Alexis de. [1835/1840] 1969. *Democracy in America.* Reprint, New York: Doubleday.

Tuch, Steven A. 1987. Urbanism, region, and tolerance revisited: The case of racial prejudice. *American Sociological Review* 52:504–10.

Tuch, Steven A., and Michael Hughes. 1996a. Whites' racial policy attitudes. *Social Science Quarterly* 77:723–45.

———. 1996b. Whites' opposition to race-targeted policies: One cause or many? *Social Science Quarterly* 77:778–88.

Tuch, Steven A., and Jack K. Martin, eds. 1997. *Racial attitudes in the 1990s: Continuity and change.* Westport, Conn.: Praeger.

Tuch, Steven A., and Lee Sigelman. 1997. Race, class, and black-white differences in social policy views. In *Understanding public opinion,* edited by Barbara Norrander and Clyde Wilcox, 37–54. Washington, D.C.: Congressional Quarterly Press.

Tuch, Steven A., and Michael C. Taylor. 1986. Whites' opinions about institutional constraints on racial equality. *Sociology & Social Research* 70:268–71.

Turner, Jonathan H., Royce Singleton, Jr., and David Musick. 1984. *Oppression: A socio-history of black-white relations in America.* Chicago: Nelson Hall.

Turner, Margery A., Michael Fix, and Raymond J. Struyk. 1991. *Opportunities denied, opportunities diminished: Racial discrimination in hiring.* Washington, D.C.: Urban Institute.

van den Berghe, Pierre L. 1967. *Race and racism.* New York: Wiley.

———. 1978a. *Man in society: A biosocial view.* New York: Elsevier.

———. 1978b. *Race and racism: A comparative perspective.* New York: Wiley.

van Laar, Colette, Jim Sidanius, Joshua Rabinowitz, and Stacey Sinclair. 1999. The three R's of academic achievement: Reading, 'riting, and racism. *Personality & Social Psychology Bulletin* 25:139–51.

Vanman, Eric J., Brenda Y. Paul, D. L. Kaplan, and Norman Miller. 1990. Facial electromyography differentiates racial bias in imagined cooperative settings. Meeting abstract. *Psychophysiology* 27:S63.

Vanman, Eric J., Brenda Y. Paul, Tiffany A. Ito, and Norman Miller. 1997. The modern face of prejudice and structural features that moderate the effect of cooperation on affect. *Journal of Personality & Social Psychology* 73:941–59.

Vanneman, Reeve D., and Thomas F. Pettigrew. 1972. Race and relative deprivation in the urban United States. *Race* 13:461–86.

Verba, Sidney, and Gary R. Orren. 1985. *Equality in America: The view from the top.* Cambridge: Harvard University Press.

von Hippel, William, Denise Sekaquaptewa, and Patrick Vargas. 1997. The linguistic intergroup bias as an implicit indicator of prejudice. *Journal of Experimental Social Psychology* 33:490–509.

Voss, Stephen D. 1996. Beyond racial threat: Failure of an old hypothesis in the New South. *Journal of Politics* 58:1156–70.

Walzer, Michael. 1994. Comment. In *Multiculturalism,* edited by Amy Gutmann, 99–103. Princeton: Princeton University Press.

Ward, Dana. 1985. Generations and the expression of symbolic racism. *Political Psychology* 6:1–18.

Weber, Max. 1958. *The Protestant ethic and the spirit of capitalism.* New York: Scribner's.

Weigel, Russell H., and Paul W. Howes. 1985. Conceptions of racial prejudice: Symbolic racism reconsidered. *Journal of Social Issues* 41:117–38.

Weiss, Kenneth. 1997. UC law schools' new rules cost minorities spots. *Los Angeles Times,* May 15, A1.

Wellman, David. 1977. *Portraits of white racism.* Cambridge: Cambridge University Press.

West, Cornell. 1993. *Race matters.* Boston: Beacon Press.

Wilcox, Jerry, and Wade Clark Roof. 1978. Percent black and black-white status inequality: Southern versus nonsouthern patterns. *Social Science Quarterly* 59:421–34.

Wilder, Daniel A., and John E. Thompson. 1980. Intergroup contact with independent manipulations of in-group and out-group interaction. *Journal of Personality & Social Psychology* 38:589–603.

Williams, Robin. 1947. *The reduction of intergroup tensions: A survey of research on problems of ethnic, racial and religious group relations.* New York: Social Science Research Council.

Williamson, Joel. 1997. Wounds not scars: Lynching, the national conscience, and the American historian. *Journal of American History* 834:1221–72.

Wills, Garry. 1987. *Reagan's America: Innocents at home.* New York: Doubleday.

Wills, Thomas A. 1981. Downward comparison principles in social psychology. *Psychological Bulletin* 90:245–71.

Wilson, Glenn D., ed. 1973. *The psychology of conservatism.* New York: Academic Press.

Wilson, Glenn D., and Christopher Bagley. 1973. Religion, racialism and conservatism. In *The psychology of conservatism*, edited by Glenn D. Wilson, 117–28. New York: Academic Press.

Wilson, Thomas C. 1985. Urbanism and tolerance: A test of some hypotheses drawn from Wirth and Stouffer. *American Sociological Review* 50:117–23.

———. 1991. Urbanism, migration, and tolerance: A reassessment. *American Sociological Review* 56:117–23.

Wilson, William J. 1987. *The truly disadvantaged*. Chicago: University of Chicago Press.

———. 1997. *When work disappears: The work of the new urban poor.* New York: Knopf.

Wittenbrink, Bernd, Charles M. Judd, and Bernadette Park. 1997. Evidence for racial prejudice at the implicit level and its relationship with questionnaire measures. *Journal of Personality & Social Psychology* 72:262–74.

Wolfinger, Raymond E. 1974. *The politics of progress.* New York: Prentice-Hall.

Wong, Cara, and Jake Bowers. 1997. Meaning and measures: A validity test of symbolic racism. Paper presented at the annual meeting of the Midwestern Political Science Association, Chicago.

Wood, Betty. 1997. *The origins of American slavery.* New York: Hill and Wang.

Wood, Gordon S. 1992. *The radicalism of the American revolution.* New York: Knopf.

Wood, Jeremy. 1994. Is "symbolic racism" racism? A review informed by intergroup behavior. *Political Psychology* 15:673–86.

Woodmansee, John, and Stuart W. Cook. 1967. Dimensions of verbal racial attitudes: Their identification and measurement. *Journal of Personality & Social Psychology* 7:240–50.

Woodward, C. Vann. 1957. *The strange career of Jim Crow.* New York: Oxford University Press.

Word, Carl O., Mark P. Zanna, and Joel Cooper. 1974. The nonverbal mediation of self-fulfilling prophecies in interracial interaction. *Journal of Experimental Social Psychology* 10:109–20.

Wright, G. C. 1977. Racism and welfare policy in America. *Social Science Quarterly* 57:718–30.

Zaller, John. 1992. *The nature and origins of mass opinion.* New York: Cambridge University Press.

Zubrinsky, Camille L., and Lawrence Bobo. 1996. Prismatic metropolis: Race and residential segregation in the City of the Angels. *Social Science Research* 25: 335–74.

AUTHOR INDEX